The Shanghai Green Gang

The Shanghai Green Gang

Politics and Organized Crime, 1919–1937

BRIAN G. MARTIN

University of California Press

BERKELEY   LOS ANGELES   LONDON

University of California Press
Berkeley and Los Angeles, California

University of California Press, Ltd.
London, England

© 1996 by
The Regents of the University of California

Library of Congress Cataloging-in-Publication Data

Martin, Brian G.
   The Shanghai Green Gang : politics and organized crime,
1919–1937 / by Brian G. Martin.
      p.   cm.
   Includes bibliographical references.
   ISBN 0-520-20114-0 (alk. paper)
      1. Ch'ing pang (Society)   2. Shanghai (China)—Politics and
government.   3. Tu, Yüeh-sheng, 1888–1951.   I. Title.
DS 796.S257M36   1996
951'.132—dc20   95-5017
                                                      CIP

Printed in the United States of America
9 8 7 6 5 4 3 2 1

For Arja

Contents

Acknowledgments

This book originated as a doctoral dissertation, "The Green Gang in Shanghai, 1920–1937: The Rise of Du Yuesheng," Australian National University, prepared under the direction of Professor Wang Gungwu and Dr. Lo Hui-min. I am very grateful to both for their unstinting support, guidance and encouragement for the project during its long years of gestation. My interest in Chinese history goes back many years, being first stimulated by the course of lectures given by Jack Gray when I was a student at Glasgow University in the late 1960s. It was he who first encouraged me to pursue the study of Chinese history.

My field work in Shanghai was facilitated greatly by Professor Tang Zhenchang of the Shanghai Academy of Social Sciences, to whom I owe special thanks. I would also like to thank Han Weizhi, the former director of the Shanghai Municipal Archives, and his staff for their helpfulness to me during my stay in the archives, as well as the staff of the Shanghai Municipal Library. Similarly, I would like to thank the staff of the Archives of the French Foreign Ministry in Paris for their assistance in gaining access to the records of the Shanghai Consulate General.

I am particularly grateful to Frederic Wakeman for his continuing interest in my work on the Green Gang, and I would like to thank him, together with Sherman Cochrane and Elizabeth Perry, for the invitation to participate in the conference on the history of Shanghai that they organized and which was held in Shanghai in September 1988. This provided me with an invaluable opportunity to exchange ideas with fellow scholars, both Chinese and foreign, on various aspects of Shanghai's modern history. I would like to mention in particular Marie-Claire Bergère. I would also like to thank Nick Clifford who very generously shared with me his profound knowledge of French diplomatic documents relating to China.

In the course of my research at the Australian National University I benefited from the friendship and the intellectual stimulation provided by many colleagues, especially Antonia Finnane, John Fitzgerald, Ann Gunn, Jeniffer Holmgren, Pauline Keating, Brian Moloughney, Terry Narramore, Warren Sun, Esta Unger, and Ye Xiaoqing.

The present work draws on a number of articles that were published previously in a somewhat different form, and I would like to take this opportunity to thank the editors of the journals and monographic series in which they appeared for permission to use portions of them. Earlier versions of chapters 1 and 2 appeared respectively as "The Origins of the Green Gang and Its Rise in Shanghai, 1850–1920," *East Asian History* 2 (December 1991): 67–86, and as "Warlords and Gangsters: The Opium Traffic in Shanghai and the Creation of the Three Prosperities Company to 1926," in *The Nationalists and Chinese Society, 1923–1937: A Symposium*, ed. John Fitzgerald, History Monographs, no. 4 (Melbourne: University of Melbourne, History Department, 1989), pp. 44–71. Material in chapters 3 and 5 has been drawn from " 'The Pact with the Devil': The Relationship between the Green Gang and the French Authorities, 1925–1935," in *Shanghai Sojourners*, ed. Frederic Wakeman, Jr., and Wen-hsin Yeh, China Research Monograph, no. 40 (Berkeley: Institute of East Asian Studies, University of California, 1992), pp. 266–304, copyright 1992 by the Regents of the University of California, and used by permission. Material in chapter 7 has been drawn from "The Green Gang and the Guomindang State: Du Yuesheng and the Politics of Shanghai, 1927–1937," *Journal of Asian Studies* 54 (February 1995): 64–91, copyright by the Association of Asian Studies, Inc., and used by permission.

Finally I would like to thank my parents and my wife Arja Keski-Nummi. Without their patience and unflagging support this project could not have been completed.

Any errors in the text are, of course, my own responsibility.

Introduction

The early twentieth century was for China an era of transition, which witnessed the final disintegration of the traditional Chinese polity and the urgent search for viable alternatives. This process involved wrenching and revolutionary changes that touched all aspects of the nation's political, economic and social structures. The forcing grounds for these changes were the major cities of China, and among these none was more important than Shanghai. It was here that new social classes emerged, new forms of economic and political organization were developed, and new types of mass media (mass circulation newspapers and radio) were first established.

The process of change in urban China, however, was complex and uncertain and did not follow a linear progression. It not only encouraged the emergence of new social forces but also witnessed the reconstitution in new forms of certain traditional social organizations. These elements of the traditional society were not merely vestigial remnants of a dying social system. On the contrary, they were, in many cases, flourishing organizations that interacted dynamically with the new social, economic and political structures and, in so doing, helped to influence the type of "modern" society that emerged in China's cities. Good examples of this phenomenon were the Chinese secret societies, traditional social organizations par excellence, which, nevertheless, successfully adapted to the new socioeconomic and political orders of the treaty ports to become an integral element of China's emerging modern urban society in the early twentieth century.

Despite the intriguing role played by secret societies in the urban environment of early twentieth century China, Western historical

research on secret societies has paid little attention to this phenomenon. Strongly influenced initially by the work of Jean Chesneaux
and Fei-Ling Davis in the late 1960s, this research, in broad terms,
concentrated on two main themes: the interaction between secret
societies and rural society and their political function as a focus for
popular opposition to an exploitative state system prior to the 1911
Revolution.[1] The approach taken by these works reflected the tenor
of the times in the China of the Cultural Revolution and, in particular, the Maoist emphasis on secret societies as catalysts of popular
revolt against the feudal state, and hence their official designation as
"progressive" organizations with protosocialist and protonationalist
characteristics. For other historians the importance of secret societies
derived from the contribution that an analysis of their activities
made toward an explanation of the larger question of why peasants
rebel.[2]

A few scholars have discussed certain aspects of secret societies
in urban China in the context of investigations of other issues, such
as the formation of the working class in Shanghai and Tianjin,
the Guomindang's relations with the Shanghai bourgeoisie, and the
Communist seizure of power in Tianjin.[3] That key areas of the
modern history of urban China cannot be written without some
discussion of secret societies only serves to underline the importance
and complexity of their economic and political roles in Chinese urban society.

In the absence of scholarly studies of urban secret societies, those
works that have addressed the issue directly, such as the books by
Sterling Seagrave and Pan Ling on the Shanghai Green Gang, have
been of a distinctly popular kind.[4] Both these works provide extremely vivid and entertaining accounts of the activities of the Green
Gang and its leaders, notably Du Yuesheng, in Shanghai of the
1920s and 1930s, but neither is (nor claims to be) a work of historical scholarship. Seagrave's account, in particular, with its con-
spiratorial view of Chinese history in the 1920s and 1930s and of
Jiang Jieshi's rise to power (which, he argues, was due to the mach-
inations of Du Yuesheng), sacrifices historical fact for sensationalist
effect. Pan Ling's work, by contrast, is more solidly anchored in the
secondary Chinese literature, especially the biographies of Du Yuesheng by Zhang Jungu and Xu Zhucheng, and it presents a much
more balanced account of Du Yuesheng's career than that provided
by Seagrave. Her approach, nevertheless, remains closer to that of a

novelist than of a historian, and her work has many of the characteristics of the traditional Chinese genre of *yanyi*, that is, a fictionalized reconstruction of historical events.[5]

By means of a study of the activities of the Shanghai Green Gang, one of the most powerful of these societies in early-twentieth-century China, the present work addresses the issues of the role of secret societies in urban China and their relationship to the state systems of the Republican period. It focuses in particular on one major group within the Shanghai Green Gang, that controlled by the French Concession Green Gang bosses, and it devotes much of its attention to the career of the most powerful of these bosses, Du Yuesheng. Through a detailed study of the Shanghai Green Gang, this work seeks to demonstrate the proposition that secret societies were resilient social organizations that not only could adapt successfully to the complex environment of a modernizing urban society but could emerge as powerful forces within that society.

In line with the lack of attention given to urban secret societies, there has been no major scholarly study of the Green Gang in the twentieth century by Western historians. The only partial exceptions to this observation are the two important journal articles written by Y. C. Wang and Jonathan Marshall in 1967 and 1976, respectively, and which together represent the point of departure for the present study.[6]

In China, by contrast, there has been a noticeable increase in interest in the history of Shanghai secret societies among Chinese historians in recent years. This reflects the progressive liberalization of historical scholarship in the 1980s: a more relaxed approach to the types of topics that could be the subject of genuine historical inquiry, and the opening up of archives and libraries to historians. An important development for the study of secret societies in Shanghai (indeed for urban secret societies generally) was the publication in 1986 of *Jiu Shanghai de Banghui* (The Gangs of Old Shanghai), a compilation of memoir literature by former secret society members and Guomindang political and labor leaders with secret society affiliations. This work constitutes a basic and easily accessible first source for the study of Shanghai's secret societies, and one that has been drawn on extensively by Chinese historians.

Among the more important recent Chinese secondary works dealing with Shanghai secret societies are three that were published in 1991. The first, *Jindai Shanghai Heishehui Yanjiu* (A Study of

Secret Societies in Modern Shanghai) by Su Zhiliang and Chen Lifei, provides a comprehensive study of the organization and activities of Shanghai secret societies in the nineteenth and twentieth centuries; the second, *Shanghai Banghui Jianshi* (A Brief History of Shanghai Secret Societies) by Hu Xunmin and He Jian, is a straightforward narrative of the evolution of the Triad and Green Gang systems in Shanghai from the mid-nineteenth century to 1949; and the third, *Jiu Shanghai Heishehui Mishi* (The Secret History of Secret Societies in Old Shanghai), edited by Guo Xuyin, is a detailed study of Shanghai secret societies in the Republican period, with a major focus on the activities of the Green Gang boss Du Yuesheng. Another important work, published in 1993, that has much to say about Shanghai secret societies is Zhou Yumin and Shao Yong's *Zhongguo Banghui Shi* (A History of Chinese Secret Societies). This rich and well-documented study of secret societies from the Qing Dynasty to the People's Republic will undoubtedly become a standard text on the subject.

The present study has also benefited from the "opening up" of Chinese scholarly institutions over the past decade. The research on which it is based would have been much the poorer without access to materials held in Chinese archives and libraries, notably the Shanghai Municipal Archives and the Shanghai Municipal Library. Equally essential for this study are both the Green Gang manuals (known as *tongcao*) published in the 1930s and 1940s, which provide much information on Green Gang ritual, historical traditions, organizational structure and even membership lists, and the Shanghai Municipal Police Special Branch files, an infinitely rich source for any work on the political, social and economic history of Shanghai. Other important sources were the French, United States and British diplomatic correspondence, Chinese and Western-language newspapers, and memoir literature, notably that produced in the *Wenshi Ziliao* series, and especially the *Jiu Shanghai de Banghui*.

The analysis of the Shanghai Green Gang in the 1920s and 1930s presented here revolves around five main themes. The first of these is what might be called the "contemporaneity" of secret societies in the Republican period. Secret societies were malleable organizations with a great capacity to adapt to different social and political environments. A major contention of this study, in fact, is that secret societies, such as the Green Gang, far from being feudal anachronisms were an integral part of the society and politics of twentieth-century China, and that they were capable of adapting positively to the challenges of social and political change.

A second theme is that the hybrid Sino-foreign character of Shanghai, together with the colonial structure of power in the foreign settlements, was particularly encouraging of secret society activities. In the early twentieth century, indeed, Shanghai was composed of three separate jurisdictions—the Chinese city, the International Settlement and the French Concession. The existence of these exclusive and competing national jurisdictions greatly facilitated both the expansion of Green Gang organization and the proliferation of the rackets controlled by various Green Gang groups. At the same time the security needs of the foreign settlements, particularly the need to control rapidly increasing Chinese populations, dictated a degree of cooperation between the foreign authorities and certain powerful Green Gang bosses, with the latter co-opted into the foreign police forces as members of their respective Chinese detective squads. In other words certain favored Green Gang bosses gained tacit official recognition of their rackets in return for contributing to the effectiveness of the coercive power of the foreign settlements. Some bosses, in fact, were able to parley the security functions they performed for the foreign authorities into real political power, as occurred in the French Concession. This relationship raises larger questions concerning the nature of the imperialist system as it operated in Shanghai.

The opium traffic was the key to financial success and power for the Green Gang groups: they competed ruthlessly with one other and with other secret society groups for a share in this lucrative racket; and it was the ability of the French Concession bosses to gain control of the opium traffic that laid the basis for the emergence of the phenomenon of organized crime in Shanghai in the mid-1920s. The security of the opium traffic, furthermore, was an important factor in determining the French Concession group's attitude to Chinese and foreign authorities in Shanghai.

The relationship of the Green Gang to the major social classes, the industrial workers and the bourgeoisie, is important to an understanding of its role in urban society. Its relations with the working class were shaped by the fact that Shanghai was an immigrant society with no highly developed sense of social cohesion; and the defining characteristic of its relations with the workers was its control of labor rackets associated with the labor-contract system. The relations of the various Green Gang groups with the Chinese bourgeoisie was at first merely a function of the former's criminal activities, notably their extortion and kidnapping rackets. Although this negative aspect of the relationship continued to be significant, it was overshadowed progressively by other, more positive factors that reflected the emergence of a more complex relationship. The new relationship, initially, owed much to the dynamics of the contraband opium traffic once it had come under the effective control of the French Concession Green Gang in the mid-1920s, and to the competition between this gangster group and certain leading members of the Chinese bourgeoisie for power and influence in the French Concession. A second phase of this new relationship began with the crisis of 1932 and the participation of certain Green Gang bosses in the political organizations that the bourgeoisie created in this period, notably the Shanghai Civic Association. In the course of the 1930s this relationship was subsumed under the corporatist state system constructed by the Guomindang.

Control of the opium traffic and its dealings with the workers and the bourgeoisie inevitably involved the Green Gang leadership in the politics of the Chinese city. Not only did the Green Gang leaders maintain close relations with a succession of warlord regimes, but they also became caught up in the revolutionary politics of the 1920s through their contacts with the two revolutionary parties of the time, the Guomindang (Nationalist Party) and the Chinese Communist Party. An important focus for this latter relationship was their involvement in Jiang Jieshi's anti-Communist coup of April 1927. The support that the Green Gang bosses gave to Jiang at this time was a necessary but not, in itself, a sufficient condition for the creation of a stable relationship between themselves and the new state system established by the Guomindang after 1927–28. This was a complex relationship shaped by a number of factors and going through a number of phases during the Nanjing Decade. The turning point came with the crisis provoked by the Shanghai Incident in 1932. In the wake of this crisis Du Yuesheng emerged clearly as the most powerful Green Gang boss in Shanghai. He participated fully in the new corporatist state system created by the Nanjing government, and through this participation enhanced significantly his political and economic power. In the 1930s, in fact, Du had become a leading political figure in his own right.

Through a discussion of these themes the study analyses the role of the Green Gang as an important element in social and political history of Shanghai in the early twentieth century. The Shanghai Green Gang, in fact, provides a useful case study of the ways in which secret societies, usually regarded as quintessential elements of the traditional society, could respond positively to the challenges and opportunities provided by China's modern urban society. Through its creation of a system of syndicate crime in the 1920s, moreover, the Green Gang provides an example of how such organizations could transform themselves successfully into one of the diverse elements that served to define the modern age for the Chinese populations of the treaty ports. In this way this study of the Shanghai Green Gang might also contribute to an understanding of the complex processes of social and political change in twentieth-century China.

1 Origins of the Green Gang

In the first half of the twentieth century the Green Gang was one of the best known of China's secret societies among foreigners and Chinese alike. The fact that treaty ports such as Tianjin and Shanghai were major centers of Green Gang activity kept it constantly in the eye of the foreign community, while the Chinese population could not escape from its ubiquitous presence. Despite the general popular and official awareness of the Green Gang, however, knowledge of its origins and evolution was very confused because of the cloak of mythology and deliberate obfuscation that enveloped it.

This confusion has been shared by later historians and has given rise to considerable debate among them concerning the origins of the Green Gang. One leading historian of the Green Gang, Hu Zhusheng, for example, has observed that among the histories of modern Chinese secret societies, that of the Green Gang is the one replete with the most complex problems; while another, Jerome Ch'en, has remarked that the history of the Green Gang "is a blend of facts and fiction, often more fiction than facts."[1]

In recent years, however, archive-based research by Chinese scholars has begun to clarify the origins of the Green Gang.[2] Briefly, these studies show that the Green Gang emerged in its modern form at the turn of the nineteenth and twentieth centuries from the Anqing Daoyou ("Friends of the Way of Tranquility and Purity," or the Anqing League), a secret society active in the Subei region of Jiangsu.[3] The Anqing Daoyou drew on the traditions of the Grand Canal grain transport boatmen's associations, which were affiliated with the Patriarch Luo Sect (*Luo Zu Jiao*), a popular Buddhist sect. At the same time it also formed a very close relationship with those elements of the Gelaohui (the Society of Brothers and Elders) that were active in northern Jiangsu. Through the mediation of the Anqing Daoyou the Green Gang was able to draw on the traditions of both the Patriarch Luo Sect and the Gelaohui. The modern Green Gang, therefore, was essentially the product of the fusion of the Anqing Daoyou with elements of the Gelaohui.

THE ORIGINS OF THE GREEN GANG

The general antecedents of the Green Gang are to be found in the traditions of the Patriarch Luo Sect, a late Ming secular, salvationist Buddhist sect that had evolved from the White Lotus tradition of sectarian Buddhism. The sect's founder, Luo Qing, stressed the importance of individual enlightenment, a message that, when directed at non-elite audiences, provided powerful encouragement for the empowerment of the ordinary individual in the religious sphere.[4] In the course of the sixteenth and seventeenth centuries the Patriarch Luo Sect spread throughout China.

According to official Qing government reports dating from the mid-eighteenth century, the sect was introduced to the soldiers and boatmen of the grain tribute fleets on the Grand Canal in the early seventeenth century by three individuals, Weng Yan and Qian Jian (both from Miyun County in Zhili) and Pan Qing (from Songjiang County in Jiangsu).[5] These three were later known as "the Three Patriarchs," and by the eighteenth century the Three Patriarchs Sect (*San Zu Jiao*) was an established sub-sect of the Patriarch Luo Sect among the crews of the grain tribute fleets.

By the early eighteenth century the city of Hangzhou, the southern terminus of the tribute fleets, had become an important organizational center for the boatmen's associations. It was here that a major temple (*jiamiao*) of the Luo Sect as well as three Buddhist monasteries (*an*) dedicated to Weng, Qian and Pan were located, together with their putative graves. These monasteries served not only as devotional centers but also as hostels for the boatmen who came mainly from areas north of the Yangzi River (from Shandong and Zhili predominantly) during the months of inactivity and unemployment when the fleets had returned to their Jiangnan base after delivery of the grain tribute to Beijing. Over time the three monasteries became the centers of three sub-networks of monastery-hostels (*antang*) among the grain transport boatmen belonging to the Patriarch Luo Sect.[6] The monastery-hostel represented the basic organizational unit for the boatmen's associations (*shuishou banghui*).[7] They were controlled by retired boatmen. Indeed, in the eighteenth century, boatmen tended to join the sect only after they had retired from the grain transports, and sect members among the active boatmen on the fleets remained a minority.[8]

The Patriarch Luo Sect, in fact, functioned as a mutual aid organization among the Grand Canal boatmen providing services strikingly similar to those provided by *huiguan* (*landsmannschaften*), such as temporary accommodation, medical care, and burial for the dead.[9] At the same time it also operated as a professional body that regulated the standards and transmitted the technical skills associated with the boatmen's occupation. As Kelley has observed, these activities of the Luo Sect temples "stabilized the livelihood of a labor force crucial to the [Qing] dynasty's interests and potentially disruptive of local order as well."[10]

Despite such important contributions to the preservation of social stability in the Jiangnan, however, in 1768 the Qianlong emperor, concerned at the growing strength of the sect among the Grand Canal boatmen, enforced an earlier proscription of the Luo Sect and razed its temples in Hangzhou and confiscated its lands. This development, it has been argued, changed the nature of the boatmen's associations by intensifying the process of their transformation into an essentially secret society organization.[11]

With the destruction of the temples the focus of the associations' organization moved to the fleets themselves, and, at the same time, a system of authority similar to that of a secret society was established. In each of the fleets one of the ships was designated a "venerable worship boat" (*laotangchuan*), which flew a banner bearing the image of the Patriarch Luo, and this replaced the temple-hostels as the organizational and religious nuclei of the boatmen's associations. Each association now took its name from that of its respective fleet (*bang*).[12] The leaders were known as the "venerable officials" (*laoguan*) and were selected on the basis of generational seniority. They determined the sect's regulations, entrance requirements, identification signs, and boatmen's wages; in fact, they controlled all aspects of the lives of their boatmen followers.[13] A key role in this organization was played by the boatswain (*duoshou*) on each of the grain transport boats. He was empowered to set up a "church" (*jiaomen*) on his boat to which he recruited his fellow boatmen, and he would also place a spirit tablet to the Patriarch Luo on the ship's bowsprit. The boatswain's power was such that even the Manchu bannerman, assigned to each grain transport junk, regularly took his orders from him.[14]

This transformation was accompanied by the outbreak of factional strife between the three separate sub-networks associated with the three monastery systems dedicated to Weng, Qian and Pan. By the beginning of the nineteenth century, and as a consequence of the Qianlong emperor's dissolution of the monastery-hostels, these networks had evolved into two major factional organizations known as the *lao'an* (literally, "old peace"—which embraced the former Weng and Qian groups) and the *xin'an* (literally, "new peace"—which was the former Pan group).[15] The often murderous competition between these two factions, together with the growing power of the boatmen's associations, greatly increased the level of violence on the fleets. By the 1820s and 1830s disorder was endemic among the grain transport fleets, and Qing officials, whose authority was increasingly diminished, took action against only the more serious disorders. In 1839, for example, Lin Zexu noted that murders were carried out regularly by the boatmen's leaders, whom he described as "teachers" (*shifu*) holding positions in the "venerable worship boats"; and he also noted that these "teachers" used any means to increase their control over the boatmen, including subverting the authority of the Manchu bannermen.[16]

In the mid-nineteenth century both man-made and natural disasters (notably the change in the course of the Yellow River in 1855) combined to bring about the demise of these boatmen's associations. By the mid-1850s the transportation of tribute grain through the Grand Canal had come to a complete halt. The move by the Taiping armies into the lower Yangzi and their occupation of Nanjing in 1853 ended grain tribute shipments from Zhejiang, and the change in the course of the Yellow River in 1855 made permanent the shift to sea transport for the grain tribute from Jiangsu that had commenced in 1848.[17]

As a result of these changes it is estimated that between 40,000 and 50,000 boatmen lost their regular employment. When all those in ancillary and service occupations associated with the grain transport along the Grand Canal are included, the final figure must be calculated in the hundreds of thousands.[18] Under the pressure of these developments the organizational structure of the boatmen's associations progressively disintegrated. One later Green Gang account commented on this disaster in the following terms: "In the fourth year of Xian Feng [1855] . . . the proper sacrifices to the Great Provider ended, and as a consequence incense was not burnt to the three ancestors for over forty years."[19]

Large numbers of unemployed boatmen joined various rebel groups such as the Nian and the Red Turbans in Subei, and the Taipings in Jiangnan. Others joined the Qing military forces. Many more, however, became salt smugglers, especially in the Liang Huai region of Subei, which contained some of the largest salt pans in the country.[20] Salt was an official government monopoly and a dietary staple of the Chinese population; its high price and inelastic demand ensured a flourishing illicit trade. The boatmen's associations already had well-established relations with the salt smugglers in Subei. In the previous century, for example, the Qing government had authorized the officers and crews of the grain tribute fleets to carry a certain amount of cargo on their own account. Many used this concession to smuggle salt from the north, where it was cheap, to the ports on the Yangzi, where its retail price was very high. In this lucrative enterprise, the boatmen formed close working relations with the professional salt smugglers of the Liang Huai region, who were referred to in the records as "green skins" (*qingpi*).[21]

With the disintegration of the boatmen's associations a new organization emerged in Subei in the late 1850s and early 1860s—the Anqing Daoyou. Its membership was composed of former grain tribute boatmen, who belonged to the *xin'an* faction (i.e., Pan faction) of the boatmen's associations, and professional salt smugglers.[22] Although initially these two groups represented separate elements within a loose organizational structure, by the 1870s they had fused into a single integrated organization. The major activity of the league was salt smuggling, and its area of operations was, therefore, originally confined to the Liang Huai region of Subei, one of the largest of the twelve salt divisions under government monopoly, and the place where the salt smugglers congregated.[23] A further reason for the concentration of the league's activities on Subei was that the Jiangnan region remained a cockpit of conflict between the Taiping and Qing armies into the early 1860s.

After the suppression of the Taiping and Nian rebellions, the Anqing League extended its activities to the lower Yangzi ports, notably Yangzhou and the Lake Tai region, during the 1870s and

1880s. By the turn of the century this latter region had become a major center of the league's smuggling activities. At the same time, many unemployed boatmen made their way back to their native districts in Shandong, Henan and Zhili and brought with them elements of the Anqing Daoyou organization. Given the poverty prevailing in rural Shandong and Henan many of these returning boatmen took to banditry.[24]

At this time the Anqing Daoyou also forged close links with that section of the Gelaohui, one of the most powerful secret societies in the late Qing period, which was active in Subei.[25] The relationship between the Anqing League and the Gelaohui went back to the 1850s and 1860s when the Hunan Army was stationed in the Liang Huai region to both eradicate the Nian and eliminate salt smuggling. This force had been penetrated by the Gelaohui and many of its officers and men were members of the society. When these forces were disbanded after the elimination of the mid-century rebellions, many of the former soldiers remained in the Subei region and, utilizing their Gelaohui organization, turned to banditry and cooperated with the Anqing League in the latter's salt-smuggling operations. Many leaders from both organizations joined the other. Among the most important was Xu Baoshan, a powerful leader of the Anqing Daoyou who also became a leader of the Gelaohui, and thus controlled both organizations in his Subei bailiwick.[26] There was also a progressive adoption of organizational structures and rituals by one organization from the other.[27] By the end of the century, in fact, the two societies in Subei had, to all intents and purposes, fused into one organization.[28]

It is now commonly accepted by historians that the name Anqing Daoyou represents the first specific reference to the Green Gang in the official sources.[29] However, the evolution from *Anqing League* to *Green Gang* is still not known. One possible explanation is that the *Qing* of *Qing Bang* (the *Green* of *Green Gang*) is a transcription error for the *qing* (a similar character meaning clear or pure) in *Anqing*. The name *qingpi* (green skins) may have contributed to the error. Indeed, *qingpi* may be the direct source for *Qing Bang*.

The evidence presently available suggests that the Green Gang first emerged as an organization distinct from the Anqing Daoyou in the 1880s and 1890s. According to Tao Chengzhang, the Anqing Daoyou (which he referred to as the "Pan Sect" [*Pan Men*] or "Pan Family" [*Pan Jia*]), which was prevalent throughout the counties of the Jiangnan by the turn of the century, was commonly known as the "Green Gang" (*Qing Bang*).[30] In the late 1880s, moreover, a certain Pan Shengtai and others, who belonged to the Anqing League, organized the *Anqing Zhongxing* (Anqing Revival), which was established in association with the partial and short-lived revival of the grain tribute system on the Grand Canal.[31] The revived system involved only six fleets—the Jiang Huai Si, the Xing Wu Si, the Xing Wu Liu, the Jia Bai, the Jia Hai Wei and the Hang San—and these six fleets provided a key element in the organizational system of the modern Green Gang.[32] One of the Green Gang manuals (*tongcao*) published in the early twentieth century, moreover, states that in 1886 (the twelfth year of Guangxu) twenty-four generational status groups were created by members of the Xing status group, in addition to the existing twenty-four generational groups originally derived from the boatmen's associations and utilized by the Anqing Daoyou.[33] This event, perhaps, is the first clear reference to the creation of an organizational structure for the modern Green Gang.

The emergence of the modern Green Gang from the Anqing Daoyou occurred over a prolonged period that extended into the first two decades of the twentieth century, and its organization was effected at different times in different localities. Support for this view is provided by the Green Gang manual cited above, which suggests that the organization was carried out by members of the Xing, Li and Da generational status groups whose period of activity covered roughly the forty years from 1880 to 1920.[34] The manual also notes that a third batch of twenty-four generational status groups was created in 1921, which would suggest that the process of defining the organizational structure of the Green Gang had not yet been fully completed in the first two decades of the twentieth century.[35]

A survey of the Anqing and Green Gang organizations in the seventeen counties of the Huai region of Subei, which was conducted by Wu Choupeng in the late 1920s as part of a larger enquiry into the social and economic conditions of the region, also suggests that the modern Green Gang was established at different times in different regions, and even in different localities of the same region, over the forty-odd years from 1885 to about 1925.[36] According to this survey a majority of the Anqing League organizations (nine of the seventeen) for which some form of date was given claimed to date from the the end of the Ming or the beginning of the Qing Dynasty. This would appear to indicate that the Anqing League organizations in these counties evolved from earlier boatmen's associations. The survey also revealed, however, that just under half of these Anqing League/Green Gang organizations (eight of the seventeen) had been first established at some time in the second half of the nineteenth century, and mainly during the Guangxu period (1875–1908); and that two of them, those in Ganyu and Donghai counties, were established as late as 1914 and 1925, respectively. This would indicate a rapid expansion of these organizations in this region in the late nineteenth and early twentieth centuries. Most of the organizations that referred to themselves as Green Gang (Qing Bang), moreover, were established in this later period, including the two that were set up in the early years of the Republic.

Evidence from other areas where the Green Gang was active, fragmentary though it is, also supports the view of an expansion of the Green Gang in the first decades of the twentieth century. Green Gang organization in the major towns of Anhui, for example, appears to date only from the early twentieth century. In Anqing the Green Gang was first organized at the end of the Qing Dynasty by a member of the Da generational status group, while in Wuhu it was established only around 1920. In Wuhu, moreover, there were very few members of the Da group.[37] In Tianjin, which in the 1930s was an important center of Green Gang activity, a number of sources suggest that the Green Gang was not formally organized there until the early 1920s, and that its organization was associated with control of the city by Shandong warlords who were themselves members of the Green Gang.[38] Once established, however, the Green Gang quickly spread throughout Tianjin and emerged as the major secret society/gangster organization in the city.[39]

An important figure in the period of transition from the Anqing League to the Green Gang at the end of the nineteenth century was Xu Baoshan (1866–1913), a prominent leader of the Anqing League in Subei. His sphere of operations was in the lower Yangzi valley in the region between Yangzhou and Zhenjiang, and here he progressively built up an impressive power base. By the first decade of the twentieth century, he reputedly controlled over 700 salt-smuggling craft and had over 10,000 followers, and in 1899 he established his own organization, the Chunbao Lodge (*Chunbao Shantang*). Throughout the 1890s and 1900s Xu enjoyed fairly complex relations with the Qing authorities and with the revolutionaries. In both cases the relationship oscillated between conflict and cooperation, depending on which policy best served to maximize Xu's interests at any given time. The apogee of Xu's power occurred after 1900 when he was appointed commander of the Qing government's local anti-smuggling forces, and especially with the outbreak of the 1911 Revolution when he seized power in Yangzhou and gained control of the production and distribution centers of the salt industry. At the very moment of his triumph, however, Xu was assassinated by members of the Guomindang in revenge for the killing of Tongmenghui revolutionaries during his seizure of Yangzhou.[40]

Xu Baoshan is an extremely important figure for the later history of the modern Green Gang. His career reveals, as noted above, the intimate organizational relationship that developed between the Anqing Daoyou and the Gelaohui in the late nineteenth century. As the creation of his Chunbao Lodge indicates, Xu had become a leader of the Gelaohui while continuing to be a leader of the Anqing Daoyou. Again, a number of his key followers, such as Zhang Renkui and Gao Shikui, went on to become important leaders of the Green Gang in the Republican period, and so provided in their persons a degree of continuity between the Anqing League and the modern Green Gang. Zhang and Gao were sworn brothers and were extremely influential in the Green Gang system in the early Republic, counting leading warlords among their followers. By the late 1920s and early 1930s both had transferred their powerful personal organizations to Shanghai.[41]

Xu's career also reveals the complex relationship that existed between the leaders of the Anqing League and established authority, and the capacity of these leaders to cooperate successfully with that authority to mutual advantage. This was a pattern that was to be repeated by certain Green Gang leaders in the Republican period. Finally, a highly developed system of smuggling provided the economic basis for the power not only of Xu Baoshan but of all leaders of the Anqing League. Salt was a necessary item in the diet of the Chinese population and was highly taxed by the state; therefore demand for cheap contraband salt was both high and constant. Management of salt smuggling demanded not only a corrupt relationship with the local authorities but also a highly developed relationship with local merchants in order to ensure the effective distribution of the contraband salt. In all these ways, therefore, the salt-smuggling activities of Xu and other members of the Anqing League provided both a precedent and a reservoir of practical experience on which later Green Gang leaders could draw when they engaged in trafficking in opium during the Republican period.

THE ORGANIZATIONAL STRUCTURE OF THE GREEN GANG

An appreciation of the Green Gang's organizational structure is important to an understanding of the emergence of the modern Green Gang in Shanghai. Details of the organization and regulations of the Green Gang are provided by the Green Gang manuals that were published in the 1930s and 1940s.[42] The information contained in these manuals is a mix of fact and received tradition, and disentangling the one from the other presents its own set of complex problems. Despite the difficulties, however, they constitute the major source of information on the internal organization of the Green Gang, and have been used extensively by those Chinese and Japanese historians of secret societies who discuss the Green Gang.[43] As indicated earlier, the formal organization of the modern Green Gang was a blend of the traditions of the boatmen's associations (particularly those of the *xin'an*, or Pan faction) and those of the Gelaohui. The former provided the generational structure and the *bang* (fleet/gang) system, while the latter contributed the system of lodges (*xiangtang*—literally, "incense halls") and sworn brotherhoods. In both instances these structures were mediated through the Anqing Daoyou.

The Green Gang organized itself along fictive kinship lines with members regarding themselves as belonging to an extended clan system. They referred to the Green Gang as "the family" (*jia*) and to their membership as being "in the family" (*jiali*). An important aspect of this system was the organization of the Green Gang along generational lines in imitation of the generational structures of lineage systems. This generational structure also had some of the characteristics of a guild hierarchy of master-disciple relations. Senior leaders in the Green Gang were called "teachers" (*shifu* or *laoshi*) and their authority within the system derived from the seniority of their generational status; only these "teachers," in theory, could recruit followers, who were called "disciples" (*tudi*). New members on entering the Green Gang were given, at the same time, a generational name (*zi*), which designated their position within the Green Gang hierarchy. The new members' generational status within the

Green Gang would be the one immediately below that of their "teacher." In the first half of the twentieth century four generational status groups operated within the Green Gang, which were, in descending order of seniority, the Da, the Tong, the Wu and the Xue (with the latter occasionally being referred to as the Jue). Thus followers of leaders who belonged to the Da generational status group (the most senior of the four) were members of the Tong generational status group, which was the next one down; and those followers of the leaders of the Tong generational status group were members of the Wu generational status group, and so on.[44]

Originally there were twenty-four generational status groups (*zibei*), whose creation was ascribed to the putative founder of the Green Gang, Jin Bifeng.[45] These status groups were taken over from the Anqing Daoyou. According to the Green Gang manuals the first four generational groups (the Qing, Jing, Dao, and De) were assigned to the ancestral founders of the Green Gang: with Jin Bifeng, himself, occupying the Qing generation; Luo Qing (the founder of the Luo Sect) occupying the Jing; Lu Kui (the "Ancestor Lu") occupying the Dao; and the three "Late Ancestors" (*Houzu*), Weng Yan, Qian Jian, and Pan Qing occupying the fourth or De generation.[46]

There is some controversy over the origins of the last four generational status groups (the Da, Tong, Wu and Xue). Some sources deny that they formed part of the original generational structure of the traditional Green Gang, arguing that they were created only at the turn of the nineteenth and twentieth centuries. One source asserts that there were in fact only twenty generational groups in the original Anqing Daoyou / Green Gang structure, and that the last of these generations, the Li, coincided with the final years of the Qing Dynasty, which ended in 1911. This source asserts that it was at this time that four further generational groups (the Da, the Tong, the Wu and the Xue) were created, which were numbered twenty-one to twenty-four in the generational hierarchy.[47] Another source agrees with this periodization, and adds a further refinement by suggesting that these four generational groups were created by anti-Qing revolutionaries who sought to use the Green Gang groups in the Jiangnan, and that the generational names are an enigmatic reference to the Datong Military School (*Datong Wuxue*) that was set up in Shaoxing by Xu Xilin and Qiu Jin.[48] This latter suggestion, however, has not yet been substantiated by corroborating evidence. As noted in the previous section two further sets of twenty-four generational status groups were created in the late nineteenth and early twentieth centuries, which would suggest that the Green Gang was undergoing significant organizational changes in this period.

One further point needs to be made with regard to the generational structure of the modern Green Gang. Although membership in a senior generational group conferred influence and status within the Green Gang system, it did not necessarily confer power. Within the Shanghai Green Gang, for example, Huang Jinrong did not become a member of one of the Green Gang's generations until late in his career, but this fact did not inhibit his ability to control his followers who were Green Gang members. Until he formally joined the Green Gang in 1923, Huang was described as having an "empty character" (*kongzi*), that is, he lacked membership in a formal generational status group. Du Yuesheng, for his part, was a member of the rather lowly Wu generational status group, which was ranked twenty-third out of the twenty-four generations. This did not prevent him, however, from exercising authority over Green Gang members who belonged to the Tong group, which immediately preceded his own.

This contradiction between formal status within the Green Gang system and the exercise of actual power is fundamental to an understanding of the development of the Green Gang in Shanghai. It reflects on the one hand the normal tendency in kinship-based lineages toward the emergence of a disjuncture between the formal generational structure and the exercise of actual power. On the other hand, it also reflects the fact that the Green Gang was a relatively new organization whose structure was still evolving in the first decades of the twentieth century. As a result it was prepared to co-opt existing sources of gangster power (such as that exercised by Huang Jinrong), and, at the same time, its hierarchical structure was not sufficiently well-defined to prevent the acquisition of significant power by members whose formal status in the hierarchy was relatively low (such as Du Yuesheng).

Given this fluidity in the formal structures of the organization an important role was played by personal relations and connections (*guanxi*) in facilitating an individual's rise in the Green Gang. Of particular importance was the institution of sworn brotherhood. Within the Green Gang the system of sworn brotherhood was different from that of blood brotherhood of the Triads. It did not involve the shared drinking of a mixture of chicken blood and the participants' blood, but merely the swearing of oaths and the burning of incense.

Sworn brotherhood was a key means by which ordinary members built up personal networks within the Green Gang. It also helped underpin alliances between Green Gang leaders, and stabilized collective leaderships such as that of the Big Eight Mob (*Da Ba Gu Dang*), discussed in chapter 2. Sworn brotherhood could also be a barometer of changing power relations within individual Green Gang organizations. A leader whose power was in decline might enter into sworn brother relations with his chief lieutenants as a face-saving device, as Huang Jinrong did with Du Yuesheng and Zhang Xiaolin in 1924. In such a case sworn brotherhood was a means by which the decline of existing leaders and the rise of new ones could be formally (and symbolically) recognized, thus limiting potential disruption and ensuring the coherence of the system that was under stress. Sworn brotherhood relations were also an important means by which Green Gang leaders developed networks with members of other secret society systems, such as the Triads (Hong League) and the Sichuan Paoge. This served over time to mediate the hostility and competition between these different secret society systems and led to a degree of interpenetration of those systems.

At the same time, sworn brotherhood provided a mechanism by which Green Gang leaders also established relations with members of the political and commercial elite, and, of course, vice versa. The initiative in forging such relations was not always left to the Green Gang leaders themselves. As regards the political elite, good examples are the sworn brother relations established between Yang Hu and Chen Qun and the French Concession Green Gang leaders in 1927, and the later sworn brother relationship between Dai Li and Du Yuesheng. Among the Shanghai capitalists, Yu Xiaqing and Wang Xiaolai enjoyed sworn brother relations with Huang Jinrong and Du Yuesheng, respectively. In this way sworn brotherhood enmeshed individual Green Gang members in a thick network of relations with other Green Gang members, members of other secret society systems, and local political, economic and social elites.

A related phenomenon of importance here was the distinction that was made in the Green Gang system between "disciples" and "pupils" (*xuesheng*) of Green Gang leaders. These categories were not the same.[49] The former were those who, on joining the Green

Gang, had gone through the formal ceremony of submitting to a "teacher" and, therefore, had entered into an immediate and permanent relationship with that particular leader, which was given institutional expression by membership in a particular generational status group. "Pupils," on the other hand, were those who merely took a leader as a "master" (*xiansheng*). This did not entail the acquisition of a position in the generational structure, and such "pupils" could take a number of Green Gang leaders as their "master" at any given time. A Green Gang member, in other words, had a primary relationship with his "teacher" but could also form secondary relationships with a number of other Green Gang leaders, whom he took as his "masters." The latter relationships, however, were of a different order and subordinate to his relationship with his "teacher." At the same time, individuals outside the Green Gang could enter into a relationship with a Green Gang leader by becoming his "pupil." This did not usually involve, however, membership in the Green Gang. This distinction gained in significance within the Shanghai Green Gang in the early twentieth century, particularly after the development in the 1930s of personal organizations by some Green Gang leaders, such as Du Yuesheng's Endurance Club (*Heng She*) and Zhang Renkui's Benevolence Society (*Ren She*).

The Green Gang was also organized into separate branches or gangs (*bang*). In the Green Gang tradition as recounted in the manuals, these branches were reputedly based on the grain tribute fleets (also called *bang*) of the Grand Canal. In the early twentieth century, however, there were only six major branches in the Green Gang structure, and, as mentioned in the preceding section, these appear to have been based on, or at least had the same names as, the six fleets of the grain transport that were revived temporarily by the Qing government in the late nineteenth century. These six branches were the Jiang Huai Si, the Jia Bai, the Xing Wu Si, the Xing Wu Liu, the Hang San, and the Jia Hai Wei.[50] These branches did not have precise geographical areas of activity, and their areas of predominance depended on the movements of the leaders of the Da generational group of the respective branches, and on who among these leaders recruited followers and in what numbers. Two branches were particularly influential in Shanghai in the 1920s and 1930s, the Xing Wu Si (in the French Concession) and the Xing Wu Liu (in the International Settlement); while the Jia Bai became the most powerful branch in Zhejiang after the 1911 Revolution.[51]

According to the Green Gang manuals the induction of new members involved fairly elaborate ceremonies, which were originally modeled on those of Buddhist monasticism. Green Gang initiates, for example, dressed in robes similar to those worn by Buddhist monks, and the terminology used in the ceremony was derived from that obtaining in Buddhist temples: the process of applying for membership was referred to as "entering the monastery" (*shangxiang*), while the customary payment made on joining the Green Gang was called "making one's vows" (*shoujie*).[52] The initiation ceremony itself was called *xiangtang* and could be either fairly simple or extremely elaborate with different degrees in between; although whatever its degree of elaboration it was normally held in a local temple. In general the particular Green Gang leader who was accepting new followers and who was designated "the teacher" was assisted by six other "masters" who performed clearly defined and important roles in the ceremony. These included the introduction (*yinjian*) of applicants, their instruction in Green Gang principles (*zhuandao*), the supervision of the ceremonies (*sili*), the custody of the official seal (*yongyin*) and the drafting of proclamations (*zhangbu*).

An applicant for membership in the Green Gang first had to find a Green Gang "boss" (*laotou*) with sufficient generational status to introduce him to the leader ("teacher") whose follower he wished to become. Once he had secured an introduction he then had to write out an application form (*baishitie*) containing information on his family background for three generations, his age, his native place, and his occupation, which he then presented personally to the "teacher." A good example of the formula in use in Shanghai in the 1930s is provided by the application by the military officer Cui Xilin to become a follower of Zhang Renkui in 1931, which went as follows:

> Disciple [*mensheng*] Cui Shuxian [i.e., Cui Xilin], 31 years old, from Gaoyu County, Jiangsu Province, through the introduction of Army Commander Du Fengju and Divisional Commander Dai Jieping [both followers of Zhang Renkui and Cui's superiors], personally seeks to become the follower of Commander, the Venerable Master Zhang [Renkui].
>
> Throughout his life Cui will follow his [Zhang's] advice and wait on his instructions.
>
> The three generations are: great-grandfather, Cui Fu; grandfather, Cui Yangchun; father, Cui Ruiting. Disciple Cui Shuxian respectfully

makes his request [to be accepted as a follower by Zhang Renkui].
September 1931.[53]

On presentation of his application the applicant then joined other
initiates in the membership ceremony, which involved kowtowing
three times and burning incense before the altars containing the
tablets representing the Patriarch Luo and the three progenitors
(*zhuye*), Weng, Pan and Qian, followed by three prostrations before
the "teacher" and his six assistants. After a period of time the initiates were each given a mouthful of water, in a ceremony known as
"the mouth cleaning" (*jingkou*), which symbolized their purification
and rebirth as a member of the Green Gang. The "teacher" then put
a series of formal questions to initiates regarding their willingness to
accept the rules of the society and the prescribed punishments for
any breach of the Green Gang's code. Each of the initiates then received a certificate of membership on payment of a fee Ch$10 or
Ch$12 to the presiding "teacher." The ceremony then usually con-
cluded with a formal dinner party.[54]

The Green Gang had, at least in theory, a very strict code of conduct, which its members transgressed on pain of very severe penal-
ties including death. The key regulations were the so-called "ten
great rules" (*shi da banggui*), which were designed to ensure organizational solidarity and esprit. They forbade "disciples" to de-
ceive their teachers or disgrace the Green Gang ancestors and encouraged them to respect their seniors in the Green Gang structure,
to obey the society's rules, to deal fairly with other members of
the society, to keep the society's secrets, and to avoid adultery and
theft. They also bound all members to uphold the traditional Confucian virtues of "benevolence" (*ren*), "righteousness" (*yi*), "pro-
priety" (*li*), "wisdom" (*zhi*) and "sincerity" (*xin*). There were also a
number of supplementary rules and proscriptions, which covered
such issues as the settlement of disputes between Green Gang members, mutual assistance among members, hospitality to traveling
members, secret signs of recognition, and disciples' responsibilities
to their teachers.[55]

These rules did not merely serve an organizational function, they
also constituted, more importantly, a code of honor and chivalry,
which distinguished them from the rest of society. Green Gang
members regarded themselves as *haoxia* (literally, "men of honor
and courage"), in other words heroes, who were engaged in a
ceaseless struggle against injustice not only for themselves but also

on behalf of the poor, the oppressed and the dispossessed. This was a powerful self-image, which resonated across the centuries.

The concept of haoxia was derived from the term for swordsmen (*jianxia*) of the Warring States period as first described by the historians Sima Qian and Ban Gu. It was sustained by reference to the heroes of popular fiction, particularly those of the *Romance of the Three Kingdoms (San Guo Zhi Yanyi)* and the *Water Margin (Shuihu Zhuan)*.[56] Chinese popular culture was permeated by stories from these two works through their retelling by itinerant professional storytellers and their dramatization in Beijing Opera and in other regional operatic traditions.[57] The heroes of these works served as archetypes for certain popular virtues, such as courage, loyalty, a sense of justice and fair play, and (in the case of the *Water Margin*) opposition to oppressive government and official corruption. These virtues included an acceptance of violence, especially if undertaken to right wrongs and to oppose injustice. A particularly potent image was that of the fictional oath of brotherhood, taken by Liu Bei, Guan Yu and Zhang Fei in the peach garden, which opens *Romance of the Three Kingdoms* and which has served as an ideal type of sworn brotherhood for a number of historical secret societies, including the Green Gang. The formula of this oath as given in the novel was as follows:

> We three, Liu Pei, Kuan Yu and Chang Fei, though of different families, swear brotherhood, and promise mutual help to one end. We will rescue each other in difficulty, and we will aid each other in danger. We swear to serve the state and save the people. We ask not the same day of birth, but we seek to die together. May Heaven, the all-ruling, and Earth, the all-producing, read our hearts, and if we turn aside from righteousness or forget kindliness may Heaven and man smite us![58]

The heroic values expressed in these works still exercised a powerful influence on the minds of members of the modern Green Gang in Shanghai in the first half of the twentieth century. Wu Yugong, for example, placed the modern Green Gang in a direct line of descent from the heroes of the *Romance of the Three Kingdoms* and the *Water Margin* when he wrote the following in the preface to his 1922 novel on the Green Gang (*Qinghong Bang Shi Yanyi* [The Romance of the Green and Red Gangs]):

> When Liu Bei, Guan Yu and Zhang Fei swore an oath of brotherhood in the peach garden, although they were born on different days, they

desired to die together on the same day. When Song Jiang and Wu Yong met up at the Liangshan marshes, they swore an oath "to enjoy good fortune together and to face difficulties together." When succeeding generations of dispossessed and unruly robin hoods (*jianghu*) combined together to form mighty bands, they also observed this tenet. And so it was with the emergence of the Green and Red Gangs.[59]

Many of the names of the Green Gang groups that were active in Shanghai consciously evoked the world of the haoxia. Two such groups—for example, the "Thirty-six Mob" (*Sanshiliu Gudang*) and the "108 Warriors" (*Yibailingba Jiang*), which was organized by Chinese detectives working for the foreign settlements—took their names directly from those hero bands mentioned in the *Water Margin*.[60] The view of the world common to many Shanghai gangster bosses was shaped in part by the spirit of haoxia. Many of the Green Gang manuals, for example, were introduced by a section containing the calligraphy of Green Gang leaders whose brushwork gave expression to such sentiments as the "spirit of honor and chivalry" (*xiayi qingshen*), "loyal hero" (*zhongyi haoxia*), "one thousand years of morality and justice" (*daoyi qianqiu*), and "the correct tradition of morality and justice" (*daoyi zhengzong*).[61] Du Yuesheng, for one, delighted in hiring people to read to him stories from the *Water Margin*, the *Romance of the Three Kingdoms*, and the *Romance of the Western Han* (*Xi Han Yanyi*).[62] Du, in fact, at the height of his power in the 1930s, deliberately cultivated a public persona based in part on the spirit of the traditional hero as a means of giving himself legitimacy with the Shanghai public. It was, therefore, with no sense of irony that Pan Gongzhan (a leading figure in the Shanghai Guomindang), in his essay to commemorate Du Yuesheng's death, could extol Du as a modern exemplar of the way of "the swordsman/hero" (*xia*).[63] Although these values were often honored more in the breach than the observance, they constituted, nevertheless, an important element in the mental universe of Green Gang members in Shanghai, and so cannot be discounted entirely. They could exercise an important, if intangible, influence on their actions.

In sum the Green Gang was a newly established secret society organization. Despite its generational antecedents in the boatmen's associations and the Patriarch Luo Sect, the Green Gang's actual origins cannot be traced much beyond the last two decades of the nineteenth century. Indeed the Green Gang was still in the process of organizational definition in the first two decades of the twentieth century. This fact is of considerable importance in understanding its emergence in Shanghai. Rather than representing the adaptation of a long-established traditional secret society organization to a new Sino-foreign environment, the Green Gang in Shanghai in fact was part of a newly emergent organization still in the process of formation. The Shanghai environment, indeed, was of central importance to its organizational development.

THE EMERGENCE OF THE GREEN GANG IN SHANGHAI TO 1920

Secret societies were active in Shanghai from its inception as a treaty port in 1843. The earliest were those associated with the Triad (*Hong Men*) system, which was particularly active among Guangdong and Fujianese sailors sojourning in Shanghai.[64] In 1853 the Small Sword Society (*Xiaodaohui*), a Triad offshoot, rebelled against the local Qing authorities and seized control of Chinese Shanghai, which it held until February 1855.[65] Despite the defeat of the Small Swords and the general proscription of Triad organizations, these organizations continued to exist among the Guangdong sojourning community, and were especially important among the Chaozhou merchants involved in the opium trade, popularly known as the Chaozhou Clique (*Chao Bang*). Toward the end of the nineteenth century the term Red Gang (*Hong Bang*) was first used in reference to the Triad groups in Shanghai.[66]

By the end of the nineteenth century the Green Gang began to emerge as one of the more important secret society groups active in Shanghai. Three general factors, taken together, produced an environment in Shanghai favorable to its development and, indeed, to the growth of gangsterism in general. These were the emergence of Shanghai as a key transshipment point in the grain tribute system in the late nineteenth century; the mass peasant migration into Shanghai from the rural hinterland, especially from impoverished Subei, consequent on Shanghai's emergence as an industrial center after 1895; and the existence of separate police jurisdictions in the city, together with the colonial nature of the police systems in the two foreign settlements.

In the latter half of the nineteenth century, as noted earlier, an increasing proportion of the tribute rice from Jiangnan was transported by sea rather than by the Grand Canal, first in sea-going junks and then in steamships. One consequence of this development was that Shanghai, as the southern terminus of the sea-transport system, became an important transshipment point for the tribute rice from Jiangsu and Zhejiang.[67] As a result many former boatmen and others associated with the Grand Canal transport system moved to Shanghai in order to work on the docks, the sea-going junks and, later, the steamships, and they brought with them elements of the Anqing Daoyou/Green Gang. Tribute rice was an increasingly important cargo for the steamers of the China Merchants' Steam Navigation Company (*Lunchuan Zhaoshangju*—CMSN) after 1873, and the CMSN ships and docks in Shanghai became particular centers of Green Gang activity by the beginning of the twentieth century.[68] In the last quarter of the nineteenth century occasional references to the activities of the Anqing Daoyou/Green Gang began to appear in the Shanghai press. The first was a brief report in *Shen Bao* for June 1876 that noted the origins of the Anqing Daoyou/Green Gang among the grain transport boatmen, its involvement in banditry in the Huai Hai region of Subei after the termination of the Grand Canal grain transport system, and its gradual expansion to other areas both north and south of the Yangzi River.[69] Shanghai, therefore, emerged as a center for the modern Green Gang from the latter's inception in the decades of the 1880s and 1890s.

In the early twentieth century, Shanghai's position as the leading commercial and industrial center in China acted as a magnet for peasants and merchants alike who came from all over the country to work in its factories and commercial firms. As a result the city's population increased dramatically in the first thirty years of the twentieth century. The population for the whole of Shanghai virtually tripled in the brief twenty-year period from 1910 to 1930, increasing from just over one million to just over three million. Population increases in the foreign settlements were even more dramatic. The population of the International Settlement doubled between 1895 and 1910 (from 245,675 to 501,541) and doubled again between 1910 and 1930 when it reached just over one million; while the population of the French Concession almost tripled between 1895 and 1915 (from 52,188 to 149,000) and more than tripled again between 1915 and 1930 to just under 435,000.[70] The greater part of this increase was provided by immigrants from other parts of

China, principally the Jiangnan and Subei regions. In the International Settlement, for example, immigrants from other regions of China made up over 89 percent of the total population in 1895, over 82 percent in 1910, and over 90 percent in 1930.[71]

In addition to the indigent peasantry, these immigrants also included various social groups who lived either close to the margins of the law or entirely outside of it in their home communities, such as disbanded soldiers, salt smugglers, bandits, local thugs and rural police constables who were attracted by the enhanced opportunities for their activities provided by Shanghai. Many members of these groups, like the peasant immigrants generally, came from rural Subei, which, as noted earlier in this chapter, was a major center of Anqing Daoyou/Green Gang activity. Many of them were, in fact, members of the Anqing Daoyou/Green Gang in their own localities, and they brought with them their own forms of Green Gang organization, which served to reinforce the Green Gang system already present in Shanghai. According to a names list of Green Gang leaders compiled by a Green Gang manual in the 1930s, the overwhelming majority of those listed as resident in Shanghai (62 percent) actually came from other parts of China, notably Subei, Shandong and Ningbo.[72]

In the early years of the twentieth century, Shanghai, therefore, was a city of immigrants, and one where the social cohesion of the Chinese population was tenuous at best. In this situation the role of native-place (*tongxiang*) networks gained in significance, and these provided the basis for whatever social organization existed among the Chinese population. This fact was of enormous importance in the development of organized crime in the city. As most of the gangsters were themselves immigrants, the native-place system itself became the basic building block of gangster organizations. Many gangster bosses restricted their area of operations to their fellow provincials, as did Gu Zhuxuan in the International Settlement and Jin Jiulin in the French Concession, both of whose power bases were provided by their fellow immigrants from Subei.[73]

At the same time, Green Gang bosses sought to influence and control the new native-place associations (*tongxianghui*) that developed in Shanghai during the Republican period and that complemented the traditional, and more narrowly based, *huiguan*. Good examples of this phenomenon are Gu Zhuxuan's close relationship with the Jiang-Huai Native-Place Association (*Jiang-Huai Tong-*

xianghui) in Hongkou, and Du Yuesheng's involvement with the Pudong Native-Place Association (*Pudong Tongxianghui*), which he controlled from the time of its establishment in January 1932 and for which he financed the construction of a modern, art deco building on the Avenue Edward VII in 1936.[74] The gangsters used these native-place networks to organize protection and other rackets (such as prostitution, gambling, etc.); to interpose themselves as middlemen between their native-place group and other such groups; to mediate relations between their fellow provincials and petty officialdom in the various municipalities of Shanghai; and to gain control of the labor market and transform it into a lucrative racket.[75]

The rootlessness of this city of immigrants was also reflected in its pattern of crime. As noted above many of the criminal gangs were organized along native-place lines, and in the 1920s Shanghai's gangsters were drawn mainly from three localities—Ningbo, Shaoxing and Subei. Many of these gangs specialized in particular types of criminal activities. Shaoxing gangs, for example, were feared for their kidnapping rings, while Subei gangs had a penchant for armed robbery.[76] Kidnapping and armed robbery, in fact, had become the two major crimes in Shanghai in the 1920s and 1930s.[77] Chinese capitalists lived in constant fear of kidnapping. To lessen the risk to themselves and their families they hired armed bodyguards and fortified their homes. They also sought the protection of those who either controlled or had influence with the kidnapping gangs, such as local Green Gang bosses Huang Jinrong, Zhang Xiaolin, Gu Zhuxuan and Du Yuesheng. The provision of such protection was one early means by which these Green Gang bosses extended their networks among the city's bourgeoisie.

The victims of kidnapping, however, were not confined to members of the bourgeoisie. A well-organized system of trafficking in children flourished in Shanghai under the control of Green Gang bosses. Trafficking in boys was referred to as "lifting rocks" (*ban shitou*) and that involving girls was called "plucking mulberry leaves" (*zhai sangye*). Boys normally were sold to wealthy monasteries or as apprentices to commercial interests in Guangdong and Southeast Asia, while girls usually were sold to brothels in North China or in ports along the China coast. It was to combat the kidnapping of children, in particular, that Chinese and Western philanthropists established the Anti-Kidnapping Society (*Furu Jiuji Hui*), which, in its first twelve years of operation, rescued 3,782 people, mainly children, from kidnappers.[78]

Another source of threat to the citizenry of Shanghai was the incidence of armed hold-ups and robberies in the 1920s. Civil war had made China a major customer of Western arms merchants despite the attempt to prevent the flow of weapons to the warlords under the terms of the international Arms Embargo Agreement of 1919.[79] Shanghai was a major port of entry for smuggled weapons. Over a two-year period, 1926–27, the local Chinese Customs made 141 separate seizures of caches of weapons and ammunition passing through the port of Shanghai, which represented only a fraction of the total of smuggled armaments.[80] A sizeable proportion of these weapons found their way into the hands of local gangsters, and the Mauser automatic pistol quickly became the weapon of choice in Shanghai in the 1920s. In the five years from 1919 to 1923 the Shanghai Municipal Police (SMP) arrested over 300 gangsters on charges of armed robbery, which frequently also involved murder charges.[81] As one British member of the SMP observed, the use of these weapons created "a reign of terror" in Shanghai in which conflict between the police and gangsters took on the characteristics of "a bitter civil war in which he who shoots first has the best chance of surviving."[82]

The large influx of Chinese immigrants into Shanghai in the second and third decades of the twentieth century, and the attendant increase in criminal activities, therefore, posed serious problems of social order and control for the city's police authorities. These authorities, however, were ill-equipped to deal with such problems. Shanghai, as noted in the introduction, was not one city but three—the Chinese City, the International Settlement and the French Concession—each with its own administrative, legal and police systems.[83] The problem was exacerbated by the fact that the three municipalities were not merely civic administrations but also constituted separate national jurisdictions, with the result that routine police functions (such as criminal investigations and the maintenance of local order) could and did take on the character of exercises in international relations.[84] There was, therefore, little or no institutional cooperation between the three separate police authorities, and what cooperation did occur was on an ad hoc and individual basis. The lack of such formal cooperation between the two foreign jurisdictions was all the more remarkable given their shared interests in the maintenance of their respective colonial authorities. The degree of isolation between the foreign administrations was reflected in the admission by the acting French Consul General, Jacques Meyrier, to the French Municipal Council in the wake of the May Thirtieth Incident in 1925 that no direct telephone link existed between the police authorities of the French Concession and the International Settlement.[85]

Such a situation of divided and conflicting police jurisdiction allowed the gangsters to flourish and to extend their own organizational systems. They could set themselves up in one jurisdiction and conduct armed robberies, kidnappings and narcotics trafficking in the other two jurisdictions, and they could safeguard their base by bribing the local beat policemen and even relatively senior police officials. In 1922, for example, the French Consul General, Auguste Wilden, dismissed the entire personnel of one police post (composed of a sergeant and four constables) for taking bribes from local gangsters. Wilden noted, somewhat sardonically, that the French sergeant involved subsequently used the fortune of 600,000 francs that he had acquired in bribes to set himself up as a major industrialist in the French Midi.[86] During periodic police crackdowns the gangsters could avoid any substantial loss to their position by moving between jurisdictions. It was for eventualities such as these that the various gangster groups entered into agreements and formed loose alliances among themselves.[87] The Shanghai gangsters, in fact, successfully transferred to this Sino-foreign urban environment the rural bandits' classic strategy of establishing their "lairs" in the no-man's-land between two or more county or prefectural administrations: by 1920 Shanghai had become a veritable urban Liangshanbo.[88]

The situation was further complicated by the fact that gangsters also formed the basis of the Chinese detective squads in both the International Settlement and the French Concession. In the early decades of the twentieth century the chief of the SMP Chinese Detective Squad was one Shen Xingshan. Shen was also the principal leader of the gangster organization known as the Big Eight Mob, which controlled the narcotics traffic in the International Settlement in this same period, and many of his lieutenants were also members of the Shanghai Municipal Police's Chinese Detective Squad. Shen's successor in the 1930s was Lu Liankui (1889–1938) who, in addition to being chief of the SMP's Chinese Detective Squad, was also a Green Gang boss and a "disciple" of Ji Yunqing, one of the eight leaders of the Big Eight Mob.[89] Indeed the Big Eight Mob had such a grip on the SMP Chinese Detective Squad that one former China coast journalist ironically observed that "almost every Chinese detective on the [SMP] force had a criminal record."[90] A similar situation obtained in the French Concession (see below), where Huang Jinrong was chief of the Chinese Detective Squad of the French police.

The fact that this state of affairs continued throughout the lives of the foreign settlements would seem to indicate deliberate policy rather than mere chance occurrence. Both the International Settlement and the French Concession represented a species of colonial state. As such they were relatively weak polities whose legitimacy derived not from the active support of the populations over whom they ruled, but from the deployment of superior coercive force to ensure the passive acquiescence of the subject populations as well as to guard against any internal or external challenge to their authority. This coercive force consisted of three elements: military units deployed by the metropolitan governments, police forces, and militia raised from the foreign business community (such as the Shanghai Volunteer Corps). Of these three elements, it was military power which, in the final analysis, underpinned foreign power in Shanghai.

Although military power was the ultimate guarantor of foreign authority in the settlements, the police forces, nevertheless, were important in ensuring day-to-day control, and, in fulfilling this role, they took on functions not commonly associated with police forces in their metropolitan countries. They were, in fact, essentially colonial, paramilitary forces whose main task was to ensure the security of the colonial administrations and the lives and property of the imperial powers' citizens, and not necessarily the enforcement of law among the subject (Chinese) population, let alone the administration of justice.[91] The overriding concern, in other words, was to maintain the control of the foreign administrations. To achieve this, all means were considered including the co-option by the police forces of selected gangster groups. On the principle of "using a thief to catch a thief" both police forces recruited the most powerful and successful gangsters into their detective squads. These gangster-detectives, in effect, were "compradors of violence." In return for their assistance in maintaining order among the Chinese population, the authorities allowed them to continue with their own illicit rackets as long as they did not become too much of an embarrassment to the administration. Formally the published crime statistics of the settlements were a measure of the successful enforcement of law and order; from a different perspective, however, they also represented the degree of success achieved by the leading gangster detectives in maintaining control over their rackets and in eliminating actual or potential rivals. Throughout the 1920s and 1930s numerous members of the Chinese detective squads of both settlement police forces were involved in a range of criminal activities, such as running pickpocket gangs, trafficking in women and children, providing protection to gambling houses and brothels, and trafficking in narcotics.[92]

This general rationale was reinforced in the Shanghai situation by the enormous problems of social control posed by the continuous large increases in the Chinese population throughout this period, and by the specific problems for police control posed by the separate national jurisdictions. The result was to strengthen and, to a degree, institutionalize gangster organizations in the foreign settlements. The access to foreign authority that the gangster-detectives gained by virtue of their role in the system of control strengthened their power and enhanced their status among other gangster groups. At the street level, indeed, the two systems of power—the criminal gangs and the police detective squads—rather than standing in an antagonistic relationship, tended to reinforce one another, with the local gang boss and the detective chief not infrequently being one and the same person. The comprador role of these gangster-detectives, in fact, gave them a degree of legitimacy within the settlements' colonial power structure, and some of them, such as Huang Jinrong, were even decorated by the colonial authorities for services rendered.[93]

The gangsters also took advantage of the colonial structure of the foreign settlements in other ways in order to enhance their security. One means that proved rather effective was bribing the consuls of countries enjoying extraterritoriality in order to obtain the nominal citizenship of these states and the extraterritorial privileges that went with it. In this way the gangster bosses could ensure that any criminal cases involving themselves would be heard before these consuls in the mixed courts of the International Settlement and the French Concession, who would invariably dismiss the proceedings. In the early 1920s the Portuguese, Spanish and Chilean consuls general enjoyed a lucrative business by selling the rights of citizenship of their respective countries to a large number of local Shanghai gangsters. These gangsters included Du Yuesheng, who enjoyed Portuguese citizenship, and the Chaozhou narcotics "king," Ye Qinghe, who claimed to be a Chilean protégé.[94]

THE MAJOR GREEN GANG GROUPS IN SHANGHAI IN THE 1920S

By the 1920s Shanghai had become notorious as the major center of large-scale criminal activity in China. Although there are no reliable figures for the total number of gangsters in Shanghai, the most commonly cited contemporary estimate for the 1920s and 1930s was about 100,000, which represented just over 3 percent of the city's population at that time.[95] Most of these were members of the Green Gang, the largest secret society-cum-gangster organization in Shanghai. According to a names-list of prominent Green Gang members throughout China compiled in the early 1930s, over 10 percent were resident in Shanghai, which represented the greatest concentration of Green Gang leaders in any city in China at that time.[96]

Contrary to certain popular accounts, the Green Gang system in Shanghai did not represent a single, integrated organization subject to the control of one paramount leader.[97] Rather, it functioned as a loose structure of interlocking webs of influence and authority, which allowed for the coexistence within it of different and competing groups. According to Jiang Hao, who was himself a Green Gang leader and a member of the Guomindang in the 1930s, there were forty-eight prominent Green Gang leaders in Shanghai over the thirty-year-period from 1919 to 1949. All of these leaders recruited their own followers and exercised real, if unequal, power in their own right. Their relationships with one another oscillated between guarded cooperation and outright conflict, depending on which strategy best served their interests at any given time. Thirty-four (or 70 percent) of these Green Gang bosses belonged to the Tong generational status group, while ten (or 20 percent) belonged to the prestigious Da status group; only one, Du Yuesheng, belonged to the relatively lowly Wu group.[98] There were, in other words, different centers of power within the system at any given moment, and these shifted and changed over time. By the 1920s, for example, three or four of these groups had emerged as significant, if different, centers of power within the Green Gang system in Shanghai: Zhang Renkui's group and the Big Eight Mob in the International Settlement;

Gu Zhuxuan's group in the Chinese City (Zhabei) and the Hongkou section of the International Settlement; and Huang Jinrong's group in the French Concession.

Zhang Renkui (1859–1945) played a very important role in the consolidation of the Green Gang system in Shanghai in the 1920s. A native of Teng County, Shandong, he began his career as a lieutenant of Xu Baoshan and took over Xu's command on the latter's death in 1913. He was well-connected with the world of warlord politics, and in 1917 he became Tong-Hai defense commissioner in Subei, a post he held until 1927. Zhang was a member of the Da generational status group of the Xing Wu Liu Branch of the Green Gang, and he belonged to that generation that had forged the modern Green Gang in the 1880s and 1890s. He personified, in other words, the link between the Anqing League in Subei of the late nineteenth century and the modern Green Gang in Shanghai of the early twentieth century. His influence extended throughout the Subei region, including southern Shandong, and later it included Jiangnan and Shanghai, where he took up permanent residence in the early 1920s. By that time Zhang was the most prestigious Green Gang leader in Shanghai, and most leading gangsters sought to become his followers in order to enhance their standing and to obtain the legitimacy of a relatively high generational status within the Green Gang system. It was largely because Zhang was a member of the Xing Wu Liu Branch that this branch became one of the predominant organizations in the Green Gang system in Shanghai. According to the name list of Green Gang leaders compiled by Chen Guoping in the 1930s, over 40 percent of all members of the Tong status group of the Xing Wu Liu Branch throughout China were members of Zhang Renkui's personal organization, the Benevolence Society, which he established in 1935.[99]

In the early 1920s the Big Eight Mob was one of the most powerful Green Gang organizations in Shanghai through its control of the trafficking in contraband opium and its close links with the SMP. Its power rapidly declined in the mid-1920s, however, as a consequence of the rise of the French Concession Green Gang in circumstances that are described in detail in chapter 3.

Among the Green Gang groups that rose to prominence in the course of the 1920s was the one organized by Gu Zhuxuan (1885–1956).[100] Gu was a migrant from Subei (his native place was Yancheng County) who arrived in Shanghai in 1900 to work as a rickshaw coolie and later, briefly, as a Chinese constable in the SMP. About 1904 he joined the Green Gang when he took as his "teacher" Liu Dengjie, a local Green Gang leader who belonged to the Da generational status group of the Xing Wu Si Branch, the second largest Green Gang branch operating in Shanghai in that period. After he was dismissed from the SMP for misconduct, Gu became involved with the local entertainment industry in the Hongkou-Zhabei district, where he opened a teahouse and later gained control of the Moon Theatre (*Tianshan Wutai*) on Jiujiang Road. At the same time, he went into the rickshaw business with his brother Gu Songmao and eventually controlled most of the rickshaw hongs in Hongkou and Zhabei. Gu was a somewhat crude and uncouth individual. Extremely fat, "a great mountain of flesh" in the words of one contemporary, he had, quite literally, a murderous temper, and enjoyed regaling visitors with stories of the murders that he had personally carried out, particularly that of the Beijing Opera star Chang Chunheng.[101] In later life he became an opium addict and in the 1930s was reported to spend several thousand dollars a month to satisfy his habit.[102]

By the early 1920s Gu Zhuxuan had established his power base among his fellow Subei migrants in Zhabei through his involvement with, and later control of, the Zhabei Volunteer Corps (the local militia) and the Jiang-Huai Fellow Countrymen's Association (*Jiang-Huai Tongxianghui*). He also had close links with members of both the uniformed and detective branches of the SMP based in Hongkou, together with officials from other institutions of the International Settlement, such as the Mixed Court and the Fire Department. As Japanese influence in Hongkou increased after the First World War, moreover, Gu developed good working relations with the relevant Japanese officials. By the late 1920s, therefore, Gu Zhuxuan had established a commanding position for himself in the Hongkou-Zhabei area and was estimated to have about 10,000 followers.

The other Green Gang group that became increasingly more powerful in the 1920s was the organization in the French Concession controlled by Huang Jinrong (1868–1953). In time this was to become the dominant group within the Green Gang in Shanghai. Huang was the son of a policeman. His father, Huang Bingchuan, had been chief constable (*bukuaitou*) in the Suzhou prefectural yamen, and on his retirement he opened a teahouse, the *Sanpai Lou*, in Nandao (Chinese City). After a traditional education in a Chinese private school, Huang Jinrong was apprenticed at sixteen to his uncle's scroll-mounting shop in the Shanghai City Temple (*Cheng Huang Miao*), and three years later, in 1887, he opened his own print-mounting business at the South Gate in Nandao. Below average in height and of stocky build, Huang had a less than prepossessing appearance. His most notable features were his head, which was rather large for his body, and his full, fleshy face with its protruding eyes and wide mouth. He had, moreover, contracted smallpox as a child and was therefore given the nickname "pockmarked Jinrong" (*mapi Jinrong*), which remained with him throughout his career.

The print-mounting business did not keep him fully occupied and he spent most of his time in the company of local gangsters who frequented his father's teahouse. In 1892 he successfully sat for the examination to become a detective constable in the French Concession Police, a move that changed his life and launched him on a successful career as a policeman. According to his own account, Huang's decision to join the police reflected his belief that there were greater financial opportunities to be had in the police force than in the print-mounting business.[103] Huang used his power and influence as a police officer to build up his gangster connections: he controlled opium hongs, gambling joints and brothels; he extended his protection to thieves, armed robbers, pimps, kidnappers and murderers; and he also recruited his own petty hoodlums to run protection rackets on his behalf.[104] Although Huang maintained close relations with members of the Green Gang, and many of his own followers were Green Gang members, he himself was not a member of the Green Gang for most of his active career.

Because of his position in the police force Huang was careful not to become involved directly with his various illicit operations; it was his de facto wife, "Miss Gui" (also known as "Sister Hoodlum" [*baixiangren saosao*]), who looked after these activities on his behalf.[105] A former brothelkeeper from Suzhou, she was a shrewd and intelligent woman and was in fact Huang's principal adviser. Her role in Huang's organization and the influence she exercised over his operations revealed the highly influential role that women could play in the Green Gang system.[106] "Miss Gui" was an important gangster-entrepreneur in her own right. She controlled the nightsoil business in the French Concession through her company the Mahong Ji Nightsoil Hong (*Mahong Ji Fenhang*), and she was commonly referred to in Shanghai as the "nightsoil queen" (*fen dawang*). This was a lucrative monopoly. With a total of 400 nightsoil carts, "Miss Gui"'s company took a profit from both ends of the operation: it not only charged residents for the removal of the nightsoil but also sold the proceeds as fertilizer to the peasants of the Shanghai region. In this way it turned a monthly profit of between Ch$10,000 and Ch$12,000.[107]

Another key figure in this group was Zhang Xiaolin (1877–1940).[108] Zhang was a native of Cixi County, Zhejiang, and his early career was spent in the provincial capital of Hangzhou. In 1897 he and his brother worked as machinists in the Hangzhou Engineering School (*Hangzhou Jifang Xue*), and it was during this period that Zhang took up with local toughs and first experienced the world of the gangster-playboy (*baixiangren*). Sometime in the first decade of the century Zhang entered the Zhejiang Military Preparatory School (*Zhejiang Wubei Xuetang*), although he left before graduating. His classmates included future Zhejiang warlords such as Zhou Fengqi, Xia Chao and Zhang Zaiyang, and these relationships proved extremely important to Zhang's later career. After leaving the military school, Zhang was employed as a "runner" or "legman" (*paotui*) by Li Xiutang, the Chief of Detectives of the Hangzhou Prefecture, and he took this opportunity to engage in various extortion rackets. At the same time Zhang also pursued a career as a professional gambler, and he made a comfortable living fleecing the peasants in the Hangzhou, Jiaxing and Lake Tai districts.

In 1919 Zhang moved to Shanghai where he lived off the earnings of prostitution and gambling: he operated a gambling joint-cum-brothel called the Manting Fang on Guangdong Road, and a bull ring just off the Avenue Joffre in the French Concession. At this time he joined the Green Gang by becoming a follower of Fan Jincheng who belonged to the Da generational status group. As a member of the Tong, Zhang began to recruit his own followers and extend the range of his activities. It was during this period that he developed a relationship with Huang Jinrong and Du Yuesheng and became involved in contraband opium. Zhang was a tall, spare and distinguished-looking man, whose education and high degree of literacy set him somewhat apart from his two colleagues. He was to play a key part, through his close contacts with the Jiangnan militarists, in furthering the interests of the French Concession Green Gang group in the 1920s.

Du Yuesheng (1888–1951), the third member of this French Concession group, was one of the most remarkable figures in the history of Shanghai, and, indeed, of modern China.[109] From humble origins he rose to become not only a major criminal boss in Shanghai, arguably the architect of organized crime in the city, but also a key political figure whose services were much sought after by both leading Guomindang figures and members of the city's Chinese bourgeois elite. Du built his career along the frontier where illicit and legitimate activities met and interacted with one another, and he in fact embodied these two separate, but related, sets of activities. At the same time, Du deliberately modeled his public persona after the classic virtues of secret society "bravos," which gained him much popular respect and served to legitimize his role in Shanghai society. Reports of his power and influence reached legendary proportions among awed contemporaries, and his story has continued to fire the imagination of successive generations of Shanghai people who regarded his "rags to riches" career as emblematic of the character of the city.

Du was born into an extremely poor family in the hamlet of Dujiazhai (Du Family Residence), in the southern section of Gaoqiao district, Pudong County. Although only across the Huangpu River from Shanghai, rural Pudong was in fact a world removed from the bustling metropolis. The lives of the peasants were governed by the rigorous discipline of the agricultural cycle of planting, cultivating and harvesting, and many of them in the early twentieth century had never visited Shanghai. Even today Gaoqiao retains elements of its rural character, with small hamlets of three or four two-storied stone houses (like Dujiazhai) scattered across a patchwork of rice paddies separated by pathways of tamped earth and linked to one another by narrow gravel roads.

Du's father, Du Wenqing, had worked in the Imperial Maritime Customs as an assistant checking goods on the Shanghai wharves, and later opened a rice shop in partnership with a friend in the industrial district of Yangshupu in the International Settlement, north of Suzhou Creek. Undercapitalized, the business was not a success, and Du's mother went to work in a cotton factory to make ends meet. It was during this period that Du obtained his only experience of formal education, a total of four months in a local elementary school. Reflecting on this years later, on a visit to Yangshupu as chairman of the Da Da Steamship Company, Du confided to Yang

Guanbei, his economic adviser: "This is the place where I studied as a child. The monthly educational fee was fifty cents. My family being poor, however, on the fifth month they were unable to raise the necessary money, and so my studies came to an end."[110]

The fact that poverty had denied him an education had a profound effect on Du Yuesheng, and in later years he established the Zhengshi Middle School (*Zhengshi Zhongxue*) with the specific purpose of providing a free education to talented children from poor families in Shanghai.[111] His lack of education meant that Du was illiterate for most of his life; it was only in the 1930s that he hired scholars to teach him the basics of reading and writing, with indifferent success.

Both his parents died while Du was still a young boy, and he was raised by his maternal uncle, Zhu Yangsheng, a carpenter in Gaoqiao. Relations between them were very difficult and Du Yuesheng led a somewhat delinquent existence dividing his time between the local teahouse and gambling den where Gaoqiao's local hoodlums hung out. It was during these years of childhood and early adolescence that Du developed a taste for gambling that never left him. The demands of the gaming table, however, instilled in him a certain self-discipline that curbed his natural tendency to outbursts of violent temper, and also helped develop the skills necessary to deal effectively with others.[112]

In 1902, when he was fourteen, Du left Gaoqiao for Shanghai, and through an introduction from his paternal uncle, Du Aqing, who was a bookkeeper with the Zhang Heng Da Fruit Hong, he was apprenticed to the Bao Da Fruit Hong in Shiliupu. Later, about 1906, he moved to the Da You Fruit Hong where he worked for five years until he was dismissed for stealing the shop's takings to fund his gambling interests. In the first decades of the twentieth century the docks area of Shiliupu was one of the centers of crime and vice in Shanghai. Stretching south of the Quai de France, the Shiliupu docks, used by the shipping companies plying the Yangzi and China coast routes, were among the busiest in Shanghai. The passenger and freight traffic through the docks provided an inexhaustible source of larceny for the petty gangsters of the district, and the docks themselves were an important part of the network of trafficking in narcotics and human beings. In the warren of narrow streets and alleys running back from the docks into the Chinese City were innumerable gambling dens, opium divans and brothels where the local hoodlums (*liumang*) and "street bums" (*xiao bisan*) hung out. During his period as a shop assistant Du immersed himself in this world of vice and became acquainted with a number of local gangsters. It was at this time also that Du was first introduced to the pleasures of opium smoking, an addiction that remained with him throughout his life despite several attempts to cure himself of the habit. In later life his opium addiction seriously undermined his health and was a major contributing factor to his death at the relatively early age of sixty-three.

After his dismissal from the fruit hong, Du took up the uncertain life of a "street bum," frequenting the wharves of Shiliupu, where he was known as "Fruit Yuesheng" (*Shuiguo Yuesheng*), and deriving a precarious livelihood from small-time opium dealing, robbery and extortion. It was such activities that first brought Du Yuesheng to the attention of the Shanghai public in April 1911, when the *Minli Bao* reported that Du was wanted for questioning by the police in connection with an extortion ring preying on local opium merchants.[113] While in his early twenties Du, who as an inveterate gambler was frequently destitute, was taken under the wing of the madam of a local brothel in Shiliupu. Du called her his "foster mother" (*ganniang*), and earned his keep by doing odd jobs around the brothel, including looking after the prostitutes. It was common practice at this time for groups of nine or ten prostitutes to form sworn sisterhoods, known as "ten sisters" (*shi jiemei*), and to include a male gangster as their "protector."[114] Du was one such "protector" or "minder."

Du Yuesheng was now in his mid- to late twenties. His physical appearance was striking although by no means conventionally handsome. He had a lean, impassive face with hard, penetrating eyes, surprisingly large ears, and a full, sensuous mouth. The rather sinister character of these features was given emphasis by a drooping eyelid over his left eye, prominent eyebrows and close-cropped hair. He was above average in height with a strong, wiry build that did not yet show the effects of abuse through opium addiction. There were few prospects, however, beyond the rather limited ones offered as a small-time thug and member of a local street gang.

At this point, however, Du's fortunes began to improve. Shortly after 1910 he became a follower of Chen Shichang, the local gangster boss in Shiliupu district and a member of the Tong generational status group of the Jiang Huai Si Branch of the Green Gang. Membership in Chen's gang was important to Du for two reasons. It enabled him to join the Green Gang which, even as a member of the relatively lowly Wu generational status group, gave him access to a citywide network of gangster relationships from which he had been previously excluded. Of equal importance was the fact that Chen had a close working relationship and shared native place associations (they both came from Suzhou) with Huang Jinrong. According to Huang's own account it was Chen Shichang who recommended Du to him.[115]

This introduction to Huang Jinrong was the turning point in Du Yuesheng's career. Although Du at first held a series of not very important positions in Huang's establishment, including a period as one of his police informers, "Miss Gui," Huang's de facto wife, recognized Du's abilities and began to assist his career in Huang's organization. A form of mother-son relationship developed between "Miss Gui" and Du, who referred to her as "teacher-mother" (*shimu*) and to whom he remained fiercely loyal.[116] In later years he frequently referred to her importance in his career. It was "Miss Gui" who persuaded Huang to allow Du to manage three of the tables in his gambling house on Sheng Ji Lane, and it was his success in discharging this responsibility that first made an impression on Huang. Until this time Du's reputation had been that of an above average "man of violence," an effective gunman, robber, extortionist, and "minder" of prostitutes. His successful management of the gaming tables, however, revealed that he was also a highly intelligent individual with strong managerial and organizational capacities, and an ability to shrewdly calculate his advantage and to think strategically. These qualities were to serve him well in the 1920s when he planned and implemented the takeover by Huang Jinrong's group of the narcotics trafficking from the Big Eight Mob.

2 The Role of Opium

The most important development in the history of the Green Gang system in the 1920s and 1930s was the ascendancy achieved within that system by the Green Gang bosses in the French Concession: Huang Jinrong, Du Yuesheng and Zhang Xiaolin. This ascendancy rested on control of the illicit opium traffic in Shanghai, and on a tacit accommodation between the gangster bosses and the French Concession authorities. Their opportunity was provided by the prohibition of the opium trade, which came into effective force after 1919.

Control of the trade in contraband opium in Shanghai provided the French Concession Green Gang bosses with the necessary financial resources to develop a vast network of organized crime, which touched most aspects of the social and economic worlds of Shanghai. In addition, the structure of this contraband trade served to define the relationship between the gangsters and the local warlords and provided the context within which the leading gangsters sought to exercise political influence. The basic contours of the pattern of interaction between local gangsters and militarists-cum-politicians in the Jiangnan region were established by 1925; and this relationship provided a model for the later cooperation between the Green Gang and the Guomindang government after 1927. The accommodation between the French authorities and the Green Gang bosses, for its part, reflected both the French concerns with security and the contributions of the local Green Gang toward meeting these concerns, and the involvement of elements in the French administration in the contraband opium traffic itself.

In many respects the prohibition on opium in China had similar results to the prohibition on alcohol in the United States. In both countries prohibition encouraged the growth of a vast, illicit traffic that provided the economic basis for the development of organized crime in the major cities, and helped define the ways in which criminal organization interacted with the world of politics.

The control of the opium traffic and the understanding with the French authorities were inseparable aspects of the French Concession Green Gang's original power base. For the purposes of exposition, however, they will be discussed separately. The present chapter deals with the issue of opium, and the following chapter discusses the origins of the Green Gang bosses' relations with the French authorities.

SHANGHAI AND OPIUM: FROM LEGALIZATION TO PROHIBITION, 1858–1919

Throughout the late nineteenth century, opium was inseparable from the prosperity of Shanghai. In this period Shanghai was the principal distribution center for the legal trade in both imported and domestic opium, and the opium trade was an integral part of the city's commercial life. Most of the local foreign and Chinese merchants derived at least part of their wealth from trading in the drug. As the *North-China Herald* noted in 1914, "the whole trade of the Settlement is interconnected in this business."[1]

Trade in opium was legalized as a result of the Treaty Settlement of 1858–60, which ended the Second Opium War (the Arrow War) of 1856–60, and developed rapidly in the 1860s and 1870s. By the end of the latter decade 83,000 piculs of foreign opium were imported into China annually.[2] Although the amount of imported opium had begun to decline by the end of the 1880s, because of the growth in native opium, it nevertheless remained an important item in China's foreign trade. In the 1890s, for example, imported opium represented over one-fifth of China's total imports, and in the years immediately preceding the Qing government's prohibition on the cultivation and consumption of opium in November 1906, imports of the drug through Shanghai averaged 22,500 piculs valued at Ch$40 million per year.[3]

The conduct of this legal trade in opium was a flourishing Sino-foreign enterprise. By the turn of the century, opium imports were largely in the hands of four foreign merchant houses: David Sassoon and Co., E. D. Sassoon, S. J. David, and Edward Ezra.[4] The whole-saling and retailing aspects of the trade were handled by Guangdong merchants, of whom the most important were those from Chaozhou who formed the so-called Chaozhou Clique, and who, as noted in chapter 1, were members of the Red Gang.[5] The Chaozhou Clique operated the three major opium businesses in the International Settlement: the Zhengxia Ji, the Guoyu Ji and the Liwei Ji.[6] Both the foreign and Chinese opium merchants carefully regulated the trade, and the latter were exempt from interference by Chinese officials.

By the first decade of the twentieth century, however, a change occurred in both official Chinese attitudes and international public opinion, which favored the prohibition of the opium trade. For Chinese officials the move against opium was part of a last-ditch political strategy to reform and restructure the Chinese state in the wake of the disastrous Boxer fiasco, while international public opinion responded to the effective propaganda of the missionaries, principally American, which condemned the trade on moral grounds. In 1906 the Qing government introduced a policy of phased abolition of opium cultivation over a ten-year period. In pursuance of this policy it gained the support of both the British government, which agreed to abolish the importation of Indian opium into China in annual installments beginning in 1908, and the international community, which by the terms of the International Opium Convention of 1912 agreed to undertake effective measure against drug smuggling into China and to close all opium retail shops and opium dens in the foreign-controlled areas in the country.[7]

Faced with the prospect of the termination of all aspects of the legal trade in foreign and domestic opium by the end of 1917, the foreign and Chinese opium merchants responded by seeking to extract for themselves the maximum financial advantage from the process of phased abolition.[8] In 1913, for example, the foreign opium merchants created the Shanghai Opium Merchants' Combine for the purpose of controlling the importation and distribution of foreign opium in Shanghai. The combine and the Chaozhou opium merchants then entered into an agreement by which the latter agreed to buy their Indian and Persian opium exclusively from the combine and to work closely with the foreign merchants. An efficient monopoly was thus created, with the combine controlling the importation of Indian and Persian opium and the Chaozhou Clique controlling its distribution. Through the activities of this monopoly, therefore, the opium merchants were able to manipulate almost at will the price of imported opium in Shanghai. As the deadline for implementation of full prohibition approached the combine was able to sell off its accumulated stocks to the Beijing government through a series of rather dubious agreements. The latter, after much hesitation, finally bowed to public opinion and burned these stocks in 1919, thus bringing to an end the legal trade in opium and the operations of the Shanghai Combine.

With the demise of the legal trade in opium in 1919, however, Shanghai reemerged as the center of a vast trafficking network in illicit opium from domestic and overseas sources. The domestic system involved the transshipment of Sichuan and some Yunnan opium by Yangzi River steamers via the ports of Yichang, Hankou and Nanjing to Shanghai, and the shipment of the bulk of Yunnan opium by rail to Haiphong and other ports in French Indochina and hence by steamer to Shanghai. The overseas trafficking, for its part, involved the smuggling into Shanghai of Persian, Turkish and Indian opium either by ocean liner from ports such as Bushire in the Persian Gulf and Constantinople, or through the medium of the parcel post.[9] The trafficking in Chinese opium was facilitated by the creation of de facto opium monopolies by various warlord units in certain key places such as Shaxi, Yichang and Hankou. These military monopolies, in cooperation with the local Chinese merchants and gangsters, taxed the passage of Sichuan and Yunnan opium and guaranteed its "protection" from one sphere of influence to another.[10] For its part, the contraband trade in foreign opium was assisted by the existence of a number of foreign colonies, each with its own opium monopoly, in the vicinity of China, that acted as transshipment points for smuggling opium and its derivatives into China. Of particular importance were those in French Indochina, Macao, Hong Kong, Formosa and Vladivostock.[11] The activities of these official monopolies in the contraband traffic was supplemented by the foreign-controlled areas in China proper, such as Guangzhouwan (Guangdong), Qingdao, Dalian and, of course, Shanghai.[12] Although no detailed figures of the value of the contraband opium trade exist, a number of educated guesses have been made by knowledgeable observers, which serve to give some indication, however imprecise they may be, of the scale of the traffic. In the late 1920s D'Auxion De Ruffé, a French lawyer in Shanghai, concluded that the consumption of opium in China totaled Ch$700 million per year, and Tang

Shaoyi, then Chairman of the National Anti-Opium Association, esti-mated that China spent a total of Ch$1 billion per year on illicit opium, of which Ch$800 million was spent on Chinese-produced opium and Ch$200 million on imported opium.[13] The amount of this revenue that was generated by the opium traffic through Shanghai has been variously put at over Ch$40 million or about Ch$78 mil-lion to upwards of Ch$100 million per year.[14] Whatever the exact figure, it is clear that these revenues played an important, if undis-closed, role in the Shanghai economy. This was recognized by the Shanghai Commissioner for Customs, E. Gordon Lowder, in his report of 1924 where he noted that contraband opium was "un-doubtedly of sufficient magnitude to affect the balance of trade in Shanghai."[15] Moreover, the profits to be earned from illicit opium ensured that Shanghai remained one of the most sought after prizes in the politics of the warlord era.

GANGSTERS AND OPIUM SMUGGLING, 1912–1919: THE ROLE OF THE BIG EIGHT MOB

In Shanghai the activities of the Opium Combine in maintaining an inflated price for the drug encouraged, in turn, an enormous increase in the smuggling of contraband opium in the period from 1913 to 1917. As the Shanghai Commissioner of Customs observed, the manipulations of the combine ensured that opium was "worth seven times its weight in silver" by 1917.[16]

There had always been a certain amount of trafficking in illicit opium by groups of petty gangsters and these pursuits formed an important element in the livelihood of the 100,000-odd gangsters in Shanghai. Such opium heists were usually small-scale affairs and involved either street hold-ups of runners from one of the opium hongs, the theft of individual chests while opium shipments entered or left the godowns in which they were stored, or the interception by sampans of consignments dropped over the sides of ships into the Huangpu River as they rode at anchor off Wusong.[17]

In the second decade of the century, however, trafficking in con-traband opium grew in size and became better organized. It was the scale of such activities that prompted the Opium Combine and its ally the Chaozhou Clique to request the Shanghai Municipal Coun-cil (SMC) in January 1916 to take strong measures against the small opium retail shops, which were doing a thriving business in smug-gled opium.[18] As the Shanghai Commissioner of Customs noted, the contraband traffic in opium had emerged by 1916 as a serious competitor to the legal opium trade and, indeed, threatened to undermine the monopoly that the foreign and Chinese opium merchants had secured over the legal opium trade in Shanghai.[19]

It was during this period that a major gangster organization emerged from among the smaller gangster groups in Shanghai in the form of the Eight Mob (*Ba Gu Dang*) or the Big Eight Mob (*Da Ba Gu Dang*). Its rise was linked directly to the events surrounding the transition from the predominance of the legal trade in opium to the prevalence of the contraband traffic in the drug that occurred in the second decade of the century. The Big Eight Mob, which was part of the Green Gang system, began its career in the first decade of the twentieth century as one of the petty gangs that engaged in opium heists. However, it successfully extended and transformed its operations into a major protection racket involving the Chinese opium merchants, so that by about 1911 it had a monopoly of the transportation and distribution of the drug.[20] The Big Eight Mob derived its name from its collective leadership structure composed of eight major gangsters, and its base of operations was located in the International Settlement.[21] The effectiveness of the mob's protection racket depended on developing a close relationship with the Chinese and foreign police forces, particularly the Chinese Water Police, the Chinese Anti-Smuggling Squad and the Shanghai Municipal Police (SMP). The emergence of Shen Xingshan as the major leader or *primus inter pares* within the Big Eight Mob can be ascribed to the fact that he was the Chief of the Chinese Detective Squad of the SMP, and as such played a key role in forging a relationship between the two organizations.[22] The corruption spawned by contact with the gangsters and their contraband opium traffic was so well established within the SMP that a confidential report prepared by senior officers of the force stated that it had "seriously affect[ed] the discipline of the municipal police" before remedial action was taken in 1923.[23]

It is probable that the Big Eight Mob had a close association with the Shanghai Opium Merchants' Combine and that it provided the combine with some of its coercive muscle, particularly during the latter's campaign against opium smugglers in 1916.[24] As noted above, the Big Eight Mob had an established relationship with the opium merchants of the Chaozhou Clique. In return for the payment of a "protection fee," it provided a guarantee to these merchants that their imports of foreign opium would not be plundered by one or other of the innumerable groups of petty gangsters in Shanghai.

The development of the Big Eight Mob's protection racket brought some measure of control over the activities of the petty gangsters, many of whom joined the more powerful organization. Among these latter were the gangsters in the French Concession who made their own accommodation with the mob. Huang Jinrong, in his capacity as Chief of the Chinese Detective Squad in the French Concession, maintained a close personal relationship with the Big Eight Mob leader and his opposite number in the SMP, Shen Xingshan. Du Yuesheng himself joined the Big Eight Mob at the time when Huang Jinrong delegated to him responsibility for the conduct of his opium interests, first in Hongkou in 1918, and in the following year in the French Concession, as manager of one of the large opium hongs on the Rue du Consulat. It was as a member of the Big Eight Mob that Du was introduced to the leading Chaozhou opium merchants after 1918.[25] In the first two decades of the twentieth century the center of gangster power and activity in Shanghai lay in the International Settlement where the major opium concerns were located, and the evidence would suggest that the gangsters of the French Concession were subordinate to the Big Eight Mob.

The period of dominance of the Shanghai Opium Merchants' Combine and its allies was brought to an end with the closure of the last licensed opium retail shops in the International Settlement and the ending of the legal importation of opium in 1917. With the inauguration of a new President, Xu Shichang, in December 1918, the Beijing government ordered the destruction of the remaining opium in its possession, and this was carried out in January 1919.[26] Although the Opium Combine was disbanded, some of its individual members together with the Chaozhou opium merchants began to seek further financial gain in the contraband traffic. This decade of transition in the opium trade was significant in that it witnessed the emergence of a new phenomenon, a large-scale criminal organization in the shape of the Big Eight Mob, and the beginnings of warlord interest in the financial rewards offered by the opium traffic.

THE FRENCH CONCESSION GREEN GANG, THE BIG EIGHT MOB AND THE ANFU CLIQUE'S OPIUM MONOPOLY, 1919–1924

With the demise of the legal trade in opium in 1919 the Anfu militarists who controlled the Shanghai area established an unofficial monopoly over the contraband opium traffic. This monopoly resembled a loosely structured syndicate in which cooperation was achieved among three separate yet interlocking elements: the military, the Chaozhou opium merchants and the gangsters.[27] Each of these three elements had its own discrete functions in the syndicate. The military provided political and physical protection, while the Chinese navy provided ships for the transportation of imported opium contraband which was off-loaded from ocean liners outside Wusong harbor. The Chaozhou opium merchants, for their part, engaged in the purchase of opium contraband through the formation of temporary combines, and in the wholesale storage and distribution of the illicit opium to networks of retail shops. Finally the gangsters, principally the Big Eight Mob, provided physical protection for the transportation of the contraband opium in association with the military, and guaranteed by their involvement that there would be a minimum of interference from groups of small-time gangsters with the system of opium trafficking.

Although Lu Yongxiang had involved himself with the import of contraband opium since 1915 when he was appointed Defense Commissioner of Shanghai and Songjiang, the monopoly system was not finally put in place until late 1919. Its creation was associated with the organizational changes that occurred in August of that year when Lu was appointed Military Governor of Zhejiang by President Duan Qirui on the death of Yang Shande, and Lu's lieutenant, He Fenglin, replaced him as Defense Commissioner of Shanghai and Songjiang.[28] The two key officials associated with the syndicate were He Fenglin and Xu Guoliang, the Wusong-Shanghai Police Commissioner, and it was He who played the leading role in the creation of its organization.[29] Of the Chaozhou opium merchants associated with the syndicate, the key figures were Su Jiashan, the owner of the leading opium hong in the International Settlement and reputedly the shrewdest of the opium merchants, and Fan Huichun, who owned the largest opium business in the French Concession.[30]

The instrument of the monopoly was the Jufeng Trading Company (*Jufeng Maoyi Gongsi*). With an initial capitalization of Ch$10 million, this company nominally dealt in real estate, but its main purpose was to manage the contraband opium traffic.[31] According to an exposé of its operations that appeared in the *North-China Herald* in 1923, the syndicate levied a "fee" on all contraband opium of between Ch$0.50 and Ch$1.00 per ounce and guaranteed the safe landing of illicit opium at Shanghai in return for an additional charge of Ch$1.00 per ounce of opium landed.[32] Further information on the operations of the syndicate was provided by documents seized by the SMP in January 1925, in connection with the so-called Ezra Opium Case.[33] This case involved a Sino-foreign combine that had been organized in late 1923 to import contraband Turkish opium into China. The documents included a contract, one clause of which clearly specified that the military would protect illicit opium in transit in the Shanghai area, stating that "the Navy, Army and Police, will generally assist in the protection of the goods."[34]

Another clause of the same contract provided a schedule of fees charged for protecting opium in transit in the Jiangnan area. These ranged from Ch$600 per chest for Chinese, Ch$1,000 per chest for Turkish, and Ch$1,400 per chest for Indian opium. Other documents recorded a payment of Ch$294,495 to the military that was described as "landing charges," and a further payment of Ch$2,000 to the Chinese River Police. The syndicate rigorously enforced this protection system, and there were numerous incidents such as the one in January 1923 when an unnamed senior official had his 300 chests of opium confiscated at Wusong because he had failed to pay the appropriate fee.[35]

Individual consignments handled by the syndicate could be extremely valuable. One example was the huge quantity of Indian opium valued at Ch$20 million that was smuggled into Zhejiang via the Zhoushan islands in late 1923 at the direction of Lu Yongxiang's subordinates, including his Chief of Police.[36] Consignments of this magnitude guaranteed that the profits were enormous. Given the secretive nature of the syndicate's operations it is virtually impossible to obtain reliable figures regarding its profitability. Contemporary estimates of its annual profits varied enormously, from Ch$10 million to upwards of Ch$100 million. Qi Xieyuan, in justifying his attack on Shanghai in late 1924, alleged that both Lu and He had netted over Ch$20 million in the period from 1922 to 1924.[37] In 1923 the North-China Herald estimated the syndicate's "lowest" possible level of profits at nearly Ch$30 million a year, and other sources suggested that its profit margin was over Ch$56 million in its first year of operation.[38] Although some part of these vast profits was used to purchase armaments for Lu Yongxiang's forces and to finance the political ambitions of the Anfu Clique, a large percentage also found its way into the private bank accounts of the syndicate operators.[39] This is suggested by the fact that when Xu Guoliang was murdered in late 1923, it was reported that he left a personal estate of Ch$4 million plus a house in Tianjin worth Ch$200,000.[40]

Gangsters from the Jiangnan area played an important part in the operations of the syndicate. A key role, in fact, was performed by Zhang Xiaolin. Through his ex-classmates from the Zhejiang Military Preparatory School, Zhang established a relationship with Lu Yongxiang and He Fenglin around 1919. He acted as liaison between Lu Yongxiang's headquarters in Hangzhou and He Fenglin in Shanghai for the purpose of safeguarding Lu's interests and those of Zhejiang militarists, and at the same time directed the Zhejiang end of the syndicate's operations.[41] The activities of Zhang Xiaolin would suggest that the existence of this syndicate provided an opportunity for Zhejiang gangsters, especially those from Hangzhou and Shaoxing, to extend their operations to Shanghai.

For most of this period, however, the Big Eight Mob remained the most powerful group of gangsters involved in the syndicate's operations in Shanghai. The basis of the Big Eight Mob's ascendancy was its control of the major opium merchants in the International Settlement, of the personnel of the Chinese Water Police and Anti-Smuggling Squad and of the Chinese detectives in the SMP, through Shen Xingshan, together with its direct access to He Fenglin, guaranteed by the fact that one of its members, Jiang Ganting, was Secretary to the Shanghai-Songjiang Defense Commissioner's Headquarters.[42] The Big Eight Mob was also involved in narcotics trafficking in the Asia-Pacific region through its cooperation with Japanese traffickers, whose sphere of operations embraced Yokohama, Formosa and China. In 1921 and 1922, for example, one of the leaders of the Big Eight Mob, Dai Buxiang, was involved with one Shinji Sekito, the president of the Sanyo Shokai Shipping Company, together with the Hoshi Pharmaceutical Company, in the importation of 2,000 chests of opium into Shanghai via Formosa.[43] In undertaking such operations the mob was undoubtedly acting on behalf of the syndicate.

Although the French Concession gangsters played an ancillary role in the syndicate's operations, as a junior ally of the Big Eight Mob for most of the period of the system's existence, a change gradually occurred in the balance of power between the two groups in the early 1920s. This realignment of forces was directly related to Du Yuesheng's ambition to carve out for himself a secure power base within the gangster milieu in the French Concession. In 1920, for example, he bought a jewelry shop on the Rue du Consulat, the Meizhenhua Ji, which was managed by one of his followers, Li Yingsheng, and which he used as the headquarters for his opium operations. It was here that he dealt with other local gangsters as well as with members of the local military and police forces.[44] At the same time Du also used his share of the profits from the syndicate's activities to provide himself with a personal following, and from about 1918 onwards he progressively built up an impressive organization, which he deliberately modeled on the structure of the Big Eight Mob, and hence was popularly referred to in Shanghai as the Small Eight Mob (*Xiao Ba Gu Dang*).[45]

With the approval of Huang Jinrong, Du began to assert his own group's right to control the opium traffic within the French Concession. In pursuing this policy Du succeeded in exploiting the prevailing dissatisfaction of some opium retailers in the French Concession with the Big Eight Mob's control over their supplies of opium.[46] An indication of the intensity of this conflict is provided by the reports of the SMP, which remarked on the "alarming" increase in crime in connection with the illicit opium traffic in the International Settlement, and the arrest of 300 armed robbers in the Settlement in the five-year period from 1919 to 1923.[47] By 1923 a modus vivendi was arranged between the two groups by which the Big Eight Mob recognized the French Concession as the "territory" of the Small Eight Mob and the latter's right to supply the illicit opium to the Concession's opium retailers.[48]

The position of the French Concession gangsters was further strengthened when they succeeded in working out an agreement with Zhang Xiaolin, which eventually resulted in the latter assuming a leadership position within their organization.[49] The arrangement with Zhang provided the Green Gang leadership in the French Concession with their own independent source of access to Lu Yongxiang and the Zhejiang militarists on the one hand and He Fenglin on the other. It was not until just before the demise of the syndicate in late 1924, however, that the French Concession Green Gang clearly emerged as the predominant element in the partnership with the Big Eight Mob.

At the end of 1923 the operations of the Jufeng Trading Company were supplemented or replaced (it is not clear which) by the Wusong-Shanghai Investigation Bureau of All Prohibited Articles

(*Song-Hu Chajin Siyun Zhuijin Pinwu Chu*). This bureau was established by He Fenglin to preempt the creation of a similar office in Shanghai by the Military Governor of Jiangsu, Qi Xieyuan, who was seeking ways to gain a share of the opium traffic. Despite the bureau's name, the SMP Special Branch reported that it was an agency for trafficking in opium and that the profits were distributed between He Fenglin's military headquarters in Shanghai, Lu Yongxiang in Hangzhou and the three Green Gang bosses in the French Concession.[50] Important changes in the local political environment, however, began to affect adversely the operations of the syndicate. Indeed, the creation of the new bureau was in part a reaction to these larger political changes. On November 10, 1923, Xu Guoliang, the Wusong-Shanghai Police Commissioner and a leading member of the syndicate, was assassinated. On the one hand, some observers believed that Xu's murder was related to the political conflict between Lu Yongxiang and Qi Xieyuan for control of the Shanghai area. Xu was not a member of the Anfu Clique, and maintained a relatively independent position in the conflict that developed between Lu and Qi in the course of 1923.[51] On the other hand, however, there is considerable circumstantial evidence to suggest that the murder was related to the operations of the syndicate. It was alleged at the time that both Lu Yongxiang and He Fenglin ordered the assassination, and that it was related to a dispute over the syndicate's opium trafficking activities.[52] Writing in 1926, George Sokolsky, a prominent American journalist in Shanghai, suggested that Xu had been murdered because he had failed to consider the interests of powerful local gangsters in the contraband opium traffic.[53] It is possible, therefore, that the murder was prompted by a mix of motives.

The activities of this Anfu opium syndicate came to an end with the defeat of Lu Yongxiang and He Fenglin by Qi Xieyuan in the Zhejiang-Jiangsu War of September and October 1924. Most sources agree that the principal cause of the war was competition for control of the revenues from contraband opium, and the war itself was popularly referred to as "the opium war."[54] During this brief war the gangster members of the syndicate lent their support to the embattled Anfu militarists. The Green Gang leaders provided much-needed trucks to transport He Fenglin's troops to the front at a critical moment in the battle for Shanghai, and Du Yuesheng set up a Refugee Relief Committee (*Nanmin Jiuji Hui*) to provide relief for the large numbers of refugees from the war zones.[55] After the defeat of the Anfu forces Du provided temporary refuge for He Fenglin and Lu Xiaojia, Lu Yongxiang's son, in his house at 26 Rue Doumer in the French Concession.[56]

Despite the provision of such assistance, the complete rout of the Anfu militarists meant that the gangsters had to devise with all speed alternative arrangements for the organization and protection of the contraband opium traffic. One such measure was the agreement that Du Yuesheng reached with the Hubei warlord Zhang Yuanming in October 1924 for the continuation of the former arrangements for opium trafficking. Zhang had seized the Jiangnan Arsenal at Long-hua in the course of the war and this gave him de facto control over Chinese Shanghai south of Suzhou Creek until dislodged by the combined forces of Qi Xieyuan and Sun Chuanfang in January 1925.[57] Despite such ad hoc arrangements, however, the French Concession Green Gang bosses needed to find a more permanent basis on which to conduct their narcotics operations.

THE CREATION OF THE THREE PROSPERITIES COMPANY, 1924–1925

Prior to the demise of the syndicate the position of the French Concession Green Gang leaders was greatly strengthened by the campaign undertaken by the SMP to eradicate the trade in contraband opium within the boundaries of the International Settlement. In an attempt to counter the increasingly brazen activities of the opium traffickers in the Settlement and their adverse effects on police morale, the SMP created in 1923 a Special Anti-Narcotics Squad under the command of Assistant Commissioner M. O. Springfield.[58] The Special Squad established an elaborate network of informers, conducted regular raids on opium shops and warehouses and intensified patrols in those areas known to be used by traffickers. These measures began to take effect in the three-year period from 1924 to 1926, and the number of prosecutions for opium trafficking accounted for over 46 percent of the total number of prosecutions in the ten-year period 1918 to 1928.[59] The high point in the Special Squad's campaign came in January and February 1925, when it dealt a series of what were described as "staggering blows" against the leading opium hongs, with the discovery of two massive storage areas for illicit opium at 51 Canton Road and at 562 Foochow

Road.[60] The raids on these two major depots broke the back of the resistance of the leading Chaozhou opium merchants in the International Settlement to the police campaign.

The major casualty of this campaign was the Big Eight Mob, whose power base in the International Settlement was completely eroded. The Big Eight Mob's position as the major gangster organization involved with opium trafficking in Shanghai rested on its control of the leading Chaozhou opium concerns and on its ability to penetrate the SMP organization. In the wake of the Special Squad's raids, particularly those of January and February, the major Chaozhou opium merchants moved their operations out of the International Settlement into Chinese Shanghai and the French Concession, and thus out of the control of the Big Eight Mob.[61] Attempts to eradicate corruption within the SMP and generally to improve the force's morale, moreover, greatly reduced the influence of the Big Eight Mob within the police force, particularly within the Chinese Detective Squad.

The Green Gang leaders in the French Concession seized this opportunity to consolidate their own control over the opium traffic in Shanghai. There is some evidence to suggest that the French Concession bosses at this time engaged in their own campaign of intimidation against the opium hongs in the International Settlement, which served to complement the activities of the Special Squad in forcing the opium merchants out of the Settlement and into the French Concession.[62] The takeover of the Big Eight Mob's operations by the French Concession Green Gang group was arranged at a meeting between Shen Xingshan and Huang Jinrong.[63] Although the sources give no date for this meeting it probably occurred at some time after the Special Squad's major raids of January and February 1925, which triggered the departure of most of the leading opium hongs from the International Settlement. Much of the Big Eight Mob's organization was incorporated into the French Concession Green Gang structure, and a large number of the mob's leading personnel, such as Shen Xingshan and Su Jiashan, went on to become prominent figures in the French Concession Green Gang's rackets.[64]

The consolidation of the control of the French Concession Green Gang bosses over the opium traffic occurred at a time when warlord politics in Shanghai was entering a highly unstable period. This development helped to strengthen the gangsters' bargaining position vis-à-vis a succession of warlord rulers. Almost as soon as he had achieved victory, Qi Xieyuan was robbed of its fruits by events in Beijing, when Feng Yuxiang betrayed Wu Peifu and allied with Zhang Zuolin in the restoration of an Anfu government with Duan Qirui as Provisional Chief Executive in November 1924. This led to a further round of conflict in the Shanghai area with Qi Xie-yuan allied with Sun Chuanfang in opposition to the Fengtian forces of Zhang Zongchang, which ended with Qi's defeat and departure for Japan in January and Sun's tactical withdrawal to Zhejiang in February 1925.[65]

There is some evidence to suggest that Qi's designs on the opium traffic led to conflict with the Green Gang, and that this contributed to his difficulties in consolidating his position in Shanghai.[66] This would explain the participation of Du Yuesheng and the other Green Gang leaders in the military conspiracies of the defeated Anfu forces. All three French Concession Green Gang bosses were in-volved in the abortive scheme of Xu Shuzheng ("Little Xu"), Duan Qirui's right-hand man and leading strategist of the Anfu Clique, in mid-October 1924 to reorganize the defeated Zhejiang forces and continue the struggle along the borders of the foreign settlements, with the option of rushing the settlements in the event of their de-feat.[67] The hostility of the French Concession Green Gang bosses toward Qi would also explain the subsequent arrest by the Fengtian forces in February 1925 of the opium merchant Fan Huichun, whom Qi had appointed as his magistrate for Shanghai during his brief exercise of authority.[68] By contrast, the French Concession gangsters went out of their way to welcome Zhang Zongchang's forces to Shanghai. They entertained Zhang on a lavish scale, and assisted him in establishing his control over Shanghai. This perhaps reflected the fact that Zhang Zongchang was himself a member of the Green Gang (he belonged to the Tong generational status group of the Shaohou Branch), and that his relations with Huang Jinrong went back to the period of the 1911 Revolution when Zhang briefly served in the forces of Li Zhengwu in Shanghai.[69]

In February or March 1925 the Green Gang leadership made its arrangements with Zhang Zongchang for the conduct of the opium traffic in Shanghai. The system, however, was not as well regulated nor as carefully controlled as the one that had been organized by Lu Yongxiang during his long period of authority in the Shanghai area. With the removal of Zhang's headquarters to Xuzhou in northern

Jiangsu at the end of March 1925 the situation in Shanghai became increasingly chaotic, not to say scandalous, as Zhang's officers competed with one another for a share of the profits from the opium traffic. The situation was complicated by the fact that throughout the first half of 1925 several public organizations in Shanghai, including the National Anti-Opium Association (NAOA), the Jiangsu Educational Association and the Shanghai Students' Union launched an active anti-opium campaign, which provided effective, and unwelcome, publicity of the activities of the militarists and the traffickers.[70] These public bodies published repeated allegations that the Chinese police conducted fake opium raids and that senior officials such as Chang Zhiying, the Shanghai and Wusong Police Commissioner, and Admiral Yang Shuzhuang, Commander-in-Chief of the Navy, were on the gangsters' payroll.[71] The gangsters, for their part, were impervious to public criticism. One prominent opium trafficker, interviewed by the Chinese press, claimed that the traffickers had official protection not only at the local level but also within the central government in Beijing, and arrogantly dismissed public opinion as "worth nothing."[72]

During May 1925 trade in opium was openly conducted in the Chinese City. Opium was sold in packages bearing the official seal of the Shanghai Bureau for the Prevention of Opium and Drug Smuggling, a circumstance which compelled the Ministry of the Interior to order its closure at the end of May.[73] At the same time, opium retail shops in the Chinese City openly displayed their official military "protection" permits.[74] The open trafficking in opium had a corrosive effect on the discipline and morale of the Fengtian forces. Each unit conducted its own smuggling operations, and disputes over the ownership of individual consignments occasionally resulted in armed conflict.[75] This state of affairs reached its nadir on May 30, 1925, in a dramatic shoot-out between three Fengtian generals—the Director of Military Affairs of the First Fengtian Army, the Director of the Military Supplies Department and the Commander of the Twenty-eighth Mixed Brigade, over the distribution of the profits from a large opium consignment, which left one dead and the other two badly wounded.[76]

The first half of 1925 also witnessed renewed calls for the legalization of the opium traffic in Shanghai. At the Rehabilitation Conference held in Beijing from February to April 1925, the prominent Shanghai merchant Yu Xiaqing, supported by Sun Baoqi, proposed the creation of a government opium monopoly at Shanghai in the form of a Public Opium Sales Bureau.[77] Yu's proposal was received with some enthusiasm, as it was well known that Duan's government was chronically short of funds to meet its administrative expenses, and the NAOA delegate to the conference observed that government officials were in the process of preparing a plan for just such a monopoly.[78] Questions were soon raised in the Chinese press, however, as to the real motives underlying Yu's suggestion. Although some commentators considered that such a scheme could never be implemented because it would arouse the opposition of the powerful gangsters who controlled the traffic, others hinted darkly that, on the contrary, the Shanghai gangsters themselves might well have been the true initiators and supporters of the scheme.[79] It was suggested that Yu Xiaqing was himself involved with the contraband traffic in Shanghai, and that Sun Baoqi's own proposal in support of Yu's scheme was merely "a means of consolidating the existing irregular trade."[80] Whatever the role of the Green Gang leadership in the promotion of this scheme, the scheme itself never got beyond the proposal stage and was quietly dropped in the face of concerted opposition from Shanghai's public organizations.[81]

None of the sources provide a precise date for the organization of the instrument of the Green Gang's monopoly, the Three Prosperities Company (*Sanxin Gongsi*). The sequence of events described above, however, would indicate that it was established some time between February and July 1925. It is doubtful whether the company had as yet been formed in the period prior to the Special Squad's major push against the Chaozhou opium hongs in the International Settlement in early 1925, and while the outcome of the military struggle in Shanghai still remained relatively uncertain at the end of 1924. On the other hand, the company was definitely in existence by late July 1925, when the Chinese newspaper the *Minguo Ribao* published details of its organization.[82]

THE ASCENDANCY OF THE THREE PROSPERITIES COMPANY, 1925–1927

According to the report in the *Minguo Ribao* the Three Prosperities Company had an initial capitalization of Ch$2.7 million, although other sources suggest a higher figure of about Ch$10 million. The company provided protection for the twenty-one Chaozhou opium hongs together with the retail shops, and engaged in opium trafficking (both Chinese and foreign) on its own account.[83] Its operations were so all-embracing that it was popularly referred to in Shanghai simply as the "Big Company" (*Da Gongsi*).[84] The company was nominally a partnership of four opium merchants who included Su Jiashan. These partners had no real authority, however, and their presence was merely part of an elaborate deception to disguise the fact that the company was actually controlled and financed by the three Green Gang bosses Du Yuesheng, Huang Jinrong and Zhang Xiaolin. The company's name, "Three Prosperities," was, in fact, popularly rumored to be a reference to the three Green Gang bosses.[85] The company's General Manager was Jin Tingsun (1884-?), a Green Gang member from Ningbo who had been associated with Huang Jinrong for many years and who had been closely involved with the Anfu Clique's de facto opium monopoly. Through his control of its financial affairs, Jin was a key figure in the operations of the Big Company.[86]

Although there are no accurate sources on the company's financial structure, it probably enjoyed a similar level of profits to those estimated for the previous Anfu-sponsored monopoly. There are suggestions that the Big Company's annual income reached Ch$56 million, and there is no doubt that the profits were vast.[87] These profits were distributed three times a year at the time of the three major festivals, the fifth of the fifth lunar month, the Mid-Autumn Festival, and Chinese New Year.

Narcotics trafficking on its own account provided the greater part of the company's income with the remainder coming from its protection racket over other traffickers and dealers.[88] According to informed contemporary estimates, each of the twenty-one Chaozhou opium hongs in Shanghai paid the Big Company Ch$50,000 a month in return for a guarantee that their operations in Shanghai and Jiangnan would be free from depredations by local gangsters.[89] The Big Company also levied monthly fees of between Ch$300 and Ch$7,000 on the sixty opium wholesale shops that operated in Shanghai, and charged a variable transit fee for transporting opium through the International Settlement and Chinese territory to the French Concession. Finally, it also collected a tax from each opium divan of 30 cents a night for each opium pipe in use.[90]

At the same time as it established its system of operations in Shanghai, the Three Prosperities Company also extended the range of its activities with the absorption of a potential rival, the Subei opium combine that was based in Nantong County, on the north bank of the Yangzi River. As with the Three Prosperities Company, this combine was also formed in early 1925 in response to the temporary disruption to the opium traffic in Jiangnan in late 1924 caused by the Jiangsu-Zhejiang War.[91] The key figures in its creation were Zhang Renkui, who was Tong-Hai Defense Commissioner, together with local Nantong merchants and a small group of Chaozhou opium merchants from Shanghai.[92] Given its location on the Yangzi River, it was able to rapidly increase the scale of its operations by gaining a major share of the trafficking in Sichuan and Yunnan opium. By the end of 1925 the combine had disposed of 40,000 chests of opium valued at some Ch$40 million.[93] Despite the threat that the Nantong Combine posed to the operations of the Three Prosperities Company, the two combines, nevertheless, were able to cooperate over specific opium shipments throughout 1925.[94] Negotiations, moreover, were conducted by representatives of both combines, which resulted, at the end of 1925, in the merging of the Nantong Combine's operations with those of the Three Prosperities Company.[95] By the beginning of 1926, therefore, the two combines formed one large organization in which the French Concession Green Gang's Three Prosperities Company held the controlling interest.

This successful outcome for the Three Prosperities Company was due, in no small measure, to the stabilization of the military and political situation in Shanghai that followed Sun Chuanfang's victory over the Fengtian forces in October 1925. As a result Shanghai quickly assumed again its central role in the opium trafficking in the Jiangnan region and along the Yangzi River. One of Sun Chuanfang's first actions after he assumed control of Shanghai was to enter into an agreement with the Big Company for the creation of an unofficial monopoly. Sun had experience of such monopolies as he had participated in the one operated at Yichang when he was stationed there in 1922.[96] By early 1926 the arrangement was working well. The French Concession Green Gang leaders had been appointed to advisory positions within Sun's headquarters, and one of Du Yuesheng's followers, Gu Jiatang, held the post of Chief of Detectives of the Wusong-Shanghai Gendarmerie.[97] Sun's military forces, for their part, protected the passage of the illicit opium through Chinese territory, and eliminated any serious rival to the Big Company's operations.[98] In return for the provision of such services Sun was able to raise up to Ch$5 million per month in taxes on illicit opium.[99]

This figure was considered a necessary and, on the whole, acceptable cost of the system for the control of the Shanghai opium traffic that the Green Gang leaders forged in the course of 1925. The reality was that the Big Company's contraband business could not have operated effectively without the collusion of the Chinese authorities in Shanghai. Indeed, it could not function either without the tacit cooperation of the French authorities, and it is to this relationship that we now turn.

3   The French Connection

The relationship of the French Concession Green Gang bosses with the French authorities was as important a factor as the bosses' control of the opium traffic in their emergence to a position of primacy within the Green Gang system in Shanghai. It was this relationship that provided them with a reasonably secure base from which they could further extend their control over the opium traffic and other rackets. In the period prior to the outbreak of the Sino-Japanese War the connection with the French authorities went through three main phases: the first phase covered the period up to 1927; the second, the years 1927–32; and the final phase, 1932–37. The present chapter is concerned with the first phase of the relationship, the two subsequent phases are discussed in chapter 4. The initial phase in the relationship between the Green Gang bosses and the French Concession authorities had three main characteristics: the continuing importance of Huang Jinrong's position in the French police; the arrangements on opium distribution within the Concession entered into with senior members of the French administration; and the competition for power and influence between the Green Gang bosses and the Chinese "establishment" in the Concession, the so-called Gentry-Councillor Clique.

HUANG JINRONG AND THE FRENCH CONCESSION POLICE

Huang Jinrong's power and influence within the French Concession, as noted earlier, rested in the first instance on the position he held within the police force. Huang's position in the police and the influence that it gave him were, in turn, determined by the specific security concerns that preoccupied the French authorities in the 1920s. Unlike the International Settlement, where executive authority was exercised by a Municipal Council overseen by the Consular Body, executive power in the French Concession was concentrated in the hands of the French Consul General, who exercised it through the issuance of consular ordinances, with the Municipal Council serving in a purely advisory capacity. One of the key powers enjoyed by the Consul General was his control over the Concession's police force (*La Garde Municipale*) which, in the words of one consul general, was answerable "directly and solely to the Consul-General."[1] The personnel of this force (both French and Vietnamese) was composed almost exclusively of former soldiers, and its chief throughout the period 1919 to 1932, E. Fiori, was an artillery captain in the Army Reserve who had seen extensive service with the French Army in Morocco.[2] The paramilitary nature of the Concession police was also reflected in its responsibilities, which, besides the regular policing of the Concession, included providing for its external security. As Consul General Wilden noted in early 1924, the police provided "in case of troubles, the principal element of the body responsible for the defence of the concession."[3] Thus both in its composition and in its diverse responsibilities the French Concession Police was in fact a typical example of a colonial police force.

Despite the large powers enjoyed by the Consul General, successive consuls general were preoccupied by the relative weakness of the Concession's system of security compared with that in the International Settlement. Although this concern only became of critical importance during the events of late 1926 and early 1927, it had been a factor in the calculations of the French Concession authorities since the First World War. Indeed, Fiori had been appointed in 1919 with the specific brief to transform the police into an effective instrument for the defense of the Concession and so lessen its dependence in security matters on the International Settlement.[4] This sense of vulnerability stemmed, in part, from budgetary constraints in the early 1920s that made it difficult to maintain the strength of the police force at levels adequate even for regular policing functions, a problem that was compounded by the huge increases in the Concession's Chinese population during this same period. Another factor that contributed to this concern was the doubtful legal standing of the 1868 Règlements, which provided the constitutional basis for the Concession. It was argued that since these regulations had been supported by *force majeure* they could be invalidated by force. As one contemporary authority noted: "The Règlements have their origin in the same vague treaty provisions as the [International Settlement] Land Regulations. The Règlements have been supported by force and could be invalidated in the same manner by a strong Chinese government."[5]

The recognition of the Concession's vulnerability on security matters was aggravated by the metropolitan French government's belief that the Concession represented the most important center of French influence in the Far East. Such an attitude led the local French administration to emphasize French authority at every opportunity, and to meet all challenges, real or imagined, to that authority no matter from what quarter they might emanate. To local French officials the International Settlement itself, by the very fact of its proximity to the Concession, represented a challenge to continuing French authority within the Concession.

This preoccupation with security concerns predisposed French officials to seek allies where they could to support the efforts to maintain French authority and prestige within the Concession. One such ally was Huang Jinrong, a member of the Chinese detective squad and a gang boss. Although Huang had joined the French Concession Police in 1892, it was not until the First World War that he emerged as the leading Chinese figure in the police force and the predominant gangster boss in the Concession. Because of the large number of French police officers who returned to France for war service at this time, the French Consul General carried out a reorganization of the police force that devolved greater responsibilities on the Chinese members of the force. Consequently in 1918 Huang was promoted to Chief Superintendent and many of his close associates, such as Cheng Ziqing and Jin Jiulin, were also appointed to senior positions.[6]

Huang's usefulness to the French authorities derived from the close relations he had developed with local gangster groups associated with the Green and Red Gang systems, such as the Big Eight Mob and the Thirty-six Mob (*Sanshiliu Gudang*), although Huang himself was not a formal member of the Green Gang system. He was also active in a group called the "108 Warriors" (*Yibailingba Jiang*), which brought together the leading Chinese detectives working for the foreign authorities, and therefore provided him with a regular channel to his colleagues in the International Settlement.[7] Through these connections Huang was able to assist the chief of the Sûreté (the detective squad) to effect such periodic police "clean-ups" as that in 1922 when thirteen separate gangster mobs (with a total of 124 members) were arrested in the course of the year.[8] In much the same way Huang was able to mobilize the necessary muscle to help the French authorities break the Chinese shopkeepers' strike in the wake of the May Fourth Incident of 1919.[9] It was for such reasons that Huang earned the popular nickname "the Great Wall of security in the Concession" (*Zujie zhi'an de Changcheng*).[10]

Huang's connections with gangster and bandit groups outside Shanghai, in particular his extensive contacts with with Green Gang organizations throughout the Jiangnan and Subei, could also be used to advantage by the French authorities. On one occasion, for example, when the wife of the Concession's chief administrative officer, M. Verdier, was kidnapped by bandits while holidaying in the Lake Tai area, the French authorities turned to Huang for help. As noted in chapter 1 the region around Lake Tai was an area of Green Gang activity, and many of the bandit chiefs in this area had close relations with various Green Gang groups in Shanghai. This fact made easier the success of Huang's negotiations for the release of Mrs. Verdier, and he used as his intermediary Gao Xinbao, one of Du Yuesheng's followers, who enjoyed close relations with the Green Gang groups around Lake Tai.[11]

Another occasion, and one of greater political significance, was Huang's role in the negotiations concerning the Lincheng Incident. On May 5, 1923, bandits, led by one Sun Meiyao, held up the Shanghai-Beijing express train, the so-called Blue Express, near the town of Lincheng, Shandong. All of the train's 300 passengers, including 35 foreigners, were seized and held for ransom.[12] The incident created an international sensation and came to symbolize for many foreigners the collapse of legitimate state authority in China. The foreign powers, concerned about the implications of the incident for extraterritoriality and other foreign rights in China, brought great pressure to bear on the Chinese government to obtain the release of the foreign captives.

The French authorities were concerned particularly about the fate of an M. Berube, a French official of the Chinese Maritime Customs, and Signor Musso, a senior lawyer in the French Concession who enjoyed a close working relationship with the French administration. They sought, therefore, to use Huang Jinrong's Green Gang connections in order to make contact with the bandit leaders. Huang sought the assistance of Zhang Renkui, who was then Tong-Hai Defense Commissioner. Zhang provided him with a safe-conduct pass, and with this he proceeded to Lincheng accompanied by Zhang's leading follower, Wu Kunshan.

Huang and Wu held a number of discussions with Sun Meiyao and his representatives in the vicinity of Lincheng, as well as with the local Chinese officials. These discussions, in fact, were part of a series of protracted and complex negotiations with the bandits, which involved the Beijing government, local warlord authorities, and the representatives of three major foreign powers (Britain, France and the United States), that finally resulted in the release of the captives at the end of June 1923. As a result of his participation in these successful negotiations Huang's standing with the French authorities was greatly enhanced. One further consequence of Huang Jinrong's involvement with the Lincheng Incident was that he finally became a member of the Green Gang. In return for obtaining Zhang Renkui's cooperation Huang agreed to become one of Zhang's disciples, and so he became a member of the Tong generational status group of the Xing Wu Liu Branch of the Green Gang.[13]

Huang also used his position as the Sûreté's leading Chinese detective to further his own economic interests and to increase his influence with the leading gangster organizations in Shanghai. From his headquarters in the Ju Bao Teahouse (*Jubao Chalou*), Huang regulated the activities of armed robbers, kidnappers and narcotics smugglers, and managed his many diverse economic interests. He owned a string of theaters and bathhouses, and he either protected or controlled all of the opium hongs, gambling joints and brothels in the French Concession.[14] As part of these operations he regularly paid out bribes to his French colleagues and superiors in the police force. Two successive heads of the Sûreté, Traissac and Sidaine, Huang's nominal superiors, in fact, lost their positions in 1924 and 1925, respectively, for turning a blind eye to the involvement of Chinese detectives in the gambling and narcotics operations in the Concession.[15]

Despite his corruption of superiors, Huang's position, nevertheless, derived from his influence with French officialdom. It was his position within the Concession police force, particularly in the 1914 to 1925 period, that gave him standing with other gangster groups in Shanghai and helped him to build up his own gangster following. It enabled him to develop a close working relationship with those gang bosses who belonged to the Green Gang system, without himself formally being a member of that system until very much later in his career. Huang Jinrong, in fact, was the "comprador of violence " par excellence. His career epitomized the ambiguous relationship between gangsters and police that had developed in the Shanghai foreign settlements in the early twentieth century. He used his police power to carve out his own bailiwick and to suppress gangster rivals. Ultimately, gangsters who wished to operate in the French Concession had to come to terms with Huang. At the same time as Huang's criminal connections grew and as his power increased among the local gangsters of the French Concession, so he became even more useful and indispensable to the French authorities. Thus it was that Huang Jinrong's positions as chief of detectives and gang boss complemented and reinforced one another.

RIVALS FOR POWER: THE CHINESE CATHOLIC "GENTRY-COUNCILLOR CLIQUE"

Huang Jinrong and his associates, however, were not the only group that the French officials used to mediate their relations with the Chinese population of the Concession. Another powerful group that was closely associated with the Concession authorities was the so-called Gentry-Councillor Clique (*Shendong Pai*), which was composed of influential Chinese businessmen who were also Roman Catholics and returned students from France.[16] The two leading members of this group in the 1920s and 1930s were Zhu Zhiyao (1863–1955) and Lu Baihong (1873–1937).[17] Zhu and Lu belonged to old, established Shanghai Catholic families who could trace their Catholicism back to the seventeenth century, and both were prominent members of the Shanghai branch of the Union for Chinese Catholic Action (*Zhonghua Gongjiao Jinxing Hui*). They were also leading merchants who enjoyed close links with the Zhejiang financial clique (notably with Zhu Baosan and Yu Xiaqing) and had extensive interests in shipping, public utilities and real estate in the Shanghai area.

Other members of this clique included Wu Zonglian (a former Chinese minister to Italy), Lu Songhou (former chairman of the Nandao municipality), Zhu Yan (co-director of the Institut Technique Franco-Chinois), and Wei Tingrong (a director of the Crédit Franco-

Chinois and the Da Da Bank, and the son-in-law of Zhu Baosan).[18] Official French protection of Catholicism in China as part of its *mission civilisatrice* gave members of these Shanghai Chinese Catholic families standing and influence with the local French authorities, which was reinforced by their connections with the Jesuit order. By the early twentieth century these Catholic gentry enjoyed extremely close relations with the French and a number of them, such as Wei Tingrong and Zhu Yan, were involved in promoting French financial and educational interests in Shanghai and so contributed indirectly to the buttressing of French authority within the Concession. When the French agreed to appoint two nonparticipating Chinese councillors to the Municipal Council to advise the Consul General on matters relating to the Chinese population, as part of the Sino-French Agreement of 1914, they naturally appointed them from the ranks of these Catholic gentry.[19]

There is no doubt that a relationship of some kind existed between this Gentry-Councillor Clique and prominent Shanghai gangsters. Both Zhu and Lu dealt with at least one leading member of the Big Eight Mob in the course of their business activities in the early 1920s, and there were suggestions that some sort of recognition concerning spheres of interest in the French Concession existed between them and Huang Jingrong's group.[20] As the gangster groups sought to enlarge the areas of their interests and the degree of their influence over the French administration, however, this tacit compact broke down and both groups engaged in both covert and overt conflict for power and influence in the latter half of the 1920s. One enduring legacy of this conflict was the mutual hostility that developed between Wei Tingrong and Du Yuesheng.

THE DEAL WITH THE FRENCH AUTHORITIES, APRIL–JUNE 1925

With the consolidation of their control over the Shanghai opium traffic through the creation of the Three Prosperities Company, the three Green Gang bosses sought to secure their base of operations within the French Concession. There are indications that the gangsters first approached the influential French lawyer and legal adviser to the Concession authorities, Du Pac de Marsouliès, in order to reach some kind of tacit understanding with the French. Du Pac was associated with the Shanghai opium traffickers. He was the defense

lawyer in the Ezra opium case, which involved the leading Guangdong opium merchant Ye Qinghe, and withdrew from the case in
rather intriguing circumstances. The Acting French Consul General,
Meyrier, moreover, was aware of allegations that one reason why
Du Pac stood for the Municipal Council elections in January 1925
was his desire to set up an opium trafficking organization.[21]

The Concession authorities were receptive to these overtures. For
several years they had argued that the policy of opium prohibition
was a failure, and Chief of Police Fiori openly urged the legalization
of the trade in 1924 and 1925. He was not alone in his advocacy. It
was suggested by a number of other foreign officials including Sir
Francis Aglen, the Inspector General of Customs.[22] Two major reasons were put forward in support of a policy of legalization. First,
there was the argument that the policy of prohibition was impossible
to police adequately, and that the situation of unenforceable prohibition created a crisis of morale within the foreign police forces of
Shanghai by encouraging rampant corruption within their ranks. A
second, and more telling, argument was that the opium trade once
legalized could be licensed and thus generate revenue for all three
administrations in Shanghai. Opium farms at that time were a standard means of raising official revenues in European colonies in the
Far East, and the French officials in Shanghai had the example of
the lucrative farm in Indochina that raised fifteen million piastres in
revenue in 1923 alone, or 21 percent of the French administration's
budget for that year.[23] Moreover, the security problems that confronted the Concession authorities in late 1924 and early 1925 in
the wake of the Zhejiang-Jiangsu War graphically illustrated the
need for an expanded police force. Revenue was, therefore, the major consideration in the French authorities' response to the gangsters' overtures in early 1925, and this was confirmed by subsequent
events.

The main obstacle to a policy of open licensing of the opium trade
was the mobilization of international and Chinese public opinion by
the powerful (and basically Protestant) missionary lobby in organizations such as the International Anti-Opium Association. It was
the effective work performed by these bodies that prevented either
the Chinese government or the Shanghai Consular Body from requesting the foreign powers to reappraise the 1912 Hague Convention and allow the public licensing of the opium trade.[24]

The local French administration, however, decided to defy this pressure and entered into secret negotiations with Du Yuesheng, representing the Three Prosperities Company.[25] These negotiations were held over a three-month period, April–June 1925, and involved senior members of the municipal administration and leading French businessmen. These included the Chief of Police, Captain E. Fiori; the Chief Administrative Officer of the Concession, M. Verdier; M. Speelman (a local Dutch banker and member of the French Municipal Council); M. Blum (the Managing Director of Ullmann et Cie, the jewelry store on Nanking Road, and member of the French Municipal Council); M. Galvin (a local pharmacist); and Doctor Hibert (a medical practitioner). The sources suggest that the then acting Consul General, Jacques Meyrier, was represented in the negotiations by Galvin and Blum, and that he used the services of Li Yingsheng, the manager of the Meizhenhua Ji, the jewelry store on the Rue du Consulat owned by Du Yuesheng, as an intermediary between himself and the Three Prosperities Company.[26]

On April 28, 1925, a meeting look place at 40 Route Vallon that was attended by Du Yuesheng and Wang Jiafa (described as an "opium importer") representing the Three Prosperities Company, and Captain Fiori, M. Galvin and Doctor Hibert representing the local French authorities. At this meeting an agreement was reached on the conditions governing the opium traffic in the French Concession.[27] By its terms five opium retail shops and an opium warehouse were to be opened on a trial basis for one month, after which period the number of opium shops would be increased to twenty. Before operations commenced the Green Gang leaders would pay Ch$70,000 to M. Galvin, who acted on behalf of the police and the consulate, in order that they would "turn a blind eye" (*pour fermer les yeux*) to the proceedings. This payment would be made in two installments of Ch$35,000, and the Three Prosperities Company agreed to pay a monthly fee in advance to the French police. Finally, the gangsters undertook responsibility for all the Chinese personnel involved, together with "the people who are in the habit of handling money in this sort of business."[28] During this meeting the gangsters expressed their doubts as to whether or not the French parties to the negotiations could deliver on their promises of protection. Both Du and Wang bluntly stated that they had limited confidence in the police's ability to ensure adequate protection and, therefore, demanded a ten-day trial period before they handed any money over to the French authorities. Galvin, in response, threatened to end the negotiations unless the Green Gang bosses made the payments. At this point in the discussions Fiori ostentatiously left the meeting delegating full negotiating powers to Galvin. Fiori's action convinced Du and Wang of the seriousness of the threat and they agreed to make the payments.[29] Shortly afterward the substance of these negotiations was leaked to the press, which led to their suspension for most of May.[30]

In late May the final contract was signed and it came into effect on June 1, 1925, although only after M. Blum, on behalf of the French authorities, had reimbursed the Ch$35,000 to the Green Gang leaders.[31] The contract, which was signed by Du Yuesheng on behalf of the Three Prosperities Company, merely elaborated the points agreed to at the meeting of April 28. Among other things, it provided that the French police would arrest and prosecute only those opium traffickers who were not members of the company; that the company would give the police advance notice of its shipments, and that it would liaise closely with Captain Fiori, and "keep him informed of everything that happens"; that the company would provide its guards with uniforms and register them with the French police; and, most important, that the company would ensure that the opium traffic was conducted "discreetly" and that nobody was "compromised" by its activities. The French authorities ensured their control of this arrangement through the stipulation that the contract was renewable on a three-month basis.[32] The arrangements, therefore, were tightly controlled by the French police: all arrangements were to be made with Captain Fiori with whom the Three Prosperities Company was to maintain a close and regular liaison, and its personnel were to be registered with the French police.

Under the terms of the contract, the Big Company agreed to pay the police representative a lump sum of Ch$140,000 together with Ch$80,000 per month (Ch$960,000 a year) "during the entire duration of the traffic." In addition it agreed to pay a body described as "the European committee," presumably those members of the administration and the Municipal Council who were parties to the negotiations, Ch$250 for each chest of opium that entered the warehouse, together with Ch$500 per month (Ch$6,000 per year) for each opium retail shop that operated in the Concession.[33] Given the volume of contraband opium shipped through Shanghai such sums were considerable and went a long way to help meet the administrative costs of the French Concession.

As some informed observers later remarked, an opium tax farm had been established in effect, if not in name, in the French Concession.[34] These semi-official arrangements created quite a different situation from the corruption of individual police and municipal officials that had obtained in an earlier period. They formalized, to a degree, the relationship between the gangster bosses and the French authorities by putting it on a new, more regular and systematic basis. The Green Gang bosses were now better placed than before to develop their political influence in the Concession over the longer term. The agreement on opium, indeed, opened up new vistas of opportunity for the gangsters.

THE CONTINUING POWER OF THE GENTRY-COUNCILLOR CLIQUE IN THE FRENCH CONCESSION, 1924–1927

These new opportunities, however, were not immediately realized, mainly because the Gentry-Councillor Clique continued to mediate the political relationship between the Chinese residents and the French Concession authorities for most of the 1920s. In late 1924 the Consul General, Auguste Wilden, turned to this group for assistance in dealing with the security crisis facing the Concession as a result of the confused military and political situation in Shanghai in the wake of the Zhejiang-Jiangsu War. The fact that the French chose not to seek help from the gangsters reflected the limited role that the French still assigned Huang Jinrong's gangster organization.

The Gentry-Councillor Clique responded to Wilden's request by organizing a militia corps between November 1924 and April 1925 that was officially known as the French Concession Chinese Volunteers (Compagnie des Volontaires Chinois de la Concession Française).[35] This corps consisted of between 150 and 200 men and was controlled by Zhu Zhiyao and Lu Baihong, who were its President and Vice President respectively. Its commander was Wei Tingrong. Although the Gentry-Councillor Clique met most of the company's costs out of a special fund, the French authorities supplied most of its armaments (200 rifles) together with a Ch$5,000 grant for outfitting the volunteers. The volunteer corps also boasted six machine guns and an armored car.

This Chinese Volunteers Corps was similar to the merchant militias organized in Chinese Shanghai, and it greatly enhanced the power and influence of the Gentry-Councillor Clique in the Concession. The French were well pleased with the performance of the volunteers and considered them to be a major support to the police in the maintenance of public order, especially during the first anniversary of the May Thirtieth Incident in 1926. As a result Wei Tingrong was awarded the Concession's highest decoration, the Gold Medal of the French Municipality (*Médaille Or de la Municipalité Française*) in recognition of the services he performed for the French Concession as commander of the Chinese Volunteers.[36]

The position of the Gentry-Councillor Clique was further enhanced by the role that French officials allocated to it in their reform of the Concession's administration. Both Meyrier and his successor as Consul General, P. E. Naggiar, were concerned at the growing influence of non-French foreigners on the Municipal Council and the threat that they believed this posed for French authority in the Concession. The problem was demographic: the French were a minority of the foreign population in the Concession. In 1926 out of a total population in the Concession of 308,000, there were 300,000 Chinese, 7,000 non-French foreigners, and only 1,000 French.[37] As part of their strategy for dealing with this problem, the French authorities decided to appoint Chinese representatives to the Municipal Council with, for the first time, full rights of participation in the council's affairs. This had a double advantage from the administration's standpoint: it met to some degree Chinese nationalist demands for greater representation in the council, and at the same time it shored up the French position within the council.

One of Naggiar's first acts on taking up the position of French Consul General in April 1926, therefore, was to appoint two leading members of the Gentry-Councillor Clique, Lu Baihong and Lu Songhou as full members of the French Municipal Council.[38] In a speech at a reception for Sun Chuanfang in early May, Lu Baihong expressed his satisfaction with Naggiar's actions, which not only provided the Chinese bourgeoisie with full representation in the Municipal Council for the first time, but also served to further strengthen his clique's position within the Concession.[39]

By the end of 1926 Naggiar had decided to abolish completely the elected Municipal Council. On January 14, 1927, he replaced it with an appointed Provisional Commission (*Commission Provisoire d'Administration Municipale*) on the basis of Article 8 of the 1868 Règlements. Technically the elected Municipal Council was only suspended temporarily because of "events affecting the order and security of the concession"; in fact it was never restored. Of the seventeen members appointed to the Provisional Commission by the Consul General, five were Chinese, and all of them were leading members of the Gentry-Councillor Clique. In a very real sense the major beneficiaries of Naggiar's administrative coup (apart from the French administration itself) was the clique of Chinese Roman Catholic gentry associated with Zhu Zhiyao and Lu Baihong.[40]

THE CHANGING POWER BALANCE AMONG THE FRENCH CONCESSION GREEN GANG BOSSES

The extension of the power and organization of the Green Gang group in the French Concesssion in the mid-1920s, through the control of the contraband opium traffic and the understanding reached with the French Concession authorities, was accompanied by changes within the group itself that saw the emergence of a new leadership combination. This change in the power balance within the leadership was at the expense of Huang Jinrong who lost his position of primacy within the organization and was forced to share increasingly more of his power with his two erstwhile lieutenants, Du Yuesheng and Zhang Xiaolin. The result was the emergence of a collective leadership after 1925, and this triumvirate was popularly referred to as the "three big bosses" (*san daheng*).

In 1924 Huang's leadership was seriously weakened by the so-called Lu Lanchun Affair, which involved Huang in a conflict with Lu Yongxiang's warlord group. The occasion was the disparaging remarks made by Lu Xiaojia, Lu Yongxiang's son, during a performance by the famous female Beijing opera star Lu Lanchun in Huang's theater, the Gong Wutai, which provoked Huang to assault Lu. Vowing vengeance Lu requested assistance from He Fenglin. This request presented He with a dilemma: on the one hand the relationship with Huang and the French Concession Green Gang was of major importance in managing the Anfu Clique's opium monopoly; on the other hand Huang had made the son of his commanding officer lose face and thus by extension had insulted Lu Yongxiang himself. He decided finally to assist the younger Lu and a few days later, soldiers in plainclothes arrested Huang in the Gong Wutai and took him to He's headquarters at Longhua.

On learning of Huang's arrest both Du Yuesheng and Zhang

Xiaolin set about trying to obtain his release. Zhang handled the direct negotiations with He Fenglin drawing on his close relations with the Zhejiang warlords. These negotiations, however, proved to be protracted, and Huang was only released after a sizeable sum of money, which Du had raised from the Chaozhou opium merchants, had been handed over by the gangsters.

His arrest and imprisonment constituted an enormous loss of face for Huang Jinrong and revealed in stark fashion the limitations on his authority and influence in a key relationship for the Green Gang bosses. Shortly after his release Huang entered into a sworn brother relationship with Du and Zhang, which symbolically expressed the new equality between the three Green Gang bosses. This arrangement in fact provided Huang with a face-saving means by which he could relinquish real power in the group and retire to the status of an honored elder. From this period on all policy decisions were made by Du and Zhang.[41]

Huang's embarrassment was compounded the following year when Wei Tingrong of the Gentry-Councillor Clique engineered his resignation as Chief of the Chinese Detective Squad.[42] This was related to the clique's attempts to disrupt the negotiations between the Green Gang bosses and the French authorities on the prospective opium farm. In early May 1925 an open letter to the acting Consul General, Meyrier, was published in the Shanghai press, which called on him to suppress the opium retail shops scheduled to open "in a day or two" so as to ensure that "the reputation and integrity of the French in Shanghai should be upheld."[43] Although the clique failed in its attempt to prevent the opium agreement between the French authorities and the Green Gang bosses it did succeed in forcing Huang's resignation from the police force. He retired in 1925. Although less than two years later, in January 1927, the French reappointed Huang to the post of senior adviser to the police, this was no more than an honorary position. By then real power within the French Concession Green Gang hierarchy had shifted decisively to his two "sworn brothers," Zhang Xiaolin and Du Yuesheng.[44]

The power exercised by Zhang and Du after 1924 rested on different but complementary bases. Zhang's power derived from his close associations with the Jiangnan warlords, Lu Yongxiang and He Fenglin, and he developed similar relations with both Sun Chuanfang and Zhang Zongchang after the defeat of Lu Yongxiang in the Zhejiang-Jiangsu War of September 1924. His power within the French Concesssion Green Gang system, therefore, reflected his familiarity with the world of warlord politics and his acceptability within that world. He was in other words the key person who mediated the relationship between the Green Gang bosses and the warlord political systems in Shanghai.

Du Yuesheng, for his part, concentrated his efforts on securing control of the Green Gang's narcotics operations in Shanghai. In the early 1920s he built up a close working relationship with the major Chaozhou opium merchants, and he played a key role in the establishment of the Three Prosperities Company, whose management he controlled in association with Jin Tingsun. It was Du, moreover, who negotiated the agreement with the French authorities on behalf of the Green Gang bosses, and this role provided him with a good basis to develop his own connections with those authorities. Through his involvement with the Three Prosperities Company, in short, Du controlled a large part of the financial resources of the French Concession Green Gang, and this provided him with the necessary leverage to progressively extend his power and influence. By late 1924, when he was mentioned by name in an open letter published in the *North-China Herald*, Du was already considered to be a major power in the gangster world of Shanghai. The letter described Du as "the chief loafer of the French Concession, an opium and arms smuggler. He claims Portuguese citizenship, and pretends to be immune from arrest in the French Concession for whatever he may do. It is strange that the *Sin wen pao* [*Xinwen Bao*] published his name as Dou 'someone' instead of in full. I presume they knew the character of the man, and were afraid to print it, for fear of inviting trouble from Dou's loafer gangs."[45] This new leadership combination within the French Concession Green Gang had not long been in place before it faced dramatically new challenges in the shape of the revolutionary politics of the Guomindang and the Chinese Communists. These developments placed further strains on the Green Gang triumvirate, and indeed the whole Green Gang system in Shanghai, as it sought to come to terms with the political ferment of the years 1925 to 1927.

4   In the Chinese Revolution

In addition to warlord regimes the links between the French Concession Green Gang bosses and the Chinese political world in the 1920s also included the two major revolutionary parties that actively sought to recast the mould of Chinese politics, the Nationalist Party, or Guomindang (GMD), and the Chinese Communist Party (CCP). These relations became increasingly important as revolutionary politics came to Shanghai in 1925–27.

For the Green Gang bosses relations with such political groups were of an essentially pragmatic nature and reflected their propensity to deal with any and all organizations in pursuit of their own specific interests. In other words the gangster bosses did not distinguish necessarily between their relations with these political parties and those they enjoyed with the local warlords and French authorities. By the late 1920s the GMD and the CCP, for their part, could not ignore the important role that the French Concession Green Gang, in particular, played in the political and economic world of Shanghai, as a consequence of its control of the contraband opium traffic and its relationships with the local Chinese warlord and French authorities. Jiang Jieshi, indeed, found the Green Gang bosses to be indispensable allies in his coup de main against the CCP; while the CCP leadership itself, in the pursuit of its political strategy of organizing the working class, had to take account of the labor rackets run by the Green Gang.

THE GREEN GANG AND THE GUOMINDANG: EARLY RELATIONS TO 1926

The relationship between the Shanghai Green Gang and the Guomindang had its origin in the period of the 1911 Revolution when Chen

Qimei, the head of the Tongmenghui's Central China Bureau, utilized the Green and Red Gangs to capture Shanghai and subsequently
to assist him in the consolidation of his own position as military
governor (*dudu*) of Shanghai. Members of the Green Gang formed
the rank and file of Chen's "Dare-to-Die" Corps (*Gansi Dui*), which
were commanded by Green Gang leaders such as Liu Fubiao and
Ying Guixin during the 1911 Revolution in Shanghai.[1] There is
some suggestion that Chen Qimei himself joined the Green Gang
and held a leadership position in that organization in order to ensure
his authority over the gangsters.[2]

Chen certainly helped to establish the Mutual Progress Association of the Chinese Republic (*Zhonghua Minguo Gongjin Hui*) in
order to mobilize the Green Gang in support of his military gover-
norship. Created in 1912 in Shanghai under the direction of Ying
Guixin, this organization sought to include all the Green Gang members in the lower Yangzi Valley, and its leadership was drawn from
prominent Green Gang members of the Da generational status
group. The Mutual Progress Association did not last long; it was
suppressed by Yuan Shikai's government by the end of 1912, and its
former leader, Yin Guixin, went over to Yuan Shikai. The assassination of the senior Guomindang parliamentarian, Song Jiaoren, by
Ying Guixin on Yuan's orders in 1913 embarrassed Chen Qimei and
compromised his strategy of using the Green Gang to further the
political goals of the revolutionaries. This strategy was disrupted
further by Chen's own assassination in 1916, and although his lieutenant, Han Hui, attempted to maintain the link between the Shanghai Green Gang and the Chinese Revolutionary Party (*Zhonghua
Gemingdang*), a predecessor of the GMD, it was finally broken with
Han's own assassination in 1917.[3]

It was during the period of the 1911 Revolution and its aftermath
that Jiang Jieshi, following the example of his mentor Chen Qimei,
also developed relations with the Green Gang bosses in Shanghai.
These links date from the time Jiang personally commanded one of
Chen Qimei's "Dare-to-Die" Corps, which was sent from Shanghai
to assist in the liberation of Hangzhou.[4] Jiang's relationship with the
Green Gang has remained a contentious issue over the past seventy
years. Both Chinese and foreign authors have made repeated allegations concerning Jiang's membership in the Green Gang and his relationship with Huang Jinrong.[5] Jiang himself admitted in a letter to
Hu Hanmin and Wang Jingwei in 1924 to having led a wild and

dissolute life when he worked as a broker on the Shanghai Stock Exchange in 1919 and first became familiar with the "playboy world" of Shanghai.[6] Huang Zhenshi, a former Green Gang boss and a follower of Huang Jinrong, asserts that Jiang Jieshi did indeed become a follower of Huang Jinrong through the good offices of Yu Xiaqing in 1919. Jiang's purpose was to find a solution to his financial embarrassment as a result of his failures on the stock exchange, and to obtain the necessary funds to join Sun Yat-sen in Guangzhou.[7] It should be noted, however, that at this time Huang himself was not a formal member of the Green Gang. On the other hand, at least part of this account is corroborated by the SMP Special Branch who noted that when Jiang did leave Shanghai finally for Guangdong in 1919 it was Huang Jinrong, along with Yu Xiaqing, who provided him with financial assistance.[8] Evidence does exist, moreover, in the form of an entry in a names list in a Green Gang manual, that would appear to establish that Jiang Jieshi was indeed a member of the Green Gang.[9] According to this source Jiang was a member of the Wu generational status group of the Xing Wu Liu Branch of the Green Gang.

After the death of Han Hui in 1917, regular contact between the Shanghai Green Gang and the Guomindang does not appear to have been reestablished until the mid-1920s, at a time when the Green Gang organization itself was undergoing profound changes with the emergence of the French Concession bosses to a position of predominance in the system. With the commencement of secret recruitment in Shanghai of cadets for the Whampoa Academy, unspecified "important members" of the Guomindang approached Du Yuesheng in 1924 and requested his protection. Du agreed and it was in this context that he first became familiar with a number of Guomindang politicians, including Chen Lifu (a nephew of Chen Qimei), Shao Lizi, Zhu Minyi and Yang Hu.[10]

During the May Thirtieth Movement in 1925 Du worked closely with the Guomindang representatives in Shanghai in their attempts to control the political direction of the movement. On the outbreak of the May Thirtieth Incident, Du held discussions on the crisis with Ma Chaojun (a GMD trade union organizer), who was then in Shanghai organizing branches of the Association for the Study of Sun Yat-sen Thought (*Sun Wen Zhuyi Xuehui*) among Shanghai students on behalf of the Right GMD.[11] Du also took an active part in the meeting organized by Ye Chucang, Ma Chaojun and Liu

Luyin and held in the Shanghai GMD headquarters at 44 Route Vallon on the evening of the May 30, which decided on the strategy of the triple strike by merchants, students, and workers to begin from June 1.[12] Du's involvement with the Guomindang's political response to the May Thirtieth Incident was a good tactical move in the light of the controversy then surrounding the creation by the Green Gang bosses of a de facto opium monopoly in the French Concession. It successfully diverted Chinese public attention away from the agreement with the French authorities and gave the gangster bosses a patriotic image in the popular mind.

THE GREEN GANG AND THE CHINESE COMMUNIST PARTY (CCP), 1921–1925

During the 1920s relations between the Green Gang and the fledgling Chinese Communist Party were extremely ambiguous. The Shanghai Green Gang leadership, although never in sympathy with the Chinese Communists' objectives, as they understood them, did not have any profound ideological hostility toward the Communists.[13] They treated the Communists, at least initially, as merely another factor in the politics of Shanghai, and were prepared to deal with them on the same basis as they dealt with Sun Chuanfang and other militarists, when it was in their interests to do so. The Chinese Communist Party, for its part, did not pursue a consistently hostile policy toward the Green Gang, and its strategies alternated between the poles of outright opposition and guarded cooperation.

The Green Gang viewed Shanghai's industrial proletariat as an important source of revenue and a useful pool from which to recruit new members. In the early 1920s the Green Gang bosses exercised a "stranglehold over the Shanghai workers" that was derived from their control of the labor-contract system known as *baogong*.[14] These Green Gang bosses had early perceived the financial rewards to be gained from the baogong system and by the 1920s had transformed it into one of their most lucrative rackets. Their control over the system was facilitated by the fact that the majority of workers in Shanghai, as noted earlier, were immigrants from the rural hinterland who were socially fragmented along native place lines, and for whom Shanghai was a completely alien environment.[15]

In most of the Shanghai factories the foremen and inspectors who controlled the baogong system were petty Green Gang leaders, and by their manipulation of the system they completely dominated the lives of the workers. They adapted Green Gang organizational principles to ensure the effectiveness of control over the workers under their charge. All workers in those factories where the Green Gang controlled the baogong system were forced to enter into "disciple" and "grand disciple" relations with their foremen; indeed, it was impossible to get a job in these factories without joining the Green Gang. The Green Gang foremen and labor bosses manipulated these relationships in order to extort regular "gifts" and bribes from their worker "disciples," as well as using the workers for their own criminal purposes.[16] By inflating the numbers of their "disciples" such methods gave the Green Gang labor contractors "face" (*mianzi*) with their gangster colleagues and increased their standing within the local Green Gang system. The majority of their worker "disciples," however, should be considered not so much participating members of the Green Gang but, rather, victims of the system.

When the Chinese Communist Party, therefore, began its policy of systematically organizing the Shanghai workers into trade unions in the early 1920s, it had to take account of the Green Gang's dominant position among the workers. As Li Lisan, the CCP's chief trade union organizer in Shanghai in 1924–1925, remembered: "The greatest problem for [the CCP's] work among the Shanghai workers was the problem of the Green Gang."[17]

In its analysis of the Green Gang the Communist leadership was aware that the phenomenon of gangsterism was not merely a labor issue but one that went to the heart of Shanghai society as a whole. Writing in 1920, one year before the founding of the Chinese Communist Party, Chen Duxiu, the party's first general secretary, painted a dark picture of the power of the Green Gang. He observed that by their control of the factory and transport workers and the police (both the uniformed branch and detectives), the Green Gang bosses influenced all "those activities which have a profound [impact] on the population of the city," and this fact, together with their criminal activities, meant that their power rivaled that of the Shanghai Municipal Council itself. In Chen's view the Green Gang was an integral part of Shanghai's urban society and, therefore, it could not simply be eliminated by legislation. He regarded his solution, the open organization of legal trade unions, as "not merely a matter of concern to the workers, it is also a question which affects directly the social peace and order of the whole of Shanghai."[18]

In dealing with the power of the Green Gang labor bosses, how-ever, the CCP was handicapped initially by the small number of party members in Shanghai, and particularly the paucity of working-class members. In 1924, according to Li Lisan, there were less than ten CCP members in Shanghai, only two of whom were workers and neither of these worked in the cotton factories, the largest employers of blue-collar workers in Shanghai.[19] Lack of sufficient working-class party members, together with a lack of experience on the part of the young student CCP members, helps explain the CCP's failure to address the question of the Green Gang during its first organiza-tional efforts among the Shanghai workers. It was only after the de-feat of the Communist-inspired strikes in the Japanese and Chinese cotton factories in Pudong, largely as a result of the cooperation between the factory managements and the Green Gang labor bosses, that the CCP changed its tactics.

At the instigation of Li Qihan, a leading Communist trade union organizer and, after 1921, secretary of the CCP's Chinese Labor Secretariat, the Communist Party adopted the tactic of infiltrating the Green Gang. The purpose was two-fold: to use the Green Gang networks to make contact with the workers in the cotton and to-bacco factories in Zhabei and Pudong, where the control of the gangster labor bosses was particularly effective; and to attempt to influence the Green Gang from within in the interests of the party's trade union policy. Li himself joined the Green Gang in about 1920 through the introduction of a woman cotton worker who attended the workers' school he ran in Xiaoshadu, and he became a disciple of a local boss who belonged to the Tong generational status group.[20] The new tactic of infiltration was first put into effect by Li Qihan and Zhang Guotao, a young CCP trade union activist, during the strike in the British-American Tobacco Company's Pudong fac-tory in August 1921. Both Li and Zhang established contact with the strikers by using Li's Green Gang connections and helped to ensure a successful outcome to the strike with the creation of a Communist-influenced trade union.[21]

Despite initial successes, however, the CCP became increasingly frustrated with this tactic as the Green Gang labor bosses not only proved resistant to penetration and manipulation by CCP labor ac-tivists, but were able to manipulate the Communist activists in their own interests. As early as 1921 Zhang Guotao had voiced his con-cerns about the newly-established CCP developing too close a relationship with the Green Gang bosses and expressed his belief that the success of trade union organization in Shanghai depended ultimately on destroying the power that these bosses exercised over the workers.[22] With the arrival of Li Lisan in Shanghai in the autumn of 1924, a new policy was developed that attempted to introduce the elements of class struggle into the Green Gang system.[23] Li Lisan was a seasoned trade union activist and experienced in dealing with gangsters in the labor movement. By his own account, he, in fact, merely applied to his relations with the Shanghai Green Gang methods that he had developed and refined earlier in dealing with the Triads as a labor organizer with the miners of Anyuan, Hunan.[24] Li Lisan's premise was that the Green Gang was a degenerate form of secret society, whose relations with the workers were based solely on exploitation. He, therefore, sought to break down the Green Gang's organizational coherence by distinguishing between the gangster bosses and the rank-and-file of their "disciples." The Communists began to attack Green Gang labor bosses as "capitalist stooges," while at the same time attempting to win over the rank-and-file gang membership. This met with some success, notably during the strike in the Japanese cotton mills in February 1925, and Li Lisan was able to build up a following among some Green Gang rank-and-file members among the factory workers.[25]

The Green Gang labor bosses responded to this challenge by joining with anti-Communist, right-wing members of the Guomindang in the establishment of the Shanghai Federation of Trade Unions (*Shanghai Gongtuan Lianhehui*) in August 1924.[26] This body had very close ties with the Chinese capitalists. Yu Xiaqing, the Chairman of the Shanghai Chinese Chamber of Commerce, for example, was not only involved with the organization of the federation, but also made available the Chamber's premises for the holding of its inaugural meeting.[27] The federation, denounced by the CCP as "a gangster trade union" (*liumang gonghui*), was strongly anti-Communist and sought every opportunity to counter growing Communist influence among the Shanghai work force.[28] During the strike in the Japanese cotton mills in February 1925, for example, the federation co-operated with the Green Gang labor bosses in the mills to undermine the CCP's control of the strike by organizing an "Anti-Communist Alliance of Male and Female Workers" and distributing leaflets calling for a return to work.[29] With the organization of the Shanghai General Labor Union (*Shanghai Zonggonghui*—SGLU) in the wake of the February strike, the CCP sought to eliminate the influence of the federation. During the period of the general strike following the May Thirtieth Incident (June–September 1925) a state of undeclared war existed between the SGLU and the federation with the former generally having the upper hand.[30] The federation, however, had a powerful ally in Yu Xiaqing, who used both it and the Green Gang to break the strike.[31] With the end of the strike and the closure of the SGLU by the martial law authorities the federation gained a temporary respite and was able to consolidate its position in the cotton mills.[32]

Despite this struggle with the Green Gang labor bosses, Li Lisan, nevertheless, also succeeded in cooperating with other Green Gang groups in Zhabei. At the height of the crisis in mid-1925, for example, the CCP and the SGLU entered into a tactical alliance with certain Green Gang groups, which allowed the latter to participate actively in the anti-British and anti-Japanese boycott under the auspices of the SGLU. In return the gangsters extended their protection to the SGLU personnel and premises in Zhabei. The available evidence would suggest that this agreement was in the nature of a deal struck between Li Lisan, the Communist head of the SGLU, and Gu Zhuxuan, the Zhabei Green Gang boss.[33]

With the proscription of the SGLU, the CCP went underground but, nevertheless, continued to extend its trade union organization among the workers of Shanghai and to build on the dramatic advances it had made throughout 1925. In the course of 1926 the CCP gained renewed confidence to set about effectively undermining the Green Gang's position within the labor market in a systematic way: the abolition of the baogong system became a key strike demand; it launched attacks on "scabs" and initiated a policy of physical assault on factory foremen which was implemented by the Workers' Pickets.[34]

THE GREEN GANG AND REVOLUTIONARY POLITICS: THE NORTHERN EXPEDITION, JULY 1926—FEBRUARY 1927

The Green Gang and the Guomindang: Jiang Jieshi's Overtures

By the second half of 1926 it was clear to Jiang Jieshi that Shanghai was the key to the politico-military strategy of the Northern Expedition. He needed to secure for himself the economic resources of

Shanghai in order to finance the Northern Expedition. Control of Shanghai and its hinterland, moreover, would place Jiang in a strong strategic position in any future political conflict within the Guomindang. Major obstacles, however, forced Jiang to tread cautiously. In the autumn of 1926 Shanghai still appeared to be securely under the control of Sun Chuanfang's Allied Army; it had also emerged as the strongest center of trade union and CCP power in China; finally, the city remained the center of foreign economic and political interests in China, which the foreign powers showed every intention of defending.

Jiang was aware of the changes that had occurred in the structure of power within the Green Gang in Shanghai in the mid-1920s as a result of the emergence of the three French Concession bosses to a position of predominance in the system. From his perspective, securing the support of these Green Gang bosses could contribute to the solution of these problems. The Green Gang leaders' friendly contacts with Sun Chuanfang and his military and civilian officials, for example, could be effectively used by the Guomindang in its strategy of subverting warlord authority in Shanghai. The Green Gang itself could provide the nucleus for a paramilitary force with which to destroy the power of the SGLU's Workers' Pickets. Even the Green Gang's relations with the authorities of the foreign settlements, through their involvement with the settlements' police forces, could be turned to advantage as a channel for securing the tacit approval of the foreign authorities for the National Revolutionary Army's takeover of Chinese Shanghai. It was considerations such as these that led Jiang in late 1926 to resume contact with Huang Jinrong, with whom he had been out of touch since 1919.

The principal motivation of the French Concession Green Gang bosses, for their part, in all their dealings was a calculating self-interest, and there is no reason to doubt that this attitude determined their response to the overtures from the Guomindang. Their actions and alliances were determined simply by what would best preserve and enhance Green Gang interests, especially their control of the opium traffic. The evidence, fragmentary though it is, suggests that the support of the French Concession Green Gang bosses for the Guomindang was achieved only after four months of negotiations, from November 1926 to February 1927. During this period these bosses continued to enjoy a mutually beneficial relationship with Sun Chuanfang who remained reasonably secure in Shanghai. Indeed, as late as January 1927 the Green Gang was still cooperating with Sun Chuanfang's police in hunting down "radicals" in Zhabei and Nandao.[35]

The French Concession Green Gang leadership was apparently uncommitted to either side in the early stages of the conflict between the Guomindang right wing and the Chinese Communists.[36] On the other hand the leadership was divided as to where it should lend its support in the military struggle between the warlords and the Guomindang after the launching of the Northern Expedition. At least one of the bosses, Zhang Xiaolin, considered the Guomindang's policies to be inimical to the interests of the Green Gang, and although this hostile view might not have been shared by the other two bosses, yet it is probable that they still considered the Guomindang to be an unknown quantity in late 1926.[37]

Simultaneously with the launching of the Northern Expedition in July 1926, Niu Yongjian was sent to Shanghai as the Guomindang's special representative entrusted with the dual task of subverting Sun Chuanfang's military subordinates and coordinating the activities of the anti-warlord and revolutionary forces in Shanghai with the advance of the National Revolutionary Army.[38] At the same time, it would appear that Niu was charged with the secret mission of monitoring and controlling Chinese Communist activities. On September 4, 1927, Niu established the seven-member Jiangsu Party Affairs Committee (*Jiangsu Dangwu Weiyuanhui*), under his chairmanship, to coordinate the Guomindang–Chinese Communist sabotage activities in Shanghai, and to provide a forum that would endorse Niu's decisions on the timing of the armed uprisings.[39]

It would appear that Niu approached the Green Gang leadership in the autumn of 1926 in order to enlist their support for the National Revolutionary Army. Du Yuesheng, for one, maintained at least unofficial contacts with Niu Yongjian and the Jiangsu Party Affairs Committee.[40] Niu was a native of Shanghai and had been associated with Chen Qimei in both the 1911 and 1913 Shanghai revolutions, and it is probable that he had been chosen for this assignment because of his extensive contacts among the political and financial power brokers of Shanghai, and these would almost certainly have included the French Concession Green Gang bosses.[41]

The first clear evidence of Green Gang interest in the possibilities of cooperation with the Guomindang occurs in the context of the autonomy movement that developed in Shanghai in the winter of

1926 as a direct result of Sun Chuanfang's worsening military situation. This movement brought together different political groups and the local capitalist elite in a Shanghai Citizen's Federation (*Shanghai Shimin Gonghui*) with the intention of preserving Shanghai from the ravages of civil war. The autonomy movement was actively encouraged by Niu Yongjian, who hoped to manipulate it to the advantage of the Guomindang.[42] The Green Gang leaders, faced with an increasingly unstable political situation in Shanghai, played an active role in this federation, and it was in this context that Huang Jinrong, apparently, had a meeting with Jiang Jieshi at Jiujiang in mid-November 1926.[43] The exact nature of this conference remains obscure, although it has been suggested that it was at this meeting that Jiang not only secured the Green Gang's support for his planned purge but also settled its detailed strategy.[44] Other evidence suggests, however, that the French Concession Green Gang bosses still kept their options open in the winter of 1926, and that, indeed, they did not finally commit themselves to the Guomindang cause until late February 1927.[45]

The following would seem to be a reasonable reconstruction of the attitudes of the French Concession Green Gang leadership toward the Guomindang. In late 1926 they appear to have adopted a noncommittal attitude toward the Guomindang, and maintained an evenhanded approach toward both sides in the Guomindang-warlord conflict. They responded to overtures from the Guomindang and developed contacts with the Guomindang's Shanghai underground, while at the same time maintaining their relations with Sun Chuanfang. This evenhanded policy accounted for their passive involvement in Guomindang espionage in early December 1926, when they passed on to Niu Yongjian intelligence reports sent to them by Zhang Boqi, the Commander of the Ningbo Forts in the Zhejiang army, concerning the dispositions of Sun Chuanfang's troops in Zhejiang.[46] It also accounted for their espionage activities on behalf of Sun Chuanfang in early 1927, when detectives controlled by the Green Gang infiltrated "radical circles" in Zhabei and Nandao.

The Green Gang leadership's major concern was to determine what benefits they would obtain from a Guomindang victory in the civil war. A major factor in these calculations, undoubtedly, was the Guomindang's attitude to their monopoly of the opium traffic in Shanghai. There are strong indications that the agreement reached between Jiang Jieshi and the Green Gang bosses contained a provision for Green Gang control of any future Guomindang opium monopoly.[47] Concern about the future of their opium interests certainly exercised the minds of the Green Gang bosses at this time. As late as mid-March 1927, for example, Du Yuesheng approached the CCP's Shanghai District Committee (*Shanghai Qu Weiyuanhui*) with the offer of placing all Green Gang groups in Shanghai under the command of the CCP in return for the latter's agreement not to move against the opium traffic. The committee, however, remained noncommittal.[48]

As Sun Chuanfang's military position deteriorated in the winter of 1926–27, Du Yuesheng and Zhang Xiaolin engaged in a vigorous debate over strategy in the event of a Guomindang victory.[49] The debate was over means and not ends, as both Du and Zhang shared a common preoccupation with the need to ensure the long-term interests of the Shanghai Green Gang. Zhang argued the need to support the warlord position, because he feared that a Guomindang victory would bring to an end the political, economic and social conditions that enabled the Green Gang to maintain its ascendancy in Shanghai. Du Yuesheng, for his part, took a pragmatic position, and argued that the Green Gang's best strategy would be to respond positively to the Guomindang's overtures, and to cooperate with it, in order to ensure that the Shanghai Green Gang's interests would be accommodated in the Guomindang's new order.[50]

The different strategies offered by Zhang and Du reflected their differing assessments of the opportunities offered by a Guomindang victory. Zhang Xiaolin, as noted earlier, had very close ties with the world of warlord politics, which had enabled him to gain a position of leadership within the French Concession Green Gang system. The imminent elimination of the structure of warlord power by the Guomindang, therefore, posed a direct threat not only to Zhang's interests but also to his position within the Shanghai Green Gang.[51] Du Yuesheng, on the other hand, could afford to be more pragmatic. His power rested on the organization and smooth functioning of the system of contraband opium, and, although he had good working relations with the warlord regime, nevertheless, he could work with any power that would guarantee the continued operations of the traffic.

A turning point was reached in February 1927 when Jiang Jieshi appointed the French Concession Green Gang bosses as his "resident" special agents in Shanghai.[52] In effect this appears to have been an attempt to secure Jiang's control over the Green Gang leaders' actions, since it placed them in a formal command structure under the authority of Yang Hu, Head of the Special Services Bureau of Jiang Jieshi's military headquarters.[53] In response the Jiangsu Provincial Government was reported to have issued warrants for the arrest of Du Yuesheng and Zhang Xiaolin as suspected Guomindang agents. Sun Chuanfang, however, took the unusual step of issuing an official proclamation denying the validity of these reports. Sun's action reflected both his own ambivalent attitude toward the Guomindang and his need to preserve his modus vivendi with the Green Gang bosses.[54]

On February 24, 1927, the three French Concession Green Gang bosses took the decision to support the Guomindang.[55] Two factors seem to have influenced this decision. The first was the total shipwreck of Sun Chuanfang's military position, which rendered redundant the carefully constructed cooperation with Sun that had underpinned the interests of the French Concession Green Gang bosses since 1925. They also had doubts about Zhang Zongchang's capacity to consolidate his position both militarily and politically in the Shanghai area. The second factor influencing this decision was the Green Gang bosses' concern regarding the threat that the organized trade union movement, under Communist direction, posed to their vested interests in Shanghai. Although the February general strike and uprising had been suppressed, it had given a clear indication of the strength of the workers' movement, which had been capable of turning "pompous Shanghai" into a "graveyard" for three days.[56]

The Green Gang and the CCP: Wang Shouhua's Conciliatory Policy and the Uprising of February 1927

In late 1926 there was a further change in the CCP's tactics toward the Green Gang, and an attempt was made to return to a more conciliatory policy than that pursued since late 1925, in order to reach at least a guarded understanding with the Green Gang leaders. This change in policy coincided with Wang Shouhua's replacement of Li Lisan as Chairman of the Labor Union Committee of the CCP's Central Committee in October 1926.[57] It is probable that Wang Shouhua was the architect of this conciliatory policy, and that he had been instructed by the Central Committee to develop a friendly relationship with the Green Gang leadership.[58] In late January 1927, for example, the CCP's Shanghai District Committee reaffirmed its decision to maintain its relationship with Du Yuesheng.[59] Throughout this period of CCP conciliation with the Green Gang, from early November 1926 to late February 1927, Wang Shouhua liaised on a regular basis with Du Yuesheng,[60] and a halt was called to CCP attacks on Green Gang factory foremen.[61]

The reasons for this change of strategy are not hard to identify. The policy of conciliation coincided with the development of the autonomy movement in Shanghai and it represented the CCP's contribution to the attempts being made by Niu Yongjian to transform the movement into some kind of "united front" in the interests of the National Revolutionary Army. It is possible that the CCP was also seeking to develop its own contacts with the Green Gang leadership in order to use the Green Gang network to strengthen the Shanghai General Labor Union's position vis-à-vis the Guomindang. The CCP had become suspicious of Niu Yongjian's policy toward the party following Niu's failure to warn the CCP of the defeat of Xia Chao's revolt in late October 1926.[62] The conciliatory policy was also a recognition by the CCP of the strong position that the Green Gang maintained in Shanghai through its control of police coercive power. As noted in chapter 3, the French Concession Green Gang had gone through an important reorganization of its own in 1924–25, which had greatly increased its power and which had coincided with the growth in the power and influence of the Shanghai General Labor Union.

This conciliatory policy culminated in Wang Shouhua's attempts to gain Green Gang support for the general strike and uprising of February 19–24, 1927.[63] By late February 1927, however, the Green Gang leadership had no intention of allying themselves with the CCP, and were in fact on the point of cooperating with Jiang Jieshi.[64] The Green Gang bosses, in fact, participated fully in the attempt to contain the general strike and repress the uprising. During the general strike Du Yuesheng used his position as chairman of the French Concession Chinese Chamber of Commerce to prevent Chinese merchants and their employees in the French Concession from joining the strike, and thus ensuring that it did not take root in the French Concession.[65] It is possible that Du also played a role in persuading the Chinese General Chamber of Commerce not to join the call for a general strike. In fact Du was praised by the foreign community for doing "much to bring the strike to an end."[66] It would appear, therefore, that Du played a crucial role in ensuring the failure of the February general strike, since the lack of support from the Chinese Chamber of Commerce and from the shopkeepers' associations was a critical factor in its failure.[67]

The role that the Green Gang bosses played in the failure of the February general strike and insurrection destroyed the CCP's policy of conciliation. These events finally disabused the CCP of any illusions they might have entertained of using the Green Gang in the interests of the Shanghai General Labor Union. Almost immediately after the end of the strike the systematic murders of Green Gang factory foremen and inspectors by CCP controlled assassination squads, resumed at an accelerated rate. According to SMP reports between February 19 and March 23 a total of eleven foremen were murdered and five wounded in Shanghai, and at least two ex-foremen were executed by workers tribunals in Pudong.[68] Again, during March, the abolition of the baogong system reemerged as a central demand of the Shanghai trade unions.[69] By late February, therefore, the CCP had swung back to a policy of outright hostility toward the Green Gang, and the Green Gang leaders themselves now regarded the destruction of the Communist controlled trade union organizations as a matter of vital importance if their former control of the labor organizations was to be restored.

THE GREEN GANG AND REVOLUTIONARY POLITICS: THE "NANCHANG POLICY" AND THE MARCH UPRISING, 1927

By the end of February 1927, therefore, the French Concession Green Gang bosses had definitely committed themselves to support of the Guomindang. During this month they lent their support to Jiang Jieshi's "Nanchang policy" of destroying CCP organizations piecemeal, and they actively participated in the subversion of warlord commanders in Shanghai conducted by Niu Yongjian.

The aim of Jiang's "Nanchang policy" was to eradicate CCP influence in local Guomindang branches and to destroy its control over the organized mass movements in those areas that were occupied by Jiang Jieshi's divisions of the National Revolutionary Army. It was in fact a policy of piecemeal destruction of the CCP's power bases, which avoided the critical political complications that a major purge would have entailed. This policy originated in December 1926—January 1927, when Chen Guofu secretly arrived in Nanchang (December) and organized an "Anti-Bolshevik League," and Yang Hu was dispatched (January) to establish contact with the Green Gang groups in the major cities of the Jiangnan: Jiujiang, Anqing, Wuhu and Nanjing.[70] The policy was not implemented until the middle of March 1927, however, and it would appear that Jiang Jieshi deliberately timed its implementation to coincide with the holding of the Third Plenum of the Guomindang's Second Central Executive Committee in Wuhan from March 10–17.[71] Jiang had disapproved of the holding of this plenum and had refused to attend, and the plenum removed Jiang from the chairmanship of the Central Executive Committee.[72] In retrospect, the holding of the Third Plenum and the initiation of the "Nanchang policy" can be seen as the opening moves in the final split of the Guomindang into right and left factions.[73]

The Green Gang groups in the lower Yangzi were intimately involved with the implementation of the "Nanchang policy." On March 17, the last day of the Wuhan Plenum, Jiang Jieshi launched simultaneous attacks against the CCP in Nanchang and Jiujiang.[74] In both assaults local Green Gang members were used as shock troops in the destruction of the trade union and mass organizations, together with the local Guomindang branches. According to Chen Duxiu, Jiang Jieshi paid out Ch$600,000 to Green Gang thugs (*liumang*) in Jiangxi in order to create anti-Communist disturbances.[75]

The purge conducted in Anqing on March 23 provides a good illustration of the techniques used in the implementation of the "Nanchang policy."[76] Immediately on Jiang Jieshi's arrival in Anqing, on March 19, his lieutenants, notably Yang Hu and Chen Lifu, began to establish their own mass organizations to oppose those controlled by the CCP and the left wing of the Guomindang. These right-wing Guomindang organizations had such names as the Anhui General Union, the Anhui Peasants Association, the Anhui Students Association, etc., names deliberately chosen to confuse the rank-and-file members of the legitimate mass organizations. In all, Yang and Chen organized five mass organizations. Their membership, however, was negligible; for example, the Anhui General Union only had between 100 and 200 members and was composed almost entirely of members of the local Anqing Green Gang.

The next priority was to create an armed force to deal with the local Workers' Pickets, and Yang Hu organized a 100-man "Dare-to-Die" Corps from among the local Green Gang membership, recruiting them at the flat rate of Ch$4 per man plus a sliding scale of rewards for injuries received: Ch$100 for minor wounds, Ch$500 for major wounds, Ch$1,500 for death. Finally, there was the need to deliberately provoke incidents with the CCP mass organizations in order to provide the justification for military intervention and the closure of the CCP organizations. In Anqing this was achieved by Guo Morou's move on March 22 to close down the Anqing General Labor Union on the grounds that it was a "false" union and had insufficient membership to warrant its existence. The Anqing General Labor Union took up the challenge and protested to Jiang Jieshi that it was being "oppressed," and Jiang promised to investigate the matter. The following day, March 23, the five Right Guomindang "mass organizations" staged a mass meeting to welcome Jiang Jieshi and enforced the closure of all Anqing's shops for the day. This was the cue for the coup. During the demonstrations of welcome a fracas developed between the demonstrators and workers belonging to the CCP mass organizations, and the upshot was the attack and occupation by the Green Gang "Dare-to-Dies" of the Anhui Provincial Guomindang Branch, the Anqing Municipal Guomindang Branch, the Right Bank Army's Political Department and several trade union headquarters.

After the coup Jiang Jieshi created an Anhui Political Affairs Committee under the chairmanship of Chen Tiaoyuan, a former warlord and Green Gang member, which included, according to Guo Morou, Green Gang leaders and leaders of the Anhui Big Sword Society. This committee supervised the implementation of the "White Terror" in Anqing.[77] Thus the Anqing purge provides a clear example of the techniques of the "Nanchang policy," which were later adapted and repeated in Shanghai.

Meanwhile, in Shanghai, Niu Yongjian was orchestrating the subversion of local warlord commanders. By mid-March Niu had successfully suborned Li Baozhang, formerly Sun Chuanfang's Defense Commissioner for Shanghai and Songjiang, with the promise of a command in the National Revolutionary Army, and Admiral Yang Shuzhuang, Commander of Zhang Zuolin's Bohai Fleet, and had entered into negotiations with the Commander of Sun Chuanfang's air force.[78] In March 1927 the key warlord commander in Shanghai was Bi Shucheng, who commanded the 137th Brigade of

Zhang Zongchang's Eighth Shandong Army and was concurrently Defense Commissioner of the Shanghai and Wusong districts. In the subversion of Bi Shucheng, Niu Yongjian enlisted the assistance of the Green Gang bosses.[79]

The gangsters' strategy was to introduce Bi to the Shanghai good life in the form of one of the most famous prostitutes in Shanghai and so lure him away from his duties.[80] The strategy worked and Bi not only ignored Zhang Zongchang's order of March 17 to proceed to Sun Chuanfang's assistance at the Songjiang front, but shortly afterwards betrayed the complete secret battle plans of the warlord forces to Niu Yongjian, with Du Yuesheng acting as intermediary.[81] By March 20 Niu could inform Bai Chongxi, commander of the Eastern Route Army of the Northern Expedition forces, to delay his advance into Shanghai as Bi was on the point of surrendering.[82] The March Uprising, however, rudely interrupted Niu's and Du's careful timetable for Bi's defection, and Bi fled to Shandong where he was court-martialed and shot, ironically, for having "secret relations with the Reds" on April 5.[83]

Throughout March the Shanghai General Labor Union had laid the groundwork for a further uprising and general strike, and the decision was taken finally at an emergency meeting on the evening of March 20, on the recommendation of Wang Shouhua, Zhou Enlai, Luo Yinong and Zhao Shiyan.[84] At noon on March 21 a general strike was called, which involved between 500,000 and 800,000 striking workers and led to a total stoppage of work throughout Shanghai's large-scale industry, its municipal utilities and commercial concerns. At the same time the Workers' Pickets of the Shanghai General Labor Union launched armed attacks on all concentrations of warlord forces, and within thirty-six hours the SGLU had effective control over all of Chinese Shanghai.[85] Foreign Shanghai was stunned by the suddenness and completeness of the victory of the Workers' Pickets, and the *North-China Herald* confessed that March 21 was "one of the most hectic days that it [i.e., Shanghai] has experienced since the area became an International Settlement."[86]

The Green Gang leadership, absorbed as it was in its role in the subversion of Bi Shucheng, was caught completely off balance by the suddenness, strength and scope of the March Uprising.[87] Unlike the February Uprising, the CCP do not appear to have informed the Green Gang bosses of the impending strike, nor to have solicited their support. Indeed, one of the major objectives of the Workers'

Pickets was to eliminate the police forces in Chinese Shanghai, which represented a key element in the Green Gang's network of influence in Shanghai.[88] Thus, attacks on the police stations led to several armed clashes between the Green Gang and Workers' Pickets in the course of the Uprising. In Hongkou the local Green Gang boss, Sun Jiefu, who controlled the local police force, sent his Green Gang force, of between 200 and 1,000 men, to assist the embattled police in an attempt to recapture those police stations occupied by the Workers' Pickets. This conflict between the local Green Gang and the Workers' Pickets was only brought to an end through the personal intervention of Du Yuesheng who persuaded Sun "with some difficulty" to call off his Green Gang followers.[89]

In the late afternoon of the same day, March 21, Green Gang units also became involved in spontaneous conflicts with the Workers' Pickets in Zhabei, when local Green Gang groups, with some assistance from Sun Jiefu's men, attempted to recapture the Huzhou Guild, which had just been occupied by the Workers' Pickets. Again, the Green Gang groups withdrew only after Du Yuesheng's personal intervention. These Green Gang units then took advantage of the confusion in Zhabei to go on a looting spree which again brought them into conflict with the Workers' Pickets.[90] In Pudong a stalemate existed between the Workers' Pickets and the Pudong Merchants' Militia, which was controlled by Du Yuesheng, after the Workers' Pickets had successfully captured Pudong's Third District Police Station. Initial overtures from the Workers' Pickets to form a joint administration for Pudong were rejected by the Merchants' Militia. It was only after the failure of an attempt by Green Gang elements from metropolitan Shanghai to come to the assistance of the Pudong Militia on the evening of March 21, that Du Yuesheng ordered the militia to reach a temporary agreement. As a result Pudong was jointly governed by the Workers' Pickets and the Merchants' Militia through the agencies of a Provisional Bureau of Public Safety (*Pudong Linshi Bao'anju*) and a Pudong Workers' Delegates Congress (*Pudong Qu Geye Renmin Daibiao Dahui*). Relations between the militia and the Workers' Pickets, however, remained uneasy, with the militia adopting an obstructionist attitude and attempting to gain control of several public utilities. The CCP, therefore, did not have undisputed control over Pudong in the wake of the March Uprising, and several minor armed clashes between the Pudong Militia and the Workers' Pickets continued to occur until the eve of the

April purge.[91] A similar arrangement for the tactical cooperation between the local Workers' Pickets and the Green Gang militia was reached in Wusong.[92]

The Shanghai Green Gang leadership, taken off-guard as they were by the March Uprising, appear to have formulated no clear policy to deal with the situation, and were merely carried along by the force of events. Du Yuesheng, at least, seems to have decided to allow events to work themselves out, and attempted to monitor developments from his home on the Rue Wagner, which became a virtual Green Gang command post.[93] Du's tactics, as revealed by his actions during March 21–22, were temporary expedients to prevent any major confrontation between the Green Gang and the CCP organizations that now effectively controlled Chinese Shanghai, and to provide time for the gangster bosses to come to terms with the new power alignments in the city. On the one hand he put a stop to any direct conflict between the Green Gang and the Workers' Pickets, as in Hongkou and Zhabei; on the other hand he entered into tactical agreements with the Workers' Pickets, as in Pudong and Wusong.

The energies of the CCP leadership, for its part, were fully occupied in establishing its authority in Chinese Shanghai, and it therefore wished to avoid any unnecessary confrontation with the Green Gang bosses. The local CCP leadership, therefore, was willing to reach some kind of modus vivendi with local Green Gang groups in those areas where the latter continued to exercise a significant degree of control. The CCP, however, also regarded these agreements as mere expedients, and after March 22 a situation akin to a "Mexican stand-off" existed between the Green Gang and the Workers' Pickets, in which neither side was as yet sufficiently powerful on its own to move decisively against the other.

The Shanghai General Labor Union now enjoyed almost total control over Chinese Shanghai. After March 22 the Workers' Pickets were not only numerous, totaling between 3,000 and 5,000 men, they were also well-armed with the weapons surrendered by the warlord troops and police, and were in a position to take over most of the police functions in Chinese Shanghai. The CCP, moreover, controlled the municipal administration through its dominant position in the Shanghai Provisional Municipal Government, which was established on March 22.[94]

As a result of the uprising, Jiang Jieshi's position in Shanghai was extremely precarious. He had only one reliable division in the Shanghai area, Liu Zhi's Second Division, whose strength of 3,000 men was hardly equal to the combined force of the Workers' Pickets. His nearest reinforcements were at Hangzhou, where He Yingqin had a force of only 10,000 men.[95] Jiang, moreover, could not rely on the loyalty of either Xue Yue's First Division or Yan Zhong's Twenty-first Division, as both these commanders had "leftist tendencies."[96] Jiang, still apparently unsure of the attitude of the Guangxi Clique to his proposed coup, finally called at least two meetings with Li Zongren, during the last week of March, at which he tried to gauge Li's attitude to the conditions in Shanghai.[97] In this situation of qualified military weakness, the Green Gang bosses' support became not merely a desirable end for Jiang Jieshi but a crucial factor in the success of his plans.

THE GREEN GANG AND REVOLUTIONARY POLITICS: THE PREPARATIONS FOR THE ANTI-COMMUNIST COUP, MARCH—APRIL 1927

The final preparations for the coup were undertaken in great secrecy during the fortnight March 27–April 11. Although there are indications that the CCP leadership had some knowledge of Jiang's activities, they had no idea as to the timing and extent of a possible coup, and appear to have been taken completely by surprise when the purge was initiated on April 12.[98]

From the moment of his arrival in Shanghai, Jiang Jieshi established contact with the French Concession Green Gang bosses. According to Huang Jinrong's own account, as told to a senior Chinese detective in the French Concession police in 1939, he and Du Yuesheng personally met Jiang's airplane at Longhua Airfield on March 26, where he introduced Jiang to Du.[99] Jiang later paid a personal call on Huang Jinrong at the latter's home.[100] Most of Jiang's dealings with the Green Gang bosses, however, were done through his two personal representatives Yang Hu and Chen Qun, who were later joined by Wang Boling.[101] Within the first few days after Jiang's arrival in Shanghai, Yang and Chen held two meetings with the Green Gang bosses, which decided the strategy for the coup and the Green Gang's role in it.[102]

Yang Hu and Chen Qun's mission was to coordinate the activities of all the gangster groups in Shanghai with a view to the elimination of the Chinese Communists. Of the two, it appears that it was Chen

Qun who devised the basic strategy, although Yang as the senior representative had to give his final approval.[103] Their first priority was to achieve a sufficient standing with the Green Gang bosses in order to establish some control over their actions and ensure that their own orders would be carried out. They, therefore, had themselves inducted into the Green Gang as "disciples" of Zhang Renkui, who, as noted elsewhere, was at that time one of the most powerful and prestigious leaders of the Green Gang in China.[104]

In this way Yang and Chen hoped to use their status as Zhang Renkui's disciples to control the Shanghai Green Gang bosses. As disciples of Zhang, the two Guomindang representatives became members of the Tong Green Gang generational status group, which meant that they were the generational peers of both Huang Jinrong and Zhang Xiaolin, and the generational superiors of Du Yuesheng who belonged to the inferior Wu generational status group. Yang and Chen judiciously complemented their formal position within the Green Gang system, however, by entering into "sworn brother" relations with Du Yuesheng, Zhang Xiaolin and Huang Jinrong, thus creating a personal bond between themselves and the Green Gang bosses.[105]

In the last days of March, Yang and Chen's overriding priority was to adapt the "Nanchang policy" to Shanghai conditions and ensure its implementation. This involved the creation both of a "front" trade union organization to challenge the Shanghai General Labor Union and wean the trade unions from its control, and of a paramilitary force capable of defeating the Workers' Pickets. Both aims were achieved by the end of the first week in April with the establishment of the Shanghai General Federation of Labor (*Shanghai Gongjie Lianhe Zonghui*), a Green Gang controlled labor organization, and the Chinese Mutual Progress Association (*Zhonghua Gongjin Hui*).

The first moves in setting up the General Federation of Labor (GFL) were taken in early March, although its operations were not finally approved by the Wusong-Shanghai Police Department until April 2. With headquarters in the French Concession, it initially controlled the employees in those public utilities and transport services located in the Concession.[106] From the outset the GFL was designed as a rival to the Shanghai General Labor Union and its function was to remain in readiness to replace the SGLU as soon as the purge was launched. The GFL's manifesto declared that the workers needed to free themselves from their "unfortunate circumstances," that is, their subservience to the CCP, and that the only way for them to achieve their goal was to obey the Three People's Principles and to participate in an undefined "popular revolution."[107] The GFL was to play a key role in the events of the purge.

The Chinese Mutual Progress Association (MPA) was established at the end of March.[108] Most sources agree that its creation was a Guomindang initiative, and that it was a conscious attempt to adapt to the conditions then prevailing in Shanghai the Tongmenghui precedents of creating hybrid organizations as bridges between the revolutionaries and secret societies, through which the revolutionaries could mobilize the secret societies in the interests of revolutionary goals. The name, Chinese Mutual Progress Association, was itself a conscious evocation of the earlier Mutual Progress Association that had been organized by Chen Qimei in Shanghai in 1912. When the Green Gang bosses published a notice in the Shanghai Chinese press announcing the establishment of the MPA, they claimed that it was merely a continuation of the earlier organization.[109] The creation of the MPA, therefore, is an indication of the continuing influence that the revolutionary strategies of Chen Qimei exercised over the minds of the Guomindang right wing in the 1920s, and in particular Jiang Jieshi.

The MPA was conceived by the Guomindang as an umbrella organization that would embrace all the secret societies active in Shanghai and thus ensure the coordination of their efforts in the purge. The leadership of the MPA, therefore, should have ideally included other secret society organizations, such as the Triads (*Hong Men*), as well as the Green Gang.[110] In fact from its inception the MPA functioned as a totally Green Gang organization. All twelve of the major leadership positions within the MPA were held by senior Green Gang members, including its figurehead civilian commander, Pu Jinrong.[111] The only non–Green Gang leader who participated regularly in the MPA's council was Jiang Ganting who was a Shanghai Triad leader and the former secretary to the Shanghai-Songjiang Defense Commissioner. Jiang, however, was very much the exception that proved the rule. He held no formal leadership position within the MPA and his entrée into the MPA inner circles was secured by his close association with the Green Gang triumvirate, and especially with Du Yuesheng, on whose payroll he had been for years past.[112]

Within the Green Gang's predominant position in the MPA, power was even further concentrated in the hands of Du Yuesheng. It was Du who exercised the real authority within the MPA.[113] The core of the MPA leadership was provided by Du's Small Eight Mob, five of whose leaders held leadership positions within the MPA.[114] Du, moreover, had sworn brother relations with two other MPA leaders, Ma Xiangsheng and Jin Tingsun.[115] Pu Jinrong, himself, had been Du's candidate for the position of overall leader of the MPA. It is more than probable that Du had engineered Pu's selection because he wanted a "straw man" in the nominal overall leadership position, in order to enable Du himself to control the MPA from behind the scenes. Pu, in fact, was heavily in Du's debt. He had been an employee of the Three Prosperities Company and his son, Pu Xianyuan, was one of Du's "disciples." Moreover Pu had sworn brother relations with Jin Tingsun and Gao Xinbao, both of whom were close associates of Du.[116]

It would appear from the available evidence that the Guomindang never established firm organizational control over the MPA. Although Yang Hu and Chen Qun participated in the MPA's war councils, neither of them had any formal standing in its organization. Du Yuesheng, in fact, ensured that his own followers were placed in key leadership positions and effectively transformed the MPA into an instrument of his own personal power. The Guomindang's inability to establish effective control over the MPA stemmed in part from a basic misunderstanding of the nature of the Green Gang power structure as it operated in Shanghai. The Guomindang representatives confused formal hierarchical status with actual power, as instanced by Yang Hu and Chen Qun's desire to be inducted into the Green Gang as "disciples" of Zhang Renkui. In Shanghai in the 1920s, however, as noted in chapter 1, Green Gang generational status signified a merely formal honor and carried no real authority in its own right. What really mattered was personal ability and the capacity to maintain and enhance Green Gang economic and political interests, as Du Yuesheng had demonstrated by his unification of the illicit opium traffic in the mid-1920s. Indeed generational status counted for so little in the Shanghai context that both Gu Jiatang and Ye Chuoshan could function effectively as two of Du's key subordinates in the Small Eight Mob, despite the fact both were superior in formal generational status to Du.[117] This misunderstanding of the true power structure within the Shanghai

Green Gang created serious problems for the Guomindang in its attempts to manipulate Du in its own interests, problems which only became apparent after the purge.

In the fortnight preceding the coup, the MPA leadership met on a daily basis. At Du's suggestion the overall military command of the MPA forces was given to Zhang Boqi, the ex-commander of the Ningbo Forts.[118] An important consideration in these military preparations was the need to secure an adequate supply of weapons. This had become an urgent problem with the Workers' Pickets' acquisition of the surrendered weapons from the defeated Shandong military and local police forces. The MPA obtained their supply of weapons and the money to purchase them from three main sources. In the first place the Green Gang leaders tapped their own resources. Du commissioned the compradors of foreign firms specializing in arms supply to purchase as many as possible at almost any price, while Zhang Xiaolin personally paid out Ch$80,000 on weapons purchases. These weapons were stored in Huang Jinrong's home in the French Concession.[119] Funds for weapons purchases were also obtained through the Guomindang, from loans provided by the Chinese merchants of Shanghai. Of a Ch$15 million loan advanced to Jiang Jieshi by Shanghai financiers in early April, Ch$500,000 was earmarked for weapons purchased on behalf of the MPA.[120] There were also, some contributions from the foreign authorities and business community in Shanghai. The French Concession authorities, for example, supplied Du Yuesheng with a large quantity of rifles and ammunition, some reports giving a figure of 5,000 rifles.[121]

During the first ten days of April, the MPA forces were involved in a series of skirmishes with the Workers' Pickets in maneuvers designed to probe the strengths and weaknesses of the latter's dispositions in Chinese Shanghai. These skirmishes reflected the increasing tension in Shanghai as the final political decisions regarding the implementation of the coup were made.[122] On April 2, the very day that the Guomindang Central Supervisory Committee members in Shanghai requested local Guomindang military commanders to arrest Communist activists, the MPA cooperated with Liu Zhi's Second Division in an attack on Workers' Pickets' strongholds in Zhabei. Five major centers were seized, including the Workers' Pickets headquarters in the Eastern Library Building, over 340 "pickets" were arrested and sent to Longhua for "interrogation," and a large number of weapons caches were seized.[123] Further skirmishes occurred later in the week in Pudong and Nandao.[124]

By April 3 the battle lines between the MPA and the Workers' Pickets were firmly drawn. In reaction to the events of April 2 and 3, the Shanghai General Labor Union, on April 5, declared that it would call a general strike if anyone attempted to destroy the Workers' Pickets, and on the following day it ostentatiously armed them in a public ceremony in defiance of the martial law provisions promulgated on March 30 by Bai Chongxi.[125] By the late afternoon of April 11, the CCP definitely knew that a coup was in preparation, as elements of the Second Division of Zhou Fengqi's Twenty-sixth Army took up their planned positions in the streets of Chinese Shanghai, shortly after 4 P.M. Throughout the evening a continuous stream of secret reports was received by Workers' Pickets headquarters, now located in the Commercial Press Recreational Club, to the effect that an attack by the MPA and the military was imminent. In response to these reports the Workers' Pickets headquarters sent a letter to Zhou Fengqi's headquarters that same evening, requesting the help of the Twenty-sixth Army in the event of any "unfortunate incident." No reply was received. The Workers' Pickets detachments in Zhabei, Wusong, Pudong and Nandao were placed on full alert.[126]

THE GREEN GANG AND THE COUP OF APRIL 12, 1927

The Events of April 11

Du Yuesheng was personally involved with two of the key events of the coup, the assassination of Wang Shouhua and the negotiations with Stirling Fessenden, Chairman of the Shanghai Municipal Council.[127] In early 1927 Wang Shouhua was the key CCP leader in Shanghai. As President of the Shanghai General Labor Union and Chairman of the Labor Union Committee of the CCP Central Committee, Wang directly controlled the Shanghai trade union movement and particularly its fighting arm, the Workers' Pickets. His elimination was therefore considered by Jiang Jieshi as a prerequisite for the success of the coup since it would, it was hoped, create such confusion among the forces of the Workers' Pickets in Shanghai that they would be unable to mount an effective defense against the shock troops. Yang Hu and Chen Qun, therefore, were entrusted with the detailed planning of the assassination, and they involved Du Yuesheng because of his close relations with Wang.[128]

The decision to murder Wang was taken at a meeting at Du Yuesheng's home on the Rue Wagner on April 9, the same day that Jiang Jieshi left for Nanjing. Those present included Du and Zhang Xiaolin, the two Green Gang bosses; Yang Hu and Chen Qun, the Guomindang representatives; Zhang Boqi, the military commander of the MPA; and Du's four chief lieutenants in the Small Eight Mob: Ye Chuoshan, Gu Jiatang, Rui Qingrong and Gao Xinbao. The strategy adopted was for Du to send a dinner invitation to Wang in order to lure him out of the fortress of the Shanghai General Labor Union's headquarters in the Huzhou Guild. The invitation was for 8 P.M. on April 11. Many of Wang's colleagues warned him against accepting the invitation, but Wang felt that he had to go otherwise the gangsters would hold him in contempt and this would destroy the relationship that he had carefully developed with them over the preceding months. Wang argued that the Green Gang bosses had always kept their word to him in the past, and if he went he might be able to persuade the gangsters not to participate overtly in any possible conflict between the CCP and the Right GMD. Wang, therefore, accepted the dinner invitation, although not without some reservations.[129] The actual assassins were Du's four lieutenants—Gu Jiatang, Ye Chuoshan, Rui Qingrong and Gao Xinbao—who supervised the preparations, and carried out the abduction and murder. As soon as Wang arrived at Du's home he was overpowered, bundled into a car in which he was murdered, and his body either dumped or buried in a shallow grave in Shanghai's western districts. The whole operation took less than an hour, and had been completed by 9 P.M.[130] Although Chen Qun attempted to suppress all information on Wang's fate, by April 15 the Shanghai General Labor Union certainly knew that he had been murdered, when it specifically cited his assassination as one of its ten major indictments against Jiang Jieshi.[131]

Sometime later on the night of April 11, after he had supervised Wang's murder, Du Yuesheng held a meeting with Stirling Fessenden (1875–1943), Chairman of the Municipal Council of the Shanghai International Settlement.[132] His purpose was to obtain Fessenden's agreement to the passage of his MPA forces through the International Settlement. This agreement was crucial to the success of the purge, since without free passage through the International Settlement, the MPA forces, based as they were in the French Concession, would be unable to speedily reach their targets in Zhabei. Du arranged the meeting at his home through the Chief of the French Concession Police, E. Fiori. According to Fessenden's own account Du "went to the point in a business-like manner," and Fessenden, after some hesitation, agreed to Du's request. Fessenden later claimed that he was motivated solely by his fears of a Communist attempt to take over the foreign settlements.[133]

Du Yuesheng's approach to Fessenden can best be understood in the context of a developing rapprochement between the Right Guomindang conspirators and the Shanghai foreign authorities. Jiang Jieshi and his allies in the Right Guomindang feared the possibility of full-scale foreign intervention in defense of the Shanghai foreign settlements. To forestall such a development and win foreign support for the coup, they sought to capitalize on the foreign authorities' fears of a Communist-inspired attack on the foreign settlements and on their generalized fears of international Communism. Du Yuesheng played this card well in his conversations with Fessenden. The Shanghai foreign authorities, for their part, were prepared to follow their standing policy of cooperating with any Chinese power that could guarantee the security of Chinese Shanghai.

The Shanghai Purge, April 12–13

In the last few days before the purge the MPA leadership drew up detailed battle plans that carefully coordinated the activities of the shock troops with those of Zhou Fengqi's Twenty-sixth Army. The function of MPA forces as "shock troops" and their organization was reminiscent of the "Dare-to-Die" Corps of the 1911 Revolution. The MPA forces were organized into two "tiger regiments" (*biaojun*), and the First Tiger Regiment was in turn divided into three "columns." The objectives of the First Tiger Regiment, the largest of the two, were the concentrations of the Workers' Pickets in Zhabei: its first column was to attack the Workers' Pickets headquarters in the Commercial Press Recreational Club; its second was to attack the Shanghai General Labor Union headquarters, located in the Huzhou Guild; and the third was to seize the Commercial Press Printing Works, which was occupied by a 100-man detachment of Workers' Pickets. The Second Tiger Regiment's objectives were located in Nandao, and centered on the Chinese Tramways Company's premises, which were occupied by large detachments of Workers' Pickets.[134] The total strength of the MPA strike forces probably numbered about 2,000 men.[135] The decision to launch the purge in the early hours of the morning of April 12 was taken when it was learned that the Shanghai General Labor Union had scheduled a mass meeting to welcome Wang Jingwei's return to China for April 12.[136]

The purge began at about 4 A.M. on the morning of April 12, and was signaled by a bugle blast from Jiang Jieshi's headquarters followed by the siren whistle of a Chinese gunboat in the harbor.[137] The aim of the initial operations was to destroy the Workers' Pickets as a credible armed force. Within the first one and a half hours the MPA units attacked all their major targets in Zhabei and Nandao. The Guomindang forces employed a ruse to throw the Workers' Pickets off-guard. A military officer conspicuously disarmed MPA units in an effort to persuade the Workers' Pickets that the military was neutral in the conflict. To maintain the pretense that the military was merely attempting to mediate between rival workers' organizations, the MPA units were all dressed in blue denim workers' overalls with arm bands bearing the character "worker" (*gong*). This stratagem was used effectively to gain control of the Huzhou Guild and the Commercial Press Printing Works, but failed with the Commercial Press Recreational Club, which contained the headquarters of the Workers' Pickets.[138] By 4 P.M. on April 12, all of the positions of the Workers' Pickets had fallen, except for the Commercial Press Recreational Club, which held out until the following day, when it too was forced to surrender.[139] The events of April 12 had broken the power of the Workers' Pickets throughout Chinese Shanghai, and at least a third of the Workers' Pickets' forces, between 900 and 1,000 men, had surrendered.[140]

Almost as soon as the military situation had been stabilized the Right Guomindang moved to establish its control over the Shanghai trade unions. On April 12, the MPA leadership issued a circular telegram stating that their aim was to wrest control of the Shanghai General Labor Union from the "black sheep," that is the CCP, and to reorganize it along the lines of the Three People's Principles. On the afternoon of April 12, Chen Qun, in his capacity as Director of the Political Department of the Eastern Route Army's Front Headquarters, issued a memorandum in which he called for "harmony" between labor and the Guomindang, and warned of the need to discipline labor when it "becomes a disturbing element, when it arrogates to itself tasks which are detrimental to the [national?] movement and [is] disturbing of law and order."[141]

In accordance with these principles, the Guomindang new order in labor organization was quickly put in place. On the afternoon of April 13 the Green Gang-controlled Shanghai General Federation of Labor took over the Huzhou Guild, swore themselves into office, and immediately dissolved both the Shanghai General Labor Union and their own organization, the latter having already served its purpose. They then created a new organization, the Committee for the Unification of Shanghai Trade Union Organizations (*Shanghai Gonghui Zizhi Tongyi Weiyuanhui*—UUC), to coordinate the activities of all trade unions in Shanghai. The personnel of this new committee, however, did not differ greatly from the old federation; it almost wholly consisted of Green Gang members.

As a harbinger of things to come, the committee's first decision was to carry out a registration of all trade unions that were affiliated with the now outlawed Shanghai General Labor Union, with a view to their reorganization and the elimination of "dangerous elements" among the workers. This trade union reorganization was entrusted to two Green Gang members, Zhang Boqi, the military commander of the MPA and his vice-commander.[142] The Shanghai General Labor Union went underground and issued a call for a general strike for April 13, which was answered, at its peak, by over 100,000 workers. The strike failed, however, in part because it was a gesture of protest and lacked any concrete objective, and in part because the military muscle of the Workers' Pickets had been eliminated. The Shanghai General Labor Union unilaterally ended the strike on April 15, but not before over a hundred unarmed demonstrators, protesting the arrests of Workers' Pickets, had been massacred on Baoshan Road on April 13.[143]

AFTERMATH: THE GREEN GANG AND THE "WHITE TERROR," APRIL–AUGUST 1927

As soon as the military struggle was won the instruments of repression and the organizational framework of the "White Terror" were set up. On April 14 the Shanghai Party Purification Committee (*Shanghai Shi Qingdang Weiyuanhui*) was established under the direction of Yang Hu and Chen Qun, respectively Chairman and Vice-

Chairman. Over the next six months until Jiang Jieshi's resignation in August, Yang Hu and Chen Qun, in fact, enjoyed a virtual monopoly of military and political power in Shanghai. In addition to their joint control of the Shanghai Party Purification Committee, Yang was also the Wusong-Shanghai Garrison Commander after May 11, 1927, while Chen was Director of the Political Department of the Wusong-Shanghai Garrison Command, and Chairman of the UUC.[144] The fact that Chen held senior positions in both the Party Purification Committee, which oversaw the extermination of Communists and leftists, and the UUC, which implemented the reorganization of the trade unions, indicates that there was no essential difference between the two operations, they were merely two aspects of the same process. This identification of interests was made quite clear by Chen himself, who was in the habit of ending his speeches to UUC members with the following statement: "I presently represent the Front Headquarters of the Eastern Route Army, and the Party Purification Committee. At the same time I also represent the Committee for the Unification of Trade Union Organizations. I, therefore, will kill anyone engaged in reactionary [i.e., Communist] activities."[145]

The French Concession Green Gang bosses were intimately involved with the implementation of this organized terror in Shanghai. The commander of the Party Purification Committee's "Action Squad" (*Xindong Dadui*) was Rui Qingrong, one of Du Yuesheng's most trusted lieutenants, whose services Du had "lent" to Chen Qun for the duration of "Party Purification." Rui's squad, which was composed entirely of his own personal Green Gang following, went into operation immediately. On the afternoon of April 14 it raided five "Communist" organizations: the Shanghai Provisional Municipal Government; the Guomindang Special Municipal Party Branch; the Shanghai Students' Federation; the offices of the "Common People's Daily" (*Pingmin Ribao*), the organ of the Shanghai General Labor Union; and the China Relief Association (*Zhongguo Jinan Hui*). In the course of this blitz Rui's "Action Squad" arrested over 1,000 Communist suspects. On the same day gangster members of the old federation closed down various trade union offices in Nandao and Pudong.[146] The terror launched by the Shanghai Party Purification Committee and implemented by the Green Gang was indiscriminate and capricious. Anyone could be arrested as a "Communist."[147]

No Communist suspect who was arrested in these early days of the terror underwent a public court trial and most were summarily executed. In interviews with Chinese journalists, Chen Qun always became evasive when questioned as to the number of "Communists" executed or awaiting execution.[148]

The Green Gang bosses were involved also with the implementation of the purge in the counties of Shanghai's hinterland and elsewhere in the Jiangnan. Du Yuesheng, for example, personally accompanied Chen Qun, Yang Hu and Rui Qingrong when they brought "party purification" to Ningbo.[149] He also, together with Huang Jinrong and Zhang Xiaolin, conducted the purge in Baoshan County, and delegated one of his lieutenants, Gao Xinbao, to implement the purge in Qingpu and Songjiang counties.[150] By early May the French Concession Green Gang bosses had set up their own Anti-Communist League and had activated the Green Gang networks in the lower Yangzi and North China in the interests of fighting Communism.[151]

The Green Gang bosses, especially Du Yuesheng, gave strong support to the UUC throughout 1927. It is significant that the UUC's trade union strength was concentrated in those districts of Shanghai where the Green Gang's influence was greatest, notably Pudong where the Green Gang controlled the BAT (British-American Tobacco Company) Union, and had little or no support in those districts, such as Zhabei and Nandao, where the CCP-controlled General Labor Union had been most active.[152] No trade union was safe from this encroaching miasma of terror. Even "reorganized" unions, such as those for the employees of Wing On and Sincere Department Stores, were not immune from threats and intimidation when they dared to criticize the corrupt practices and terroristic methods of the UUC.[153] The UUC was even capable of turning on the Shanghai GMD Party Branch. When Zhou Zhiyuan, the head of the GMD Branch's Workers and Peasants Department, ordered his secretary, Zhang Junyi, to engage in secret organization work among the Shanghai trade unions in an attempt to undermine the UUC's position, Chen Qun had Zhang arrested and murdered in short order.[154] Some indication of the fear generated in Shanghai by the campaign of terror carried out by the UUC and its Green Gang allies is provided by a witticism current at the time: "wolves and tigers (hu) hunt in packs (qun)," a bitter pun on the names of Yang Hu and Chen Qun.[155]

The terror became an integral part of the Guomindang's administrative system during the first six months of its rule in Shanghai. It was progressively extended in its scope until eventually it was a weapon used against all classes of Shanghai society, in order to coerce them into acquiescence of Guomindang policies. When wealthy Chinese businessmen, for example, balked at the ceaseless financial demands made on them by Jiang Jieshi, many found themselves denounced as "Communists" and thrown in prison until they made the payments demanded of them. By such measures Jiang was believed to have raised about Ch$50 million to meet his military expenses.[156]

The French Concession Green Gang bosses played an active part in the extension of the terror. All three held leadership positions in the "Self-Defense Militia" (*Ziwei Tuan*) which was organized in July by the Shanghai Federation of Commerce and Industry (*Shanghai Shangye Lianhehui*), a body which had been set up by some leading businessmen to support Jiang Jieshi.[157]

The resignation of Jiang Jieshi from his government posts on August 11, 1927, heralded the end of this policy of terror. Fearing just such an outcome and its implications for their relations with the new Guomindang authorities, Du Yuesheng and Zhang Xiaolin sent an urgent letter the following day to their "elder brother" Zhang Jingjiang, a senior member of the Guomindang and a confidant of Jiang Jieshi. Expressing their concern that the CCP could take advantage of the "unclear" political situation and current industrial unrest to engage in "rash actions" and so render "unmanageable" the situation in Shanghai, Du and Zhang strongly urged Zhang Jingjiang to eliminate the CCP "while there is yet time."[158] The intervention by the Green Gang bosses, however, was unsuccessful and the Shanghai Party Purification Committee was wound up in early September, although the UUC continued in operation until May 1928. In the six months from mid-April to early September 1927 it was estimated that over 5,000 leftists, Communists, members of the Guomindang "left wing" and sundry others, had been killed by the apparatus of the terror.[159]

Through their crucial assistance to Jiang Jieshi in April 1927 the Green Gang bosses became an officially recognized element within the Guomindang's new national polity. In mid-May 1927 the three Gang bosses were formally appointed counselors with the rank of Major General to Jiang Jieshi's military headquarters.[160] Although these appointments were in fact merely honorific titles they had great symbolic importance. They legitimized the Green Gang's position in Jiang Jieshi's new national polity; they formalized the special relationship that had developed between the Green Gang and the Guomindang in the preparations and implementation of the purge, and this relationship was to be one of the characteristics of Chinese political life in the 1930s; and finally, these titles implicitly acknowledged the special position and interests of the Green Gang in the local politics of Shanghai.

5 "The Pact with the Devil"

The events of early 1927 in Shanghai, the threat posed by the CCP after the March Uprising and the approach of the GMD's Northern Expedition, altered fundamentally the parameters of power within the French Concession. It placed the relationship between the French authorities and the Green Gang bosses on a new basis, and saw the emergence of Du Yuesheng as the key figure in that relationship. Over the next few years Du proceeded to consolidate his good working relations with key members of the French Concession administration and to enhance his political position within the Concession. The influence of the Green Gang bosses, and in particular Du Yuesheng, within the Concession reached its apotheosis during the consulship of Edgar Koechlin (December 1928–March 1932). The erosion in French authority in the Concession during those years created a serious political crisis for the French administration in 1932, and led to a major reassertion of French authority during the consul generalship of Jacques Meyrier (1932–35). Du Yuesheng, nevertheless, continued to exert significant influence in the Concession until the outbreak of the Sino-Japanese War in 1937.

THE FRENCH AUTHORITIES, THE GREEN GANG AND THE EVENTS OF JANUARY–APRIL 1927

In early 1927 the French authorities in both Paris and Shanghai were extremely concerned about the security implications of the entry of the Guomindang's National Revolutionary Army (NRA) into the Jiangnan region and the Communist-inspired workers' uprisings in Chinese Shanghai in February and March 1927. They were troubled particularly by the implications for the French Concession of the reports of the seizures of the British concessions in Hankou and Jiujiang in early January 1927. During the first two months of 1927 the French Foreign Ministry feared that the weaker defense forces available to the Shanghai French Concession relative to those in the International Settlement would encourage the Chinese to consider the Concession a "soft option" and attack it.[1] As a minute to the French Cabinet from the Ministry of Foreign Affairs in January 1927 indicated, Paris was especially concerned by the adverse implications for France's political and economic position in the Far East generally of any failure to resist effectively a possible attack on the Concession.[2]

This crisis, which appeared to have the potential to threaten the very existence of the Concession, forced the French authorities to look very hard at their defense resources. In the course of this review they dismissed the Chinese members of the police force and the Chinese volunteer units organized by the Gentry-Councillor Clique as incapable of providing an effective defense "in the event of anti-foreign disorders."[3]

The influence of the Gentry-Councillor Clique was based essentially on its extensive networks within the Chinese business community of Shanghai and, to a degree, with the warlord units that controlled the Chinese City and its environs. It had not developed, however, significant connections with the new forces on the Chinese political stage, the GMD and the NRA. The clique, therefore, was of little use to the French during the crisis months of early 1927. The gangster bosses, on the other hand, as noted in chapter 4, did enjoy a working relationship with the various revolutionary parties active in Shanghai, and also had links with Jiang Jieshi. The French authorities, therefore, turned to them and in particular to Du Yuesheng. These French overtures neatly balanced those from the Right GMD who were also seeking the gangster bosses' assistance against the Communists in Shanghai.

Du agreed to assist the French in maintaining order in the Concession in return for French-supplied weapons. On February 26, therefore, Naggiar, the French Consul General, dispatched a request for 300 rifles plus 150 revolvers and 1,000 steel helmets.[4] These were some of the weapons that Du's gangsters used to execute the anti-Communist coup in mid-April. Du quickly implemented his side of the bargain when he personally intervened to prevent Chinese merchants and their employees in the French Concession from joining the Communist-sponsored general strike of February 20–24. The French, for their part, facilitated Du's preparations for the anti-Communist purge. In addition to supplying weapons, they provided an armed police guard for the headquarters of the Chinese Mutual Progress Association, at 18 Song Shan Road in the French Concession.[5] As noted earlier, the Chief of the French Concession Police, Captain Fiori, arranged a meeting between Du Yuesheng and Stirling Fessenden at which the latter granted Du's armed gangsters the right of passage through the International Settlement to attack the Communist positions in Zhabei.[6] The close cooperation between the French police and Du Yuesheng's gangsters was officially acknowledged in 1928 by the acting Consul General Meyrier in a dispatch to the French Minister in Beiping.[7] It is probable that the French used the gangster bosses as their intermediaries in establishing contacts with the GMD's NRA, an important element in their strategy to maintain the security of the Concession during the first four months of 1927.[8]

THE POST–APRIL 12 COUP DEAL: OPIUM AND THE SECURITY OF THE CONCESSION

By their actions the Green Gang bosses, and most particularly Du Yuesheng, effectively served the political interests of the French authorities at a time of acute crisis in early 1927. The crucial assistance that the gangster bosses had provided the authorities during the crisis months of February–April began the process by which they progressively displaced the Gentry-Councillor Clique as the major center of Chinese power in the French Concession. An important aspect of the accord reached in February 1927 between Du Yuesheng and Captain Fiori was the agreement by the police chief to protect the extension of the gangsters' economic power (in the form of opium and gambling rackets) in the Concession. This marked the beginnings of a clear community of interests between the French authorities and the gangsters, in which the former tolerated the latter's rackets in return for their assistance in the maintenance of the security and internal order of the Concession. The French, themselves, ruefully referred to this arrangement as "the pact with the devil" (*le pacte avec le diable*).[9]

An important aspect of this pact was the reaffirmation of the 1925 agreement on opium trafficking and the extension of the narcotics distribution network within the Concession. The sale of opium was conducted on such an open basis in the Concession that the local Chinese regularly referred to the system as an "official monopoly."[10] An indication of the degree of involvement of French officialdom in the opium traffic were the strenuous efforts they made in the late 1920s to try and persuade the representatives of the other foreign powers to overturn the 1912 International Opium Convention and put the opium trade back on a legal (and officially taxable) footing. The French authorities had argued for several years the practical benefits for both China and the foreign powers with interests in China of a policy of control rather than prohibition, and therefore gave strong support to the Anti-Opium Law proposed by the Nanjing government in early 1928, which would have established a form of official monopoly.[11]

In the context of these Chinese moves to promote an official monopoly, Du Yuesheng approached the senior officials of both foreign settlements in order to obtain their agreement to putting the opium traffic on a semi-official basis. In February 1928, the acting French Consul General, Meyrier, informed the French Minister, de Martel, in Beiping that he had held discussions with Du Yuesheng in which the latter had offered to make regular monthly payments of between Ch$20,000 and Ch$60,000 to the French Mixed Court in return for the nonimplementation of the Chinese government's anti-opium laws in the French Concession. Meyrier told de Martel that he supported the conclusion of such an agreement in part because of Du's power within the Concession and the need for the French administration to retain his support. He also noted that a similar agreement had been entered into secretly between Stirling Fessenden and Du Yuesheng, by which the gangster boss agreed to make anonymous payments to the SMC's treasury of between Ch$50,000 and Ch$100,000 a month in return for the nonoperation of the anti-opium laws in the International Settlement. The French government was sympathetic to the possibility of such arrangements, but forbade the conclusion of any formal agreement until, and unless, the other interested powers agreed to such a course of action.[12]

When the Shanghai Consular Body held its discussions on the proposed Anti-Opium Law in early March 1928, therefore, Meyrier strongly argued the case for the creation of a monopoly system in the Shanghai foreign settlements. In the course of his argument Meyrier revealed the proposal that had been put to him by Du Yuesheng.[13] In July of that year Naggiar, the newly appointed head of the Asiatic Department of the Ministry of Foreign Affairs, put the same argument to members of the British Embassy in Paris.[14] Unfortunately for the French (and indeed the SMC), the British and American governments refused to consider a revision of the Hague Convention, and so the policy of official connivance in the drug traffic continued in the French Concession. This connivance even extended to the French armed forces in the Far East, with reports that French gunboats on the upper Yangzi were used to convoy French-flagged vessels known to be engaged in running guns to Sichuan and opium to Shanghai.[15]

In addition to his opium rackets, Du Yuesheng also developed major gambling interests in the Concession after 1927, which greatly increased his financial power. He conducted negotiations with Fiori and Verdier in the course of 1927 that resulted in the opening of five large gambling houses catering to wealthy Chinese in the Concession in early 1928. These were under the direct control of Du Yuesheng and were managed by key lieutenants of his Small Eight Mob, and protected by a special squad of 500 gangsters under the command of one of his principal lieutenants, Gao Xinbao. The largest and most notorious of these gambling houses was the Fusheng, also known as "Number 181" from its address on the Avenue Foch. This was a large three-story foreign-style house that catered to all types of Western and Chinese forms of gambling, for whose use Du paid 4,000 silver taels each month. Besides such prestigious locations, Du also controlled innumerable gambling dives catering to working-class gamblers in the area around Bao Xing Li.[16]

THE CONSOLIDATION OF GREEN GANG POLITICAL POWER IN THE FRENCH CONCESSION

Du Yuesheng also used the pact with the French authorities to further his political ambitions within the Concession. The instrument of this policy was the French Concession Chinese Ratepayers' Association (*Fazujie Nashui Huaren Hui*—CRA). This organization was established in mid-January 1927 with the avowed purpose of representing the interests of the Chinese ratepayers in the Concession. From the outset, however, it was controlled by Du Yuesheng and his colleagues. The three Green Gang bosses were joint chairmen of a twenty-one-man Preparatory Committee, which formally established the association during the first six months of 1927, and whose headquarters was located either in or near Du's home on the Rue Wagner. The Preparatory Committee numbered at least two more gangsters in its membership, Shang Mujiang (a close associate of Zhang Xiaolin) and Cheng Zhusun.[17] The Green Gang bosses also firmly controlled the association's supervisory committees and the joint chairmanships "elected" by the association's members in 1929 and 1931.[18]

The gang bosses launched their drive for political power in the Concession in the immediate aftermath of the anti-Communist purge. In late April 1927 the CRA began to put pressure on the French authorities to meet its demands for the election of all Chinese members of the Provisional Commission (instead of their appointment by the French Consul General); to increase the numbers of Chinese members from five to eight; and to appoint six Chinese advisers to the Consulate General.[19] These aims had the dual purpose of promoting the CRA itself (and hence the gang bosses) as the legitimate spokesman for the Chinese residents of the Concession, and to undercut the position of the Gentry-Councillor Clique whose members made up all the Chinese representation on the Provisional Commission.

The French authorities' decision in July 1927 to follow the International Settlement and raise the Concession's rates by 2 percent provided the gang bosses with the ideal issue to push their political demands. In early July the CRA presented the Provisional Commission with its demands, including the ambit claim that all matters concerning the Concession's administration should be submitted to the CRA for its approval. If accepted, this demand would have enabled the CRA to appropriate the functions of the Provisional Commission. It was, in fact, an obvious attempt by the gangster bosses to pressure the French by capitalizing on current Chinese nationalist hostility to extraterritoriality and the GMD's intervention in the contemporaneous rates dispute in the International Settlement. The other demands dealt with the real issues at stake: the abolition of the rates increase and the election of the Provisional Commission's Chinese members by the CRA.

In mid-July the CRA appointed Du, Zhang Xiaolin and Shang Mujiang to negotiate with the French authorities on its behalf. As a result of these negotiations a compromise was reached that gave both sides something of what they sought. Although the Green Gang bosses failed to obtain the election of the Chinese members of the Provisional Commission, they did win the right to have the CRA elect nine Chinese advisers to the commission. All nine advisers were drawn from the CRA's Executive Committee and included Du Yuesheng, Zhang Xiaolin, Cheng Zhusun and Shang Mujiang. The French, for their part, obtained the gangsters' acceptance of the increased rate on the basis of a review after a six-month period.[20]

Despite this compromise the CRA continued to press throughout the latter half of 1927 for the election of the Chinese members of the Provisional Commission. In an open letter to the Concession's Chinese ratepayers of late November 1927, the CRA argued that the effectiveness of the existing Chinese councillors was severely restricted by the fact that they were appointed by the French Consul General and not elected by the Chinese ratepayers. In the context of the competition between the Green Gang bosses and the Gentry-Councillor Clique, this statement was not merely, or even primarily, a plea for greater democracy in the Provisional Commission, but an attack on the clique's self-assumed right to represent Chinese interests in the Concession. At the same time the CRA attempted to strengthen its legitimacy by appropriating current GMD terminology on political democracy. In the letter, it described its aims as "to promote the capacity for self-government" and to develop "the spirit of self-government."[21]

In January 1928 Du Yuesheng and Zhang Xiaolin used the resumption of negotiations on the increased rate to bargain for Zhang's admission to the Provisional Commission. In return, the French continued to collect the increased rate and, as a sop to the ratepayers, they agreed to increase the police force by 200 men. Zhang's appointment to the Provisional Commission was one of the last acts of Naggiar as Consul General, and he acknowledged that it was a quid pro quo for the services rendered by the gangster bosses during the security crisis a year before.[22] Zhang's membership in the Provisional Commission was a major victory for the Green Gang bosses, and it was consolidated eighteen months later by Du Yuesheng's own appointment as a councillor in July 1929. In his inaugural speech on taking his seat in the Provisional Commission on July 17, Du stated that the basic work of the commission was that of Sino-French administration.[23] This was a calculated remark which implied that in future the main business of government in the Concession could only be pursued on the basis of a collaboration between the representatives of the Chinese population and the French authorities. By stating that this should occur within the Provisional Commission, moreover, he was asserting a parity between that body and the French administration that it had never enjoyed nor had been meant to enjoy. The reason Du made such a claim was that the Provisional Commission had now become (as of mid-1929) the power base of the gangster bosses in the Concession.

If the membership changes to the Provisional Commission in 1928 and 1929 represented an increase in power for the Green Gang bosses, by the same token they represented a serious diminution in the power of the Gentry-Councillor Clique. Both Zhang and Du gained their seats on the commission at the expense of Lu Songhou and Wu Zonglian, two aged members of the clique. Although the clique still retained three of the five Chinese seats, real influence had shifted to Du and Zhang. This was clearly revealed by the Wei Tingrong affair in mid-1929. Within a week of his taking his seat on the commission, Du had his old rival Wei Tingrong kidnapped and spirited away to Pudong. Such a brazen attack on a leading member of the Gentry-Councillor Clique caused consternation within French officialdom. According to an SMP report, the French authorities threatened to close down the opium traffic unless Wei was released. The incident also created a rift between Du and Zhang Xiaolin. The relationship between the two bosses had never been easy and had become increasingly difficult with the marked increase in Du's power and authority since 1927. It is possible that Zhang considered that Du had overreached himself and had endangered the basis of the gangsters' power in the Concession (their control of the opium traffic) for the dubious satisfaction of settling accounts with a bitter rival. Whatever the reason, Zhang abruptly resigned his position as co-chairman of the CRA on August 1, 1929, and left Shanghai for Dalian. The affair was finally brought to an end when, after a tense three months, Wei was finally released in mid-September 1929 in a raid conducted by all three police forces in Shanghai.[24] Whatever the immediate costs to Du's position, he had, in kidnapping Wei, delivered a symbolic message to the Gentry-Councillor Clique on where power now lay in the new balance of forces within the French Concession.

The coping stone to the edifice of gangster political power in the Concession was provided by Consul Koechlin's agreement in late 1930 that the CRA should elect the Chinese members of the Provisional Commission. This was the result of protracted negotiations conducted throughout 1930, and the gangsters again made use of the rate issue as a lever. Among other factors that influenced Koechlin's decision was undoubtedly the crucial role played by Du Yuesheng in bringing to an end the long-drawn-out strike of the French Tramways Union from June to August 1930. On October 31, therefore, Koechlin sent a letter to the CRA in which he conceded the principle of election of the Chinese councillors, and requested that the CRA endorse the five Chinese members already serving on the commission. The CRA complied and on November 18, 1930, it convened a special congress which formally endorsed the five sitting Chinese members, and elected nine special advisers to the various committees of the Provisional Commission.[25] These developments represented a complete victory for the Green Gang bosses, and in particular Du Yuesheng. He now controlled the Provisional Commission, and the leaders of the Gentry-Councillor Clique were dependent on his favor for the retention of their positions on the commission. A new balance of forces had emerged in the power structure of the French Concession.

THE GREEN GANG AND THE MAINTENANCE OF SOCIAL AND INDUSTRIAL ORDER IN THE FRENCH CONCESSION: THE FRENCH TRAMWAYS UNION 1928–1931

In addition to his assistance to the French authorities in ensuring the external security of the Concession in 1927, from which he derived important political gains in the Provisional Commission, Du Yuesheng's position in the Concession was enhanced further by his successful mediation of industrial and social disputes. Such mediation was an important aspect of the pact between Du and the French authorities and represented, from the latter's point of view, a significant contribution to the maintenance of the internal security of the Concession. In the words of the British Consul General in Shanghai, the Green Gang bosses were

> extremely useful intermediaries in dealing, by Chinese methods, with any Chinese troubles which arise, whether political ..., industrial ..., or even peace and good order [in the French Concession]. They can continue their opium dealings just so long as the concession benefits—very materially—and is spared much of the trouble to which foreign authorities in China are so often heirs.[26]

The most important industrial disputes in this period occurred in the principal public utilities concern in the Concession, the French Tramways and Electric Light Company (*La Compagnie Française de Tramways et d'Éclairage Électrique Changhai*—FTC), and in particular the strikes of December 1928 and June–August 1930.[27] In undertaking the mediation of these strikes Du was concerned with increasing his standing with and, hence, his "indispensability" to the French authorities. He was interested, however, in more than this. By the latter half of 1930 Du was intent on building up an independent power base within the Concession, and as part of his strategy he sought to gain control over organized labor in the French settlement. One major purpose of his mediation of the 1928 and 1930 strikes, therefore, was to gain control of the French Tramways Union (*Fadian Gonghui*—FTU), which he accomplished by 1931. Through its provision of water and electricity supplies as well as public transport, the FTC, in fact, occupied a strategic position in the social and economic life of the French Concession. This concentration of strategic services in the one company, in turn, ensured the importance of the FTU since any strike in the FTC had the potential to paralyze the whole Concession.[28] Once he had control of the FTU, therefore, Du had the advantage over the French authorities.

Du's strategy was facilitated by the fact that industrial disputes, such as those in the FTC, were not matters solely of concern to the Concession authorities. Agencies of the Chinese Municipal Government of Greater Shanghai, such as the Bureau of Social Affairs (*Shanghai Shi Shehui Ju*—BSA), together with the Shanghai GMD Party Branch, claimed an interest in the Chinese populations of the foreign settlements, and both organizations were actively involved in the 1928 and 1930 disputes in the French Tramways Company. This was a local manifestation of the new Nationalist government's general policy to reclaim those areas of the nation's sovereignty that had been lost to the foreign powers. As part of this policy the Chinese authorities in Shanghai took every opportunity to assert their claims to authority over the Chinese population and their welfare in the foreign settlements, and this attitude ensured that even relatively minor incidents became the subjects of diplomatic exchanges.

This was the context within which Du conducted his mediation of social and industrial disputes in the Concession. The French used him to "manage" their relations with the local Chinese authorities in the resolution of disputes involving the Chinese population of the

Concession, while the Chinese authorities found Du to be a useful instrument in furthering their own political interests in the Concession. Du, for his part, used his relations with one to gain increased leverage with the other and so increase his own power and influence. Good examples of this triangular relationship in a situation in which local fracases could become international incidents were provided by the Wu Tonggen Affair of September 1928 and the Xin Dingxiang Affair of October–December 1930.[29] In both cases a Chinese worker was murdered by French marines (a tram driver in the case of Wu and a sampan ferryman in the case of Xin), public protests were mobilized by the Shanghai Party Office and the Shanghai trade unions, in which demands were made for the abolition of extraterritoriality, and the affairs became the subject of diplomatic exchanges between the Chinese and French authorities. On each occasion both parties accepted Du's mediation of the incident, and in each case he negotiated a compromise settlement that took the immediate heat out of the affair, met the needs of the local French and Chinese authorities and provided some material relief to the victims' bereaved families.[30] By his successful mediation of these incidents Du strengthened his relations with both Chinese and French officialdom. At the same time, by his preparedness to finance a settlement out of his own pocket, he further enhanced his reputation in the popular imagination.

The French tramways strike of December 3–30, 1928, was the first major test of the understanding regarding social order in the Concession between the French authorities and the Green Gang.[31] Several days into the strike, Du Yuesheng emerged as the French Tramways Company's representative and, by December 10, he had successfully negotiated a settlement that allowed for a return to work while meeting some of the strikers' demands. The FTC, however, rejected this agreement and Du was forced to withdraw as mediator. With the collapse of the agreement, the strikers, not surprisingly, felt betrayed by Du and the GMD strike committee. This situation, in turn, provided the opportunity for the CCP activist Xu Amei (1906–1939) and other radical members of the FTU to reorganize the strike committee and gain control of the strike.[32]

Meanwhile Du Yuesheng sought to reverse the serious loss of "face" he had suffered as a result of the FTC's refusal to accept the settlement he had negotiated. He, therefore, used his control of the French Concession Chinese Ratepayers' Association to bring strong pressure to bear on the FTC for his reinstatement. The radicalization of the strike finally forced the FTC to turn once more to Du Yuesheng.[33] In seeking to end the strike Du worked closely with the BSA and the GMD Shanghai Branch.[34] To achieve an immediate return to work he was also prepared to meet the strikers' financial demands by paying Ch$7,000 out of his own pocket.[35] By means of a combination of negotiations, bribery and calculated threats, Du Yuesheng succeeded in breaking the strike and obtaining a return to work on December 30.[36]

With the successful termination of the 1928 strike Du Yuesheng sought both to deepen his influence over the FTC workers and to increase his control over the FTU itself. Through the activities of his two key Green Gang followers in the FTC, Li Linshu, a senior inspector in the traffic department, and Shao Ziying, a senior company clerk, Du was able to consolidate his influence over the traffic department workers and the FTC's clerical staff.[37] In February 1929 Du succeeded in splitting the FTU when the traffic employees, as the result of an orchestrated campaign of intimidation instigated by Li Linshu, broke away to form their own union, the Traffic Employees' Club (*Chewubu Tongren Julebu*).[38] The FTU, although still under the control of Xu Amei, was now effectively limited to the machine-shop workers. This division among the FTC's blue-collar workers was to be a determining factor in the 1930 strike.

The strike of 1930, which lasted for 54 days (June 20 to August 13), was the most important industrial dispute to occur in the French Concession. Unrest had been developing for some time as rising rice prices eroded the workers' standard of living.[39] Du Yuesheng, for example, was able to prevent a strike in May by persuading Xu Amei that a strike at that time would be considered to be Communist inspired and, therefore, counterproductive.[40] Late in the following month, however, Xu could no longer resist increasing pressure for industrial action from among union members and brought the FTU out on strike.[41] A complication for the FTU was that Xu Amei's relations with Du Yuesheng indirectly had led to his expulsion from the CCP for failing to support the new Li Lisan leadership's decision for a general strike in "Red May." Henceforth Xu was denounced as a "yellow unionist" and a "scab" by official CCP organs.[42]

Not all the FTC's workers were affected by the strike, which was limited initially to the workers in the machine shops. The traffic staff, who belonged to the Traffic Employees' Club, refused to join the strike, undoubtedly at the direction of Du Yuesheng in an effort to keep the strike within manageable limits.[43] This division among the workers' ranks led to confrontation and escalating violence.[44] By early July a situation of stalemate existed between the FTC and the FTU, while violence between striking and nonstriking workers increased significantly. Xu Amei, therefore, finally had to approach Du Yuesheng who urged a return to work and, as a quid pro quo, promised that he would guarantee the payment of strike pay. Xu's acceptance of these terms temporarily split the strike leadership, but unity was quickly restored when Du proved unable to fulfill his promise to secure the release of a number of arrested strikers.[45]

The violent confrontation between strikers and the French riot police on the Rue Brenier de Montmorand, on July 21, changed fundamentally the character of the strike.[46] The scope of the strike was enlarged when the FTC's Chinese clerical staff, in protest at the French police action, joined the strike the following day.[47] The incident also released a great outpouring of nationalist and anti-imperialist emotion among the Shanghai public and put a serious strain on Sino-French relations. Not only did the Municipal Government of Greater Shanghai approach Koechlin over the incident, but the Nanjing government lodged a strong protest with the new French Minister to China, Auguste Wilden.[48] The French authorities themselves were under pressure from Paris to resolve the dispute.

The strike had now become embroiled with China's foreign relations; this fact intensified efforts to bring it to an end and, in the process, greatly enhanced the significance of Du Yuesheng's role in these efforts. Koechlin delegated Verdier and Fiori to approach Du.[49] Du had created a climate favorable to his intervention by orchestrating demands from the FTC's clerical staff as well the French Concession Chinese Ratepayers' Association for his mediation.[50] During the discussions with the French representatives, however, Du was curiously reluctant to accede to their request, and Fiori felt compelled to remind Du that his opium and gambling rackets would be placed in jeopardy if the dispute remained unresolved.[51] An explanation of this paradoxical situation is that Du sought to mediate the dispute in his own right and not simply as the representative of the FTC; in other words, he wished to avoid another damaging loss of "face" as had occurred during the 1928 strike.

Du's attempts to reach an accommodation with Xu Amei, however, failed when Xu sabotaged his efforts to obtain an early return to work by denouncing as unsatisfactory the provisional agreement drafted by Du on August 5.[52] With this failure, Du seriously set about the task of breaking the strike by using the Green Gang to harass the strikers and by excluding Xu Amei and radical strike leaders from the negotiations on August 12 that led to an end to the strike.[53] By these means Du ensured a return to work on August 13. He himself bore most of the financial costs of the settlement, a sum that was estimated to be as high as Ch$300,000.[54] This was, however, a small price to pay to safeguard his opium and gambling interests in the Concession. With the end of the strike Xu was sacked by the FTC, and Du succeeded in neutralizing the radical union leadership.[55]

The struggle between Xu Amei and Du Yuesheng for control of the French Tramways workers continued for another year, and reached a climax in September 1931 with Xu's arrest, trial and imprisonment. Xu Amei's arrest enabled Du Yuesheng finally to take full control of the FTU by appointing two new leaders to head the union, Zhang Fubao and Shi Chuanfu, both of whom were members of his Green Gang coterie.[56] The French police noted that with Xu's arrest and the takeover of the FTU "serenity returned to the workers' thoughts."[57]

THE CRISIS OF AUTHORITY IN THE FRENCH
CONCESSION, 1931

The drama of Xu Amei's demise and Du Yuesheng's consolidation of his control over the FTU occurred against a backdrop of gathering crisis in the Concession. This crisis turned on the nature of the relationship between the Green Gang and the French authorities. By early 1931 Du's control of the Provisional Commission and the local trade unions together with his close and complex relationship with the French authorities had caused many informed foreign observers to conclude that the gangsters and not the French administration ran the Concession. The British and International Settlement authorities were particularly concerned by this development and the adverse implications it held for the foreign position generally in Shanghai.

In late 1929, for example, the SMP provided the British Consul General with a confidential report on the situation in the French Concession which stated that Captain Fiori was Chief of Police in name only and that real power was exercised by Du Yuesheng and his gangster colleagues.[58] Eighteen months later, in March 1931, the British Consul General observed that not only did the Green Gang bosses have complete control of the Concession's affairs but that they were in a position to destroy the French administration if they considered it in their interests to do so.[59] These sentiments were echoed by the Shanghai-based American journal *The China Weekly Review*, which observed in an editorial in July 1931 that the Green Gang bosses were in fact the real power in the French Concession and constituted a form of "super-government not greatly different from the regime of Al Capone which operated in Chicago."[60] The French authorities themselves admitted to the erosion of their authority in the Concession by 1931–32. In a dispatch to Paris in May 1932, Meyrier, the recently appointed Consul General, observed that Du Yuesheng's organization, which had initially acted as a "willing tool" (*instrument docile*) of the French, had become a formidable power in its own right, and one that sought to take over the Concession's administration and to substitute itself "for the French authorities, either by agreement or by force" (*de gré ou de force, à l'autorité française*).[61]

By mid-1931, therefore, it was commonly believed that public order had so broken down that a crisis of authority existed in the French Concession. Thus it was seriously suggested that the commanders of the United States and British defense forces in Shanghai be formally requested to station some of their troops in the residential section of the Concession in order to protect the lives and property of their nationals resident there.[62]

These developments were a cause of some concern to the French government in Paris, not only because of the threat they posed to French authority in Shanghai, but also because of the great damage they inflicted on French prestige in the Far East generally. For these reasons France dispatched in mid-1930 Auguste Wilden, a retired former Consul General in Shanghai, as the new French Minister to China with the specific brief to investigate the situation in the Shanghai Concession. After his arrival Wilden's investigations made very slow progress due to the obstructive tactics adopted by the French officials in Shanghai, notably Koechlin, whom Wilden described as "obviously hostile," and Fiori who was "evasive and furtive." Finally Wilden reluctantly concluded that it was impossible to reform the situation through the existing local French officials, who were too deeply involved with the gangsters, although he did not finally succeed in persuading Paris of the need to replace Koechlin and Fiori until late 1931.[63]

While Wilden searched for an appropriate strategy to deal with the problems in the Concession, the situation deteriorated further with the publicity given to the gambling rackets in early 1931. Between 1929 and 1931 the SMC had progressively closed down all the gambling houses and the two dog-racing tracks (Luna Park and the Stadium) in the International Settlement, which meant that by 1931 the only remaining gambling rackets in the foreign settlements of Shanghai were those located in the French Concession under the control of the Green Gang bosses. One reason for the International Settlement's policy was its desire to prevent the gambling question (which was formally proscribed under Chinese law) from becoming an issue in the negotiations between the Chinese government and the foreign powers concerning extraterritoriality. Accordingly, many foreign officials feared that the continued open operations of the Green Gang's gambling houses in the French Concession could seriously undermine the position of the foreign powers in the face of the Chinese government's diplomatic offensive in early 1931 for the rendition of the foreign settlements. It was for this reason that the British Consul General, J. F. Brenan, put pressure on Koechlin in February 1931 to clean up the gambling rackets. However, the French authorities merely procrastinated and responded with a few carefully managed raids that left the Green Gang gambling houses largely undisturbed.[64]

The pressure, nevertheless, was increasing on Green Gang interests, and Du Yuesheng used his power within the Concession to try and keep the local French officials in line. As a lever on the French authorities he ended his previous lukewarm attitude to the Nationalist government's campaign against extraterritoriality, and swung the CRA in support of the government's negotiations for the rendition of the French Mixed Court, which were then just getting underway.[65] At the same time, Du used his control of industrial labor to bring pressure to bear on the local French officials and prevent them from capitulating to Wilden's blandishments.

Although the strike in July 1931 by the garbage collectors of the French Municipality had its own separate causes, there are strong circumstantial reasons to suggest that Du used the strike to demonstrate his power in the Concession in order to intimidate the French authorities.[66] The strike spread rapidly to include over 90 percent of the French Municipal Council's work force and thus effectively paralyzed the French Concession. This was the context in which a number of observers spoke of a crisis of authority in the Concession. From the point of view of the gangsters the strike did have a salutary effect on the local French officials. When Captain Fiori, in response to pressure from the Consular Body, launched his drive against gambling in September 1931, it was conducted in such a way as to minimize its impact on Green Gang interests.[67]

THE FRENCH AUTHORITIES MOVE AGAINST DU
YUESHENG, FEBRUARY–JULY 1932

The outbreak of conflict between Chinese and Japanese forces in the Shanghai area on January 28, 1932, brought the crisis in the French Concession to a head. Both sides tried to manipulate the security crisis to their own advantage: Du Yuesheng and the gangsters in a bid to preserve their power and influence; Wilden and those French officials associated with him in order to ease out Koechlin and Fiori and to curb Du Yuesheng's influence on the Concession. Immediately hostilities commenced between Chinese and Japanese forces, Vice Admiral Herr, commander of the French Far East Fleet and overall commander of French forces in Shanghai, took over all authority from the civil officials of the Concession and proscribed the opium and gambling rackets. At the same time Koechlin called out Du's gangsters ostensibly in support of the French forces in the defense of the Concession, and the streets were filled with over 1,000 of Du's "special agents" sporting tricolor armbands and carrying weapons supplied by the French police. Their purpose was to create such confusion as to effectively disrupt the French forces' security operations, and so compel the martial law authorities to rescind their proscriptions on the opium and gambling rackets. Herr, however, had apparently been forewarned of Du's tactics and he moved decisively against the gangsters and within a few days he had cleared them from the streets.[68]

Wilden simultaneously, in accordance with an earlier decision, announced the appointment of Meyrier and Fabre, respectively Consul General and Chief of Police in the Tianjin French Concession, as the new Consul General and Police Chief in Shanghai.[69] Koechlin, now under considerable pressure, was compelled to seek Du's resignation as a member of the Provisional Commission. Du tendered his resignation in a letter dated February 15, 1932, in which he cited, among other things, his financial and commercial commitments and his involvement with the Shanghai Martial Law Committee, which precluded his further membership of the Provisional Commission. Koechlin formally accepted Du's resignation at the next meeting of the Provisional Commission on February 29, 1932.[70]

A strange sequence of events now unfolded. Within a fortnight of the public acceptance of Du's resignation from the Provisional Commission, three leading members of the Concession died within a week of one another from what Meyrier described as "a sudden illness" (*une maladie foudrayante*): Du Pac de Marsouliès of "double pneumonia," ex-Consul General Koechlin of "smallpox" en route to France, and Colonel A. Marcaire, commander of French land forces in Shanghai, of "pneumonia."[71] Rumors circulated almost immediately that all three had been murdered by Du in revenge for the actions taken against his interests in the Concession, but no convincing evidence has been found to substantiate them.[72] Nevertheless, the circumstances of the deaths, the fact that they were of key French officials involved in the pact with the gangsters, that they all occurred in just over a week (March 11–19, 1932) and the lack of any adequate explanation as to the manner in which the alleged fatal diseases were contracted, are certainly suspicious.

Whatever the true nature of these deaths, they did usher in a five-month period (March to July 1932) of bitter conflict as Du Yuesheng deployed all his resources in an effort to preserve his position in the face of the determined efforts by Meyrier and Fabre to prize him out of the Concession. During this period protracted negotiations were held between Du and Meyrier for the removal of the Three Prosperities Company from the Concession. These negotiations were conducted in an extremely tense atmosphere. As Meyrier observed at the time, he and Fabre had to tread very carefully because Du's loss of face had made his organization even more dangerous.[73] During this period, in fact, Meyrier and Fabre were first offered bribes and then had their lives threatened. When these tactics failed to move the local French officials, Du used his connections with leading Chinese to have them intercede on his behalf with senior French officials and politicians. As a result Zheng Yuxiu (Soumay Tcheng) and Song Ailing (Madame H. H. Kung) went to Paris in mid-April 1932 to lobby French government officials and French politicians on Du's behalf, while Huang Huilan (Madame Wellington Koo) lobbied Wilden in Beiping.[74] Both attempts, however, were unsuccessful.

With the failure of these missions Du fell back on his last remaining (but most powerful) weapon—his control of organized labor in the Concession. He used his control of the FTU to orchestrate a strike in the French Tramways Company, and timed its outbreak for the week preceding Bastille Day (July 14, 1932) in order to maximize its impact on the French authorities.[75] This stratagem worked and with the outbreak of the strike on July 7, French troops and police were mobilized to patrol the main thoroughfares of the Concession.[76] After the strike had been in progress for four days, Meyrier made contact with Wu Tiecheng, the Mayor of Greater Shanghai, in order both to end the strike and seek an arrangement for the removal of Du's opium business from the Concession. An agreement was finally reached after further negotiations by which Du could run his narcotics operations from Nandao under the auspices of Wu's newly created opium monopoly in Greater Shanghai, and the French would assist in the transportation of his opium stocks out of the Concession. Once this agreement was reached Du terminated the strike. By November 1932, therefore, Meyrier could assure the British Consul General that the opium combine had been removed from French territory and that Du Yuesheng was no longer allowed to interfere in the Concession's affairs.[77]

THE REASSERTION OF FRENCH AUTHORITY IN THE CONCESSION 1932–1935

Meyrier's primary task during his three years as Consul General was the assertion of French consular authority in the Concession, which had been seriously eroded during the tenure of his predecessor Koechlin (December 1928–March 1932). In his inaugural speech to the Provisional Commission on March 14, 1932, Meyrier outlined his three priorities: the preservation of order and security in the Concession, the improvement of its administration and the enhancement of its prosperity.[78]

Police corruption, the legacy of Fiori, was the first item on the agenda of his program of administrative reform. With the very able assistance of Fabre he dismissed large numbers of corrupt officers from the force and implemented a wholesale reform of the police structure. Great care was taken in the selection of officers and the lines of responsibility within the police hierarchy were strengthened, so that by 1935 the Concession had a more disciplined and tightly controlled police system than at any time since the First World War.[79]

In the sphere of municipal administration Meyrier reasserted the primacy of the office of the Consul General over the Provisional Commission. He rarely attended the meetings of the commission and communicated with it through his Consul, Coiffard, who acted as its President. This restored the traditional relationship between the Consul General and the Municipal Council/Provisional Commission that had been undermined in the period 1929–32 when Du Yuesheng had transformed the Provisional Commission into his personal power base with Koechlin attending all its meetings in his capacity as President. Meyrier also restored key members of the Gentry-Councillor Clique to their former role as the main intermediaries between the French administration and the Chinese population. Meyrier had a long-standing relationship with this group and had worked very closely with them in the mid-1920s, first as Consul under Wilden and then as acting Consul General. This was particularly true of Wei Tingrong, for whom Meyrier had apparently a very high regard, and whom he used as a personal adviser on matters affecting the Chinese residents of the Concession. Wei's consistent opposition to Du Yuesheng further increased his standing with Meyrier.[80]

Besides implementing these administrative reforms, Meyrier prosecuted vigorous anti-opium and anti-gambling policies. In late September 1932, the French police played a prominent role in the seizure of a large consignment of opium valued at between Ch$250,000 and Ch$500,000.[81] Moreover, there was a marked increase in the number of arrests of drug traffickers and proprietors of opium divans. Almost ten times as many traffickers were arrested in 1932 as in 1931 (475 as opposed to merely 48), and almost five times as many opium divan proprietors (2,053 versus 465).[82] The crackdown continued throughout 1933 and 1934, when a total of 11,130 drug-related arrests were made. The arrest rate for drug-related offenses, however, decreased noticeably after Meyrier returned to France in January 1935. In 1935 the number of arrests totaled 3,234 and in 1936 they totaled a mere 788.[83] Meyrier also created a Gaming Squad (*Brigade des Jeux*) for the express purpose of eradicating all forms of Chinese gambling from the Concession. This squad made just over 1,700 arrests each year between 1934 and 1936.[84]

It was never part of Meyrier's purpose, however, to completely remove the influence of the Green Gang from the Concession. This would have been a major undertaking that was probably beyond the resources available to the French administration. Nor was it necessarily in the interests of the French authorities to do so. They still found the gangster bosses, including Du Yuesheng, a useful and necessary adjunct to their administrative resources; a point that was acknowledged explicitly by Meyrier. The aim of Meyrier's reforms, therefore, was to ensure that the gangster bosses never again exercised undue influence over the French administration, and to once again make of them a "willing tool" in the hands of the French authorities. Meyrier had expressed this view during the crisis of early 1932 in his dispatch to the Minister of Foreign Affairs when he observed that although the French authorities could no longer depend on Du Yuesheng, nevertheless, they needed to keep on good terms with him.[85] This pragmatic approach was reinforced by the enormous expansion of Du's power and influence throughout Shanghai in the years after 1932, when he became an integral part of the Guomindang state system.

The influence of the Green Gang bosses, therefore, was still apparent in the Concession after 1932. Zhang Xiaolin, for example, not only retained his membership in the Provisional Commission but was honored by the French administration on his sixtieth birthday in June 1936.[86] The CRA continued to "elect" the Chinese members of the Provisional Commission, three of whom came from its own ranks, as well as the special advisers to the commission's various committees, who included such prominent Green Gang members as Shang Mujiang and Jin Tingsun. Du Yuesheng's control of the CRA, in fact, was strengthened after the association's 1933 election, which abolished the system of co-chairmen and replaced it with one chairman (Du) and two vice-chairmen. The new CRA Executive Committee elected in 1933 also contained at least four members of Du's recently established Endurance Club.[87] Du, indeed, was one of the official guests at the farewell dinner for Meyrier on his return to France in January 1935.[88]

Throughout the 1930s Du Yuesheng continued to mediate disputes in the Concession. A good example was his role in negotiating a settlement of the rickshaw registration dispute of July–August 1935. In an attempt to limit the number of rickshaws operating in the Concession, the French administration decided on a policy of compulsory registration on the lines of a similar system that had been established in the International Settlement by the SMC.[89] The rickshaw owners, not surprisingly, strongly objected to the registration process and they launched a business strike in late July, and encouraged their coolies to take strike action. At the same time, representatives of the Rickshaw Owners' Association (*Renlicheye Gonghui*) approached Du Yuesheng to act on their behalf in discussions with the French authorities. In early August, therefore, Du held a number of meetings with Baudez, the acting Consul General, together with the Chinese authorities of the Shanghai city government and the Bureau of Social Affairs. The latter had become involved in the dispute after an incident between French police and striking rickshaw coolies at the Pont Ste. Catherine on August 6. In consultation with representatives of the Shanghai city government, the Bureau of Social Affairs and the Rickshaw Owners Association, Du worked out a compromise agreement, involving both the waiving of the registration fee imposed by the French administration and the postponement of the registration process for a period of two months, which became the basis for the final settlement.[90]

Although Du's role in this dispute appeared to be similar to the one he had played during the French Tramways disputes of the late 1920s and early 1930s, its basis, in fact, was quite different. Then he represented the French capitalists and the French administration; in the mid-1930s, on the other hand, he represented Chinese capitalists and conducted his negotiations in close consultation with the Chinese authorities and not the French administration. Du's mediation certainly remained important for the French authorities, but it now derived its significance from his influential position in the Guomindang political system both nationally and locally, and was not dependent on his relationship with the French.

6 Instability and Crisis

The relationship between the French Concession Green Gang bosses and the new Guomindang regime in Shanghai as it evolved over the period 1927–31 was a highly complex one. Participation in the anti-Communist coup of April 1927 was a necessary precondition, but not of itself a sufficient one, for ensuring the stability of that relationship. Other factors that were of equal importance included the politics of opium, the political instability of the regime itself, and, as we have seen, the gang bosses' relations with the French Concession authorities. At the same time, the influence within Shanghai society of the French Concession Green Gang continued to grow. This was largely due to the activities of Du Yuesheng who emerged clearly as the senior member of the group, as demonstrated by his mediation of relations between the French and Chinese authorities.

THE ROLE OF OPIUM IN GUOMINDANG—GREEN GANG RELATIONS, 1927–1931

Opium was of fundamental importance in the new relationship of the Green Gang bosses with the Guomindang regime, just as it had been in their relations with the earlier warlord regimes. The security of their opium interests, as noted in chapter 4, was a prime consideration for the three Green Gang bosses in their dealings with both the Communist and Guomindang representatives in Shanghai in February–April 1927. Despite the understanding reached with Jiang Jieshi in early 1927, however, the politics of opium during these years remained very complicated, with periods of accommodation between the gangster bosses and the Guomindang regime alternating with periods of covert hostility. This reflected the fact that the interests of Du Yuesheng and his two colleagues and those of the Nationalist government frequently diverged. The former sought the preservation and even enhancement of the existing contraband system for personal enrichment, while the latter sought to regulate the traffic as a source of government revenue.

It was the poverty of its fiscal resources that forced the Nanjing government to consider the possibility of an official opium monopoly, and the Finance Minister Song Ziwen (T. V. Soong) attempted to create such a monopoly on several occasions. All attempts, however, had to take account of the entrenched interests of the Green Gang. In mid-1927 Jiang Jieshi's urgent need for funds to finance the final phase of the Northern Expedition led the Nanjing government to consider the creation of an opium monopoly. In order to minimize both public disquiet and the concerns of the foreign powers who were parties to the Hague Convention of 1912, the monopoly was instituted under the guise of prohibition. According to the regulations the consumption of opium was to be phased out over a period of three years during which time a licensing system was to be instituted. In late June, therefore, a National Opium Suppression Bureau (*Guomin Jinyan Ju*—NOSB) was established under the jurisdiction of the Ministry of Finance, and the sale of licensed opium in Jiangsu and Zhejiang was farmed out to a private company, the Xin Yuan Company, under the supervision of the NOSB.[1]

The three French Concession Green Gang bosses were among the original promoters of this company, together with some of the leading Chaozhou opium merchants. Not long after the Xin Yuan Company was established, however, the Green Gang bosses resigned because they could make larger profits from their own Three Prosperities Company in the French Concession free from the supervision of agencies of the Nanjing government. The withdrawal of the gangster bosses was followed by a retail war between the Three Prosperities Company and the official monopolist Xin Yuan Company, in which the latter established its own distribution network in the French Concession to compete with that of the Green Gang bosses. As this "war" progressed into late 1927, however, the advantage shifted increasingly in favor of the gangster bosses, who were able to use their connections with the Guangxi Clique, as well as their political connections with the French authorities, to bring into Shanghai large amounts of opium in defiance of the government monopoly. In November 1927, for example, Bai Chongxi, one of the leaders of the Guangxi Clique, intervened in favor of the Green Gang bosses in a dispute between the Three Prosperities Company and the Xin Yuan Company over a large consignment of Persian opium.[2]

After Jiang Jieshi's resignation in mid-August 1927, Du Yuesheng reached an agreement on the opium issue with the "September government," a coalition of the former Wuhan and Nanjing regimes, which canceled the license of the Xin Yuan Company and gave its tax farm in the Jiangnan region to the Zi Xin Company, a subsidiary of the Three Prosperities Company.[3] In the new system the NOSB was replaced by the Jiangsu Opium Suppression Bureau (*Jiangsu Sheng Jinyan Ju*) as the official regulatory body, and licensed opium shops were established in Chinese Shanghai during the first half of 1928 that received their supplies from the Zi Xin Company.[4]

In order to give this licensing system an established basis in law, the National government drafted an Anti-Opium Law in March 1928, and it also sought to win the support of the foreign powers for a licensed monopoly system. As noted in chapter 5, this latter attempt failed, and as a consequence the semi-official licensing system was terminated in August 1928 with the abolition of the Jiangsu Opium Suppression Bureau. The interests of the Green Gang had been well served by this system of semi-official monopoly, which had enabled them to extend significantly their narcotics operations.[5]

The tacit, if occasionally tense, accommodation between the Nanjing government and the French Concession Green Gang bosses was also prone to scandal, as shown by the Jiang'an Affair in late 1928.[6] On the night of November 21, 1928, a violent dispute occurred between a party of troops from the Wusong-Shanghai Garrison Command and a police detachment from the Municipality of Greater Shanghai over the unloading of 20,000 ounces of opium from the China Merchants' Steam Navigation Company's (CMSN) steamer, the S. S. Jiang'an, which was anchored at the CMSN wharf on the Nandao bund next to the French Concession.[7]

The true nature of this affair still remains unclear, although it would appear to have been related to the tensions between Jiang Jieshi and the Guangxi Clique regarding control of the proceeds from the opium traffic. The consignment, apparently, had been sent by Song Ziwen from Nanjing to Xiong Shihui, the Wusong-Shanghai Garrison Commander, for distribution. Xiong, in conjunction with Dai Fushi (the Shanghai Commissioner of Police), had established retail outlets for opium throughout Chinese Shanghai. Zhang Dingfan, the Mayor of Chinese Shanghai and a senior member of the Guangxi Clique, who had been informed about the dispatch of this consignment by Feng Yuxiang, decided to take the opportunity presented by the incident to settle accounts with his political rival, Xiong Shihui. Once his police had seized the consignment he sent a telegram to the Nanjing government in which he accused Xiong and Dai of having violated the government's anti-opium regulations, and he made sure that the Shanghai newspapers gave the affair extensive coverage.[8] Zhang's tactics of ensuring maximum publicity for the affair acutely embarrassed the Nanjing government.[9] Jiang Jieshi was furious.[10] Not only did the scandal come very close to him personally, but it also occurred at an extremely inconvenient time for his government which had just hosted a national conference on opium suppression (November 1–10) and passed a new Opium Suppression Act (November 24).[11] The government was forced to respond, and a special commission, headed by Zhang Zhijiang, Chairman of the National Opium Suppression Committee and a close supporter of Jiang, was set up to investigate the matter.[12] The political implications of the affair, however, were so potentially damaging for the government that the committee's report merely condemned a few scapegoats, including Dai Fushi, but ignored the wider ramifications of the issue. This provoked the resignation of Mayor Zhang and, with this act, political interest in the affair subsided.[13]

If this opium scandal was an embarrassment for Jiang Jieshi, it was also a serious matter for the Green Gang bosses. Their concern was two-fold. In the first place, the operations of the Three Prosperities Company at this time depended on close cooperation with both the Garrison Command and the Municipal Government of Chinese Shanghai. Any overt conflict between them, as occurred in the Jiang'an Affair, could involve serious problems for the company's operations.[14] Second, the affair generated a great deal of unwelcome publicity for the gangster bosses, with reports in the Shanghai press of their involvement in the distribution of the disputed opium consignment.[15] They were now seized with the fear that any genuine inquiry into the current scandal would jeopardize their relations with key political and military figures in both Shanghai and Nanjing, on whose cooperation the success of the traffic depended. The gang bosses, therefore, attempted to divert attention from their involvement by themselves joining in the chorus of public condemnation of the scandal and in the calls for the punishment of those involved.[16] By early 1929, however, the scandal had blown over, and the Three Prosperities Company resumed its regular operations.

The attempts by the Nanjing government to regulate the opium traffic in the late 1920s and early 1930s involved the development of a rather complex relationship between Song Ziwen, the Minister of Finance, and Du Yuesheng, acting on behalf of the Green Gang opium consortium, which oscillated between periods of serious tension and guarded cooperation. In February 1928, for example, Song's untiring search for revenues led him to attempt to extort a "loan" of Ch$1 million from the Zi Xin Company on pain of closure of the operations of the Three Prosperities Company. Du Yuesheng, however, refused to pay on the grounds that the government "ceaselessly" demanded loans but failed to provide adequate protection for the company's opium operations. He then called Song's bluff by demanding that the monopoly under which the Zi Xin Company operated be wound up, together with the refund of monies already paid by the gangsters to the government.[17]

On the other hand one example of the mutual interest of the government and the Green Gang bosses being served by a degree of cooperation was the opium consignment involved in the Jiang'an Affair of late 1928. Another was the "arrangement" that Song entered into with Du and Xiong Shihui in May 1930 for the importation of a large consignment of Persian opium into Shanghai valued at about Ch$14 million.[18]

The most serious confrontation between Song Ziwen and Du Yuesheng occurred in the context of a further proposal for a government opium monopoly in February 1931 by Dr. Wu Liande, Head of the government's National Quarantine Service. Wu estimated that such a monopoly would net the Nanjing government annually between Ch$50 million and Ch$100 million.[19] The proposal had the support of Liu Ruiheng, the Chairman of the National Opium Suppression Committee, and Frederick Maze, the Inspector General of the Chinese Maritime Customs. It was reported also that the scheme, in fact, had been suggested to Chinese officials by Dr. J. Rajchman, the League of Nations adviser to the National government, when he proposed that China should use a government opium monopoly as security for the raising of foreign loans.[20] Wu's proposal gained strong political support when Jiang Jieshi delivered a speech in May to the National People's Convention in which he announced the government's intention to adopt a "scientific method" to deal with the opium problem.[21]

The French Concession Green Gang bosses strongly opposed, at first, the creation of such a monopoly, which they considered would adversely affect the existing operations of their Three Prosperities Company.[22] At the end of April, however, Jiang Jieshi summoned Du Yuesheng and his two colleagues to a conference in Nanjing at which a deal was done between Du and Jiang. In return for Du's assistance in his anti-Communist drive, Jiang agreed that Du could select all the officials involved in the proposed opium monopoly. Du Yuesheng, in other words, would have effective control over the system.[23] Once this agreement had been concluded opium suppression bureaus were established in six provinces, including Jiangsu and Zhejiang.

Within a month, however, the arrangement with the gangsters broke down in somewhat obscure circumstances involving the activities of Song Ziwen. Song had set up his own organization in Shanghai, including a force of 200 special police, which he used to bring pressure to bear on the Three Prosperities Company. In early July, for example, Song directed the Shanghai Opium Suppression Bureau (*Shanghai Shi Jinyan Ju*) to confiscate a large amount of opium valued at Ch$1 million from an unnamed concern, presumably either the Three Prosperities Company itself or one of its affiliates, on the pretext that it had failed to pay stamp duty on the merchandise.[24] In the event, the opium suppression bureaus were abolished abruptly in mid-July, and many informed observers believed that this was because of the renewed opposition of the Green Gang bosses, notably Du Yuesheng, to the involvement of the Ministry of Finance in the opium traffic.[25]

A fortnight later, July 23, 1931, an unsuccessful attempt was made to assassinate Song Ziwen at Shanghai's North Station on his arrival from Nanjing. Although the circumstances of this incident are obscure, a number of informed observers at the time, including the United States Consul General in Shanghai, believed that the Green Gang bosses were behind the attempt and that it related to their conflict with Song over the proposed opium monopoly.[26] In this way another attempt by the Nanjing government to create an official opium monopoly came to naught, and again the opposition of the Green Gang bosses played a considerable role in this outcome.

The failure of the Nanjing government to establish effective control over the opium traffic in this period left Du Yuesheng free to expand his narcotics operations through arrangements with independent regional militarists. In 1928, for example, Liu Xiang, the Sichuan warlord, began to set up a number of morphine factories around both Chongqing and Wanxian. By late 1930 there were twenty such factories and their number had increased to twenty-eight by 1932. Not long after the first of these factories was established Du entered into an agreement with Liu Xiang by which Du purchased the partially refined product of these morphine factories and undertook the final refining process in Shanghai. The deal was arranged through the good offices of Fan Shaozeng, a subordinate of Liu Xiang and one of the principals involved with the management of the Sichuan morphine factories. Fan was also a leader of the Paoge (a Sichuan secret society affiliated to the Gelaohui), and he not only used his secret society connections to develop a relationship with Du Yuesheng, but also joined the Green Gang by becoming a follower of Zhang Renkui.

A subsidiary of the Three Prosperities Company, the Xin Ji Company, was set up in Chongqing under the management of two of Du's senior associates in the narcotics business, Chen Kunyuan, the "morphine King" (*mafei da wang*), and Ye Qinghe, the "opium King" (*yapian da wang*). This company bought an average of Ch$250,000 worth of morphine a month in Chongqing, which it sent on to Shanghai for further refining. By 1933 Du's Green Gang group controlled all the Sichuan morphine traffic that was transported down the Yangzi River. This morphine was refined in a number of narcotics plants in Shanghai controlled by Du's organization, one of which was located in the Du Family Temple, Gaoqiao, Pudong, which Du had built in 1931 to honor his ancestors.[27]

THE GREEN GANG BOSSES AND GUOMINDANG POLITICS, 1928–1931

The "Sichuan connection" reflected the second factor that conditioned the relationship between the Green Gang bosses and the Nationalist government in this period. The extreme political instability of the regime's ruling coalitions compelled the gang bosses to maintain relations with a broad spectrum of factional groups (including opponents as well as supporters of the regime).

Despite his control of the greater part of the regime's military resources, Jiang Jieshi had not yet effectively consolidated his political power in these early years. Consequently he was compelled to resign temporarily from his offices on two separate occasions, in August 1927 and again in December 1931, for lack of the political strength to withstand a coalition of other Guomindang factions. If Jiang could not rule in his own right without an accommodation with the senior civilian leadership of the party, however, neither could these leaders govern effectively without Jiang. Both attempts at civilian rule, Wang Jingwei's attempt to govern in coalition with the Guangxi Clique in the second half of 1927 and Sun Ke's brief government of December 1931—January 1932, ended in failure.

More successful was the coalition forged between Jiang Jieshi and Hu Hanmin's Guangdong Clique in 1928, which lasted until early 1931. This coalition, however, continued to face serious challenges from the other military and political factions, notably the conflict with the Guangxi Clique in April 1929, and the alliance between Feng Yuxiang, Yan Xishan and Wang Jingwei's Reorganizationist faction which led to open warfare with the Nanjing government in 1930. Eventually the Jiang-Hu coalition broke down with Jiang's arrest of Hu in February 1931 over Hu's opposition to Jiang's proposed constitution for the Republic of China. This incident initiated a protracted political crisis for the regime and involved the creation of a separate Guomindang government in Canton in May 1931, which repudiated Nanjing's authority.

The ability of the three Green Gang bosses to deal with a wide range of political factions in this period derived from the fact, as made clear in chapter 5, that they enjoyed an established, independent power base within the French Concession. This gave them a certain freedom of action in the world of Chinese politics, which enabled them to work with a variety of political leaders without being completely identified with any one of them. Du Yuesheng, for example, developed close and extensive ties with the Guangxi Clique in the wake of the coup of April 1927. This reflected the fact that it was Bai Chongxi's forces, the Eastern Route Army, which carried out the anti-Communist coup in Shanghai, and that these forces remained an important element in the politico-military situation in

the Shanghai region until early 1928. It was not surprising, therefore, that Du and the Guangxi Clique cooperated closely in the narcotics traffic in Shanghai at this time. These links were strengthened
further by the cooperation between Du and the clique in matters
of labor control. The Committee for the Unification of Shanghai
Trade Union Organizations (UUC), with which Du Yuesheng was
closely involved throughout 1927,[28] was also the instrument of
Bai Chongxi and the Guangxi Clique, with Bai's headquarters providing many of its officials and most of its finances.[29]

It was in this context, therefore, that Li Zongren, as well as Bai
Chongxi, met and dealt with Du Yuesheng and Huang Jinrong, despite his professed distaste in doing so.[30] The relationship between
the leaders of the Guangxi Clique and Du Yuesheng, in fact, proved
to be an enduring one. In early 1929, for example, prior to the
Guangxi revolt, the Nanjing government approached Du Yuesheng
and requested him to prevent Li Zongren, who was visiting Shanghai at the time, from leaving the city and joining the other Guangxi
leaders. Du, however, refused on the grounds that he could not get
involved in political differences between rival cliques at the expense
of personal friendships.[31] Over two years later, when the Guangxi
leaders came to Shanghai to attend the peace conference in late
1931, Du sent his private motor-launch to meet their steamer off
Wusong, and placed them under his personal protection during their
stay in Shanghai.[32]

The French Concession Green Gang bosses also maintained relations with Wang Jingwei during this period. In 1930, for example,
Du Yuesheng kept in touch with Wang Jingwei's Reorganizationist
faction in Beiping through Wang's right-hand man, Chen Gongbo.
Indeed, it would appear that he was not only privy to, but also directly involved with, some of the Reorganizationists' moves against
Jiang Jieshi.[33] Over a year later, during the Shanghai Peace Conference (October 27–November 7, 1931), which attempted to work out
a modus vivendi between the Nanjing and Canton governments,
one of Du Yuesheng's followers, Deng Zuyu, acted as a liaison between the French Concession Green Gang bosses and the delegation
from the Canton government.[34] At the same time, Huang Jinrong,
for his part, extended his personal protection to Wang Jingwei when
the latter held his faction's Fourth National Congress in Shanghai in
December 1931. Huang also provided the location, his recently acquired Great World Amusement Center (*Da Shijie Yule Zhongxin*),

for the congress.[35] The Green Gang bosses, in fact, provided one channel of communication between the different political factions during the negotiations to work out an acceptable compromise government in October–December 1931.

An important dimension of the Green Gang bosses' relations with Guomindang factional leaders was their ability to provide assistance in private matters as well as in public affairs. This was particularly the case with Du Yuesheng who, even more than his two colleagues, made himself indispensable to a wide range of members of the new Guomindang power elite in the years after 1927, by helping them resolve potentially embarrassing scandals in their private lives. When Jiang Jieshi, for example, divorced his second wife, Chen Jieru, in order to marry Song Meiling in the autumn of 1927, Du Yuesheng was one of those who helped mediate the settlement that provided Chen with a financial allowance and ensured her departure for the United States.[36] According to an SMP report, Du was particularly adept at defusing potential sexual scandals among the elite, and it mentioned specifically Sun Ke in this regard.[37] By such means Du not only succeeded in ingratiating himself with powerful individuals in the regime, but also came to know a great deal of the intimate details of their private lives, a fact that increased significantly his influence with them.

DU YUESHENG BECOMES A SHANGHAI "NOTABLE": THE DEDICATION OF THE DU FAMILY TEMPLE, JUNE 1931

As their diverse relations with the Guomindang and French authorities demonstrate, the French Concession Green Gang bosses had consolidated their position as the major Green Gang group operating in Shanghai after 1927. Of the three bosses, it was clear that Du Yuesheng was the dominant figure. Only forty-two years of age in 1931, Du was not only the key member of the group but was also the most influential Green Gang leader in Shanghai.

With the increase in his power and influence after 1927, Du sought to legitimize his position in Shanghai society. The means he chose were conventional but effective: involvement with philanthropic works and patronage of scholars to gain an entrée into Chinese "high culture." Philanthropy was an obvious choice. Charitable works provided a community-sanctioned means of expressing an important self-image of the secret society member: that of the open-handed "hero" who protected the weak and the powerless and who, in the popular phrase, "scattered gold as if it were dirt" both among his followers and the poor. Involvement in philanthropic activities was also one practical way in which, traditionally, the Confucian gentleman demonstrated his responsibility to his community, a role to which Du Yuesheng aspired. In Shanghai, moreover, Chinese merchants had been involved with charitable activities in a systematic way since the time of the 1911 Revolution, and such involvement was an important element in the development of a culture of civic responsibility among them.[38] Du's interest in philanthropy, therefore, was one further means by which he strengthened his network of relations with the Chinese merchant community.

In the late 1920s and early 1930s Du Yuesheng became a major contributor to schools, hospitals and poor relief. In 1930 he established the Zhengshi Middle School, which provided free education for the children of poor families, at a cost of Ch$600,000 and with Chen Qun as its first principal.[39] Later, Du also established a primary school in Gaoqiao as part of his efforts to transform his native place into a "model" district. He also took an interest in public health and was president of two public hospitals, the Shanghai Emergency Hospital and the Ren Ji Hospital in Ningbo. The government later rewarded Du for his interest in public health by appointing him Deputy Chairman of the Chinese Red Cross Association (*Zhongguo Hongshizi Hui*).[40]

Those in need also benefited from Du's largesse. He financed, for example, an orphanage and an old people's home, and he also provided out of his own pocket a monthly living allowance for over 200 very poor households in Shanghai.[41] Another area of Du's philanthropic activities concerned the victims of natural and manmade disasters. He had first become involved with this kind of relief in the 1920s, when he helped raise financial assistance for flood victims in Zhejiang in 1922 and provided relief to refugees from the conflict between Lu Yongxiang and Qi Xieyuan in 1924.[42] By the early 1930s, involvement with disaster relief had become a regular part of his activities, and he played a particularly important role, together with Yu Xiaqing, Wen Lanting, Wang Yiting, and other Shanghai capitalists, in raising funds for the relief of the victims of the disastrous Yangzi floods of July and August 1931.[43] Du, in fact, had succeeded in establishing for himself a reputation for "good works" in the eyes of the Shanghai public. He was frequently referred to as "big philanthropist Du Yuesheng" (*dashanshi Du Yuesheng*), and, in 1931, John Powell's influential *Who's Who in China* could describe him without any sense of irony as a "liberal contributor towards philanthropy and education."[44]

In fashioning this public image Du received important assistance from a number of prominent Chinese scholars whose straitened financial circumstances caused them to accept his financial support. A key figure in this group was Yang Du (1875–1931). Yang had been a prominent member of Chinese intellectual and political circles in the first two decades of the twentieth century, closely associated with such figures as Kang Youwei, Liang Qichao and Yuan Shikai. After the failure of Yuan Shikai's imperial aspirations in 1916, with whose promotion Yang had been intimately involved, his political career entered a steep decline. During the 1920s he eked out a precarious living from selling his calligraphy and paintings. At this time he also made contact with the new revolutionary parties, joining the GMD in 1926 and, two years later in 1928, being secretly recruited by Zhou Enlai into the underground CCP. In the autumn of 1928, only months after he had joined the CCP, Lu Chongpeng introduced him to Du Yuesheng who appointed Yang as his secretary on a monthly salary of Ch$500, a post he held until his death from tuberculosis in September 1931.[45]

Deploying the full range of his scholarly and literary skills, Yang Du set about creating a public persona for Du Yuesheng as a paragon of traditional virtue, who combined the values of both the "swordsman/knight" and the Confucian "gentleman." In this endeavor Yang was joined by Zhang Binglin (1868–1936), the prominent scholar and famous revolutionary of 1911, who also held discussions with Du on the themes contained in the popular novels *Romance of the Three Kingdoms* and *Water Margin*.[46] The major focus of the exercise was the dedication ceremonies for Du Yuesheng's family temple, the *Du Jiasi*, in Gaoqiao on June 9–10, 1931. Du commenced building the temple complex in 1930, which covered about eight mou of land and contained a modern-style two-story memorial hall/library and a private academy, in addition to the traditional single-story family temple. Yang Du was appointed secretary of the committee that organized the dedication ceremonies, which included such leading Shanghai capitalists as Yu Xiaqing, Wang Xiaolai and Yuan Ludeng, as well as Du's two colleagues, Huang Jinrong and Zhang Xiaolin.

In his capacity as secretary, Yang penned the formal eulogy on the completion of the temple in May 1931, in which he adumbrated the theme for the celebrations that the establishment of a temple to Du's ancestors clearly demonstrated Du's embodiment of the virtues of both the swordsman/knight and the Confucian gentleman. In the eulogy Yang praised Du, who was "of an old and renowned clan," for engaging in an important and time-honored ritual, and placed his temple in direct descent from the famous clan temples and mausoleums of the past. Yang observed that Du not only had "the nature of a knight-errant" (*haoxia*) as revealed by his generosity, concern for the less fortunate and integrity ("keeps all his promises"), but also revealed by his actions a commitment to the values of "a true [Confucian] gentleman" (*junzi*), in that he demonstrated virtue (*de*) without conceit, merit (*gong*) without boastfulness, modesty and self-discipline (*qianhuaiziyi*).[47]

Yang developed this theme further in his commemorative essay on the temple written a few weeks later where he described Du Yuesheng as "the great knight of the modern age" (*jinshi daxia*) and placed him in the tradition of the wandering knights (*youxia*) of the Warring States period. Yang observed of Du:

> His conduct and sense of justice are similar to the character of the wandering knights of ancient times. He is generous and honorable, and does not make promises lightly, and is a person who can be trusted in times of trouble. He places no importance on possessions and money, but, instead, emphasizes the importance of friendship ... Those who request help at his gate immediately receive a reply, and for this he is renowned both north and south of the Yangzi.... All admire him for his style.[48]

For Yang, however, Du was more than just a latter-day "wandering knight," he was also a representative of the Confucian ideal of the true man (*renren*—"a person of humanity") who by his actions demonstrates benevolence and compassion. By building his family temple Du demonstrated his filial piety (*xiao*), which, according to Yang, is the basis of humanity (*ren*), which is, in turn, "the first principle" of Confucianism.[49] Yang concluded his essay by observing that Du, like the famous knights of the Warring States period, united in his person the qualities of the warrior (*xia*) and the Confucian scholar (*ru*).

In his own commemorative essay, Zhang Binglin reinforced Yang's identification of Du with key aspects of China's classical culture. He created an idealized and honorable genealogy for Du

Yuesheng, tracing the clan's origins back to the legendary emperor Yao and to the Xia Dynasty, and linking it with that of the royal family of the Han Dynasty. Zhang also provided a "golden age" for the Du clan which, according to him, extended from the Han to the Tang dynasties during which no less than eight ancestors held the senior bureaucratic position of imperial secretary. After this period there was an inevitable decline into obscurity and poverty, which came to an end with the emergence of Du Yuesheng himself, who was now in the process of reviving the clan's fortunes.[50]

By these means Yang Du and Zhang Binglin sought to legitimate the position Du Yuesheng enjoyed in contemporary Shanghai society by giving him the attributes of an romanticized cultural hero with elements drawn from both the Chinese popular and classical traditions. By rendering his public personality in such idealized—not to say mythical—terms, they obviated the need to explain the incongruities in both his background and the real sources of his power. This process of idealization did not merely provide a justification of Du's present power, but also sought to give it the appearance of being part of the natural order of things. It might be observed here that intellectuals such as Yang Du and Zhang Binglin, in order themselves to be able to accept the power of someone like Du Yuesheng, both psychologically and intellectually, needed to "understand" it by placing it fully within the discourse of Chinese "high" culture. This was as important as Du Yuesheng's own desire to obtain that culture's sanction for the power he exercised.

The dedication ceremonies, themselves, had a stylized quality to them and were literally a dramatization of the power and influence of Du Yuesheng. For two days Shanghai was transformed into a stage for the enactment of a ritualized drama whose plot was the celebration of the social triumph of a major gangster. The ceremony began with a huge parade, which included Green Gang members, government officials, merchants, trade unionists, police, soldiers and boy scouts, and which wended its way from Du's home in the Rue Wagner through the French Concession to the Quai de France (the French Bund). Members of both the French Concession Police and the SMP lined the route of the procession, and in the vanguard were honor guards carrying the congratulatory scrolls from leading business and political figures. There were scrolls from senior members of the National government, including Jiang Jieshi, Hu Hanmin, Kong Xiangxi (H. H. Kung) and Song Ziwen, as well as from Mayor

Zhang Qun, other members of the Shanghai city government and the Shanghai GMD Branch. Leading individuals and institutions in the French Concession also had their congratulatory scrolls carried in the procession, including those from Koechlin, Fiori, Verdier, members of the Gentry-Councillor Clique, the French members of the Provisional Commission, the Association of Chinese Officers of the French Concession Police, the management and senior staff of the French Tramways Company, and the members of the French Tramways Union. There were also congratulatory scrolls from leading figures of the former warlord regimes including Duan Qirui, Cao Kun, Wu Peifu, Zhang Zongchang, and Xu Shichang.

Du had organized special launches, flying pennants with the character for his name inscribed on them, that plied back and forth between Shanghai and Pudong carrying thousands of guests over the two-day period. He also provided free theatrical performances by leading Beijing Opera stars (including Mei Lanfang, Ma Lianliang and Cheng Yanqiu), who had been brought to Shanghai specially for the occasion.[51] For the duration of the festivities, the Shanghai Post Office set up a temporary post office in Gaoqiao that issued a special postmark for cards and letters "to commemorate the dedication ceremonies of the Du Family Temple." In the course of the celebrations Du received innumerable gifts and he himself personally distributed over Ch$70,000 to his followers and servants.[52]

The success of the dedication ceremonies for his family temple represented a public acknowledgment of Du Yuesheng's newly acquired status in Shanghai society. It was a concrete expression of the fact that he was now one of the central figures whose public careers helped define the nature of that society. At the same time, Du's relations with the Guomindang were about to undergo a profound change that would not only enhance his position in Shanghai, but also provide the basis for a national role in the regime itself. This development was precipitated by the serious political and foreign policy crises that confronted the regime at the end of 1931 and the beginning of 1932.

THE CRISIS OF 1932: THE GUOMINDANG AND THE SHANGHAI ELITE

Nineteen thirty-two was a turning point in the relations between the French Concession Green Gang organization led by Du Yuesheng and the Nanjing government. During the first half of that year both the Guomindang regime and Du Yuesheng's organization faced critical challenges to their respective positions. In surmounting these separate challenges they both discovered a new need for each other, which provided the basis for a new accommodation between the regime and Du Yuesheng's French Concession Green Gang group. In the course of the year the government was reconstituted on a broader and more integrated basis, and one which provided a definite role for the leading Shanghai capitalists. At the same time, Du Yuesheng lost his independent power base within the French Concession and was forced, therefore, to seek an accommodation with the Nanjing authorities. In this endeavor he was successful and, as a result, he and his Green Gang group became an integral part of the new Guomindang power structure in Shanghai.

In the winter of 1931–32 the combination of a serious foreign policy crisis and a protracted domestic political crisis produced a severe regime crisis for the Nanjing government. The house arrest of Hu Hanmin by Jiang Jieshi, as mentioned earlier, initiated a major political crisis in the course of which calls were made for Jiang's impeachment and a separate government was set up in Canton. The Japanese invasion of Manchuria, following the Mukden Incident of September 18, 1931, forced the Guomindang politicians to seek a solution to the domestic political crisis in order to provide an effective response to the Japanese action. After prolonged negotiations and the convening of a peace conference in Shanghai, a compromise was reached by which Jiang resigned his posts and a new government was formed under Sun Ke in December 1931. This government was not long-lived. It lacked any real authority and it did not have the support of either Jiang Jieshi or the Shanghai financiers. It finally collapsed in the face of renewed Japanese aggression, when Japanese forces invaded Shanghai on January 28, 1932. This further crisis led to the formation of another government in which Wang Jingwei and Jiang Jieshi played key roles as President of the Executive Yuan and Chairman of the Military Affairs Commission respectively.

In the following months the Nanjing government's confused response to the crisis provoked by Japan, coming on top of the prolonged political crisis of the previous year, eroded its authority and undermined its legitimacy in the eyes of the Chinese public. The decline in the government's stocks was only compounded by the removal of the capital from Nanjing to Luoyang on February 3, and by the growing popular belief that the withdrawal of Cai Tingkai's Nineteenth Route Army from the Wusong-Shanghai area on March 2–3, 1932, was due to inadequate support from the Nationalist government.[53] In early March the American Consul General in Nanjing reported on the general disillusionment felt by the Chinese elite toward the Guomindang regime. He noted the prevalence of the belief that Jiang Jieshi, his "military regime" and the Guomindang itself were all "finished" and that certain responsible Chinese advocated a League of Nations mandate for China.[54] It was against this background of profound public disillusionment with the regime that Jiang Jieshi, himself, remarked in midyear that the "Chinese revolution has failed."[55]

In Shanghai the Japanese invasion led to the temporary suspension of regular administrative authority in the Chinese City.[56] After their occupation of Zhabei the Japanese military proceeded to set up a puppet government to administer the area. This was the so-called Shanghai Northern District Citizens' Municipal Maintenance Association (*Shanghai Beishi Renmin Difang Weichihui*), which was run by local Zhabei gangsters, such as Hu Lifu and Chang Yuqing, who belonged to Gu Zhuxuan's Green Gang group.[57] Indeed, the Shanghai Municipal Police firmly believed that Gu and his brother, Gu Songmao, were behind the puppet government and financed the venture. This government, in fact, was nothing more than a glorified extortion agency whose main administrative function was to run gambling houses, opium divans and brothels.[58] In early May, discussions were held between these gangsters and officers of the Japanese consulate in Shanghai about the possibility of creating a separate Japanese Concession in Shanghai that would include the districts of Zhabei, Jiangwan, Wusong, Baoshan and Liuhe.[59] These discussions were suspended, however, following the implementation of the ceasefire agreement on May 5.

The administrative vacuum created by the temporary erosion of government authority in Shanghai was filled on an ad hoc basis by the elite of the Shanghai bourgeoisie. On January 31, members of this elite organized the Shanghai Citizens' Maintenance Association (*Shanghai Shimin Difang Weichihui*—SCMA), which undertook a comprehensive range of administrative, financial and troop support functions throughout the period of conflict in Shanghai.[60] It provided material support for Chinese forces at the front and relief for refugees from the war zone, together with any other measures that were necessary to ensure local order. At the same time, it maintained as many of the essential economic activities of Chinese Shanghai as was possible in the crisis, through its regulation of the Chinese financial markets and of Chinese commercial and industrial operations. Under its auspices, for example, the Shanghai Bankers' Association (*Shanghai Yinhangye Tongye Gonghui*) set up a Joint Reserve Board (*Yinhang Lianhe Junbei Weiyuanhui*) on March 15, 1932, to counter the financial panic then prevailing in Shanghai by guaranteeing the deposits of the Chinese commercial banks, and so provide some semblance of financial stability.[61]

The SCMA had a total membership of ninety-four, drawn from the leading Chinese financiers, industrialists and businessmen in Shanghai, and its operations were in the hands of a Chairman (Shi Liangcai), and two Deputy Chairmen, who were assisted by a fifteen-member Executive Committee.[62] It was organized into five sections dealing with troop support, refugee relief, economics, international relations and general affairs; and it also organized, separately, ten committees covering such issues as food supply, rear support, communications, management of relief supplies, and merchant militia, as well as larger issues such as civil aviation, foreign policy and domestic politics, and the question of extraterritoriality.

During the crisis the SCMA raised over Ch$930,000 in contributions for troop support and refugee relief; it ran sixty-five refugee camps (*shourong suo*), which looked after 32,700 out of a total of 43,300 refugees in Shanghai; it supplied the Chinese troops with a total of 14,200 piculs of rice; and it assisted with the provision of 39 field hospitals. It also responded to the pleas for help from the Bureau of Social Affairs (BSA) in supporting the workers dismissed from the Japanese textile mills through its role in the creation of the Shanghai Municipal Committee for the Relief of Unemployed Workers (*Shanghai Shi Shiye Gongren Jiujihui*), and in the provision of 600 piculs of rice to feed the unemployed workers. The Repatriation Unit of the SCMA's Relief Section, moreover, hired fifteen steamers and returned a total of 18,701 unemployed workers and refugees to their native places, principally in Jiangbei.[63] The SCMA conducted its activities over a four-month period (January 31–June 6), and during the height of the crisis its Executive Committee sat in almost permanent session. In early June it was reorganized on a permanent basis and renamed the Shanghai Civic Association (*Shanghai Shi Difang Xiehui*—SCA).

The cooperation of the Shanghai bourgeois elite with the local Guomindang authorities, however, did not prevent the SCMA from voicing trenchant criticisms of the regime itself. In fact the ineffectiveness of the Nanjing government and the obvious dependence of the municipal authorities on the work of the SCMA during the crisis, encouraged the bourgeois elite to formulate political demands of its own. An opportunity was provided by the controversy associated with the convening of the National Emergency Conference (*Guonan Huiyi*) in Nanjing in mid-April. When this conference was first proposed by Cai Yuanpei in November 1931 its purpose was to encourage a wide-ranging discussion of all aspects of the national emergency, including political and military issues as well as economic and foreign policy matters. The conference, however, was repeatedly postponed by the government, and when it was finally convened the terms of its discussions had been narrowed to exclude debate of the one-party rule of the Guomindang and political reform. Led by Shi Liangcai, the sixty-six Shanghai delegates (many of whom were members of the SCMA), boycotted the conference and sent a telegram laying out their political demands of the Nanjing regime. This was nothing less than a political manifesto in which they asserted their right to offer advice to the government on matters of national importance, and called for immediate guarantees of freedom of speech, press and popular assembly, the establishment of an elected Control Yuan within two months, and the promulgation of a democratic constitution within eight months.[64]

DU YUESHENG AND THE 1932 CRISIS

The reaction of Du Yuesheng to the crisis in early 1932 was complex and reflected the diversity of his interests in Shanghai. Du and his two Green Gang colleagues had been involved in the anti-Japanese commercial boycott since its inception in mid-1931. After the September Eighteenth Incident and the Japanese occupation of Manchuria, Du was appointed to the Standing Committee of the Shanghai Municipal Resist Japan National Salvation Association (*Shanghai Shi Kangri Jiuguo Weiyuanhui*), which was established at a mass meeting in the Chinese Chamber of Commerce on September 22, 1931.[65] The Green Gang bosses also participated in the various relief organizations that the leading members of the Shanghai bourgeoisie set up to assist Manchurian refugees. Du and Zhang Xiaolin, for example, were members of the standing committees of the Shanghai Northeast Refugees Relief Association (*Shanghai Dongbei Nanmin Jiuji Hui*) and the Federation of Shanghai Charities for Providing Relief Funds for Refugees in the Northeast (*Shanghai Ge Zishan Tuanti Zhenji Dongbèi Nanmin Lianhehui*), along with Wang Xiaolai, Shi Liang-cai and Yu Xiaqing. Huang Jinrong was a member of the Federation of Shanghai Charities Supervisory Committee, while Du was a member of the Standing Committee of another related organization established by the Chinese Chamber of Commerce, the Shanghai Municipal Chamber of Commerce's Committee to Raise Funds for the Support and Relief of the Northeast (*Shanghai Shi Shanghui Choumu Yuanjiu Dongbei Juankuan Weiyuanhui*).[66]

Involvement in organizations associated with the anti-Japanese boycott provided new opportunities for the Green Gang leaders to engage in racketeering, especially extortion. The "patriotic" nature of these associations, moreover, served to legitimize such activities.[67] Among the instruments for enforcing the boycott in 1932 were three organizations controlled by Du Yuesheng and Huang Jinrong that the French police regarded as merely mechanisms for extorting money from certain members of the business community. These were the Secret Investigation Group for National Salvation and Resistance against Japan (*Jiuguo Kangri Anchatuan*) and the Blood and Soul Group for the Extermination of Traitors (*Xuehun Chujian Tuan*), both controlled by Du Yuesheng, and the National Salvation Assassination Society (*Jiuguo Ansha Tuan*), which was organized by Huang Jinrong's senior lieutenant, Chen Peide.[68] These groups later were used as snipers as part of Chinese resistance to the Japanese landing party in the Hongkou-Zhabei area.[69]

In carrying out their activities during the boycott these gangster organizations worked in association with certain prominent Chinese businessmen, such as Wang Xiaolai, who found in them a useful means for the elimination of their commercial and political rivals in the name of "national salvation." The activities of these strong-arm gangster organizations, therefore, provided one channel by which the Green Gang bosses, notably Du Yuesheng, forged close links with certain leaders of the Chinese bourgeoisie during the crisis of 1931–32.

Another means by which Du Yuesheng strengthened his organizational links with the Shanghai bourgeoisie was through his participation in the activities of the SCMA. Du played a key role in this organization.[70] He was one of the association's two Deputy Chairmen (the other was Wang Xiaolai), while his colleague, Zhang Xiaolin was a member of the Executive Committee. Du also provided the SCMA with its headquarters, his ex-gambling joint at 181 Avenue Foch, and made the largest single contribution to the association's administrative expenses. Du's bank, the Zhonghui Bank (*Zhonghui Yinhang*) was a founding member of the aforementioned Joint Reserve Board set up by the Shanghai Bankers' Association under the auspices of the SCMA to stabilize the Shanghai financial market during the crisis.[71]

At the same time both Du and Zhang were members of SCMA sections charged with raising financial contributions for the National Salvation Fund (*Jiuguo Juan*—NSF) and with providing material support for the troops at the front. The Zhonghui Bank was one of the thirty-three modern-style and native banks which were designated as official agents for the collection of NSF contributions. In fact, the Zhonghui Bank held the fourth largest deposits of NSF contributions, amounting to Ch$52,271 or almost 6 percent of total contributions of Ch$931,618. Du was also a member of two important committees of the SCMA, the Committee to Study the Question of a Merchant's Militia (*Shangtuan Wenti Yanjiu Weiyuanhui*) and the Committee for the Management of the Fund to Resist the Enemy and Support the Troops (*Kangdi Weilao Jin Chuli Weiyuanhui*). Finally Du's follower, and senior economic adviser, Yang Guanbei, was Deputy Head of the SCMA's Repatriation Unit, which supervised the relocation of war zone refugees and unemployed workers back to their native districts.

The participation by Du Yuesheng in the SCMA was an important step in the extension of his influence among the leaders of the Chinese bourgeoisie and in the broadening of his power base beyond the confines of the French Concession. This was because the SCMA (and its successor the SCA) was the key body that articulated the political interests of the Shanghai bourgeois elite as a whole, and represented those interests to the Guomindang authorities. Du participated fully in the political activities of the SCMA in the course of 1932. He and Zhang Xiaolin, for example, joined the other Shanghai delegates in boycotting the National Emergency Conference in April, and both put their names to the circular telegram that demanded major political reforms of the Guomindang regime. Huang Jinrong, alone of the three Green Gang bosses, attended, a decision which was not unrelated to his appointment by Wang Jingwei as an adviser to the Executive Yuan on the eve of the conference.[72] DuYuesheng also played an active part in the Anti–Civil War League (*Feizhi Neizhan Datongmeng*), which was organized by leading Shanghai financiers, and was elected to its Standing Committee, along with Wang Xiaolai, Lin Kanghou and two others, at the league's congress in August.[73]

A major determinant of Du Yuesheng's actions in 1932 was the decisive moves taken by the French authorities to remove his gambling and narcotics rackets from the French Concession. The French, as has been discussed in chapter 5, took advantage of the crisis caused by the Shanghai Incident to bring pressure to bear on Du to divest him of his official positions in the Concession, which inaugurated a bitter five-month conflict. At one point, at the beginning of May, Du Yuesheng made arrangements with the Zhabei puppet government to transfer his opium and gambling interests to Zhabei in the event that the outcome of his negotiations with the French proved unsuccessful. By the end of May some of Du's gambling and opium interests had in fact been transferred to that part of Zhabei that bordered on Hongkou.[74]

Despite his activities in the SCMA and in support of the Chinese troops, Du Yuesheng maintained contacts with the Hu Lifu puppet government in Zhabei from its inception, as did his Green Gang colleagues in the French Concession. Shortly after this government was established in early April, for example, Huang Jinrong wrote a letter to Hu Lifu in which he expressed his support and sympathy for Hu's organization. When two members of the puppet government, Wang Ziliang and Gu Jiacai, were incarcerated by the Chinese authorities in late April, it was Du who interceded on their behalf and secured their release. Both men were members of Du's narcotics combine, the Three Prosperities Company.[75]

With the final collapse of the puppet government at the end of May, Du Yuesheng had to seek alternative arrangements for securing his gambling and narcotics interests. At the same time as he increased the pressure on the French authorities in order to improve his bargaining position, Du entered into negotiations with the Mayor of Shanghai, Wu Tiecheng, for the removal of his narcotics interests to Nandao. The context of these latter negotiations was provided by the Nanjing government's moves in October 1932 to extend its semi-official opium monopoly from Hankou, where it had operated for several years as the Hubei Special Tax Bureau (*Hubei Teshui Qinglihui*), to Jiangsu and Shanghai. This reflected the decision taken by senior Guomindang leaders at the Lushan Conference in June 1932 to set up a de facto opium monopoly because of the serious financial problems that faced the government as a result of the crisis of 1931–32.[76]

In early November 1932 Du Yuesheng visited Hankou to seek official permission to conduct the public sale of opium in Shanghai in return for the payment of Ch$3 million a month to the Minister of Finance, Song Ziwen. Some days earlier, Du had secured the appointment of his nominee, Yang Hu, as commander of the Shanghai Peace Preservation Corps (*Shanghai Shi Bao'andui*) and thus ensured the necessary armed protection for the transportation of his opium shipments. Du then wound up the operations of the Three Prosperities Company and incorporated its functions within a "Special Service Department" (*Tewu Bu*) of the Peace Preservation Corps. Once a deal had been struck with Wu Tiecheng this "Special Service Department" was placed under the control of the Shanghai Bureau of Public Safety (*Shanghai Shi Gong'an Ju*), and hence of Wu himself. Finally, in December, Du Yuesheng also secured the "farm" of the opium operations in Jiangsu province.[77]

By the end of the year, therefore, Du had succeeded in reaching an agreement with the Guomindang authorities that not only allowed the transfer of his narcotics operations from the French Concession to Chinese territory but that also gave them a semi-official status. This opium deal, however, was only one element in a larger accommodation between Du Yuesheng and his Green Gang group and the Nanjing government. This accommodation occurred within the context of the new configuration of power in the regime that had emerged from the crisis of 1932.

7 Gangster Politician
Du Yuesheng and the Guomindang State

In reaction to the crisis of 1931–32 and the consequent erosion of the authority of the government, Jiang Jieshi conducted a major political reorganization of the regime after 1932, an important element of which was the implementation of a form of state corporatism. As applied in Shanghai, this reorganization, particularly the creation of corporatist institutional structures, provided Du Yuesheng with a range of new opportunities, and enabled him to conduct a far-reaching restructuring of his own power base. He was, in fact, the only Green Gang boss to respond successfully to the new political realities in Shanghai, and he was able, as a result, to achieve a position of dominance over the various Green Gang groups, as well as to play an important role in the politics of the city.

The restructuring of his power base, however, was only the first step in Du's response to the Nationalist government's refurbished political system. His purpose was to become part of that system. One of the more remarkable developments in the politics of Shanghai in this period was the relative rapidity with which Du's network of personal power underwent a process of institutionalization. By mid-1937, on the eve of the Sino-Japanese War, Du had become, in effect, an integral part of the Guomindang's corporatist system in Shanghai. These twin processes of reconstruction and institutionalization can be observed across the range of Du's activities in the 1930s: his close working relationship with the GMD's powerful CC Clique; his involvement with labor control and the government's opium policy; his role in the Shanghai Civic Association; the organization of the Endurance Club, and his successful assertion of primacy within the Shanghai gangster leadership; and the development and expansion of his economic interests in Shanghai.[1]

THE GUOMINDANG CORPORATIST STATE

In the wake of the crisis of 1932 Jiang Jieshi adopted a complex, multi-pronged strategy to rebuild and enlarge the regime's power and authority. The main elements of this strategy were the forging of a political alliance with his main factional rival, Wang Jingwei; his assertion of personal control over the Guomindang Party Branches; and an emphasis on the elimination of the Communist challenge. It also involved the adaptation to Chinese conditions of aspects of the system of state corporatism.

Corporatism, in the view of one leading scholar in the field, is a system by which society is organized into a fixed number of single, compulsory, functionally defined bodies or "corporations." These are recognized by the state as the officially sanctioned representatives of the interests of broad socioeconomic groups in return for the acceptance of certain controls on the selection of the leaders and on the articulation of the interests of such "corporations."[2] The attractions of corporatism for the Guomindang government as it sought solutions to the political crisis of 1931–32 are not hard to find. In the 1930s corporatism was considered to be a progressive political ideology that sought the effective integration of society with the state, and which postulated a "third way" distinct from both capitalism and communism.[3] As one enthusiastic advocate of the period exclaimed: "The twentieth century will be the century of corporatism just as the nineteenth century was the century of liberalism."[4]

Corporatism as a political theory, moreover, resonated in official Guomindang ideology, which, as articulated by Sun Yat-sen in his *Three Principles of the People* (*Sanmin Zhuyi*), had a distinct statist character. As Arif Dirlik has pointed out, the Guomindang's conception of politics was in fact consonant with state corporatism. In the view of the Guomindang, the state was an agency, under (temporary) party dictatorship, for the reconciliation of the conflicting interests of various classes, none of which in itself had a right to govern society.[5]

It is not surprising, therefore, that state corporatism, a coercive ideology of state building with a strong anti-Communist flavor, proved attractive to Jiang Jieshi. Its appeal was only enhanced, moreover, by the fact that corporatism was a major component of the ideology of the Italian Fascist State, which Jiang himself saw as providing a blueprint for future society.[6] Indeed many factions close to Jiang were influenced strongly by the example of fascism, and some, notably the "Blue Shirts" and the CC Clique, believed that fascist ideology should eventually replace the official Guomindang ideology, the Three People's Principles, as the guiding ideology of the state.[7] The fact that these Guomindang factions turned to fascism at this time is instructive. It reflected the failure of the Three People's Principles to meet the needs of the Guomindang state for an integrative ideology that could counter effectively the serious political and ideological challenge of communism.

Elements of a corporatist system were to be found in the relationship between the Shanghai trade unions and the Guomindang authorities after 1932.[8] On the one hand the government ensured its control over trade union organization and activity by the provisions of the restrictive Trade Union Law promulgated in 1929 (and subsequently amended in 1931 and 1933), and by the creation of a municipal Bureau of Social Affairs at the end of 1928. One of the important functions of this bureau was to monitor trade union activities and mediate industrial disputes, and after 1933 it became the designated government supervisory authority over trade unions.[9]

On the other hand the Guomindang government recognized certain unions that operated in key industries or utilities as having a major role to play in the industrial order of Shanghai. These were the "seven big unions": the Postal Workers' Union, the British-American Tobacco Company Workers' Union, the Journalists' Union, the Commercial Press Workers' Union, the Nanyang Tobacco Company Workers' Union, the Chinese Electricity Company Workers' Union, and the Shanghai-Ningbo Railwaymen's Union; and to their number could be added the Chinese Seamen's Union.[10] These formed the core of the "yellow unions" (*huangse gonghui*), and, after 1932, their leadership formed the senior echelons of the Guomindang trade union movement. After some difficulties these unions finally succeeded in establishing their peak organization in 1933, the Shanghai Municipal General Trade Union (*Shanghai Shi Zonggonghui—* SMGLU), which cooperated closely with the Bureau of Social Affairs in the management of industrial relations in Shanghai.[11]

Similarly, the relationship between the Nanjing government and the Shanghai bourgeoisie also demonstrated certain characteristics of state corporatism. In his study of the Guomindang and the Shanghai merchant elites, Joseph Fewsmith noted the emergence of a system of state corporatism prior to 1930 with the extension of state control over the Shanghai Chamber of Commerce (*Shanghai Shi Shanghui*) in the wake of the passage of the Trade Association Law and the Chamber of Commerce Law in 1929.[12] This process, however, gathered pace and was given an added urgency by the serious regime crisis provoked by the events of 1931–32. In order to repair the damage done to the regime's legitimacy by these events, Jiang Jieshi allowed for the strictly limited, but nevertheless important, involvement by the leading members of the Shanghai bourgeoisie, through such organizations as the Shanghai Civic Association, in aspects of the regime's decision-making process. In this way their interests were given institutional representation in the political system.

The moves to co-opt the leading members of the Shanghai bourgeoisie were prompted by the erosion of the legitimacy of the regime in the eyes of key sections of the Chinese public, notably leading intellectuals and members of the bourgeoisie, on which depended the restoration of its authority. At the same time the Nanjing government could not ignore the important contributions made by the Shanghai Citizens' Maintenance Association (SCMA) to social order and basic economic health in Shanghai at a time when the local municipal administration was in a state of near collapse. The huge economic costs of the conflict in Zhabei, estimated at between Ch$1.5 billion and Ch$2 billion, also underlined the importance for the government of an accommodation with the leading members of the Shanghai bourgeoisie.[13]

It was such considerations that induced the Nanjing government to extend official recognition to the Shanghai Civic Association (SCA), the successor to the SCMA. Government leaders, especially Song Ziwen, believed that the SCA would make an important contribution to the government's financial, industrial and defense policies, as well as to the restoration of economic prosperity and social order in Shanghai.[14] The Nanjing government, therefore, regarded the SCA as an important organization through which to cooperate with the upper stratum of the Shanghai bourgeoisie and to gain their support for key Government policies. The importance of the SCA was that it brought together the leaders from all areas of Shanghai economic life—finance, commerce and industry—in the one organization. If membership numbers are any indication, the SCA became even more representative of the Shanghai economic elite as time went on. Its membership tripled in five years, rising from 80 in June 1932 to 156 in 1935 to 241 in May 1937.[15]

At the municipal level the Shanghai Municipal Government set up a nineteen-member Provisional Municipal Council (*Shanghai Shi Linshi Shi Canyihui*) in mid-October 1932 to provide it with advice on administrative matters. The councillors brought together representatives of Shanghai's industrial, financial and business interests (all of whom were members of the SCA) with labor leaders and local Guomindang Party figures, under the chairmanship of Shi Liangcai.[16] The council, as Pan Gongzhan observed, was a genuine corporatist body, with councillors selected from representative professional groups to "represent" "the people."[17] It was organized into eight sections, which mirrored the bureaus of the municipal government, such as Social Affairs, Public Safety, Finance, Public Works, Education, etc. Furthermore, it debated and reviewed all aspects of municipal administration, from road construction, house rents and health regulations to the annual budgets, the issuance of municipal bonds and the management of government revenues.

This accommodation between the Guomindang regime and the Shanghai bourgeoisie was, in sum, a form of corporatism based on mutual weakness. The Nanjing government had been seriously weakened by the events of 1932 and needed to reassert its authority. However, it had to confront the serious political and financial limitations on that authority, and find ways to ameliorate them. One means of meeting the situation was to co-opt the leading elements of the Shanghai bourgeoisie. In the years immediately after the Shanghai Incident, in other words, the Nanjing government could be described as an early example of a weak authoritarian regime of a type that has become much more familiar in countries of the Third World since the demise of colonialism. The Shanghai bourgeoisie, for its part, was given an opportunity by the crisis of the regime in 1932 to assert its political interests in a meaningful way. It did this effectively through its involvement in the SCMA and in its public criticism of the National Emergency Conference. The Guomindang regime had to take note of its views. On the other hand, the bourgeoisie's political strength was neither very great nor very soundly established, and had been eroded by the past policies of the Guomindang government itself. The best it could hope for, therefore, was to negotiate an increase in its influence on government policies, and this it largely achieved in the years after 1932.

DU YUESHENG'S RELATIONS WITH THE CC CLIQUE

The form of state corporatism promoted by the Guomindang, therefore, was designed to compensate for the regime's political and institutional weaknesses, and it sought to co-opt all major social groups on a pragmatic basis. In Shanghai these included, in addition to the trade unions and the bourgeoisie, secret society/gangster organizations belonging to both the Green Gang and Triad systems. A number of attempts, for example, were made by the Guomindang to establish organizations to serve as links between itself and different Triad groups, the most successful being the creation of the Triad Promotion Association (*Hong Xing Xiehui*) in 1936. The most important of these links that the Guomindang regime forged with secret society organizations, however, was that with Du Yuesheng and his Green Gang group, which was integrated progressively into the regime's processes of corporatist intermediation in the city.

One important aspect of these links was the close relationship that Du Yuesheng enjoyed with the Guomindang CC Clique, and which became one of his key political alliances in Shanghai after 1932. This was not surprising, as the CC Clique, which had been organized in mid-1927 by the Chen brothers (Chen Guofu and Chen Lifu) to promote Jiang Jieshi's interests within the party, was charged with control of the local party organization in Shanghai, as well as establishing control over the city's labor, educational and economic organizations.[18] Du's contacts with the leadership of the CC Clique went right back to 1924, when he had extended his protection to Chen Lifu who was then engaged in setting up an underground Guomindang organization in Shanghai.[19] It was only after the 1932 crisis and the arrival of Wu Xingya to head up the CC Clique operations in Shanghai, however, that Du developed a close, regular relationship with the clique.

Wu Xingya had been responsible for CC Clique strategy in Hubei and Anhui in the years 1928–31, and in the 1930s he was the third most powerful figure in the clique, after the two Chen brothers. In 1932 he was appointed Chairman of the Shanghai GMD Branch's Executive Committee and Chief of the Shanghai Municipal Government's Bureau of Social Affairs. Wu's primary objective was to strengthen the CC Clique's operations in the city and to gain control over the municipal party branch and sub-branches. To achieve this he worked closely with two local CC Clique members, Wu Kaixian (who headed the "Jiangsu faction") and Pan Gongzhan. After his arrival in Shanghai Wu Xingya moved quickly to gain control of the local party structure. In September 1932 he manipulated the Shanghai GMD Branch's Eighth Congress to ensure that his nominees, all CC Clique members, were "elected" to the Executive and Supervisory committees. This process was repeated in all the district sub-branches of the Shanghai GMD Branch. No further congresses were held, and this new power configuration, in which the CC Clique dominated the local party apparatus, remained stable for the rest of the Nanjing Decade.[20]

Wu Xingya also desired to establish a good working relationship with the Green Gang organization in Shanghai. Some sources have noted in this regard that one reason for his appointment as head of CC Clique operations in Shanghai was his prior membership in the Green Gang, and the fact that he had sufficient generational seniority to deal on an equal footing with Du Yuesheng and Yang Hu.[21] Whatever the truth of this Wu and Du first began to work closely together during the crisis of 1932, when the two men (in their respective capacities as the newly appointed Chief of the Bureau of Social Affairs and as the Deputy Chairman of the SCMA), cooperated to contain the social problems created by the Shanghai conflict. Du's successful mediation of the anti-Japanese strike wave, and, in particular, his assistance in the solution of the politically inspired Postal Workers' strike in late May 1932 impressed Wu.[22]

Another key figure in the Shanghai CC Clique whom Du began to cultivate in 1932 was Wu Kaixian, one of the four members of the Shanghai GMD Branch's Standing Committee "elected" in September 1932. He was also the leader of the so-called "Jiangsu faction" within the CC Clique, and one of Wu Xingya's two deputies in the CC Clique's Shanghai organization.[23] In mid-1936 Du Yuesheng strongly supported Wu Kaixian's moves to establish his control over local Chinese merchants, which was part of a political struggle within the Shanghai GMD Party Branch, and provided assistance to Wu when the latter set up his own organization, the Nineteen Thirty-six Club (*Bingzi She*) to achieve this.[24]

Although Du did have followers among local GMD members

prior to 1932, the most important one being Chen Junyi, it was only after 1932 that he engaged in a systematic recruitment of Shanghai party members by means of his new organization, the Endurance Club.[25] Du recruited his followers not only from the Shanghai GMD Party Branch but also from the district sub-branches, especially the Second District Sub-branch (the French Concession), the Fifth District (Pudong), the Sixth District (Zhabei), and the Ninth District (Longhua). In the 1930s, therefore, Du had about a dozen followers who were not only key local party members, but were also important members of the CC Clique in Shanghai. They included Lu Jingshi, Wang Manyun, Huang Xianggu, Zhang Binghui, Xu Yefu, Wang Gang, Hou Dachun, and Cai Hongtian.[26]

One important area of cooperation between Du Yuesheng's Green Gang organization and the CC Clique was the latter's special service operations against Communists, leftists, liberals and sundry other enemies of the Guomindang regime. One of Wu Xingya's first acts on his appointment in 1932, for example, was to establish the so-called Action Club (*Gan She*), in order to further the CC Clique's interests in Shanghai (particularly in the areas of propaganda, education, and youth affairs). This was a highly secret organization that, according to a former member, was greatly influenced by the Italian Fascist Party and German National Socialism, and whose purpose was to promote fascism within the Guomindang as a means of strengthening the position of Jiang Jieshi.

Pan Gongzhan, who was Deputy Head of the Action Club, for example, drew up a list of operational slogans for the organization, which included exhortations to "firmly trust in Fascism" and to "pledge one's life to the struggle for the realization of Fascism," as well as to "protect and support to the death the supreme leader Chairman Jiang." According to reports of the SMP Special Branch, Wu Xingya had been ordered by a conference of the CC Clique held in Lushan in August 1933 to establish "fascist cells" within the Shanghai party branch, "loyal" military units, and schools and universities in Shanghai.[27] Lu Jingshi, Du Yuesheng's leading lieutenant in the 1930s, was very active in the Action Club. He controlled the club's Workers' Action Battalion (*Gongren Xingdong Da Dui*), an organization of blackshirted bully-boys that cooperated closely with the Bureau of Public Safety in raids on left-wing presses and book stores, and in the "storming" of universities, such as Jinan, and secondary schools, to purge them of left-wing students and faculty.[28]

Another of Du Yuesheng's Green Gang "cronies," Yang Hu, was involved with the training of an assassination corps that the CC Clique special services had organized from the ranks of Communist "turncoats" led by the former CCP security boss Gu Shunzhang. This corps proved to be extremely effective, and in the course of one year, July 1933–July 1934, it was reported to have contributed to the elimination of 4,500 Communists.[29] By 1933 the local Japanese press reported that Du's Green Gang group was so heavily involved with the activities of the Guomindang special services that the French police could not rely on their Chinese Detective Squad (composed of Green Gang members) to investigate crimes committed by these special service units in the French Concession. In an attempt to solve the problem, the French police began to recruit Red Gang (Triad) members into its Chinese Detective Squad specifically to investigate the activities of the special service squads.[30]

By late 1936 the CC Clique organization in Shanghai had entered a period of decline that was related to its growing competition with a rival anti-Communist organization, the Blue Shirts (*Fuxing She*, or the Revival Society), which had established its own "special service" squad.[31] The competition between the two organizations for control of Shanghai's cultural and educational institutions grew in intensity in 1935 and 1936.[32] At this point an obscure conflict within the Action Club leadership broke out between Li Shiqun (head of the club's intelligence services and a Green Gang member) and Wu Xingya in May–June 1936. Wu's sudden death from natural causes in August resulted in the collapse of his personal organization. There immediately followed a struggle for control of the organization between Wu Kaixian and Pan Gongzhan resulting in the paralysis of the CC Clique's activities in Shanghai.

It is not clear what role, if any, Du played in these developments, although it would appear that he gave his support to Wu Kaixian. By this time, however, Du's own position was so strong that the collapse of the CC Clique's position in Shanghai did not adversely affect him. In any event he had already established contact with the Blue Shirts. Du had known Dai Li, the head of the Blue Shirts' special services (*Juntong*) since the mid-1920s, and the two were sworn brothers.[33] Between 1935 and 1937, furthermore, he developed a close working relationship with the head of the Shanghai Area of the Juntong, Wang Xinheng. Wang was a frequent guest of Du's Endurance Club, and he drew many of his recruits for the Juntong from Du's gangster groups and from members of the Shanghai General Postal Workers' Union (which was controlled by Du).[34]

In the years 1932 to 1937 the two key individuals in Du Yuesheng's network of power in Shanghai were Lu Jingshi and Yang Hu. Lu provided the link between Du and local political and labor circles, while Yang gave Du access to the military units in Shanghai. Lu Jingshi became a member of Du's Green Gang group in May 1931 along with Zhu Xuefan and other leaders of the Postal Workers' Union. In 1932 he joined the CC Clique through Wu Kaixian and was appointed to the Shanghai GMD Branch's Eighth Executive Committee in September of that year. Although Lu was an active and influential member of the CC Clique, his first loyalty remained to Du Yuesheng. No less a figure than Chen Lifu remarked that Lu's loyalty to Du surpassed his loyalty to the Guomindang.[35] It is not surprising, therefore, that Du considered Lu to be his most capable follower and that he always gave particular weight to his advice.

Lu was very active in party and governmental affairs in Shanghai, becoming a member of the Shanghai Municipality's Provisional Council in 1932. In 1934 he was appointed a member of the Shanghai Municipality New Life Movement Acceleration Committee (*Shanghai Shi Xin Shenghuo Yundong Zujinhui*), the organization which was charged with responsibility for implementing Jiang Jieshi's New Life Movement in Shanghai. Over the next two years he became the Director of this organization's Youth Service Groups (1935) and Vice-Chairman of the New Life Labor Service Corps (*Xin Shenghuo Laodong Fuwu Tuan*) in 1936. At the same time he was head of the CC Clique's Shanghai Workers' Movement Promotion Association (*Shanghai Gongren Yundong Zujinhui*) and of its paramilitary wing, the Workers' Action Battalion.

In late 1935 Lu was appointed Chief Judge of the Military Court of the Wusong-Shanghai Defense Commissioner's Headquarters (*Song-Hu Jingbei Silingbu de Junfa Chuzhang*), and in this capacity he worked closely with Yang Hu, after the latter was appointed Defense Commissioner in early 1936. In his judicial capacity, Lu was also appointed in May 1936 to the three man Standing Committee of the Shanghai GMD Branch's Committee for Re-educating Political Prisoners in Shanghai (*Shanghai Zhengzhifan Jiaohui Weiyuanhui*).[36]

Yang Hu, for his part, was a long-time Green Gang "crony" of Du Yuesheng, who controlled significant coercive power in Shanghai in the period 1932–37. He held the post of Commissioner of the Shanghai Municipal Peace Preservation Corps from November 1932 to April 1936. This was the paramilitary force that was raised to fill the security gap created by the Sino-Japanese ceasefire agreement of May 5, 1932, which had proscribed the stationing of Chinese troops in either Pudong or Zhabei.[37] According to the SMP, Yang Hu had, in fact, been Du Yuesheng's nominee for the post. In April 1936 Yang Hu was appointed Wusong-Shanghai Defense Commissioner (*Song-Hu Jingbei Siling*), the most senior military post in the Shanghai area, and one which had previously been held by Mayor Wu Tiecheng. Yang held this post until the withdrawal of the Guomindang administration from Shanghai in November 1937, and in this period he was the most powerful military figure in the Shanghai area. He was also among the most corrupt. According to the SMP, Yang made over Ch$2 million during his tenure as Defense Commissioner.

In addition to these military posts Yang also controlled both the Chinese Seamen's Union (*Zhonghua Haiyuan Gonghui*) and the Guomindang's Chinese Seamen's Special Party Branch (*Guomindang Zhonghua Haiyuan Tebie Dangbu*).[38] One important reason for this odd combination of posts was that Yang played a key role in the protection of Du Yuesheng's narcotics operations. His capacity to perform this role was enhanced by the control he exercised over sailors on coastal and river steamers through the Seamen's Union, and was a useful complement to his control of the Shanghai area through his military posts.[39] It is not surprising, therefore, that when the mayoralty of Shanghai became vacant with Wu Tiecheng's departure from Shanghai upon his appointment as Governor of Guangdong, Du Yuesheng "strongly recommended" Yang Hu's candidacy to Jiang Jieshi as Wu's successor. Although ultimately unsuccessful, the fact that Du made the attempt revealed just how powerful he had become in Shanghai on the eve of the Sino-Japanese War.[40]

DU YUESHENG AND LABOR CONTROL

It was not until 1932 that Du Yuesheng became involved in the Guomindang's policies of labor control in a systematic way. Prior to that year his involvement in "industrial relations" issues had been limited to his cooperation in the purge of Shanghai trade unions, which was conducted by the UUC in the course of 1927, and to his

mediation, largely at the behest of the French Concession authorities, of disputes in the French Tramways Company. The harbinger
of change in this situation was the decision, in May 1931, by Lu
Jingshi, Zhu Xuefan, Zhang Kechang and nine other key people in
the Nanjing government's Department of Communications, the
Central Postal Administration and the Shanghai Post Office to join
the Green Gang and become followers of Du Yuesheng.[41] Lu's purpose, according to Zhu Xuefan's account, was to use his membership in Du's Green Gang group to strengthen his own control over
the Postal Workers' Union and to enhance his standing as a major
figure in the Guomindang's trade union organization.

These moves were also part of the process of accommodation
between reformist trade union leaders and key factions in the Nanjing government, such as the CC Clique, which provided part of the
foundation for the Guomindang's emerging system of state corporatism. In this context these overtures to Du reflected the need of
reformist trade unions, such as the Postal Workers' Union, to obtain
powerful allies where they could to counter-balance the continuing
influence of those anti-unionist elements within the Nanjing government who had ensured the passage of the repressive GMD Trade
Union Law in October 1929. The repeal of this law, or its extensive
amendment, was a constant preoccupation of trade union leaders,
such as Lu Jingshi and Zhu Xuefan, in the early 1930s.[42]

At the same time, the fact that the leadership of the Postal
Workers' Union joined Du's Green Gang group, enabled him to
extend his influence into one of the seven major trade unions in
Shanghai. With leading Guomindang trade unionists as his followers,
moreover, Du enjoyed a direct entrée into trade union politics in
Shanghai. Indeed, by 1932 Du Yuesheng's penetration of organized
labor in Shanghai was so effective that it was the envy of the CCP.[43]

It was the crisis of 1932, in fact, that prompted Du's involvement
in labor disputes beyond the French Concession, when he participated in the mediation of the anti-Japanese strike wave among
Chinese textile workers.[44] Of particular importance was Du's mediation of the postal workers' strike of May 22–27, 1932. This was
essentially a political rather than an economic strike. The leadership
of the Postal Workers' Union took the opportunity of the weakness
of the government and the general ill-repute in which it was held
during the Shanghai crisis, to give vent to long-held criticisms of the
postal administration. The government, however, did not look with

equanimity on a strike in a strategic industry, the postal service, at a time of national crisis, and therefore moved quickly to end it by invoking legislation which stated that postal workers, as government employees, did not have the right to strike. At the same time the Shanghai Guomindang authorities entered into negotiations with the leadership of the Postal Workers' Union. Du was invited to participate in the mediation effort that arose out of these negotiations, because it was known that the leaders of the Postal Workers' Union were his followers. Other mediators included key CC Clique members, Wu Kaixian and Pan Gongzhan. The strike was ended successfully on May 26, and Du, together with Pan and Wu, were members of the fifteen-man Special Committee that was set up to oversee the implementation of the agreement.[45]

As noted earlier it was Du's involvement in the mediation of this postal workers' strike that provided the basis for his rapport with leaders of the CC Clique organization in Shanghai. Labor control was an important area of activity for the CC Clique, and Du Yuesheng's follower Lu Jingshi, who joined the CC Clique after the termination of the postal workers' strike, was very active in the clique's labor activities. Of particular importance was his control of the clique's so-called Workers' Action Battalion, which was regularly used to forcibly terminate strikes, as in the case of the strike at the Hengfeng Cotton Mill in September 1933.[46]

At the same time, Du Yuesheng, with the encouragement of the CC Clique leadership in Shanghai, engaged in industrial mediation on a regular basis. In this activity he worked very closely with the Shanghai Municipal Bureau of Social Affairs, and the degree of closeness was such that, during Wu Xingya's tenure as Bureau Chief (1932–36), three of the bureau's four section heads were followers of Du Yuesheng. Du, in fact, actively sought to place his followers in key positions within the local Guomindang's apparatus for managing mass work and labor relations. A case in point was his recommendation to Wu Xingya that Xu Yefu be appointed head of the bureau's Third Section, which dealt with labor-management disputes.[47] By such means Du succeeded in consolidating his position within the Guomindang's system of labor control in Shanghai.

Du now mediated disputes in all the major industries in Shanghai. Some of his more important efforts included mediation of strikes in the Shanghai Power Company's plant in September–November 1933; in the British-American Tobacco Company factory, Pudong,

June 1934; in the Hong Xing Hosiery Factory, July 1936; in the Japanese cotton mills, November 1936; in the Shanghai Electrical Construction Company, February–April 1937; and among the crews employed by the Ningbo-Shaoxing Steam Navigation Company, March 1937.[48]

After 1932 Du Yuesheng also strengthened his control over both the Postal Workers' Union and the SMGLU. He did this through the activities of his follower Zhu Xuefan in both organizations. In 1935 Zhu set up his own Green Gang group, the Resolute Club (*Yi She*), and actively recruited members in both the Postal Workers' Union and the SMGLU. In his memoir Zhu notes that Du Yuesheng and the Green Gang bosses who formed part of his group (i.e., Jin Tingsun, Ma Xiangsheng, Peng Baiwei and Yang Hu) held a preponderant position in the Postal Workers' Union; and that the two largest organizations of postal workers were both controlled by Du's followers, Zhang Kechang and himself. Within the SMGLU, members of the five-man Standing Committee who controlled its operations were either followers of Du himself or of Du's close colleague Jin Tingsun. Zhu Xuefan, for his part, used his position within the SMGLU to extend his Resolute Club network among the unions in a number of enterprises throughout Shanghai. These included all the major utilities and industrial companies in both the International Settlement and the Chinese City. As a loyal follower of Du, Zhu's activities not only increased his own power and influence but also, indirectly, that of Du Yuesheng as well.[49]

The SMGLU's influence over the industrial workers in Shanghai remained fairly weak throughout the 1930s. This was because all the major factories and industrial concerns were located either in the International Settlement itself or on the External Roads (under SMC control) and outside Chinese jurisdiction. In an attempt to rectify this situation and tighten Guomindang control over these industrial workers, the Shanghai party branch and the Bureau of Social Affairs, in association with Du Yuesheng, organized the Livelihood Mutual Aid Association (*Shenghuo Huzhu She*—LMAA) in August 1936. This organization had a membership of about 300 by April 1937 and gave priority to the establishment of branches among transport workers. The LMAA was designed, in the view of the SMP Special Branch, to circumvent the SMGLU and to further Du Yuesheng's control over organized labor in Shanghai. As this SMP Special Branch report noted, all fifteen promoters of the LMAA were

Guomindang Party members (indeed they were all members of the CC Clique's Shanghai organization), all were followers of Du Yuesheng, and many were members of his Endurance Club.[50]

The creation of the LMAA, therefore, represented the merging of the interests of Du Yuesheng and the Guomindang on labor issues, which in turn reflected the complete integration of Du Yuesheng into the regime's system of labor control. In other words, by 1936 Du was an integral part of the corporatist structures that the Nanjing government had constructed to regulate its relations with organized labor.

DU YUESHENG AND THE POLITICS OF THE SHANGHAI BOURGEOISIE: THE SHANGHAI CIVIC ASSOCIATION

Leadership of the SCA was an important means by which Du Yuesheng created for himself a key role in the politics of the Shanghai bourgeoisie, and in mediating its relations with the Guomindang authorities. Du took over the SCA chairmanship on the assassination of its first chairman, Shi Liangcai, in November 1934. Shi, the proprietor of *Shen Bao*, Shanghai's preeminent newspaper, had been a moving force in the mobilization of the Shanghai bourgeoisie during the crisis of 1932.[51] He saw himself, and was seen by others, as the political leader of the Shanghai bourgeoisie. Shi's personal ambition was boundless, and ultimately he overreached himself. He appears to have wanted to share power with Jiang Jieshi, and to have believed that the aftermath of the 1932 crisis provided the ideal opportunity. According to Huang Yanpei, Shi told Jiang at a meeting in Nanjing: "You control a large army of several hundred thousand men; I have several hundred thousand readers of my two newspapers, *Shen Bao* and *Xinwen Bao*. If you and I cooperated what could we not do!"[52]

Shi's murder, therefore, revealed the limits to the accommodation that the Nanjing government was prepared to make with the bourgeoisie. The regime, it might be inferred, would not countenance cooperation on the basis of two independent centers of power, as this would merely be a tactless reminder of its inherent weakness; this was Shi Liangcai's mistake. The regime could only countenance one power center, its own. Once this was accepted, however, the political process itself could take on the character of a series of pragmatic adjustments to take account of a continuously changing, if unequal, balance of weakness between the regime and major social forces, such as the Shanghai bourgeoisie. It was this process that Du Yuesheng well understood.

Du's role in Shi Liangcai's assassination remains enigmatic. Allegations were current at the time that he was "the prime instigator" of the murder, but nothing could be proved. It is now clear that the assassination was carried out by Dai Li and his Juntong on the orders of Jiang Jieshi. Jiang was angered by the *Shen Bao*'s lack of enthusiasm for his anti-Communist campaigns and its calls for a stronger stand against Japan by the Nanjing government, and, moreover, he had come to believe that Shi was a secret Communist sympathizer.[53] Whatever his involvement might have been, Du benefited enormously from the murder. He was appointed Chairman of Shi's newspapers—*Shen Bao, Xinwen Bao, China Evening News*, and *China Press*; and of course he became Chairman of the SCA. In many respects Shi's murder was a necessary precondition for Du's emergence as a leading political figure on the Shanghai scene.

His political style, however, was quite different from that of Shi Liangcai. As Chairman of the SCA, Du worked closely with Wang Xiaolai, Chairman of the Chinese Ratepayers' Association of the International Settlement. In mid-1936 Du gave Wang important support in a complex political conflict with his arch rival, Wang Yansong, a silk merchant and prominent member of the Shanghai GMD Party Branch, for control of the Shanghai Chamber of Commerce. Du had an interest of his own in opposing Wang Yansong. Wang and his supporters had extorted money from one of Du's prominent followers and member of the Endurance Club, Zhang Rongchu, during the anti-Japanese boycott in 1931. Zhang's case was used as the means to disgrace Wang Yansong, who was briefly imprisoned in Nanjing. The upshot of the conflict was that Wang Xiaolai was elected Chairman of the Chamber of Commerce, and Du was elected to its five-man Standing Committee for the first time, in July 1936. Between them Wang and Du now controlled the Chamber of Commerce, and this gave them a commanding position within the Shanghai bourgeoisie.[54]

Du Yuesheng used his position first as Deputy Chairman and then Chairman of the SCA to both project himself as a local leader representing Shanghai interests, and as an important figure on the national political stage. In this dual role he actively supported the implementation of the Guomindang policies of "self-government" in Shanghai, and obtained the municipal government's agreement for the organization of his native place, Gaoqiao, as a model district. In pursuit of this latter objective, Du, in his capacity as Deputy Chairman of the SCA, organized the Gaoqiao Rural Progress Association (*Gaoqiao Nongcun Gaijinhui*) in February 1934, which over the next thirty-four months engaged in a number of rural reconstruction projects. These included the planting of 600 trees along the roads in the district; the digging of a ten li (about three miles) irrigation canal; the establishment, with the help of the Shanghai Commercial and Savings Bank, of a credit society for the local peasantry; efforts to improve the quality of the local cotton crop; and the opening of a school for women and a local primary school.[55] Du's native-place pride, however, was not untinged with financial self-interest. According to the American journalist Ilona Ralf Sues, who visited the project in 1936, Du extended money to the credit society at 12 percent interest, half again as much as that charged by other banks.[56]

The Progress Association also assisted in the implementation of the Guomindang policy of *baojia* in Gaoqiao on an experimental basis.[57] *Baojia* was a traditional system of collective security used by several Chinese dynasties by which village populations were organized into a hierarchy of units of mutual responsibility loosely based on a decimal system (ten families formed a *pai*, ten *pai* formed a *jia*, and ten *jia* formed a *bao*, and so forth).[58] During the 1930s the Guomindang government, initially in the context of its campaigns against the Communists in central China, used a remodeled version of the baojia system as an instrument for the extension of state control at the local level under the rubric of "local self-government."[59] The participation of the Gaoqiao Rural Progress Association in this system is a further example of the cooperation of elements of the bourgeois elite, through organizations such as the SCA, and the local Guomindang authorities in the process of state building in Shanghai. Du Yuesheng expressed his own belief in the shared interests of the Shanghai elite and the Guomindang government in the extension and consolidation of the state's power at the local level in a retrospective article on the activities of his Gaoqiao Rural Progress Association that appeared in the *Xinwen Bao* on December 22, 1936.[60]

In addition to their exertions in the field of rural reconstruction both Du Yuesheng and the SCA were also involved in the successive attempts by the Guomindang government to organize elections for a proposed National People's Congress (*Guomin Dahui*—NPC) in the course of the year from mid-1936 to mid-1937. One response of the government to its crisis of legitimacy in 1931–32 had been to emphasize its commitment to the implementation of the period of constitutional rule at the earliest opportunity. As a result the Legislative Yuan, under the presidency of Sun Ke, prepared a number of draft constitutions between 1932 and 1935.[61] As part of this process the first plenary session of the Guomindang's Fifth Central Executive Committee met on December 5, 1935, and decided both to promulgate the third draft constitution on May 5, 1936, and to convene the NPC on November 12, 1936, in order to mark the commencement of the period of constitutional government in Nationalist China.

In order to qualify to vote in the elections for the proposed NPC the Chinese population first had to be registered as citizens, and a citizenship registration campaign was launched in August 1936. The official reason for the registration was the need to obtain adequate information on each individual, which did not then exist because of the absence of a proper population census. The Guomindang, in fact, regarded membership of the national polity as an exclusive rather than inclusive process, in which membership was determined by the degree of one's loyalty to the party-state. Citizenship registration, in other words, was a potent political weapon that enabled the Guomindang government to decide who was and was not a "citizen" and, therefore, who could participate in the political process.[62]

Within the French Concession the process of citizenship registration was undertaken by the Election Office for the Second Special District, which was run jointly by the French Concession Chinese Ratepayers' Association and the Second Special District Guomindang Branch. When the French authorities, concerned about the implications of the process of registration for their own authority in the Concession, halted the process in mid-August, Du Yuesheng discussed the issue directly with the French Consul General. As a result of Du's intervention the French authorities acknowledged that a "misunderstanding" had occurred and undertook not to interfere further with the registration campaign, which was thereupon resumed in the Concession.[63] During August, Du, in his capacity as Chairman of the Shanghai Civic Association, also officiated at various citizenship and oath-taking ceremonies, including one held by the Chinese Chamber of Commerce that involved 470 employees of the chamber itself and affiliated associations.[64] At the same time, Du Yuesheng's close Green Gang associate, Yang Hu, chaired a citizenship ceremony that involved about 1,000 members of the Chinese Seamen's Union.[65]

In the event the meeting of the NPC was postponed for a year, until November 12, 1937, on the grounds that insufficient time had been allowed to conduct the citizenship registration and hold the elections.[66] Elections for the postponed NPC were held finally in July 1937, and Du Yuesheng stood as one of the three candidates for the French Concession; the other two being his Green Gang associate, Jin Tingsun, and his financial adviser and business ally, Qian Xinzhi. All three candidates had the support of both the French Concession Ratepayers' Association and the Second Special District Citizen's Federation, which festooned the streets of the Concession with banners supporting their slate.[67]

The twenty Shanghai candidates for the NPC were elected on the basis of a combination of occupational and geographical constituencies, with twelve delegates representing organizations such as trade unions, business associations and peasant associations, and the remaining eight representing the different areas of Shanghai. The SCA was well represented and, in fact, its members formed the majority of the delegates. Not only were the delegates representing the business community drawn from its ranks, so also were many of those representing geographical constituencies, and, indeed, even one who ostensibly represented the peasantry. Among the ranks of the elected delegates who were also members of the SCA were to be found Wang Xiaolai, Yu Xiaqing, Lin Kanghou, Guo Shun, Qian Xinzhi, and of course Du Yuesheng. Indeed, in their composition the Shanghai delegates to the NPC clearly represented Du Yuesheng's own network of power. In addition to his colleagues from the SCA, they also included two of Du's leading Green Gang followers, Lu Jingshi and Zhu Xuefan, who represented the Shanghai trade unions, as well as his Green Gang colleague Jin Tingsun.[68] These elections, however, were overtaken by the Marco Polo Bridge Incident, which initiated the Sino-Japanese War; on August 13 the war came to Shanghai, and the NPC never met.

In addition to its participation in the political processes of the Guomindang state, the SCA, under the chairmanship of Du Yuesheng, was also an important source of support for the regime during periods of national crisis. Two major examples are provided by the December Ninth Movement of 1935 and the Xi'an Incident of December 1936. On December 9, 1935, about 6,000 students in Beiping demonstrated against continued Japanese incursions in North China, in particular against the creation of the East Hebei Autonomous Council, a semi-autonomous regime that was under the effective control of the Japanese military. The students also opposed the Nanjing government's policy of continuing appeasement in the face of Japanese military aggression, which led the Chinese government to create its own autonomous organization in North China, the so-called Hebei-Chahe'er Political Council. By the end of the first week the number of students involved in the demonstrations in Beiping had more than doubled to 15,000, and the movement spread to the other major cities of China, including Shanghai.[69]

On December 24 there were major student demonstrations in Shanghai, and the Mayor, Wu Tiecheng, was presented with a request from the students for permission to go to Nanjing to present a petition to the government. Mayor Wu, however, refused and forbade any further demonstrations in line with instructions he had received from the Minister of Education, Wang Shijie.[70] On the following day, Christmas Day 1935, Wu held a meeting with Du Yuesheng and other members of the SCA to discuss the student situation in Shanghai. At this meeting Du and his SCA colleagues expressed their approval of the Mayor's actions, and offered their assistance to the municipal government in the preservation of peace and order in Shanghai.[71] In this way the SCA, under the chairmanship of Du Yuesheng, actively assisted the Shanghai Municipal authorities in its attempts to limit the political consequences of the December Ninth Movement in Shanghai.

A year later an even more serious political crisis confronted the Nanjing government as a result of the detention of Jiang Jieshi by Zhang Xueliang in Xi'an on December 12, 1936. Zhang's purpose was to persuade Jiang to end the civil war with the Communists and form a united front with them against Japan.[72] Du Yuesheng was one of the first members of the Shanghai elite to rally to Jiang's support. Du, together with Wang Xiaolai and Qian Xinzhi, sent an urgent telegram to Zhang in the name of the SCA and the Shanghai Chinese Chamber of Commerce in which they offered to go themselves to Xi'an as hostages in return for Jiang's release.[73]

It is possible that Du hoped to use his long-established relationship with Zhang to gain Jiang's release. Du had had business dealings involving contraband opium with Zhang in the past; and in March 1933 he had extended his personal protection to Zhang when the latter came to Shanghai at a time when he was the subject of numerous assassination attempts and death threats because of his reputed loss of Manchuria to the Japanese.[74] Although nothing came of Du's offer, it should not for that reason be dismissed as merely an empty political gesture, given the fact that by the end of 1936 he was a key element in the Guomindang's structure of power in Shanghai. On Jiang's release from Xi'an on Christmas Day 1936, Du was among the first to travel to Nanjing to offer his sympathy and congratulations to the Generalissimo.[75] It is clear, therefore, that by 1937 Du Yuesheng had established the SCA as an organization that exercised influence, not only at the level of local Shanghai politics, but also at the level of national politics.[76]

DU YUESHENG AND OPIUM

As noted in chapter 6 the agreement reached between the local Shanghai authorities and Du Yuesheng over the latter's opium interests in late 1932 was a basic element in the accommodation between Du and the Guomindang regime. As a result of this agreement Du became part of the Nanjing government's semi-official opium monopoly. Because the purpose of this covert monopoly was to raise additional revenue for Jiang Jieshi's anti-Communist campaigns, it was run by the Hubei Special Tax Bureau (also known as the Hankou Special Tax Bureau) under the control of Jiang's military headquarters in Nanchang. Du's role in these operations was to control the Shanghai opium merchants and to collect taxes on opium at the rate of 15 cents per ounce on behalf of the official Special Tax General Bureau (*Teshui Zongju*) which was established in Shanghai. At the same time Du controlled the operation of the system in Jiangsu through his Green Gang followers and colleagues, who held all the key positions in the so-called Jiangsu Province Opium Suppression Bureau. When the opium monopoly in Jiangsu was canceled in September 1933,[77] Du reopened his Three Prosperities Company in Nandao, and this quickly became, in the words of an SMP Special Branch report, "the chief distribution office and supply agent for opium in Shanghai."[78]

Two key official figures in this covert monopoly were the Minister of Finance, Song Ziwen, and the Mayor of Shanghai, Wu Tiecheng. Both had close relations with Du. By 1933 Du and Song had reached an understanding that ended the serious conflict of 1931. Indeed on at least two occasions, in August 1933 and December 1935, Du extended his protection to Song when the latter's life was threatened.[79] Wu Tiecheng, for his part, was on Du's payroll, and received a "personal donation" of Ch$500,000 a month from Du, as had his predecessor as mayor, Zhang Qun. According to the SMP Special Branch it had been Song Ziwen and Du Yuesheng together who had secured Wu Tiecheng's appointment as Wusong-Shanghai Defense Commissioner, in order to guarantee protection for the operation of the covert opium monopoly in the Jiangnan area.[80]

This covert monopoly, however, was hostage to scandal and could cause serious political embarrassment to the Nanjing government. A case in point was the morphine scam of November 1933. In mid-1933 Du Yuesheng, together with Wu Tiecheng, Song Ziwen and Lu Liankui (Assistant Superintendent in the SMP and a Green Gang boss) organized the Xia Ji Company (*Xia Ji Gongsi*) to refine a quantity of morphine that had been seized by the Chinese authorities in Hankou. The operation had the approval of Jiang Jieshi who wanted the morphine refined for "medicinal purposes." However Du used this agreement as a useful cover to refine his own consignments of morphine rather than those of Jiang Jieshi. When Huang Jinrong informed Jiang of Du's scheme in late 1933, the resulting uproar almost cost Wu Tiecheng the mayoralty of Shanghai, and seriously compromised Du's relations with Jiang. It was only with some difficulty that Du was able to retain his position in the semi-official monopoly.[81]

In order to avoid these recurring scandals associated with the covert policy, Jiang Jieshi's Nanchang headquarters introduced in June 1934 a new strategy of the phased suppression of opium over a six-year period. Although the objective was to end all dealing in opium by 1940, the scheme was in fact a system of official monopoly. Under its terms all dealing in opium was restricted to government agencies and licensed merchants, while only registered smokers would be allowed to buy opium. As part of this scheme the Shanghai Municipal Government set up a Shanghai Municipal Opium Suppression Committee (*Shanghai Shi Jinyan Weiyuanhui*—SMOSC) in July 1935 under the control of a three-man Standing Committee consisting of Du Yuesheng, Wang Xiaolai, and Yan Fuqing, President of the Chinese Red Cross.[82] The functions of this committee were to supervise the registration of addicts, suppress unlicensed dealers, and conduct propaganda on behalf of the government's policy of opium prohibition.

In fact the operations of the SMOSC enabled Du to promote his opium interests quite openly as the Shanghai representative of the official monopoly. The means by which he effected this was his control of the licensing and addict registration systems in Shanghai.[83] Furthermore, Du could now count on the public cooperation of government agencies such as the Chinese Maritime Customs. According to Ilona Ralf Sues, after 1935 the customs turned over all stocks of confiscated opium to the SMOSC for destruction. Many customs staff believed, however, that these confiscated stocks merely found their way back via the committee into the illicit traffic.[84] In 1936 and 1937, moreover, protracted and ultimately inconclusive negotiations were held between the Shanghai Municipal Government and the Shanghai Municipal Council (SMC) for the extension of the Chinese suppression policy to the International Settlement.[85] These negotiations essentially took up where the earlier negotiations in 1928 had left off, and they held out the prospect for Du of extending his opium operations legally into the International Settlement, thirteen years after the SMP had successfully eliminated large-scale narcotics trafficking in the Settlement.

THE ENDURANCE CLUB

The various threads of Du Yuesheng's growing network of power and influence were brought together in the Endurance Club. This club was established in November 1932 (although it did not formally open for business until February 1933) with the express purpose of coordinating Du's various interests and effectively projecting his power in Shanghai. The key figures in this organization were Lu Jingshi, Wan Molin and Chen Qun. It was Lu who played the principal role in the club's planning and organization, while Chen Qun, a professional politician and former secretary to Du, suggested the club's name, and Wan Molin, Du's erstwhile butler, took charge of the club's day-to-day administration.[86]

On Lu Jingshi's advice, the Endurance Club was created as a deliberately elitist organization whose membership was restricted to those with social standing; that is, politicians, government and military officials, industrialists, financiers and professionals. In other words it was conceived as a vehicle for the promotion of Du Yue-sheng's interests within the local Chinese political, economic and social establishment. Membership, therefore, was not open to all of Du's followers, and the majority of his gangster coterie were excluded. Thus the Endurance Club was distinct from, but complementary to, Du's Green Gang group. Prospective members of the club underwent a membership ceremony similar in many respects to that of a secret society, and which involved their acknowledgment of Du as their "master." They were not inducted, however, into the Green Gang, and Du refrained from instructing them in the secret language of the Green Gang.[87]

The membership of the Endurance Club remained relatively small, numbering in the hundreds rather than the thousands, although within those limits there was a remarkable expansion of membership prior to the outbreak of the Sino-Japanese War. In the four years from February 1933 to May 1937 membership increased more than four-fold, from 130 to 564.[88] According to the data on the 402 members for whom details are available, the majority, 54 percent, were businessmen and industrialists. These were followed by politicians and government officials, 24 percent, and next came professionals (lawyers, journalists, medical practitioners, educationalists, etc.), 13 percent. The smallest groups of members were trade union officials, 6 percent, and military officers, 3 percent.[89] However, it should be noted that the trade union members were entirely composed of Post Office employees. The overwhelming majority of Endurance Club members, 80 percent, lived and worked in Shanghai, and most of the remainder came from the nearby provinces of Zhejiang and Jiangsu. An interesting figure is the 5 percent of members who lived and worked in Nanjing, which indicates that Du Yuesheng's organizational network was well-entrenched within the national capital itself.[90] The composition of the membership of the Endurance Club, therefore, reflected the expanding pattern of the social, economic and political networks of Du Yuesheng in Shanghai after 1932.

The Endurance Club had a formal organizational structure, complete with periodic congresses, a nineteen-member executive committee, and a nine-man standing committee. Organizationally, the Standing Committee of the Executive Committee was the highest decision-making body of the club; and between 1934 and 1936 the membership of the Standing Committee of the Second Executive Committee consisted of Lu Jingshi, Cai Futang, Zhang Kechang, Xu Maotang, Zhang Rongchu, Zhang Zilian, E Shen, Zhang Shichuan, and Chen Dazai.[91] In June 1936 in an attempt to encourage greater involvement by the membership in the activities of the club an Advisory Council (*Pingyi Hui*) was established. It consisted of fifty members, or ten percent of the club's total membership at that time, who met every second month, and its aims were to strengthen the club's organization and to promote the cohesion of its membership.[92]

This formal structure, however, meant very little in practice. The Endurance Club was Du Yuesheng's organizational instrument and everything was in fact directly controlled by him. The membership voted as Du directed, and he would select a list of officeholders, which would be read out at the Congress and formally voted through by the membership. Power did not reside in the formal structure but in Du and his immediate coterie, Lu Jingshi and Wan Molin.[93] Lu Jingshi emphasized the character of the Endurance Club as Du's personal organization in his speech to the club's Third Anniversary Congress. In this speech he observed that the club had only one leader and only one center and that was Du Yuesheng, and went on to remark that all Endurance Club members had to "serve Mister Du like dogs and horses."[94]

DU YUESHENG'S ASCENDANCY WITHIN THE SHANGHAI GREEN GANG SYSTEM AND RELATIONS WITH THE TRIADS

By the mid-1930s Du's Endurance Club was the most powerful personal organization within the Shanghai Green Gang because of its links with the Shanghai bourgeoisie and with Guomindang politicians and government officials. It also reflected the position of primacy that Du Yuesheng then enjoyed within the Green Gang structure.[95] By the mid-1930s Du had succeeded in eliminating his major rivals and in asserting his preeminence over his two erstwhile colleagues, Huang Jinrong and Zhang Xiaolin.

By 1935 the most serious threat to Du's position was provided by the ambitions of the Green Gang boss Gu Zhuxuan, who had emerged as a very powerful figure in the Green Gang system in Shanghai. By the 1930s, for example, Gu had a personal following of well over 7,000 "disciples," over 6,000 of whom were resident in

Shanghai, while a further 1,000 were scattered throughout the various counties of the Subei region.[96] In the early 1930s, Gu began to extend his power beyond his bailiwick in Zhabei/Hongkou and into other areas of Shanghai.[97] In late 1930, for example, he became a "pupil" of Huang Jinrong in order to extend his influence into the French Concession. During the Shanghai Incident, in April 1932, he was, as noted earlier, the principal figure behind the creation of the pro-Japanese Zhabei Puppet-Government. The major activity of this government was the establishment of gambling and opium dens, and it is probable that Gu attempted to capitalize on Du Yuesheng's conflict with the French authorities over the removal of Du's narcotics and gambling operations from the Concession.[98] Du, therefore, had good reason to take Gu's challenge seriously.

In the autumn of 1935, however, Gu's position suddenly collapsed when he was arrested by the French police for the murder two years earlier of Tang Jiapeng, the manager of the Great World Amusement Center and a follower of Huang Jinrong. Gu was tried, found guilty and sentenced to fifteen years imprisonment. He successfully appealed the sentence, however, and was released in December 1936 after having been imprisoned for fifteen months. Although some sources suggest that Du Yuesheng framed Gu, the evidence suggests that Gu did in fact arrange Tang's murder in 1933. It is possible, however, that Du encouraged the investigation by the French police in 1935, and he certainly stood to gain by Gu's incarceration. His trial and imprisonment eliminated Gu as a serious rival of Du Yuesheng, and when he emerged from prison his power was greatly diminished. Du followed up Gu's discomfiture by eliminating the power of Gu's cousin and ally in the French Concession, one Jin Jiulin.[99]

By 1934 the close cooperation between the three French Concession Green Gang bosses, which had ensured the supremacy of their organization within the Green Gang system in Shanghai since the early 1920s, had effectively broken down. The reason was that neither Zhang Xiaolin nor Huang Jinrong had accommodated themselves to the political realities of the new Guomindang corporatist system as successfully as had Du Yuesheng. As a result both Zhang and Huang lost substantial authority and power to Du, which enabled him to emerge as the undisputed Green Gang boss in Shanghai in the course of the 1930s.

Although Zhang Xiaolin cooperated with the authorities of the new Guomindang state after 1927, he never developed the same close working relationship with them as did Du, and which he himself had enjoyed with the authorities of the previous warlord regimes in the 1920s. During the 1930s Zhang's position within the Green Gang structure derived from his large network of followers within the French Concession, and his diverse business interests, many of which were in association with Du Yuesheng, such as the Lin Ji Timber Company (*Lin Ji Muhang*), which traded in timber products from the Soviet Far East.[100] Of particular importance was his standing and influence with the French authorities, which continued even after the closure of the gambling dens and the removal of the narcotics operations from the Concession in 1932. Zhang, nevertheless, experienced an erosion of his power after 1932 as increasing numbers of his Green Gang followers left him for service with Du Yuesheng. At the same time, Du was able to use his political connections to exclude him from particularly lucrative financial deals. A case in point was the government's currency reform of 1935, when Du obtained prior knowledge of the government's plans but failed to inform Zhang, because he wished to exploit the financial advantage for himself. Zhang deeply resented Du's actions in this affair.[101]

Huang Jinrong, for his part, was in a state of virtual semi-retirement by 1930. Beginning with the Lu Lanchun Affair of 1924, Huang's power within the Green Gang had steadily declined in the second half of the 1920s, although he remained an influential figure within the French Concession Green Gang organization. At the same time Huang lost touch with the centers of power in the new Guomindang state after 1927, and particularly after 1932. Although he, alone of the Green Gang leaders in 1927, was personally known to Jiang Jieshi, and indeed had introduced his colleagues to the latter on the eve of the anti-Communist purge, his relationship with Jiang dated from 1919, that is, the period prior to Jiang's emergence as a political leader within the reorganized Guomindang. Despite his involvement in the anti-Communist purge in April 1927, Huang had not maintained contact with Jiang in Guangzhou in the 1920s, and, unlike Du Yuesheng, he did not develop relations with the new political groups and politicians, such as the Chen brothers and their CC Clique, Kong Xiangxi, Song Ziwen and other prominent political and financial figures who made up Jiang's network of power in the 1930s. His isolation from Jiang's network is illustrated by his decision to offer Wang Jingwei his protection in 1931.

Huang also failed to diversify the recruitment of his followers by including petty politicians and businessmen, as was done so effectively by Du Yuesheng through his Endurance Club. His followers, therefore, continued to be drawn in the main from the gangster demimonde, and only two of them, Tang Jiapeng and Ding Yongchang, demonstrated any skill in furthering the interests of their boss in the changed environment of the 1930s. Huang did not develop any substantial relationship with the Chinese business or financial communities of Shanghai to the degree that Du Yuesheng, or even Zhang Xiaolin, succeeded in doing in the 1930s. Indeed, he refused to do so, and contented himself with maintaining his interests in those concerns, such as theaters, amusement centers, hotels and bathhouses, associated with the popular entertainment industry of Shanghai; in fact, those traditional "legitimate" business interests preferred by Shanghai gang bosses. The only serious new business venture that Huang undertook in the 1930s was the Great World Amusement Center, which he took over from Huang Chujiu in 1931.[102]

It is not surprising, therefore, that Huang's power declined markedly in the 1930s, especially in relation to that of Du Yuesheng, and that he became increasingly marginalized within the power structure of the Shanghai Green Gang. As this process unfolded, serious tensions and covert conflict emerged in the relationship between Huang Jinrong and Du Yuesheng. In 1933, as noted above, Huang attempted to undermine Du's relationship with Jiang Jieshi by revealing to the latter the full extent of Du's role in the morphine scam of that year. Although Du was able to extricate himself successfully from the ensuing controversy he did so only with some difficulty, and Huang came very close to realizing his objective. Some two years later, in early 1936, Du struck a blow against Huang's prestige when his leading follower, Lu Jingshi, the newly appointed head of the Martial Law Division of the Wusong-Shanghai Garrison Command, arrested Chen Peide, one of Huang's foremost followers and the Chairman of the BAT Trade Union, as a suspected Communist. The immediate cause of this incident was competition between Lu and Chen for control of the SMGLU, but the deeper cause was the covert conflict between Huang and Du. Huang was outraged and demanded that Yang Hu, the Wusong-Shanghai Garrison Commander, release Chen immediately; at the same time, he complained to Jiang Jieshi who ordered Yang to conduct an investigation into the affair. On his release Chen accused Lu of deliberately slighting the authority of Huang Jinrong.[103]

A further incident occurred in December of the same year when one of Huang's closest Green Gang associates, Cheng Ziqing, a Chinese Chief Detective Inspector with the French Concession Police's Sûreté, was accused by the Guomindang authorities of spying for the Japanese in Shanghai. Cheng asked for Huang's help in clearing up the allegations against him, and Huang was compelled to request Du Yuesheng to use his contacts in the local administration to resolve the "misunderstanding." Du wrote to Geng Jiaji, the French Secretary of the Municipality of Greater Shanghai, who investigated the case and recommended the withdrawal of the accusations against Cheng.[104] This incident revealed starkly Huang's lack of standing with the local Guomindang authorities by the mid-1930s, which greatly limited his own capacity to help even old colleagues when they ran afoul of these authorities without recourse to Du Yuesheng's assistance.

Neither Zhang nor Huang accepted passively their diminished power vis-à-vis Du Yuesheng, and both took measures to undermine his position in the mid-1930s. Zhang, for example, set up a couple of organizations whose principal purpose was to oppose Du's Endurance Club. One of these was called the Chinese Mutual Progress Association, which was an unmistakable reference back through the organization of the same name of 1927 to the original Mutual Progress Society created by Green Gang leaders in 1912. The other was called the Hut of Tolerance (*Ren Lu*), which was, perhaps, a whimsical rejoinder to the name of Du's organization, the Endurance Club.[105]

Similarly, Huang Jinrong approved the establishment of the Fidelity Club (*Zhongxin She*) in the summer of 1936 with the purpose of covertly undermining Du's Endurance Club by exploiting tensions and contradictions among its membership. Neither attempt by Zhang and Huang was successful. The problem was that Du Yuesheng was just too powerful; with his political connections he completely isolated his two former colleagues. Huang Jinrong ruefully reflected on this fact in a conversation with Xue Gengxin of the French Concession Police in 1939, when he complained that Du no longer addressed him respectfully as "Uncle Huang," as he once had done, but merely used the more familiar "Elder Brother Jinrong." Huang felt deeply Du's lack of respect for him.[106]

In addition to Du Yuesheng's creation of the Endurance Club and his assertion of primacy within the Green Gang system, Du also established a close relationship with the leadership of the Triads. This development further strengthened Du's central position within the secret society organizations of Shanghai and his key role in mediating the relationship between these organizations and the Guomindang political authorities in the 1930s. By the 1920s the Triad organization in Shanghai, as noted earlier, had entered a period of decline and was very much weaker than that of the Green Gang. The marginalization of the Triads in Shanghai was compounded by the close relationship that elements of the Green Gang leadership established with the Guomindang authorities from the late 1920s on.[107] This situation bred enormous resentment of the Green Gang among Triad members, which was only exacerbated by the necessity for Triad leaders to join the Green Gang organization if they wished to prosper in Shanghai. Good examples of this phenomenon were the careers of Wang Yucheng, Xu Langxi and Zheng Ziliang. All three were prominent Triad leaders, both Wang and Xu played an active part in the 1911 Revolution, and both set up their own Triad lodges (the Five Elements Mountain—Wuxing Shan—by Wang, and the Valley of Clouds Mountain—Guyun Shan—by Xu); while Zheng was a leader of the Triad Chaozhou Gang which ran the opium divans in Shanghai. Nevertheless, all three found it necessary to join the Green Gang in order to effectively pursue their activities in Shanghai; both Wang and Xu belonged to the Da generational status group of the Green Gang, while Zheng belonged to the Tong generational status group.[108]

From 1929 onwards periodic attempts were made by Triad leaders and certain local Guomindang politicians to revitalize the Triad system in Shanghai both to counteract the severe fragmentation of that system, which had accompanied its marginalization after 1916, and to restore its political links with the Guomindang. The first attempt occurred in 1929 with the creation of the Five Sages Mountain (*Wuxing Shan*) by five Triad leaders in Shanghai; Xiang Songpo, Ming De, Zhu Zhuowen, Mei Guangpei and Zhang Zilian. Despite its avowed aim of challenging the Green Gang's dominant position in Shanghai and the fact that its leadership had very close links with the Guomindang, this organization lacked any substance and never posed a serious challenge to the Green Gang ascendancy in Shanghai.[109] A second, and more structured attempt was made

in 1936 when Wang Yucheng and several other Triad leaders organized the Triad Promotion Association (*Hong Xing Xiehui*—
TPA). This association brought together over thirty separate Triad
groups in Shanghai, each of whom nominated five of its members
to represent it on the TPA; the latter body therefore had over 150
members and served to coordinate the activities of these Triad
groups. The TPA was also the official liaison body between the various Shanghai Triad organizations and the local Guomindang authorities, and it had the enthusiastic support of Jiang Hao, a member
of the Executive Committee of the Shanghai Municipal GMD Party
Branch who was also a member of the TPA.[110]

Du Yuesheng had well-established connections with certain Triad
leaders through their common involvement in the contraband opium
traffic. As part of the operations of the Three Prosperities Company,
Du maintained close relations with two Triad leaders in particular:
Yang Qingshan, who was one of the three leaders of the Triad organization in Hankou and who controlled the transportation of Sichuan opium through Hankou; and Zheng Ziliang, the boss of the
Chaozhou Gang.[111] In the 1930s Du expanded his connections with
the Triad groups in Shanghai to take account of the restructuring of
the Triad organization undertaken under the auspices of the Guomindang. The key figure in Du's relations with these politically ori-
ented Triad organizations was Zhang Zilian. Zhang was one of the
five leaders of the Five Sages Mountain and was head of the Xinliantang (the Lodge of Trust and Integrity) which was one of the five
lodges that composed the Five Sages Mountain. He was also, however, a prominent member of Du Yuesheng's Endurance Club, and
was a member of the Standing Committee of that body's Second
Executive Committee which was appointed in 1934. In the mid-
1930s Zhang became a leading member of the TPA, and it was his
position on that body's Executive Committee that enabled Du to
influence the TPA's activities. Zhang's work on Du's behalf was
complemented by that of Mao Yun, who was also a member of Du's
Endurance Club as well as being a member of the TPA and of the
Shanghai GMD Party Branch.[112] In this way Du was able to exercise
some control over the Triad organizations in Shanghai and to monitor their relations with the local Guomindang.

In conclusion, the nature of Du Yuesheng's relations with the
Guomindang changed significantly after 1932, and this change was
intimately associated with the establishment of a system of state

corporatism by the Nanjing government. Du, in fact, was co-opted by the Guomindang state and became an important element in the new corporatist system as it functioned in Shanghai. The key aspects of this co-option were Du's alliance with the CC Clique, which provided the political context for his involvement with the corporatist structures in Shanghai; his rapprochement with the reformist leaders of the major "yellow unions," such as Lu Jingshi and Zhu Xuefan, which, together with his relations with the CC Clique, ensured for Du a major role in the Guomindang's industrial policy; and his chairmanship of the Shanghai Civic Association, which enabled him to play a prominent role in the mediation of relations between the municipal and national authorities and the Shanghai bourgeoisie. It was this active involvement with the structures of the Guomindang's corporatist state that clearly distinguished Du's activities after 1932, and which enabled him to emerge as an influential political power broker in his own right in Shanghai. At the same time Du's co-option by the Guomindang corporatist state gave him a crucial advantage over his erstwhile Green Gang colleagues and enabled him both to consolidate his power within the Green Gang system and to extend his influence over the Triad organizations in Shanghai. In many respects Du was the means by which the Guomindang incorporated the secret society organizations in Shanghai into its new corporatist political system. It was this corporatist system that also provided the institutional framework within which Du expanded his economic interests after 1932.

8 Gangster Entrepreneur
Du Yuesheng and the Shanghai Economy

The growth in the power and influence of Du Yuesheng in the 1930s was accompanied by, and inseparable from, the expansion of his economic interests. This expansion also went through two distinct phases. The first covered the period from about 1928 to 1931 and its main features were the more or less continuing close cooperation between Du and his two Green Gang colleagues, Huang Jinrong and Zhang Xiaolin; the regular use of coercive gangster tactics to gain economic advantage with individual Chinese businessmen; and a reliance on the power of the French Concession authorities. The second phase from 1932 to 1937, on the other hand, was characterized by the differentiation of the economic interests of the three Green Gang bosses, as Du asserted successfully his own interests over those of his erstwhile colleagues; a more positive and cooperative relationship with the leading members of the Shanghai bourgeoisie, especially those associated with the SCA, and a consequent moderation of gangster tactics; and a close and generally constructive relationship with the Guomindang authorities that superseded in importance the previous relationship with the French authorities, thereby gaining for Du a respectability that served him well in the highest political, financial and social echelons.

OVERTURE: RELATIONS BETWEEN THE FRENCH
CONCESSION GREEN GANG AND THE CHINESE
COMMERCIAL WORLD OF SHANGHAI, 1928–1931

The instrument by which Du penetrated successfully the financial and commercial world of Shanghai after 1930 was the Zhonghui

Bank. It opened for business in March 1929, and served as a conduit for the revenues generated by the gambling houses and the opium retail shops. According to one reliable source, the establishment of this bank had been suggested by Qian Xinzhi, who had urged Du to use the modern banking sector as a means of recycling the profits from his narcotics and gambling activities by investing them in legitimate business activities.[1] Qian was a key figure in China's modern banking circles through his position as Vice President of the Bank of Communications from 1922 to 1927, and in the course of 1928 he established a working relationship with Du Yuesheng, one of the first of Shanghai's leading Chinese capitalists to do so.[2]

The original board of directors of the Zhonghui Bank brought together leading Green Gang cronies of Du Yuesheng, such as Jin Tingsun and Li Yingsheng, with leading Shanghai financiers. Prominent among the latter were Xu Maotang, comprador for the P. & O. Banking Corporation from 1922 to 1937, and Zhu Rushan, Chinese manager of the *Union Mobilière Société Française de Banque et de Placement* (*Tonghui Xintuo Yinhang*). The bank also enjoyed the patronage of the French Consul, Koechlin, who was a member of its Board of Directors, a further indication of the close political and economic relationship between the French authorities and Du Yuesheng that developed after 1927. Although Du was Chairman of the Zhonghui Bank's Board of Directors he played only a nominal role in the running of the bank, and its management was largely in the hands of Xu Maotang.[3]

In its first two years of operations the Zhonghui Bank's regular business was not well developed, nor was the bank itself well managed. By 1931, in fact, it had incurred large debts.[4] At the same time, it was undercapitalized by the standards of other Shanghai commercial banks. Its initial capitalization was Ch$1 million, but only half of this amount was paid up in 1929 with the remainder not finally paid until 1931.[5] This was not a problem for the bank, however, since its main function was to channel the profits from Du Yuesheng's narcotics interests and his major gambling houses in the French Concession, notably the Fusheng or 181 Avenue Foch, into legitimate business activities. Given their clandestine or semi-clandestine nature, it is impossible to provide accurate figures for these profits. They must have been considerable, however, when one considers the official estimates of the narcotics traffic in Shanghai and the suggestion that the Fusheng gambling house alone had a monthly turnover of over Ch$2 million. The Zhonghui Bank also extended loans to the leading opium hongs on the security of their opium consignments.[6]

Initially neither Xu Maotang nor Zhu Rushan were willing investors in the Zhonghui Bank. Both agreed to invest substantial sums only after succumbing to some gangster-style blandishments from Du. Xu, for example, was obligated to Du after the latter had helped him obtain his father's inheritance, which had been contested by his father's concubine. When Du Yuesheng asked Xu to make a substantial investment in his new bank, therefore, Xu could not refuse. In fact he invested more money in the bank than did Du himself, and provided the initial capitalization of Ch$500,000. Xu also became a follower of Du and a founding member of the Endurance Club when it was established in late 1932.[7]

As the experience of Xu Maotang makes clear, Du Yuesheng, in his relations with Chinese capitalists, continued to rely on the gangster techniques of cultivating obligations and judicious use of intimidation. Good examples of this approach were the Green Gang bosses' involvement with the Shanghai Cotton Goods Exchange and their takeover of the business interests of Huang Chujiu. In 1930, Du Yuesheng and Zhang Xiaolin used intimidatory tactics to obtain a share of the extremely profitable business of the Shanghai Chinese Cotton Goods Exchange (*Shanghai Huashang Shabu Jiaoyisuo*). Their opening gambit was to send a group of gangsters to disrupt business on the floor of the exchange, which forced its temporary closure. The directors of the exchange, however, refused to enter into any negotiations with either Du or Zhang. Du, therefore, sent a second batch of gangsters to harass the members of the exchange as they entered and left the building. When the Shanghai Municipal Police refused to intervene, on the grounds that they dealt only with disturbances outside and not inside the exchange, the directors were forced to negotiate with the Green Gang bosses. As a result of these negotiations Du and Zhang not only were elected to the exchange's Board of Directors in the elections held in late 1930, but were made presents of parcels of shares in the exchange by one of its major shareholders, Wu Ruanyuan.[8]

Not long after this incident, the Green Gang bosses initiated moves against the business interests of Huang Chujiu. Huang ran a number of pharmacies and amusement centers, the most important of which was the Great World Amusement Center, which he had established in 1916 on the Avenue Edward VII in the French Concession. His business dealings were of a somewhat dubious nature on occasion and, according to the Shanghai Municipal Police, Huang enjoyed "friendly" relations with the three Green Gang bosses in the French Concession.[9] In fact Huang's business concerns were just the sort of enterprises that attracted the attention of the gangster bosses, and Huang Jinrong, in particular, had a long-standing interest in acquiring the Great World.

The Green Gang bosses' opportunity came in 1930 when the Day and Night Bank (*Da Shijie Riye Yinhang*), which Huang Chujiu had set up in 1921 and through which he financed his various business ventures, experienced financial difficulties. This bank was attached to the Great World Amusement Center and it attracted the business of small, working-class depositors by its generous opening hours of up to eight o'clock every evening. By early 1931 it was estimated that Huang's bank had a total of 13,000 depositors with over Ch$3 million in deposits. The bank, however, was very poorly managed, and Huang used it, in effect, as his personal treasury.[10] The Green Gang bosses turned this situation to their advantage, and encouraged a "run" by depositors on the bank by circulating reports of its insolvency, which precipitated a major financial crisis for Huang Chujiu. With his business dealings unraveling in late 1930, Huang's health gave way and he died on January 19, 1931.

On the very day of Huang's death a Liquidation Committee including such leading Shanghai merchants as Yu Xiaqing, Wang Xiaolai and Wang Yansong was established to wind-up his affairs. The French Concession Green Gang bosses were invited to join this committee, but they demurred and refused to cooperate with it.[11] The activities of the Liquidation Committee were frustrated by the obstructive tactics of Du Yuesheng and Huang Jinrong. After just one week the committee discontinued its operations citing unspecified "difficulties."[12] The fate of Huang Chujiu's bankrupt enterprises hung in the balance throughout the first half of 1931 as proceedings dragged on in the French Mixed Court. The sale of the Great World Amusement Center, in particular, was continually postponed until May when a company of which Huang Jinrong was the chairman, and appropriately named the Victory Company (*Shengli Gongsi*), obtained the lease on the Great World for a six-month period for a mere Ch$10,000.[13] Thus did Huang Jinrong obtain control of the Great World for a fraction of its market value (which was estimated at Ch$1.2 million in 1931), and it became the centerpiece of his business interests in the 1930s.

THE CONSOLIDATION OF DU YUESHENG'S ECONOMIC INTERESTS, 1932–1937

After 1932 Du Yuesheng successfully consolidated and expanded further his diverse commercial and financial interests in Shanghai, which provided the economic basis for his developing relationship with the Chinese bourgeoisie. As noted above, three factors contributed to this expansion. In increasing order of importance they were, first, the continued use of gangster tactics of intimidation that had proved so effective in the period prior to 1932. Second, the new political and economic relationship that was forged with key elements of the Chinese bourgeoisie, such as Wang Xiaolai and Liu Hongsheng, in the course of the Shanghai Incident. Most important of all, however, was the new political relationship that Du Yuesheng had established with the Guomindang during and immediately after the crisis of 1932; and particularly the role that the Guomindang authorities had reserved for Du in their economic strategy of seizing control of strategic business concerns under the rubric of "national enterprise" (*guoying*) or "joint official-merchant enterprise" (*guan-shang heban gongsi*).

The network of Du's business interests extended into all areas of the Shanghai economy in the years 1932 to 1937. Of particular importance, however, were his banking and shipping interests, and his interest in the city's food supply through his involvement with the fish hongs and the establishment of the Shanghai Municipal Fish Market. Du's activities in these areas are representative of the range of his business interests in Shanghai in the mid-1930s, and they provide the basis for this chapter.

Banking

The mid-1930s witnessed the dramatic expansion of Du's involvement with the financial world of Shanghai through the increased range of the business activities of the Zhonghui Bank, and his acquisition of interests in other banking institutions, especially in the Commercial Bank of China (*Zhongguo Tongshang Yinhang*).

Despite the problems that beset the Zhonghui Bank in its first years of operation, after 1932 it greatly expanded its field of operations and emerged as the primary vehicle for furthering Du's business interests. In 1932, for example, the bank transformed its previous debts into a healthy net profit of Ch$190,000. The following year its capitalization was doubled to Ch$2 million, which was increased further in 1936 to Ch$3.5 million with the acquisition of the Jiangsu-Zhejiang Commercial and Savings Bank (*Jiang Zhe Shangye Chuxu Yinhang*).[14] At the same time, the total assets of the Zhonghui Bank rose steadily from just under Ch$11 million in 1932, to over Ch$13 million in 1933, to just over Ch$15 million in 1935. By the mid-1930s Du's bank was a stable and successful medium-sized commercial bank, with a total staff of over 100. It was, in fact, one of that group of nine middle-sized banks which, together with the "big five" commercial banks (that is, the Shanghai Commercial and Savings Bank, the Jincheng Banking Corporation, the China and South Sea Bank, the Continental Bank, and the National Commercial Bank), controlled 80 percent of the assets of all Chinese commercial banks.[15] As befitted its enhanced status Du Yuesheng built a new headquarters for the bank, the Zhonghui Building (*Zhonghui Dalou*), on the Avenue Edward VII, at a total cost of Ch$1,560,000. Du had an extensive office on the second floor of the building that could only be reached by means of a bulletproof private elevator, and this served as the nerve center of his financial and commercial operations in the mid-1930s.[16]

Using the Zhonghui Bank as a base Du expanded his interests in the Shanghai banking world. As noted above, he took over the Jiangsu-Zhejiang Commercial and Savings Bank in 1936. He also established the Minfu Union Commercial Bank (*Minfu Shangye Chuxu Yinhang*) in August 1933, and two years later he was instrumental in the establishment of the China Investment Bank (*Guoxin Yinhang*), in association with his fellow Green Gang boss Zhang Xiaolin and leading Shanghai bankers such as Lin Kanghou.[17] Du also had a major interest in both the Pudong Commercial Bank (*Pudong Shangye Chuxu Yinhang*), which had been set up in 1928 and of which he became Chairman some years later, and the Bank of Asia (*Yazhou Yinhang*), which was established in 1934 by Li Yaozhang and others.[18] Du's interest in the development of modern-style banks continued into the period of the Sino-Japanese War, when he set up two banks in Chongqing, the Yong Cheng and the Fu Hua, in association with the Sichuan warlord Fan Shaozeng, one of his major business partners in the narcotics traffic, and Gu Jiatang, a leading member of his Small Eight Mob.[19]

In promoting his financial interests Du Yuesheng was assisted greatly by his relationship with the Guomindang authorities, both in Shanghai and in Nanjing. This was demonstrated clearly by his role in the Guomindang's "banking coups" of 1935, and, in particular, in the government's takeover of the Commercial Bank of China in June 1935. The marked increase in the size and scope of the operations of the Zhonghui Bank, in fact, was related directly to the events of 1935. By 1934 the Chinese business community was under a great deal of pressure both from the international economic depression, whose full impact it experienced for the first time, and from the destabilizing effects on the Chinese financial system of the large outflows of silver as a consequence of the United States government's silver-purchase policy. The Nanjing government took advantage of this situation to assert its control over the financial life of the nation by means of a takeover of the leading commercial banks and the implementation of a comprehensive reform of the currency.[20]

As Parks Coble has shown in his study of the relations between the Shanghai capitalists and the Guomindang state, the Finance Minister, Kong Xiangxi, assigned Du Yuesheng a major role in the government's takeover of the Bank of China (*Zhongguo Yinhang*) and the Bank of Communications (*Jiaotong Yinhang*) in late March 1935.[21] According to an SMP report Kong requested Du to negotiate with the shareholders of the two banks because these "shareholders were all on friendly terms with Mr. Tu, in whom they had much confidence . . . ."[22] In other words, Kong used Du's network of personal relations with the Chinese financiers in Shanghai as one element in his strategy for taking over the banks. Du, in his capacity as Chairman of the SCA, called a meeting on February 13, 1935, at which discussions were held between Kong and the Chinese financiers on the measures necessary to relieve the Shanghai business community of the worst aspects of the depression.[23] At this meeting, which was attended by representatives of the Shanghai Chinese Chamber of Commerce, the Shanghai Bankers' Association, the Shanghai Native Bankers' Association, and Zhang Jia'ao of the Bank of China, Du and Kong suggested that the Bank of China and the Bank of Communications, together with the Central Bank of China (*Zhongyang Yinhang*), should form a three-bank group to provide loans to the Chinese business community.

Du followed up this suggestion in early March by forming a special committee of the SCA to review these relief proposals, in which he invited the participation of leading bankers.[24] There was, however, a hard edge to Du's discussions, and it was probably during this period that he gave an unambiguous warning to Zhang Jia'ao not to thwart the takeover of the Bank of China.[25] Once the takeover had been completed successfully in late March, Du Yuesheng was appointed an executive director of the Bank of China and later that same year a director of the Central Bank of China.[26] This latter appointment caused Sir Frederick Leith-Ross, Chief Economic Adviser to the British government who led a British mission to China in 1935–36 to advise the Chinese government on currency reform, to protest to Kong that such an appointment would not enhance the standing of the bank. Kong replied, somewhat implausibly, that although Du had a murky past, he was now a reformed character and regularly attended the Kongs' Sunday services. Leith-Ross was later informed by a member of his mission, Cyril Rogers of the Bank of England, that Du Yuesheng was in fact one of the most sensible and helpful directors of the Central Bank.[27]

Du and his fellow Green Gang boss, Zhang Xiaolin, also played an important role in the government takeover of the Commercial Bank of China, which was one of three commercial banks targeted in the "little coup" of June 1935.[28] The Commercial Bank of China was the oldest modern Chinese commercial bank, having been established by Sheng Xuanhuai in 1896.[29] By the 1920s the bank was controlled by Fu Xiao'an, a prominent member of the Zhejiang financial clique, who held the position of Managing Director. In early 1927, however, Fu fell foul of the new Guomindang government because of his support for Sun Chuanfang, and he was forced to flee to Dalian when the Guomindang authorities ordered his arrest as a "reactionary" and the confiscation of much of his property.[30]

Fu remained in exile for over four years during which time he cultivated Du Yuesheng and Zhang Xiaolin and persuaded them to intercede on his behalf with the Guomindang authorities. As a result the arrest order was lifted and Fu returned to Shanghai in October 1931, and, as the price for their efforts, Du and Zhang were appointed to the Board of Directors of the Commercial Bank in June 1932 and given regular access to loans from the bank. These loans varied from several tens to several hundreds of thousands of dollars, and since they were never repaid, they were, in fact, a form of extortion. Such payments were one reason for the burden of bad debts, which totaled 57 percent of all loans, borne by the Commercial Bank in the early 1930s.[31]

In mid-1935 Kong Xiangxi deliberately provoked a financial crisis for the three banks as a preliminary to their takeover by the government. He did this by ordering both the Bank of China and the Bank of Communications to buy up the banknotes of the three commercial banks and then present them for immediate redemption, thus precipitating a liquidity crisis for the banks. Faced with this squeeze on his cash reserves Fu turned to Du for assistance, and the latter stated that his own bank, the Zhonghui Bank, was willing to provide Fu with the necessary loans to redeem the Commercial Bank's banknotes. This offer was something of a double-edged sword. If accepted it would have provided immediate relief for Fu's liquidity problems, but it also would have given Du enormous influence with the Commercial Bank, if not de facto control. Given that the Zhonghui Bank was a much smaller bank than the Commercial Bank, moreover, it was not an unreasonable question to ask where the money would come from to honor Du's offer. The inference was that on this occasion Du was acting as a front for the Guomindang government, a conclusion that was borne out by subsequent events.

Du also brokered an arrangement by which Fu transferred the ownership of his newly completed headquarters, the Commercial Bank Mansions (*Zhongguo Tongshang Yinhang Daxia*), valued at Ch$1.8 million to Kong's group, as a means of raising some of the cash necessary to redeem his bank's notes. At the same time, Du cooperated with Kong in increasing the pressure on Fu. When the latter was unable finally to raise further funds to redeem the Commercial Bank's banknotes, Du circulated rumors that the bank had closed its doors and thus encouraged a run by depositors on the bank. This tactic was strikingly similar to the one used against Huang Chujiu's Day and Night Bank in 1930. The run on the Commercial Bank finally forced Fu's hand and he relinquished control of the bank by formally turning over its account books to Du Yuesheng.

Following its takeover, the Commercial Bank was reorganized as a government-sponsored commercial concern, officially termed a "joint official-merchant enterprise," under the control of Du Yuesheng. On June 7, 1935, at a special meeting of the Commercial Bank's Board of Directors, Du was nominated Chairman, with Zhang Xiaolin as his deputy, and both represented the government shareholders in the bank. The same meeting reduced Fu Xiao'an's position to that of Executive Director. After 1935 nearly all the bank's senior officers belonged to Kong's group, either directly or as followers of Hu Mei'an, the bank's new Deputy Managing Director and a senior member of Kong's clique. These changes at the top were mirrored by changes at all levels of the bank's organization, which brought in a large number of Green Gang followers of both Du Yuesheng and Zhang Xiaolin, the most notable of whom included Gu Jiatang, Lu Jingshi and Yang Guanbei. It has also been alleged by a former senior officer of the bank that the nature of the Commercial Bank's business changed noticeably after 1935, with an increasingly large amount of business being done with local opium concerns and enterprises run by Green Gang members.[32]

Du took the opportunity of the Guomindang government's currency reform in late 1935 to speculate on both the domestic and foreign exchange rates. According to one source, Du used his relationship with Kong to obtain prior knowledge of the future exchange rate between the new Chinese dollar (*fabi*) and the Sichuan dollar (*chuanbi*). He and one of his cronies, the Sichuan warlord Fan Shaozeng, then bought up large quantities of Sichuan dollars and enjoyed a huge windfall profit once the new Chinese dollar was issued.[33]

According to another account told to Leith-Ross in 1936, Du had also obtained confidential information on the future foreign exchange rate of the new Chinese dollar from Kong's wife, Song Ailing. Du, however, apparently misunderstood the information and bought up large amounts of Chinese currency. As a consequence, he faced a major financial loss that was estimated to be equivalent to over 50,000 pounds sterling. When Du's attempts to gain redress from Kong himself proved fruitless, he reverted to gangster-style intimidation by sending a coffin together with six funeral attendants to Kong's home as a none-too-subtle warning to Kong. This had the desired effect and Kong called a special meeting of the Central Bank's Board of Directors (of which Du himself was incidentally a newly appointed member), and at this meeting it was agreed that the Central Bank should take responsibility for Du's holdings of worthless Chinese currency.[34] Although Leith-Ross could not vouch for the complete veracity of this story, it does indicate, nevertheless, in a very striking way the contemporary belief in Du Yuesheng's capacity to use strong-arm tactics when his interests were threatened, even against his patrons within the Nationalist government.

SHIPPING

One of Du Yuesheng's most important business decisions after 1932 was to become a shipping proprietor in his own right. As a result of this decision he gained a share of the lucrative riverine and coastal trade based in Shanghai, and, at the same time, extended his business interests beyond the confines of the city and its immediate hinterland. Having his own fleet of ships also strengthened Du's control over the transportation of contraband opium, since it reduced his dependence on other shipping companies, and neatly complemented his monopoly over the distribution of the drug in Shanghai and the Jiangnan region.

Du Yuesheng's acquisition of a shipping line was made easier because of the significant leverage he already exerted over the proprietors of both docks and shipping companies through his control of stevedoring and seamen's organizations.[35] In the 1920s and 1930s all the major Shanghai Green Gang bosses had an interest in the rackets on the Shanghai waterfront. They controlled the stevedores who worked the Shanghai docks through Green Gang followers who monopolized the posts of dock foremen-cum-labor contractors (*baogongtou*). These gangster-foremen recruited their own followers from among the stevedoring gangs, which were usually organized along native-place lines, such as the Pudong, Subei and Shandong gangs. Each of the foremen controlled his own particular "turf," which was usually a section of a dock, and in the 1930s there were estimated to be 266 such "feudal kingdoms" (*fengjian wangguo*) on Suzhou Creek and along both banks of the Huangpu River. As a Shanghai adage put it: "Good men do not eat dock rice. If one wishes to eat dock rice, then one must submit to an 'old man' [*laotou*, that is, a gangster boss]."[36] These local gangster bosses could call on the support of their patrons, the major gang bosses, when they got into difficulties or had serious conflicts with rival gangs over "turf."

Du Yuesheng was the most influential gang boss on the waterfront with most followers among the gangster-foremen. One of his followers, Yu Xianting, was Chairman of the leading stevedores' union on the Shanghai docks, the China Merchants' Five Docks Joint Trade Union (*Zhaoshangju Wumatou Liangonghui*).[37] The power that Du could exercise through his control of these stevedoring gangs was indicated by the fact that proprietors of stevedoring companies, such as Liu Hongsheng, regarded it as essential to reach an accommodation with him. Liu, for example, developed close relations with Du and his two colleagues, Huang Jinrong and Zhang Xiaolin, and would entertain them regularly at his home on Chinese New Year and other festivals. When his son, Liu Nianzhi, assumed the management of Liu's stevedoring company, the China Docks Company (*Zhonghua Matou Gongsi*), the younger Liu felt the need to take Du as his "old man." In other words he became one of Du's Green Gang followers in order to facilitate his management of his father's stevedoring company.[38]

Du Yuesheng also controlled the sailors who worked on the various coastal and riverine shipping lines. The mechanism through which he exercised this control was the China Seamen's Union (*Zhonghua Haiyuan Gonghui*), whose secretary, as noted in chapter 7, was none other than Yang Hu, one of Du's leading Green Gang associates. Du's influence with the seamen was well illustrated by the speed with which he mediated a settlement of the strike by sailors employed by the China Merchants' Steam Navigation Company (CMSN) in early January 1932. This strike, which began on January 7 and at its peak involved 1,300 sailors, was the result of longstanding grievances over terms and conditions of service. Principal among these was the demand that the CMSN recognize the organization of a trade union among the company's sailors. Once the strike was declared, it was the sailors themselves who requested Du to mediate the dispute, which he did successfully, together with the shipping magnate Yu Xiaqing, in a series of meetings held over a three-day period, January 9–11. Once a compromise settlement had been negotiated the strike was ended, and the sailors returned to work on January 12.[39]

The shipping company that was the target of Du Yuesheng's ambitions was the Da Da Steam Navigation Company (*Da Da Lunchuan Gongsi*—DDSN), whose financial and managerial problems made it vulnerable to Du's takeover strategy in 1932–33. The DDSN had been established by Zhang Jian, a leading gentry-entrepreneur, in 1904 as part of the operations of the industrial complex that he had built up in Nantong since the mid-1890s. By the mid-1920s the DDSN dominated the shipping routes between Shanghai and the Subei ports, especially those of Haimen, Nantong, and Yangzhou, and which were referred to as the "little Yangzi routes" (*xiao Changjiang xian*).[40]

In the late 1920s and early 1930s the DDSN experienced numerous problems, which reached crisis proportions in the years 1931–32, seriously weakening the company and making it a ready target for the intrigues of Du Yuesheng. After Zhang Jian's death in 1926 the DDSN, together with the other enterprises of the Nantong complex, went into a slow but steady decline. As a result the DDSN faced increasing competition from other shipping companies and it progressively lost its predominant position on the Subei run. This economic decline of the Zhang family enterprises was compounded by political problems, when Zhang Cha, Zhang Jian's brother, fled to Dalian after being designated a "reactionary" in 1927 by the new Guomindang government for his assistance to Sun Chuanfang during the Northern Expedition. As a consequence, after 1927, the operations of the DDSN were subject to periodic interference from the Guomindang authorities.[41]

In 1931 the company experienced a major disaster when two of its steamers were destroyed by fire with the loss of over 1,000 passengers. Overcrowding was one of the main causes of this disaster, and the following year the Harbor Board fined the DDSN for violating the shipping regulations by carrying passengers in excess of the numbers stipulated by law.[42] The final blow to the company's solvency came with the collapse of the DDSN's banker, the Deji Native Bank (*Deji Qianzhuang*), in the wake of the Shanghai Incident. As a result of this bankruptcy the DDSN lost all its funds, estimated at over Ch$200,000, deposited with the bank. The collapse of the Deji Bank also caused a revolt of the shareholders against the DDSN management, which, after Zhang Cha's flight, had been in the hands of Bao Xinzhai, and this provided Du Yuesheng with his opportunity to seize control.[43]

Du's bid for control of the DDSN in 1932–33 was both carefully planned and systematically executed. A pivotal role was played by Yang Guanbei. Yang was a trained economist and lawyer whose family held major investments in Zhang Jian's Nantong complex. Yang himself had a detailed knowledge of the inner workings of the Nantong enterprises both through his position as one of the directors of the Da Sheng Cotton Mill (*Da Sheng Shachang*) and his shareholdings in the Shanghai Nantong Real Estate Company (*Shanghai Nantong Dichan Gongsi*). At the same time, he had well-established links with the Guomindang, which dated from the period of the Northern Expedition when he worked in the Political Department of Bai Chongxi's military headquarters where he established good working relations with both Chen Qun and Yang Hu. Through these connections Yang was introduced to Du Yuesheng, and he quickly became one of Du's leading followers and key economic advisers.[44]

Taking advantage of the DDSN's financial disarray Yang Guanbei sought to gain leverage in the company by arranging for the Zifeng Native Bank (*Zifeng Qianzhuang*) to purchase a nominal shareholding of Ch$3,000 in the DDSN on behalf of himself and Du Yuesheng. As a shareholder Du could now bring pressure to bear on the company's directors from the inside, and, in alliance with a large group of disaffected shareholders, he demanded a thorough reform of the DDSN management. When the resulting reorganization preserved the dominant interests of the Zhang family and thus failed to meet Du's requirements, he used his connections with the local Guomindang authorities to bring further pressure to bear on the DDSN management. Du wrote a letter to Wu Xingya, Head of the Bureau of Social Affairs of the Shanghai Municipal Government, in which he complained of rampant corruption within the DDSN. In response Wu convened a general meeting of shareholders, which he then directed to reorganize the company's Board of Directors and appoint a new Chairman together with a new Managing Director.[45]

During the negotiations over the composition of the new Board of Directors Du strengthened his position by resort to strong-arm gangster tactics. He ordered one of his senior Green Gang followers, Dai Buxiang, to seize control of the Da Da Docks (*Da Da Matou*) in Shiliupu. In the ensuing conflict between Dai's gangsters and those of the gangster-foreman of the docks, one Zhang Jinkui, members of the Bureau of Public Safety led by its chief, Cai Jingjun, intervened and sealed the docks. As a result the DDSN steamers could neither load nor unload cargo, and the company's business ground to a halt. The circumstances and the timing of this fracas strongly suggest some degree of collusion between the Chinese police authorities and Du Yuesheng. After this affray Zhang Jinkui drew the obvious conclusion and joined Du's Green Gang group, a move that gave Du complete control of the Da Da Docks.[46]

The closure of the docks had a direct influence on the outcome of the negotiations, and when the new board met in 1933, Du's victory was complete. He had gained unquestioned control of the DDSN. Under the new arrangements Du Yuesheng was Chairman of the

Board of Directors, while his two followers, Yang Guanbei and Xu Yihe, were Manager and Deputy Manager respectively. The Zhang family's interests were represented by Zhang Jian's son, Zhang Xiaoruo, who was appointed Managing Director. This was a purely nominal position, however, since all decisions on company policy were taken by Yang Guanbei.[47]

Once he had gained control of the company Du left its day-to-day management in the hands of Yang Guanbei who ran it without further reference to the shareholders. According to the memoirs of a former senior employee of the DDSN, no general meeting of shareholders was called after 1932–33, and very few meetings of the full Board of Directors were ever held. Despite this, and the fact that the DDSN failed to declare a dividend for the remainder of the 1930s, the shareholders were effectively intimidated by the potent combination of Du's gangster muscle and his political connections and dared not protest.[48] At the same time, Du placed his own Green Gang followers in key management positions. In addition to the posts held by Yang Guanbei and Xu Yihe, Yang Zhixiong became the company's new Supervisor; Zang Ruiqing, the new Warehouse Manager; and Chen Runqing, the company's new General Inspector.[49]

Once he controlled the DDSN, Du Yuesheng also used his relations with his fellow Green Gang bosses to enhance the company's business prospects. In an important move to rehabilitate the company's operations, he secured protection for its activities in Subei through the Green Gang boss Gao Shikui. As a member of the prestigious Da generational status group of the Jiang Huai Si Branch of the Green Gang, Gao was an important "elder" in the Green Gang system in Shanghai in the 1930s. He also exercised significant influence among the Green Gang groups in the Subei region, as his original power base at the turn of the century had been provided by his control of the docks along the route of the Grand Canal in northern Jiangsu.[50] In the early twentieth century the Subei region suffered from endemic banditry which, in conjunction with periodic natural disasters and a resource-poor economic environment, resulted in major disruptions to the rural economy.[51] In the late 1920s the situation worsened with the outbreak of a revolt by the Small Sword Society in which local Green Gang leaders were involved.[52] As a consequence of this highly volatile situation the operations of the DDSN, like those of other commercial enterprises in the region, were disrupted by the depredations of bandits and Small Sword rebels. Gao now used his influence and prestige on behalf of Du to obtain the agreement of the leading bandit chief and Green Gang boss in the Lake Hongze region, one Wu Laoyao, not to attack the DDSN steamers on the Subei run. Yang Guanbei followed up this agreement by appointing influential local Green Gang bosses as the managers of the DDSN's branch agencies in Subei.

At the same time, Yang also organized the Da Xing Trading Company (*Da Xing Maoyi Gongsi*), in conjunction with the Shanghai Commercial and Savings Bank (*Shanghai Shangye Chuxu Yinhang*) and the Bank of Communications, to act as a purchasing agent in Shanghai for Subei merchants, allowing them to avoid the inconvenience and danger of traveling to Shanghai to make their purchases. The company also strengthened the grip of Du Yuesheng over the commercial activities in Subei. Indeed, by the late 1930s the DDSN, under the control of Du Yuesheng and through the efforts of Yang Guanbei, had been transformed into a vast trading conglomerate that not only ran separate shipping services for passengers and freight but also provided agency services for local merchants, which even included arrangements with the Shanghai banks for a bills of exchange facility.[53] In the creation of this conglomerate the Green Gang networks of Du Yuesheng played a considerable role.

These same networks were important also in reaching accommodations with rival shipping companies after 1933, and in particular with the Da Tong Renji Steam Navigation Company (*Da Tong Renji Hangye Gongsi*—DTRSN) which was the DDSN's major competitor on the Subei route. The DTRSN was established in 1924 as a partnership between Yang Zaitian, a former salt smuggler from Subei and one of the leaders of the Big Eight Mob in Shanghai, and the two leading members of the French Concession's Gentry-Councillor Clique, Lu Baihong and Zhu Zhiyao.[54] At first the DTRSN plied only those Subei routes for which it had reached a prior agreement with Zhang Jian. After 1926, however, it engaged the DDSN in serious competition, and, by employing larger steamers, it succeeded in significantly eroding the DDSN's previous dominance of the "little Yangzi run" by the early 1930s.[55]

The dynamics of this competition, however, changed dramatically after Du Yuesheng acquired the DDSN. Du's deal with Gao Shikui gave the DDSN a clear advantage over the DTRSN on the Subei routes, and the former was able to press this advantage by excluding the latter from certain ports, notably Nantong. Yang Zaitian, therefore, sought to reach an understanding with Du Yuesheng on the basis of their common membership of the Green Gang. This understanding resulted in the creation of an effective duopoly on the Shanghai-Subei run with the establishment by the two shipping companies of a common organization, the Da Da–Da Tong Joint Office (*Da Da–Da Tong Lianhe Banshichu*). By means of this joint office the two companies divided up the Subei run between themselves on the basis of mutually agreed percentages, and presented a common front toward competition from other shipping lines.

The creation of this duopoly, however, antagonized Yu Xiaqing who was anxious that his own San Bei Steam Navigation Company (*San Bei Lunchuan Gongsi*) should gain a share of the business of the Shanghai-Subei run. Du Yuesheng, however, successfully used his influence with the Guomindang authorities to frustrate Yu's ambitions. As a consequence Yu's complaints to the Shanghai Bureau of Shipping Administration (*Shanghai Hangzhengju*) and the Ministry of Communications were unsuccessful. Finally, in 1934, the Ministry of Communications convened a Committee for the Regulation of Shipping Routes (*Zhengli Hangxian Weiyuanhui*), which recommended that the Shanghai shipping proprietors themselves mediate an agreement between Du and Yu Xiaqing. The compromise that was eventually reached involved the hiring by the Da Da–Da Tong Joint Office of one of the San Bei Company's steamers to ply the Subei run.[56]

In the mid-1930s Du Yuesheng's position as a leading Shanghai shipping proprietor was reinforced by the role that he and the other Green Gang bosses played in the Nanjing government's "nationalization" of the CMSN. The takeover of the CMSN had been a longstanding objective of the Guomindang, and an attempt had been made to assert its control over the company even before the forces of the Northern Expedition reached Shanghai in March 1927. The consolidation of the new government's control over the CMSN, however, proved somewhat elusive in the years from 1927 to 1931, when all attempts were negated by the general political instability that affected the regime itself. As a result the CMSN experienced a period of acute uncertainty, which reached its nadir in July 1930 when a serious dispute between Zhao Tieqiao, the government-appointed Commissioner for the Reorganization of the CMSN, and Li Guojie, the former Chairman of the CMSN, with both parties accusing the other of misappropriation of funds and general corruption, resulted in the murder of Zhao.[57] At the same time, the leading foreign banks in Shanghai refused to extend further banking facilities to the CMSN's subsidiary, the China Merchants' Steam Navigation Wharves Company (*Lunchuan Zhaoshangju Matou Gongsi*), because its business management was in a "state of chaos," and demanded that its management be given to a foreigner and that the company be reorganized "on a sound business basis."[58]

In the wake of the political and foreign policy crises of 1931–32, the Guomindang government adopted a new and more radical approach to the question of control of the CMSN. In October 1932 the government initiated a complete takeover of the company through the systematic purchase of all CMSN shares at the rate of 50 taels per share; a process that was substantially completed by the beginning of March 1933. At the same time, the government renamed the company the National Enterprise China Merchants' Steam Navigation Company (*Guoying Zhaoshangju*).[59] This policy of nationalization by purchase was accompanied by a major reorganization of the CMSN's management with the appointment of a new Managing Director, Liu Hongsheng, together with new executive and supervisory committees. In addition to Liu Hongsheng all the senior management of the reorganized company was drawn from among those Shanghai entrepreneurs and industrialists who had been active during the crisis of 1932 and who were leading members of the SCA, such as Shi Liangcai, Wang Xiaolai, Yu Xiaqing, Qian Xinzhi and Rong Zongjing.[60]

The Green Gang bosses also held influential positions in the reorganized company. Both Du Yuesheng and Zhang Xiaolin were members of the new Executive Committee, while Du was also a member of its influential Standing Committee. At the same time both Huang Jinrong and Du's close colleague, Jin Tingsun, were members of the Supervisory Committee. The prominence of the Green Gang bosses in the new CMSN administration was unsurprising. As noted above, all had a share in the control of the Shanghai docks, and Du, in particular, exercised a major influence over the stevedores on the CMSN docks and among the sailors on the CMSN steamers. These Green Gang bosses also had a long-standing interest in the affairs of the CMSN, as its steamers were the principal means by which the Three Prosperities Company's opium shipments from Sichuan were transported to Shanghai. Both Du and Zhang were also members of the SCA; indeed, as noted earlier, Du was Deputy Chairman of the

SCA at this time. Du Yuesheng's leverage within the CMSN was increased by the fact that the company's new Managing Director, Liu Hongsheng, was involved in the stevedoring business and had enjoyed a close relationship with Du and his gangster colleagues for some considerable time. According to the memoirs of Liu's son Liu Nianzhi, the day after his father took up his appointment as Managing Director of the CMSN, he invited Du, Zhang and Huang to lunch and requested their help in running the company.[61]

Liu Hongsheng faced an extremely difficult task as Managing Director because the Board of Directors was riven by factionalism, and disputes over policy were frequent and heated. It is possible that, given the importance that Liu Hongsheng attached to cooperation with the Green Gang bosses, the increasing tensions between Du Yuesheng and Huang Jinrong after 1932 was one factor contributing to these policy disputes. Both Du and Huang were returned in the elections for the executive and supervisory committees that were held in October 1933. Problems within the CMSN management, however, reached a crisis in 1935, and in February 1936 a further reorganization took place. Liu Hongsheng resigned and was replaced as Managing Director by Cai Zengji, and the Supervisory Committee was abolished. Among other things, this reorganization strengthened Du Yuesheng's position within the CMSN at the expense of Huang Jinrong, who lost his position in the CMSN administration with the abolition of the Supervisory Committee.[62]

The Shanghai Food Supply and the Shanghai Municipal Fish Market

Another area of cooperation between Du Yuesheng and the Guomindang authorities, and also a source of major conflict between Du and Huang Jinrong, was the creation of a centralized municipal fish market at Point Island (*Dinghai Dao*) in the Yangshupu district of Greater Shanghai in May 1936. Fish and fish products constituted one of the basic food staples of the population of Shanghai in the early twentieth century. In the 1930s the Shanghai market represented about half of the estimated total annual demand for fish in China, just under Ch$51 million out of Ch$100 million.[63]

The Green Gang bosses, and in particular Huang Jinrong, had long been involved with this lucrative business. Huang controlled the twenty-three fish hongs located in the Marche de l'Est, French Concession, which, until the mid-1930s, supplied fish to all the food markets in Shanghai. The fishing grounds for Shanghai were located in the waters off the Zhoushan archipelago and these were the monopoly of the "fish barons" (*yuba*) on Zhoushan with whom the fish hong proprietors of the Marche de l'Est enjoyed sworn brother relations. The supply of fish to Shanghai, therefore, was controlled by a duopoly composed of the Zhoushan "fish barons," who owned the fishing fleets, and the Marche de l'Est fish hong proprietors, who handled the distribution of fish.[64]

Behind both stood the figure of Huang Jinrong. All of the leading fish hong proprietors, such as Wu Xintai and Zhou Mengyue, were his followers, as was Chen Yiting, Chairman of the Zhoushan Native-Place Association (*Zhoushan Tongxianghui*) and the Shanghai representative of the "fish barons." In addition one of Huang's leading followers and closest advisers in the 1930s, Huang Zhenshi, was manager of the Shanghai Municipal Association of Frozen Fish Storage Enterprises (*Shanghai Shi Bingxianye Tongye Gonghui*).[65] Du Yuesheng also had long-standing interests in the fish industry that developed out of the work he did in this area for Huang Jinrong in the early 1920s. In 1925, for example, Du organized the Dunhe Office (*Dunhe Gongsuo*) which later became the Shanghai Municipal Association of Frozen Fish Enterprises of which he was chairman. It was, in fact, as a representative of this organization that Du first gained membership in the Shanghai Chinese General Chamber of Commerce.[66]

After 1932 the Nanjing government planned to extend its control over the Shanghai fish market by setting up a central fish market as an "official-merchant joint enterprise." Work was commenced at Point Island in 1934 and completed in May 1936. The government's purpose was both financial and strategic: to gain access to the largest and most profitable fish market in China, and to control the supply of one of the basic food items in Shanghai. This latter point was not lost on the foreigners in Shanghai. H.G.W. Woodhead, for example, in his regular column in the *Shanghai Evening Post and Mercury* enlarged upon the possible security threat posed to the foreign settlements by the establishment of a central fish market on Chinese territory and under Chinese control.[67]

These moves by the local Guomindang authorities to assert their control over the fish market dovetailed neatly with Du Yuesheng's own ambition to expand his interests in the frozen fish business. It was generally believed at this time that an expansion of cold-storage facilities could triple the total annual demand for fish in China.[68] As early as 1931 Du was appointed Chairman of a committee that had been set up by the Ministry of Industry to reorganize the fishing industry of Jiangsu and Zhejiang, and he was involved in the planning of the central fish market from its inception in 1934.[69] Given Huang Jinrong's predominant position in the existing fish marketing arrangements, the expansion of Du Yuesheng's interests could only be at the expense of those of Huang. The latter had also been involved with the planning of the new market through the membership on the Planning Committee of his close adviser Huang Zhenshi. Huang Zhenshi, however, was eventually squeezed out of this position by Du Yuesheng, and this was the cause of serious tension between Du and Huang Jinrong.[70] Du also made inroads on the fish hongs, and by the mid-1930s five leading fish hong proprietors were members of his Endurance Club.[71]

The Shanghai Municipal Fish Market (*Shanghai Shi Yuye Shichang*) opened for business on May 11, 1936. The complex contained a market, godowns, a cold-storage warehouse that could hold up to 1,500 tons of fish, and an icehouse that could produce fifty tons of ice a day. Its total capitalization was Ch$1.2 million, with the business community and the government each providing 50 percent.[72] In line with its organization as a joint official-merchant enterprise (*guanshang heban gongsi*), eight members of its fifteen-man Executive Committee were government appointees and the remaining seven were appointed by the business community. The actual number of businessman on the committee, however, was more than this breakdown might suggest as the government appointees included merchants such as Wang Xiaolai and Yu Xiaqing.[73]

Du Yuesheng headed the list of appointees by the business community, and he enjoyed a commanding position in the new fish market's administration. He was appointed Chairman of the Board of Directors, and his business partner of the mid-1930s, Wang Xiaolai, was appointed Managing Director. Of the two Deputy Managing Directors, one, Tang Chengzong, was one of Du's trusted followers, and the other, Zhu Kaiguan, became a follower of Du shortly after taking up his appointment. Moreover, Du's Green Gang colleague, Jin Tingsun, was a member of the market's five-member Supervisory Committee, as was Du's financial adviser, the banker Qian Xinzhi.[74] It was Du who presided over the market's official opening ceremonies on May 11, 1936. The new fish market also recruited a large number of its employees from Du's Endurance Club and, in the course of 1936, the club's Employment Section was able to find positions in the new market for eleven club members.[75]

These new arrangements for the marketing of fish in Shanghai were extremely contentious from the outset. In the first place they did not provide a satisfactory role in the new system for Huang Jinrong and his associates, despite the latter's long involvement with the fish hongs of the Marche de l'Est. At the same time, the arrangements required these fish hongs to move from the Marche de l'Est to the Point Island site, and to work on a commission basis rather than on their own behalf as they had done previously.[76] Not unnaturally this caused great resentment among the hong proprietors, and thirteen of the leading fish hongs, led by the Gongda and Qianfeng hongs, and encouraged by Huang Jinrong, went on strike on May 17. They requested the support of the French authorities who were themselves unhappy about the compulsory move of the fish hongs from their jurisdiction, since it deprived the Concession of a lucrative source of revenue in the form of licenses. The French Consul General lodged an official complaint with Mayor Wu Tiecheng, as did the French Chargé d'Affaires with the government in Nanjing.[77]

The strike by the fish hongs lasted about three weeks and was marked by occasional instances of violence. In late May, for example, groups of gangsters organized by the thirteen hongs and belonging to Huang's coterie systematically intimidated the fish hongs located in the International Settlement to prevent them from dealing in fish from the municipal market. In response the Shanghai municipal authorities extended military and police protection to the municipal market to ensure its resumption of operations.[78] By early June an impasse had been reached, and attempts at mediation by Yu Xiaqing got nowhere.[79] Finally Du Yuesheng entered into discussions with Huang Jinrong and a compromise was reached by which the fish hongs agreed to move to the new municipal market and, in return, provision was made for Huang's interests to be accommodated in the new system by giving Huang Zhenshi a role in the operations of both the central market and the new Fisheries Bank (*Yuye Yinhang*), which the Central Bank established under Du Yuesheng's chairmanship. On June 7 the fish hongs ended their strike and Wang Xiaolai could announce publicly that the "misunderstanding" was at an end.[80] Despite this compromise Huang

Jinrong's interest in the fisheries' business had received a major, indeed, a permanent check, and Du Yuesheng emerged, in conjunction with the local Guomindang authorities in Shanghai, as the predominant force in the business of supplying fish to the Shanghai market.

The expansion of Du Yuesheng's economic interests in the 1930s, therefore, followed a definite pattern. In the first place the targets were usually companies that were experiencing serious financial difficulties, such as Huang Chujiu's establishments in 1930–31 and the Da Da Steamship Company in 1932–33, and were therefore vulnerable to financial manipulation. Favored targets, moreover, were the concerns of those capitalists who had fallen foul of the Guomindang for whatever reason, and therefore enjoyed no political protection. This was the case with the management of the Da Da Steamship Company and with Fu Xiao'an of the Commercial Bank of China. A further characteristic was the judicious use of gangster tactics of intimidation in order either to force the management of the targeted institution to take the overtures seriously, or to forcibly cut through an impasse in negotiations. Good examples were Du's dealings with the Shanghai Cotton Goods Exchange in 1930 and with the Da Da Steamship Company in 1932. Once the takeover was completed, Du immediately moved to place his own Green Gang followers in key positions throughout the organization irrespective of their lack of technical or commercial competence, and also irrespective of whatever promises had been made to existing staff during the process of negotiations. Such a development occurred in both the Da Da Steamship Company and the Commercial Bank of China. In other words Du Yuesheng did not consider such organizations merely as profit-making concerns, but regarded them also as bases of power for the promotion of his Green Gang interests.

Finally, in his economic activities Du worked with and relied on the power of the Guomindang authorities. It was this relationship that gave Du a decisive advantage both over other entrepreneurs and over fellow Green Gang bosses in his economic ventures. The pattern can be clearly observed from the instances discussed in this chapter. Wu Xingya's intervention was crucial, for example, in Du's takeover of the Da Da Steamship Company; while the expansion of Du's interests in the Commercial Bank and in the fish market of Shanghai was achieved within the context of the Guomindang's policy of extending partial state control over key areas of the Shanghai economy. In the former case Du collaborated with Finance

Minister, Kong Xiangxi, and in the latter case with the Mayor of Shanghai, Wu Tiecheng.

Du Yuesheng's business activities in the mid-1930s, in fact, revealed the mutuality of interests that had developed between himself and gangster-business concerns on the one hand and the Guomindang authorities on the other. The context of this relationship was the GMD's attempts to extend its economic control through the promotion of "joint official-merchant enterprises." Although the Guomindang authorities used Du Yuesheng as one of their agents in the furtherance of this policy, he was not simply their creature. If he had been merely this he would not have served their interests as effectively as he did. As shown in chapter 7, after 1932 Du had established a solid relationship in his own right with senior members of Shanghai's Chinese bourgeoisie. It was this fact that enabled him to mediate successfully the relationship between the Guomindang authorities and the Shanghai bourgeoisie, especially after 1934 when he chaired the SCA. In this context Du's cooperation in the implementation of the Guomindang's policy of "joint official-merchant enterprises" served his own purposes of creating and expanding an independent base of economic power for himself and his Green Gang coterie.

Conclusion

The Green Gang, far from being a hangover of China's premodern feudal society, was, in fact, an integral part of the processes of social, economic and political change that together created the "modern" character of early-twentieth-century Shanghai. It was part of the very fabric of Shanghai's complex and changing social structure. This is the central argument of the book. It is developed through a discussion of the French Concession Green Gang group: its adaptation of secret society traditions to meet the new challenges and opportunities presented by Shanghai's urban milieu; its emergence as a highly organized criminal syndicate through its control of narcotics, gambling, extortion and labor rackets; and its progressive influence over key sectors of the city's business community.

The French Concession Green Gang group, however, was more than merely a criminal organization. The book argues that it also became, through the activities of its leaders such as Du Yuesheng and (to a lesser degree) Zhang Xiaolin, part of the political system of Shanghai. The opportunities for such involvement were provided by the peculiar political structure of Shanghai. Not only was the city divided between three separate administrations, but these administrations also represented two very different types of state system, a modernizing, nationalist regime in the Chinese City and variant forms of the colonial state in the International Settlement and the French Concession. Despite their differences, however, both types of state were limited in nature: the limits on the Chinese regime reflected its weak institutionalization, political instability and the restricted reach of its sovereign power; while in the two variants of the colonial state, issues of security and public order took priority over other areas of administrative activity. As a consequence both types of state system in Shanghai sought to maximize their respective political resources by the careful co-option of other centers of power within the city.

Preeminent among these were the various gangster organizations. Green Gang leaders were co-opted into the police forces of the International Settlement and the French Concession in order to strengthen the coercive power of the colonial state, and in some situations were used also as intermediaries between the colonial state and the Chinese population through their appointment to such bodies as the French Concession's Provisional Commission. The Chinese municipality, for its part, sought to utilize the power that the Green Gang bosses enjoyed in the foreign settlements as one means of extending indirectly its political reach into those settlements. The informal influence and, more particularly, control that a Green Gang boss like Du Yuesheng enjoyed with the workers and the bourgeoisie by reason of his highly developed labor and extortion rackets, moreover, was transformed and institutionalized in the 1930s through his co-option by Guomindang state corporatism. As a result Du's Green Gang organization became an integral part of both the Guomindang's formal trade union organization and the expanding state sector of the urban economy. Du, together with his close colleagues and followers, also played prominent roles in those political organizations, such as the Shanghai Civic Association and the Shanghai Provisional Municipal Council, which mediated relations between the regime and the bourgeoisie. By the outbreak of the Sino-Japanese War in 1937, therefore, Du Yuesheng's organization had become an intrinsic element of the structure of Guomindang state power in Shanghai.

In the course of the 1930s Du Yuesheng had successfully remade himself. Although he remained the head of the most powerful organized criminal syndicate in Shanghai, this was no longer the only or, increasingly, the most important element that defined his power in the city. It was the creation of his own political networks and his involvement with the politics of the city (and indeed the nation) that enhanced and consolidated his influence in Shanghai. He had become, in other words, a leading political figure in his own right and a powerful ally of the Guomindang state.

The Shanghai Green Gang was a product of the history and culture of modern China, and its development needs to be understood in that context. At the same time, however, the phenomena of secret societies and organized crime was also prevalent in other societies and cultures both in the West and in Asia in the first half of this century. Although the secret society/gangster structures in these countries had their own, historically shaped characteristics, yet there were also a number of underlying elements that they had in common. Many of the variables, for example, that contributed to the emergence of the Green Gang as a system of organized crime in Shanghai in the 1920s and 1930s—the fragmented immigrant society; the free-wheeling urban capitalism; a weakly institutionalized national state; the existence of colonial regimes; and the stimulus of revolutionary movements—were also common, to a greater or lesser degree, to other secret society/gangster systems, although, of course, not necessarily in the particular combination found in Shanghai. The present chapter, therefore, seeks to locate the Green Gang in this broader comparative context through a discussion of some of these other systems of organized crime in the nineteenth and early twentieth centuries. Specifically, it discusses four major types: the Italian mafia, organized crime in the United States, Indonesian gangsters, and the Japanese *yakuza*.

THE RELATIONSHIP TO THE MODERN STATE: THE ITALIAN MAFIA

Scholarship over the last twenty years, particularly the works by Blok and Arlacchi, has provided us with a new, sophisticated and complex understanding of the Italian mafia.[1] Despite the very different historical situations and cultures, this research provides a basis from which to begin to make some comparative generalizations about the mafia and the Green Gang. The works by Blok and Arlacchi, for example, have shown that the mafia, far from being a single, centrally organized and unified system, was in fact a loose network of small groups of no more than a dozen or so individuals (known as *cosca*—"artichoke leaves") organized around one leading mafioso. In this it was reminiscent of the Green Gang, which was itself not a centralized but rather a loosely structured network of groups organized around powerful individuals. In the case of the Green Gang, however, this structure was reinforced by a formal generational hierarchy and a system of branch (*bang*) organizations, which provided it with a relatively greater degree of organizational coherence than that enjoyed by the mafia of southern Italy.

Mafia also grew out of and reflected a culture of violence. The ability and preparedness to use violence was the mark of a mafioso, and the successful use of violence earned him "respect" that was the basis for his cult of honor. For Arlacchi, mafia was "a form of behaviour and a kind of power" rather than a formally structured organization. As he observed, "The behaviour of the mafioso was part of a culture system whose central theme was honour attained through individual violence."[2]

A culture of violence was also important to Chinese secret societies like the Green Gang. Preparedness to resort to violence, as discussed in chapter 1, was one important means by which Green Gang members defined themselves as *haoxia* (men of honor and courage) and set themselves apart from the general population.

The mafia, moreover, despite certain arcane characteristics, was not a legacy from the feudal period but very much a product of the modern age. As Eric Hobsbawm warned us in his discussion of the mafia: "It is a mistake to believe that institutions which look archaic are of great antiquity. They may, like public schools or the fancy dress part of English political life, have come into existence recently (though built of old or pseudo-ancient material) for modern purposes."[3]

This view of the mafia also resonates in the history of the Green Gang. Although it drew on the traditions of the Patriarch Luo Sect and the Grand Canal boatmen's associations, the Green Gang was very much a product of the modern age. It was still in the process of expansion and organizational definition in the first two decades of the twentieth century.

As the writings of Blok and Arlacchi demonstrate, the mafia was the product of the political and socioeconomic changes that were set in motion by the impact of two related external forces on nineteenth century southern Italy—capitalism and the modern state. Capitalism impinged on the rural economy with the break-up of the feudal estates and the reorganization of agricultural production for the national and international markets. According to Blok a form of "rent capitalism" developed in certain areas of rural Sicily in which a landless and land-poor peasantry worked the large estates for absentee landlords, who handed over the management of their estates to *gabelloti* (overseers). Arlacchi argues that the resulting asymmetry between this mercantile capitalist economic structure and the traditionalism of the cultural structure created a "society of permanent transition."

At the same time, the formation of a modern state system began to influence political life in southern Italy. The process began in the waning years of the Bourbon Kingdom of the Two Sicilies and gathered pace after the Risorgimento and unification in 1860–70. Although the state had modern, centralizing ambitions, in southern Italy its institutions were weak, and, crucially, it failed to gain a monopoly of violence over local society. State formation, in other words, was only partially realized, and it was forced to share power with local elites. Local mafiosi were able to take advantage of the resulting power vacuum to interpose themselves between different social and political groups in this highly fragmented society. The power of these mafiosi, therefore, derived from their role as mediators and middlemen. Monopolizing the position of gabelloti they mediated the economic relations between landlords and peasantry, and many became landlords in their own right. They also mediated relations between local society and the state. With its imperfect control over the instruments of violence, the state entered into a pragmatic relationship with the mafiosi that sanctioned their use of private violence to control the public arena in the villages, as a de facto extension of state power at the local level.

Allowing for the different milieus in which they both operated, the one rural and the other urban, there were broad similarities between the conditions that gave rise to the mafia and those that enabled the Green Gang to flourish. An emergent capitalism and a weakly institutionalized state system were as important to the development of the Green Gang in Shanghai as they were to the mafia in southern Italy. In the early twentieth century the Green Gang was able to make effective use of the opportunities provided by the new social and economic structures of the emergent capitalist system in Shanghai. Of particular note was its influence on an emerging working class through its control of transitional structures such as the labor-contract system, thus enabling them to mediate relations between this working class and the industrial capitalists. The influence of Green Gang leaders, furthermore, owed much to the constraints on the reach of the power of the national state in Shanghai. As a result the Guomindang state in the decade after 1927 sought to co-opt the informal, private power of certain local Green Gang leaders, most notably Du Yuesheng, to further the interests of the state. As with mafia leaders, the power and influence of the Green Gang bosses derived, in no small measure, from their mediatory role in relations between local society and the state and between different social classes.

The arrival of fascism after 1922 resulted in major changes in the system of accommodation between state power and the mafia in southern Italy. Regarding the existence of mafia as an unacceptable challenge to his claims to control all aspects of Italian society, Mussolini used the extensive organization of the Fascist Party and its militia to fill those gaps in communication between the localities and the center on which the mafiosi had thrived. Mafia structures were systematically destroyed and their leaders sent into internal exile. By these means, the power of the Fascist state penetrated the rural areas of southern Italy to an unprecedented extent. The way Italian Fascism dealt with mafia bore some similarity to the policies that the Chinese Communist Party instituted against secret societies after it came to power in 1949. Both were activist, revolutionary parties intent on establishing control over their respective societies and, therefore, could not tolerate independent systems of power (such as mafia and secret societies). Because of their respective emphases on total control neither party was interested in co-opting such power systems, but sought, rather, their complete elimination as vestiges of a "feudal" past. The success of the Fascist state was short-lived, and mafia reemerged in the 1940s with its decline and collapse. It might be observed in passing that the Chinese Communists too have failed to eliminate the phenomenon of secret societies. The relaxation of state power that has accompanied the economic reforms of the 1980s has seen the reemergence of secret society-type organizations in various parts of China, especially in the South.

Despite the fact that mafia in southern Italy was an overwhelmingly rural phenomenon, the above discussion suggests that it did have certain elements in common with the Green Gang. Both were loosely structured networks rather than tightly organized systems, although the size and degree of organization within the Green Gang groups in Shanghai was certainly greater than the mafia "cosca." The catalyst for the development of both organizations was an emergent capitalism, and their power derived from their role as middlemen in their respective societies, mediating relations between different social groups as well as between such groups and the institutions of the state. The relationship with the modern or modernizing state was of fundamental importance to both, with the constraints on the reach of the state's power compelling it to enter into pragmatic relationships with such centers of private power as the Italian mafia and Shanghai Green Gang.

THE GANGSTER ENTREPRENEUR: AMERICAN ORGANIZED CRIME

When Western journalists in Shanghai in the 1930s sought to explain the phenomenon of the Green Gang to their readers, the comparison they invariably reached for was with organized crime in contemporary urban America, and in particular the criminal syndicate in Chicago controlled by Al Capone. Many also compared Du Yuesheng with Capone and the former was frequently referred to as either "the Al Capone of the French Concession" or "the Capone of Shanghai."[4] Others sought to refine the comparison in order to convey the complex sweep of Du Yuesheng's activities, tending to see him as "a combination of Al Capone and Rockefeller."[5] As Percy Finch put it, "[Du] was a compound of an Al Capone with social standing, a Lucky Luciano on a Wall-Street scale, and a Shanghai Rockefeller badly in need of an Ivy League to put him right with the public."[6] Despite its tendency on occasions to degenerate into journalistic cliché, there was, nevertheless, a great deal of point to the comparison of the Shanghai Green Gang with American crime syndicates.

The origins of the American criminal gang/syndicate are to be found in the ethnic youth gangs that proliferated among the immigrant communities in cities such as New York. Although these syndicates were later commonly described as "the mafia" they were not exclusively Italian but included a mix of ethnic groups, including Jews, Irish and Poles, as well as Italians. The gangs themselves were loose networks of alliances rather than a highly structured organization.[7]

This eclecticism of the American gang/syndicate was also shared by the Green Gang system. As the careers of Du Yuesheng and other Green Gang bosses indicate, the Green Gang organization was able to draw on a vast pool of young street hoodlums for its recruits. It also successfully absorbed into its system other well established petty gangster groups such as the *hunhun'r* of Tianjin and various Triad-affiliated gangster groups in Shanghai. This eclecticism could give rise to confusion, and some commentators on the Shanghai Green Gang referred to it as the "Green/Red Gang" (*Qinghong Bang*).

The key event in the emergence of organized crime in the United States was the prohibition on the manufacture, sale and transport of alcoholic beverages as a result of the ratification of the Eighteenth Amendment in 1919 and its enforcement by the Volstead Act of 1920.[8] Prohibition performed the same role for American organized crime as the opium traffic did for the Shanghai Green Gang. In both cases governmental prohibition of a commodity for which there remained a huge consumer demand provided the opportunity for criminal entrepreneurs to meet that demand by illegal means. Fabulous profits could be made from "bootleg" alcohol. In the 1920s, for example, the Torrio-Capone organization in Chicago grossed somewhere between US$60 million and US$240 million a year from beer and other alcoholic beverages. As Al Capone observed, "Prohibition is a business."[9] This recognition saw the emergence of what Fried has termed "Prohibition capitalism."[10] The gangs created their own illicit business organizations roughly patterned after those of legitimate business, entered into business dealings with Canadian breweries and distilleries, and developed a relationship with major banks. Many went on to invest their profits from "bootlegging" in legitimate businesses.

Prohibition was also the catalyst for the greater rationalization, indeed "professionalization," of the organizational structure of the gang/syndicate with the creation of syndicate cartels. These cartels, such as "the Combination" organized by Lucky Luciano, sought to regulate the competition between different syndicates, dividing up the "bootlegging" business and territory on an agreed basis, and mediating disputes. At the same time, these syndicate/cartels forged links with local politicians, political parties and police forces in order to gain protection from the enforcement of the law against the illicit trade in alcohol. Such arrangements were pioneered by John Torrio and Al Capone in Chicago and were known as "the Chicago pattern."[11] This system was different from the Tammany tradition of gangsters working for the political machine. In the Tammany system the politicians controlled the gangsters through the former's system of patronage, whereas under Torrio and Capone it was the syndicate bosses who controlled the local politicians. These organizational developments certainly bore a broad similarity to the ways in which the French Concession Green Gang emerged as the pre-eminent gangster organization in Shanghai through its control of opium trafficking during roughly the same period. There was a similar professionalization of the organizational structure with the creation of a syndicate cartel, the Three Prosperities Company, which regulated the contraband opium enterprise in association with the Chaozhou opium merchants, military and police agencies, and city politicians. This system, as refined by Du Yuesheng, might well be described as "the Shanghai pattern."

With the repeal of Prohibition in 1933 the criminal syndicates to which it had given rise did not dissolve themselves but retained their organizational coherence and redirected their energies into other activities: gambling, prostitution, and narcotics trafficking. They also used extortion as an effective tool for their penetration and takeover of legitimate businesses. One activity in particular that gained in importance during the Depression was labor racketeering.[12] Exploiting the needs of both factory owners and union officials for their services to either break strikes or protect striking unionists, various gang syndicates penetrated certain trade unions and took them over. They used these unions as a system of double extortion, appropriating the unionists' membership dues and extorting payments from related industries on pain of industrial action. A good example was Lepke Buchalter's takeover of the New York Cutters' Local No. 4, which served as the base for his control of the New York garment industry in the 1930s.[13] Other examples were the control that organized crime exerted over the Port of New York with its takeover of the International Longshoremen's Association, and its forty-year influence with the Teamsters' through its corrupt compact with Jimmy Hoffa.[14] Such developments were not dissimilar to Du Yuesheng's takeover of the French Tramways Union in the French Concession, which he used not only to control the workers but also to gain leverage with the French management. At the same time, the control of New York stevedores by organized crime had a parallel in the effective control that a number of Green Gang bosses exercised over the docks in the Port of Shanghai.

The emergence of a system of gangster capitalism in the United States in the 1930s was broadly similar to what occurred in Shanghai during the same period. The manner in which vast profits from illicit activities were used to gain access to legitimate businesses and the use of gangster methods to intimidate actual or potential business rivals were, as we have seen, also the stock-in-trade of the Green Gang. There were differences, however. As noted in the preceding chapters, Du Yuesheng and his Green Gang group not only reached accommodations with local politicians and police on an ad hoc basis, but were also integrated into the system of state power that the Guomindang government developed in the course of the 1930s. The Green Gang did not merely run labor rackets; it actually became part of the formal structures of labor organization created by the Guomindang state.

COLONIAL STRUCTURES AND NATIONALIST REVOLUTION: THE GANGSTERS OF JAKARTA

The historical study of gangster cultures in Asia is not as well-developed as that for Europe and the United States. Some works have made their appearance, in the last few years, however, which provide the beginnings for such a study. Of particular interest, from the perspective of the Shanghai Green Gang, is the emergence of gangster organizations in the great colonial cities of Asia, and their relations to both the ruling colonial state and indigenous social classes. We are able to consider one such group, the Indonesian gangsters of colonial Batavia (Jakarta), thanks largely to the pioneering study by Robert Cribb of the involvement of these gangsters in the politics of the Indonesian revolution.[15]

Colonial Batavia in the early twentieth century was a fragmented society. The population was composed of immigrants from other areas in Java as well as from other Asian countries, and these immigrant groups led a physically and socially segregated existence in the city. This fragmentation, together with the mobility of the migrant population, encouraged the emergence of middlemen "fixers," such as the labor bosses who played a key role in hiring and managing the city's labor force. Their need to use coercive power led many of these labor bosses to establish relations with local gangsters, and many gangsters, in turn, became labor bosses in their own right. Cribb notes that over time there developed networks of power between labor bosses and gangsters and that these stood in an antagonistic, although not overtly hostile, relationship to the colonial authorities. This phenomenon was not unlike the Green Gang's involvement with the labor-contract system in Shanghai.

The area surrounding Batavia (the so-called *ommenlanden*, or "lands around") had been cleared by the Dutch of indigenous people, who were replaced by large, commercially-run estates with their labor force drawn from the city. Here banditry was endemic. Over time a symbiotic relationship developed between these bandits and the estate owners, with the latter frequently employing the bandits as an informal police force on their estates to ensure order among their labor force. At the same time, the colonial government, on occasion, recruited captured members of bandit gangs into the army rather than sending them to prison.[16]

The Second World War provided enhanced opportunities for Batavian gangsters as the collapse of Dutch power and the initial period of Japanese occupation led to a massive breakdown of law and order in the countryside around Batavia. As a result the Japanese reached an accommodation with local gangsters and recruited the most powerful of them as local police chiefs. A few years later, the Japanese also sought to use the Batavia gangs as the basis for a guerrilla force to be used in the event of an Allied invasion.

It was during the Japanese occupation that links were forged between the gangsters and nationalist leaders. Even before the war certain political parties proscribed by the Dutch, most notably the Communist Party of Indonesia (PKI) developed close relations with the gangsters in the Batavia region. These gangs were directly involved in the PKI's abortive uprising in Batavia in 1926.[17] With the end of the war, the Indonesian nationalists, as part of their strategy to resist the reimposition of Dutch rule, recruited gangsters into the newly formed nationalist militias, such as the People's Militia of Greater Jakarta (*Lasykar Rakyat Jakarta Raya*). Membership in these militia units provided gangster leaders with access to power and authority within the nationalist movement. Not all nationalist politicians, however, supported the militia movement, and in the course of the revolutionary conflict, the Republican government sought to restrain and, eventually, to eliminate the gangster militias. The Indonesian Army, in particular, was hostile to the militias, which it regarded as a rival military force, and brought pressure to bear on the civilian politicians for their disbandment, which occurred finally in 1949.

The history of the gangsters of Batavia provides strong parallels with that of the Green Gang in Shanghai. Like Shanghai, Batavia had a fragmented, immigrant population that provided opportunities for gangsters to construct their power in the interstices of society, mediating relations between different social groups. The Batavia gang bosses, like their Green Gang counterparts, enjoyed an ambiguous relationship with the colonial state and the colonial (landlord) elite, and at times were co-opted by the state as extensions of its coercive power. At the same time, these gangster leaders also established relations with proscribed revolutionary parties, both nationalist and communist, and were finally given an active military role to play in the revolution against the Dutch. These developments are strongly reminiscent of the Shanghai Green Gang's relations with the Chinese Communist Party and the Nationalist Party in the 1920s and of its involvement in the anti-Communist coup of April 1927. Unlike the relationship that was forged between the Shanghai Green Gang and the Guomindang state in the 1930s, however, the Indonesian Republican government sought to reduce gangster power at a relatively early date and made no attempt to integrate it into the new state structures that it created in the late 1940s. One reason for this difference in outcomes, perhaps, was that the Batavia gangsters remained highly fragmented and never attained a degree of organizational coherence comparable to that of the Green Gang. Another reason was that the Republican government enjoyed full sovereign power after 1949, and did not have to recognize the separate sovereignty of colonial entities as did the Guomindang state in Shanghai in the 1930s. As a result it did not have the same need as the Guomindang for intermediaries, such as gangster bosses, to serve its interests in a situation of fragmented sovereignty.

"CONFUCIAN GANGSTERS": THE JAPANESE YAKUZA

A final point of comparison is with another East Asian criminal organization, the Japanese yakuza.[18] The yakuza is especially interesting because it exists within a society that belongs to the broad East Asian cultural paradigm of which China is also a part. It is not surprising, therefore, to find that there are many striking similarities between the yakuza in the early twentieth century and the Green Gang. Not the least of these is the degree of tolerance that both the yakuza and a Chinese secret society like the Green Gang enjoyed in their respective societies. In contemporary Japan, for example, yakuza groups maintain offices, carry identifying insignias and publish their own newspapers and journals. This is very reminiscent of Du Yuesheng's Green Gang group in Shanghai, which, as discussed in the text, maintained its own public organization and published its own journal.

The origins of the yakuza are to be found in the organizations of traditional gamblers (*bakuto*) and street hawkers (*tekiya*) of eighteenth-century Japan. It was the gamblers who provided the name *yakuza*. This was originally a term that referred to one of the losing combinations in the card game Hanafuda (8–9–3, i.e., *ya-ku-sa*), and by extension it denoted something that was completely useless.

The organizational structure and value system of the yakuza bore certain similarities to those of the Green Gang. Members of the yakuza were organized hierarchically along fictive clan lines with "godfathers," "elder brothers," "younger brothers," and so on. The most important relationship was between the *oyabun* (boss) and the *kobun* (follower), which was akin to that between father and son. The oyabun provided advice, protection and help to his kobun who reciprocated with unswerving loyalty to the oyabun. This relationship between boss and follower was extremely strong, and, just as the master/follower relationship was for the Green Gang, it represented the basic building block of yakuza organization.

The value system of the yakuza extolled the virtues of the violent but compassionate outlaw, who stood up for the weak and the disadvantaged against the strong and the powerful. The Japanese concepts of *giri* and *ninjo* lay at the heart of yakuza values. Giri places emphasis on a sense of moral obligation and duty, while ninjo conveys the idea of "human feeling," and, by extension, generosity and sympathy for the weak. These values were, and remain, extremely potent as indicated by the remarks made by one leading oyabun in an interview with David Kaplan in the early 1980s: "The yakuza are trying to pursue the road of chivalry and patriotism. That's our biggest difference with the American Mafia, its our sense of giri and ninjo. The yakuza try to take care of all society if possible, even if it takes a million yen to help a single person."[19] These idealized, conservative values are very similar to those espoused by the Green Gang, particularly the cult of the haoxia and its espousal of the five traditional Confucian virtues, and which provided its leaders, such as Du Yuesheng, with the rationalization for their public actions. Such gangster codes, in a sense, were an adaptation of the popular Confucian values that informed their respective societies.

The expansion of the yakuza occurred as a consequence of the social and political changes set in motion by the Meiji Restoration in the second half of the nineteenth century. With the beginnings of a modern urban economy and a burgeoning proletariat, many yakuza bosses set themselves up as labor contractors and by this means extended their control over unskilled labor, such as construction workers, stevedores and rickshaw pullers. Gambling remained a key activity for the yakuza, many of whose leaders set up legitimate businesses to act as "fronts" for gambling houses. It was through their gambling activities that the yakuza established close relationships with the local police, who tolerated the existence of these establishments in return for generous bribes.

During the Meiji period yakuza bosses also developed a pragmatic, working relationship with politicians and officials. They became closely identified, in particular, with the politics of ultranationalism. One of the earliest examples of this phenomenon was the creation of the ultranationalist and expansionist Genyosha (Dark Ocean Society) by Toyoma Mitsuru in 1881, whose members acted both as bodyguards for government officials and as enforcers for local political bosses. In 1919, Toyoma organized a national federation of gangster groups called the Great Japan National Essence Society (*Dai Nippon Kokusui-kai*) which brought together about 60,000 gangsters and operated as a huge strike-breaking organization with strong support from the Ministry of Home Affairs, the police and the military. By the 1920s both major Japanese political parties, the Seiyukai and the Minseito, had their own paramilitary forces recruited from yakuza gangs; and the yakuza also worked closely with the Japanese military in both Manchuria and North China during the 1930s and 1940s. The involvement of the yakuza in Japanese political life paralleled similar developments in China, such as the relations which the Shanghai Green Gang bosses enjoyed with the various Guomindang factions in the late 1920s and 1930s. Yakuza co-operation with Japanese military intelligence, moreover, had its Chinese equivalent in the co-operation between Du Yuesheng's Green Gang organization and Chinese military intelligence, the Juntong, in the 1930s and 1940s.

Japan's defeat in World War II did not destroy the relationship between the yakuza and the world of politics, which simply took a new form. During the postwar occupation, the intelligence arm of General MacArthur's headquarters, SCAP (Supreme Commander Allied Powers), used the yakuza to monitor left-wing unions and the activities of the Japanese Communists. This relationship was the basis for the alliances forged by Kodama Yoshio in the 1940s and 1950s between the yakuza and the new political structures of postwar Japan.

As the above discussion suggests, certain characteristics of the historical development of the Green Gang were shared by gangster organizations in other countries and cultures. A common theme to many of these gangster groups was the opportunity provided by the social fragmentation caused by the existence of a large immigrant population in a complex urban environment. This was true of the American metropolises of New York and Chicago, as well as a colonial city such as Batavia. For the leadership of many of these gangster groups the role of mediator, both between different social groups and between local society and the political world, was of central importance in their rise to power. This was as much the case for the Italian mafia, the labor-contractor gangsters of Batavia, and, to a degree, the Japanese yakuza, as it was for the Shanghai Green Gang. Again co-option of gangster groups by the modernizing state was not peculiar to the history of the Shanghai Green Gang, but was also a factor in the rise of the Italian mafia, and, indeed, in the evolution of the yakuza in early-twentieth-century Japan. The Green Gang's ambiguous relationship with the colonial state in Shanghai's French Concession and International Settlement, moreover, was also shared by the Indonesian gangsters of Batavia. Finally, the expansion of Du Yuesheng's business interests in Shanghai in the 1930s was paralleled by the contemporary rise of the entrepreneurial gangster in the United States.

This work has sought to explain the Green Gang as an important phenomenon in China's modern historical development. At the same time, however, as the above discussion suggests, the emergence of the Green Gang in Shanghai can also be viewed as part of a larger historical process, as well as being the product of historical conditions shaped by the specificities of time, place and culture. In some ways the Chinese and Shanghai contexts are local variants of this larger process. As it emerged in the early twentieth century, the Green Gang was a species of gangster organization, the product of complex and far-reaching changes within Chinese society. As such it shared certain characteristics with other similar organizations that were also the product of profound social change associated with the emergence or refinement of different forms of capitalism. In this way, it may be suggested, the Shanghai Green Gang was one variant of the phenomenon of organized crime, which was itself an intrinsic part of the complex phenomenon of the emergence of a capitalist polity.

Notes

ABBREVIATIONS

AMAE   Archives de la Ministre des Affaires Etrangeres
CF   *China Forum*
CMCDR   *China Maritime Customs Decennial Reports*
CWR   *China Weekly Review*
DLDYS   *Da Liumang Du Yuesheng*
FMC   French Municipal Council/Provisional Commission
FO   Foreign Office
Inprecorr   *International Press Correspondence*
JSBH   *Jiu Shanghai de Banghui*
JSYDC   *Jiu Shanghai de Yan Du Chang*
MAE   Ministre des Affaires Etrangeres
MBY   *Minguo Banghui Yaolu*
NCDN   *North-China Daily News*
NCH   *North-China Herald*
SB   *Shen Bao*
SMC   Shanghai Municipal Council
SMP   Shanghai Municipal Police

INTRODUCTION

1. Davis 1971; Chesneaux 1965, 1973; and Chesneaux, Davis and Nguyen Nguet Ho 1970. It should be emphasized here that these are not the only themes to have attracted the attention of Western scholars with an interest in secret societies. In recent years there has been a strong interest in the religious aspects of secret societies and of their relationship to Chinese popular culture in the late traditional period. Such an approach has informed the work of Susan Naquin and, most recently, that of Joseph Esherick. Naquin 1976, 1981; Esherick 1987.

2. Perry 1980, 1.

3. Hershatter 1986; Honig 1986; Perry 1993; Coble 1980; Fewsmith 1985; Lieberthal 1980.

4. Pan Ling 1984; Seagrave 1985.

5. This is clear from Pan Ling's discussion of her technique in the preface to her work; Pan Ling 1984, vii.

6. Wang 1967; Marshall 1976. Another historian who has dealt with the issue of secret societies in the urban environment of Shanghai is Tadao Sakai. Sakai might well be considered a special case, however, as much of his discussion relies heavily on his own experience as a Japanese intelligence officer who dealt with Shanghai secret societies in the course of his duties during the Sino-Japanese War (1937–45). His work, therefore, has the attributes of a primary source, and is so treated in the present study; Sakai 1970.

CHAPTER ONE

1. Hu Zhusheng 1979, 111; Ch'en 1970a, 65. For details of the controversy on Green Gang origins, see Martin 1991, 9–10.

2. These scholars include Hu Zhusheng, Li Shiyu, Cai Shaoqing, Ma Xisha, Chen Xiao, Han Bingfang, and Zhou Yumin. The work by Ma and Han on popular religion is particularly important. The following discussion is based on these works together with those by David E. Kelley, Atsushi Watanabe and Dai Xuanzhi. Li Shiyu 1987, 1963; Cai Shaoqing 1989, 79–86; Ma Xisha and Cheng Xiao 1984; Ma Xisha and Han Bingfang 1992, 242–339; Zhou Yumin and Shao Yong 1993, 26–41, 223–288; Kelley 1982; Watanabe 1984; and Dai Xuanzhi 1973.

3. For a discussion of Subei as both a geographical region and as an idea, and its relationship to Jiangnan and Shanghai, see Honig 1992, 18–35. A suggestive discussion of the economic backwardness of Subei that uses the concept of "internal colony" as a means of understanding the Subei experience is provided by Finnane 1993.

4. Overmyer 1985, 236–237. See also Overmyer 1976, 113–129.

5. Li Shiyu 1987, 293, citing the report of the interrogation of members of the Luo Sect in 1768 by Cui Yingjie, the Governor General of Fujian and Zhejiang.

6. Hu Zhusheng 1979, 104; Cai Shaoqing 1989, 82; Ma Xisha and Han Bingfang 1992, 262.

7. Ma Xisha and Cheng Xiao 1984, 12.

8. Ma Xisha and Han Bingfang 1992, 262; Kelley 1982, 382.

9. On *huiguan*, see Ho 1962, 208–209, 342–343; Morse 1909, 35–48.

10. Kelley 1982, 377.

11. Ma Xisha and Han Bingfang 1992, 271–272; Kelley 1982, 368, 382.

12. Wang Yangqing and Xu Yinghu 1982, 63.

13. Ma Xisha and Han Bingfang 1992, 272–273.

14. Hu Zhusheng 1979, 103–104; Ma Xisha and Han Binfang 1992, 275; Fan Songfu 1980, 153.

15. Ma Xisha and Han Bingfang 1992, 273–275.

16. Hu Zhusheng 1979, 106.

17. Hinton 1970, 16–38; Jones and Kuhn 1978, 119–128.

18. Hu Zhusheng 1979, 110; Watanabe 1984, 800.

19. Zhao Qingfu, *Anqing Cucheng,* cited in Hu Zhusheng 1979, 110.

20. Ma Xisha and Han Bingfang 1992, 291–292.

21. Ibid., 297.

22. Ibid., 292.

23. Adshead 1970, 11–12.

24. Ma Xisha and Han Bingfang 1992, 305–313; Ma Xisha and Cheng Xiao 1984, 20, 22; Tao Chengzhang [1916] 1957, 21.

25. For a discussion of the Gelaohui, see Cai Shaoqing 1984, esp. 495–500 on the role of the Qing armies in the spread of the Gelaohui.

26. For the career of Xu Baoshan, see below.

27. Hu Zhusheng 1979, 112; Watanabe 1984, 804.

28. Ma Xisha and Han Bingfang 1992, 303–305.

29. The origins of the name *Anqing Daoyou* has been the subject of some disagreement among historians. On the basis of archival research, most leading Chinese historians now believe the league took its name *anqing* from the two neighboring localities in Subei in which it was first active, that is Andong (xxx) and Qinghe (xxx) counties, at the point where the Grand Canal intersected with the Huai River. Ma Xisha and Han Bingfang 1992, 293; Ma Xisha and Cheng Xiao 1984, 20; and Cai Shaoqing 1989, 85.

30. Tao Chengzhang [1916] 1957, 21.

31. For details of the temporary revival of the canal transport system, see Hinton 1970, 38–75, and Wright 1969, 175–176. The system collapsed finally in 1901.

32. Hu Zhusheng 1979, 113. A discussion of the organizational structure of the Green Gang follows in the next section.

33. Liu Bainian 1931, 24.

34. Ibid., 50–54.

35. Ibid., 21.

36. Wu Choupeng 1935.

37. An Wensheng et al. 1983, 93, 97.

38. Hu Junsu and Li Shufen 1983, 220–221. See also Wang Zichen 1983, 209; Li Shiyu 1988, 216–217; Zhou Enyu and Liu Yanchen 1988, 231.

39. Tianjin had its own variety of local hoodlums, known as *hunhun'er* ("drifters"). Originally affiliated with the Gelaohui, the hunhun'er ran gambling dens and extortion rackets involving local peasants and fishermen in the late nineteenth century. After it was established in Tianjin, the Green Gang absorbed most of the hunhun'er into its own organization. Hershatter 1986, 125–131; and Li Shiyu 1988, 213–216.

40. Hu Zhusheng 1979, 114, 116; Watanabe 1984, 803–805, 811–812; Chen Bingzhi, Kuai Mingsun, and Wang Bingjun 1981; Zhu Fugui and Xu Fengyi 1985, 187–189.

41. The warlords Zhang Zongchang and Han Fuju were followers of

Gao and Zhang respectively; Guomindang intelligence report on the activities of the Shanghai Green Gang, February 23, 1938, in MBY 1993, 96–97.

42. Eleven Green Gang manuals were consulted for the purposes of the present work: Chang Shengzhao 1935; Chen Guoping 1946; *Daoyi Zhinan* 1931; Geng Yuying 1934; Liu Bainian 1931; Tianjing Diaosou (pseud.) 1932; Sun Yuemin 1946; Grand Master Wei 1946; Xie Tianmin 1935; Zhang Shusheng n.d.; Zhang Zhenyuan 1940.

43. Among the most important of these general histories are Cai Shaoqing 1989; Shuai Xuefu [1970]; and Ikemoto Yoshio 1973.

44. Xu Zhucheng 1983, 13; Cai Shaoqing 1989, 86–87; Zhu Zijia 1964, 50.

45. Sun Yuemin 1946, 15; Shuai Xuefu [1970], 154–157; Wang Yangqing and Xu Yinghu 1982, 63. The twenty-four generations of the Green Gang were the Qing; Jing; Dao; De; Wen; Cheng; Fo; Fa; Neng; Ren; Zhi; Hui; Ben; Lai; Zi; Xin; Yuan; Ming; Xing; Li; Da; Tong; Wu; Xue or Jue.

46. Shuai Xuefu [1970], 154–157; Liu Lianke 1940, 74–75.

47. Wang Zichen 1983.

48. Fan Songfu 1980, 154. Details concerning the activities of Xu Xilin and Qiu Jin, their organization of the Datong School, and their relations with Green Gang groups in northern Zhejiang can be found in Rankin 1971, 136–139, 164–167.

49. Jiang Hao 1986a, 66.

50. Zhang Shusheng n.d., diagrams 1–6, 52–63; Zhang Zhenyuan 1940, 48, 147–152; "The Rise and Growth of the 'Ch'ing Pang'" 1934, 117.

51. Fan Songfu 1980, 153; Wang Yangqing and Xu Yinghu 1982, 64; *Qing Bang ji Qi Yi'an* n.d., 37.

52. Qing Bang ji Qi Yi'an n.d., 36.

53. Cui Xilin 1992, 129.

54. Jin Laofo 1990, 52–54; Xie Tianmin 1935, 53–62; Jiang Hao 1986a, 56–57; Zhang Zhenyuan 1940, 77–117.

55. Jin Laofo 1990, 52–54; Jiang Hao 1986a, 57–59; Ikemoto 1973, 265–284; Zhang Zhenyuan 1940, 27–138; Xie Tianmin 1935, 27–36.

56. These were essentially cycles of traditional tales that were compiled into two works by Luo Guanzhong in the Ming Dynasty. See Hsia 1968, chs. 2 and 3; Lu Hsun 1959, 166–167, 183–184.

57. *The Water Margin* and the plays based on it were considered so subversive that Qing Emperor Qianlong proscribed them in 1736; Dolby 1976, 135. See also Mackerras 1975, 115, 137, 141, 149; and Ward 1985, 183.

58. Lo Kuan-chung 1925, 5–6.

59. Wu Yugong [1922] 1991, 3.

60. For further discussion of these groups, see ch. 2.

61. These examples are taken from the following manuals: Chang Shengzhao 1935, Zhang Zhenyuan 1940, and Sun Yuemin 1946.

62. Yang Guanbei 1952, 30(a).

63. Pan Gongzhan 1954, 4(b)–5(a).

64. The main societies that made up the Triad system were the Heaven and Earth Society (*Tiandihui*), the Three Harmonies Society (*Sanhehui*) and the Three Dots Society (*Sandianhui*). On the origins and development of the Triads, see Schlegel 1866; Xiao Yishan [1935] 1986, 1–25, 177–199; Davis 1971, 61–67; Wakeman 1970, 91–93; Cai Shaoqing 1987, 45–122; Qin Baoqi 1988, 61–134.

65. On the Small Swords, see Fass 1970; Perry 1985, 85–100; Hu Xunmin and He Jian 1991, 26–29.

66. The origins of this term are still a matter of dispute, although it has been noted that the character for "red" (*hong*xxx) is a homopheme of the character for "vast" (*hong*xxx) in the name Hong Men. One theory suggests that the transposition of the terms occurred because Qing officials habitually referred to members of the Hong Men as "red turban bandits" (*hongjinzei*). Wang Yangqing and Xu Yinghu 1982, 65.

67. Hinton 1970, 80–84; Chen Rongguang 1919, 1: 181.

68. Feuerwerker 1970, 157–158.

69. *Shen Bao*, June 15, 1876, cited in Su Zhiliang and Chen Lifei 1991, 68–69.

70. Luo Zhiru 1932, 21, table 29.

71. Ibid., 27, table 43.

72. Chen Guoping 1946, 281–313.

73. Wang Yangqing and Xu Yinghu 1982, 64.

74. On *tongxianghui*, see Goodman 1992. For Gu Zhuxuan and the Jiang-Huai Native-Place Association, see Xue Gengxin 1986, 95–96; Gu Shuping 1986, 360. For Du Yuesheng and the Pudong Native-Place Association, see SMP Files (March 27, 1933), (December 27, 1935), (October 8, 1938) D4683; SMP Files (February 6, 1940) D9319.

75. Zhu Bangxing, Hu Linge and Xu Sheng [1939] 1984, 263–265, 625–626, 665–666; *Liu Hongsheng Qiye Shiliao* 1981, 1: 314–315.

76. NCH, October 24, 1925; October 31, 1925; December 12, 1925; Luo Binsheng [1919] 1989, 217–218.

77. Opium trafficking and gambling are treated in subsequent chapters.

78. Xue Gengxin 1986, 97–98; Luo Binsheng [1919] 1989, 220–222; Pal 1963, 206–207; SMP Files (March 27, 1933) D4683.

79. Chan 1982, 49.

80. SMP Files (July 29, 1930) D1455.

81. NCH, June 16, 1923.

82. Peters 1937, 128.

83. There is as yet no Western monographic study of the police systems that operated in Shanghai prior to 1937. For an analysis of the development of modern police functions in Chinese Shanghai, see Wakeman 1989, 1988.

84. Feetham 1931, 2: 83, 159.

85. FMC, *Compte-Rendu 1925*, (Meeting of the Council, September 9, 1925), 140. The records of the French Concession Municipal Council are held in the Shanghai Municipal Archives.

86. France. MAE, *Direction des Affaires Politiques et Commerciales.* Asie: Océanie 34 E515.4 Wilden to MAE February 18, 1924.

87. The encouragement given to criminal activity by the existence of these separate police jurisdictions was one argument used by the Chinese authorities in the early 1930s for the rendition to China of the Shanghai foreign settlements; Wakeman 1989, 88–89.

88. Liangshanbo was the hideout and stronghold of the Chinese "robin hoods" at the end of the Song Dynasty as described in the Ming novel the *Water Margin*.

89. Zhang Jungu 1980, 1: 124, 136; Jiang Hao 1986a, 61, 66; Pal 1963, 186–188; SMP Files (August 1938) D8676.

90. Pal 1963, 19. On the widespread corruption within the Chinese detective branch of the SMP, particularly regarding contraband opium, see Peters 1937, 113–114.

91. On the colonial nature of the SMP and its function as an integral part of the United Kingdom's system of global imperial control, see Wakeman 1989, 63–72, 118–124.

92. Xue Gengxin 1986, 96–103; SMP Files (May 11, 1930–November 10, 1931) CS143; SMP Files (August 22, 1932) D4009.

93. Shi Jun 1986, 352.

94. NCH, August 25, 1923, October 20, 1923, August 30, 1924, October 25, 1924, February 7, 1925, March 7, 1925, May 2, 1925; League of Nations, 109; Great Britain, FO 415, confidential print (opium), FO 4749/4749/87 memorandum by Pratt, August 10, 1929. All references to Foreign Office correspondence are to this series (FO 415) unless otherwise noted.

95. Ma Yinchu 1928, 4: 280; Glick and Hong 1947, 252; Hauser 1940, 252.

96. Chen Guoping 1946, 281–313.

97. See, e.g., Seagrave 1985, 151.

98. Jiang Hao 1986a, 59–66.

99. Chen Guoping 1946, 293–297, 284; Hong Weiqing 1986, 108–114; Wang Yalu 1988, 238–239; Watanabe 1984, 811–812; Shi Yi 1962, 202; SMP Daily Intelligence Report, October 23, 1925; "Xing Wu Liu Da Zipai Zhang Gong Yixiang (A portrait of the recently deceased Mister Zhang who belonged to the Da generational status group of the Xing Wu Liu Branch)," in Geng Yuying 1934.

100. Xue Gengxin 1986, 95; Wang Delin 1986, 357–359; Wang Yangqing and Xu Yinghu 1982, 64; SMP Files (December 30, 1930) CS178; SMP Files (October 26, 1935) D7057; SMP Files (April 8, 1932) D3445.

101. Alley 1976, 25.

102. Report of Guomindang Intelligence Agent "205," February 18, 1939, in MBY 1993, 104.

103. Huang Jinrong 1951.

104. Xiang Bo 1986, 131–132; DLDYS 1965, 5–6.

105. DLDYS 1965, 7.

106. Zhang Jungu 1980, 1: 84–85; Qian Shengke 1919, 37–48.

107. Zhu Menghua 1984, 162–163; Xue Gengxin 1986, 105–106.

108. Zhu Jianliang and Wu Weizhi 1984, 160–161; Xu Zhucheng 1983, 17; Zhang Jungu 1980, 1: 139–140; DLDYS 1965, 11.

109. DLDYS 1965, 1–4, 6–7; SMP Files (February 6, 1940) D9319; Shi Yi 1962, 187–192, 48; Jiang Shaozhen 1978, 314.
110. Yang Guanbei 1952, 29(b).
111. Lu Jingshi, preface to Zhang Jungu 1980, 1: 4; *China Year Book 1931*, 74.
112. DLDYS 1965, 1; Shi Yi 1962, 187–188.
113. *Minli Bao*, April 28, 1911, cited in DLDYS 1965, 4.
114. DLDYS 1965, 2–3. For a discussion of the phenomenon of sworn sisterhoods among Shanghai women workers, see Honig 1986, 209–217.
115. Huang Jinrong 1951; Xue Gengxin 1986, 91; DLDYS 1965, 6.
116. DLDYS 1965, 7; SMP Files (February 6, 1940) D9319; Shi Yi 1962, 48.

CHAPTER TWO

1. NCH, December 19, 1914, cited in A. M. Kotenev 1927, 244.
2. Yen-p'ing Hao 1986, 132–137.
3. Yan Zhongping 1955, 76; Kotenev 1927, 244.
4. Hauser 1940, 118.
5. Gao Hongxing 1988, 46; Li Xiuzhang 1988, 56–57.
6. Chen Dingshan 1964, 34–35; Shi Yi 1962, 192.
7. Great Britain. FO, F4749/4749/87 memorandum by Pratt, August 10, 1929; CMCDR *1902–11* 1913, 3–4; Morse 1913, 362–365; *China Year Book 1914*, 688–707; Willoughby 1925, 20–37.
8. For further details of the policy of phased abolition and the response of the Shanghai opium merchants, see Martin 1989.
9. United States Department of State Decimal File, China, Internal Affairs, 893.114, Narcotics/105 Cunningham to State, March 3, 1930. All references to State Department correspondence is to this series.
10. FO, F3170/193/10 Legation to FO, October 11, 1922; FO, F82/82/87 Mills to Macleay, November 7, 1923; *China Year Book 1924–25*, 555, 565; *China Year Book 1925*, 576; Wou 1978, 76; Xue Gengxin 1980, 161.
11. For details of the workings of the Hong Kong opium "farm," see Miners 1987, 207–277.
12. FO, F4749/4749/87 memorandum by Pratt, August 10, 1929.
13. Ruffé 1928, 102–103; NCH, May 29, 1926.
14. Inprecorr, January 13, 1927; Pal 1963, 41, where he cites estimates made by the journalist Lennox Simpson ("Putnam Weale"); *China Year Book 1924–25*, 559.
15. CMCDR *1912–21* 1924, 10.
16. Ibid.
17. Shi Yi 1962, 47–48.
18. Kotenev 1927, 259.
19. CMCDR *1912–21* 1924, 10.
20. Zhang Jungu 1980, 1: 124; Liu Hong 1943, 87; Jiang Shaozhen 1978, 314.
21. Zhang Jungu 1980, 1: 124; Liu Hong 1943, 87. The eight leaders

were Shen Xingshan, Guo Haishan, Ji Yunqing, Yu Bingwen, Yang Zaitian, Xie Baosheng, Bao Haichou and Dai Buxiang.

22. Zhang Jungu 1980, 1: 136.

23. FO, F6548/69/87 Lampson to Henderson, October 22, 1929.

24. CWR, March 26, 1927.

25. Zhang Jungu 1980, 1: 124; Liu Hong 1943, 87–88; Jiang Shaozhen 1978, 314; SMP Files (February 6, 1940) D9319; DLDYS 1965, 8.

26. FO, F4749/4749/87 memorandum by Pratt, August 10, 1929; CMCDR *1912–21* 1924, 10; Kotenev 1927, 259.

27. NCH, August 11, 1923.

28. Ma Baoheng 1981, 136–139; FO, F6548/69/87 Lampson to Henderson, October 22 1929; NCH, August 11, 1923.

29. Ma Baoheng 1981, 136–139; Liu Hong 1943, 88; Xu Zhucheng 1983, 16; Chen Dingshan 1964, 36; Xiang Xiongxiao 1981, 177.

30. Liu Hong 1943, 88; Zhang Jungu 1980, 1: 246.

31. DLDYS 1965, 7; Liu Hong 1943, 88.

32. NCH, August 11, 1923.

33. The information that is presented here from the Ezra documents is derived from the proceedings of the Mixed Court as recorded in various issues of the *North China Herald* (February 21, 1925, March 7, 1925, May 2, 1925, June 6, 1925, August 22, 1925) and documents published by the Advisory Committee on Opium of the League of Nations, League of Nations Advisory Committee on Traffic in Opium and Other Dangerous Drugs. Minutes of the Seventh Session, Geneva August 24–31, 1925. Appendix C.602.M.192 1925 Xl no. 8.

34. League of Nations, 1925 Xl no. 8

35. NCH, August 11, 1923.

36. NCH, February 2, 1924.

37. NCH, September 13, 1924.

38. NCH, August 11, 1923; Liu Hong 1943, 88; Xu Zhucheng 1983, 16.

39. Ma Baoheng 1981, 136–139; NCH, August 11, 1923, September 13, 1924.

40. NCH, November 17, 1923.

41. Hu Zhusheng 1979, 119; Chen Dingshan 1964, 36; Xue Gengxin 1980, 164; Zhang Jungu 1980, 1: 141–142; Xu Zhucheng 1983, 17; DLDYS 1965, 11–12.

42. Zhang Jungu 1980, 1: 141–142; Shi Yi 1962, 193.

43. FO, F553/553/87 Eliot to Curzon, January 17, 1923.

44. SMP Files (February 6, 1940) D9319.

45. Liu Hong 1943, 88; Xu Zhucheng 1983, 16; Zhang Jungu 1980, 1: 124–128; DLDYS 1965, 7–10. The Small Eight Mob consisted of eight petty gangster leaders who were divided into two groups of four. The inner core was composed of Gu Jiatang, Gao Xinbao, Ye Chuoshan and Rui Qingrong, and the outer group of Yang Qitang, Huang Jiafang, Yao Zhisheng and Hou Quangen.

46. Zhang Jungu 1980, 1: 124–128; Xu Zhucheng 1983, 25–26.

47. FO, F6548/69/87 Lampson to Henderson, October 22, 1929; NCH, June 16, 1923.

48. Zhang Jungu 1980, 1: 96–98.

49. Zhang Jungu 1980, 1: 141–142; Xue Gengxin 1980, 164; Xu Zhucheng 1983, 17, 32.

50. SMP Files (April 9, 1924) and (May 2, 1924) IO5374.

51. NCH, November 17, 1923. Xu had been appointed Police Commissioner by Yuan Shikai on August 8, 1914.

52. NCH, November 24, 1923, December 8, 1923, January 12, 1924, September 13, 1924; SMP Files, (April 9, 1924) IO5374.

53. NCH, March 13, 1926.

54. Yu Zhi 1925a, 2–3; Chen Xizhang 1982, 2: 393; Ma Baoheng 1981, 139; NCH, May 23, 1925; Ruffé 1928, 116; Ma Yinqu 1928, 4: 280; Zhang Jungu 1980, 1: 210.

55. Qian Yongming 1952, 2(b); Fu Runhua 1948, 85; Shi Yi 1962, 199; Zhang Jungu 1980, 1: 210.

56. Zhang Jungu 1980, 1: 153, 163, 210.

57. SMP Files (November 6, 1924), (November 18, 1924) IO5782.

58. FO, F6548/69/87 Lampson to Henderson, October 22, 1929; FO, F4749/4749/87 memorandum by Pratt; U.S. Dept. of State, 893.114 Narcotics/105 Cunningham to State, March 3, 1930.

59. FO, F6548/69/87 Lampson to Henderson, October 22, 1929; U.S. Dept. of State, 893.114 Narcotics/105 Cunningham to State, March 3, 1930. The number of prosecutions for opium trafficking in the decade 1918 to 1928 totaled 21,384.

60. NCH, September 26, 1925; FO, F6548/69/87 Lampson to Henderson, October 22, 1929.

61. NCH, May 30, 1925; F4749/4749/87 memorandum by Pratt, August 10, 1929.

62. Hu Zhusheng 1979, 119.

63. Zhang Jungu 1980, 1: 132, 136–139.

64. Shi Yi 1962, 238; Zhang Jungu 1980, 1: 246–247; FO, F4749/4749/87 memorandum by Pratt, August 10, 1929.

65. Li Chien-nung 1956, 471–473; NCH, February 14, 1925.

66. NCH, March 13, 1926.

67. NCH, October 18, 1924, October 25, 1924; Zhang Jungu 1980, 1: 212; SMP Daily Intelligence Report, December 11, 1925.

68. NCH, October 18, 1924, October 25, 1924, February 28, 1925; Zhang Jungu 1980, 1: 212.

69. Zhang Jungu 1980, 1: 214–216; Wan Molin 1975, 191–194; Boorman and Howard 1967–71, 1: 123; Chen Guoping 1946, 300.

70. NCH, May 23, 1925.

71. NCH, May 16, 1925, May 30, 1925.

72. NCH, May 23, 1925.

73. NCH, May 23, 1925, May 30, 1925.

74. NCH, May 30, 1925.

75. NCH, May 23, 1925.

76. NCH, June 6, 1925; *Guowen Zhoubao*, June 7, 1925; Kotenev 1927, 264; Martin 1989, 57.

77. Yu Zhi 1925a, 2–3; NCH, February 14, 1925.

78. NCH, May 16, 1925.

79. NCH, March 14, 1925.

80. Yu Zhi 1925b, 2; NCH, March 13, 1925, May 23, 1925.

81. NCH, May 23, 1925.

82. *Minguo Ribao*, July 25, 1925.

83. Ibid.; Zhang Jungu 1980, 1: 143.

84. *Minguo Ribao*, July 25, 1925.

85. FO, F6548/69/87 Lampson to Henderson, October 22, 1929. The three other opium merchants who made up the nominal partnership with Su Jiashan were, according to the municipal police, Chang Ruitang, Wang Shaochen and Lin Chenhong.

86. Zhang Jungu 1980, 1: 130–132, 146; CWR, November 26, 1932; Hong Zhensheng 1992.

87. Zhang Jungu 1980, 1: 143. For an attempt to calculate the income of the Three Prosperities Company, see Martin 1989, 60–62.

88. Shi Yi 1962, 48; Zhang Jungu 1980, 2: 135.

89. FO, F4749/4749/87 memorandum by Pratt, August 10, 1929.

90. FO, F6548/69/87 Lampson to Henderson, October 22, 1929; U.S. Dept. of State, 893.114 Narcotics/105 Cunningham to State, March 3, 1930.

91. International Anti-Opium Association 1926, 19–20; *China Year Book 1926*, 663.

92. International Anti-Opium Association 1926, 19–20; Zhang Jungu 1980, 1: 152–153.

93. NCH, January 30, 1926.

94. Zhang Jungu 1980, 1: 153–163.

95. Ibid.

96. FO, F85/85/10 Yichang Intelligence Report, September Quarter, 1922.

97. Shi Yi 1962, 199; Zhang Jungu 1980, 1: 163; SMP Daily Intelligence Report (December 22, 1925).

98. International Anti-Opium Association 1926, 19–20; *China Year Book 1926*, 663; NCH, April 17, 1926, May 8, 1926, July 10, 1926, February 19, 1927; CF, May 1932.

99. U.S. Dept. of State, 893.114 Narcotics/625 State to Legation, January 29, 1934; International Anti-Opium Association 1926, 19–20; *China Year Book 1926*, 663.

CHAPTER THREE

1. MAE, 34 E515.4 Wilden to MAE, February 18, 1924.

2. Ibid.; NCH, February 18, 1928.

3. MAE, 34 E515.4 Wilden to MAE, February 18, 1924.

4. Ibid.

5. Johnstone 1937, 103.

6. Shi Jun 1986, 352; Huang Jinrong 1951.

7. Xiang Bo 1986, 131–132; Cheng Xiwen 1986, 148–149.

8. MAE, 16 E515.4 Wilden to MAE, July 9, 1923.

9. *Shen Bao*, June 8, 1919, cited in *Wusi Yundong zai Shanghai Shiliao Xuanji* 1980, 768.

10. Xiang Bo 1986, 132; DLDYS 1965, 6.

11. Xiang Bo 1986, 132. For a detailed discussion of banditry in the Lake Tai region at this time, see Cai Shaoqing 1993, 279–327.

12. For details of the incident consult Powell 1945, 92–124; and Chen Siyi 1986. See also the detailed account on the first anniversary of the incident in NCH, May 10, 1924.

13. Chen Dingshan 1964, 37–38; Wan Molin 1982a; Yang Hao and Ye Lan 1989, 155–156.

14. Xiang Bo 1986, 132; DLDYS 1965, 6; Xu Zhucheng 1983, 14–15.

15. MAE, 34 E515.4 Wilden to MAE, July 21, 1924, Meyrier to MAE, January 11, 1926.

16. Yang Shi 1986, 88–89.

17. Zhu Wenwei 1984; Boorman and Howard 1967–71, 2: 450–451; CWR, September 13, 1930; Fitzsimmons and Maguire 1939, 78–80; Latourette 1929, 741; Ruan Renze and Gao Zhennong 1992, 729–731.

18. CWR, January 3, 1931; *Gendai Chūka Minkoku Manshūkoku Jimmeikan* 1932, 75, 113, 147.

19. Latourette 1929, 306–318; Ruan Renze and Gao Zhennong 1992, 623–625, 730; Dong Shu 1934a, 1022; Zhu Menghua 1983, 81.

20. Huang Yongyan 1986, 289; Yang Shi 1986, 88–89.

21. MAE, 41 E515.4 Meyrier to the Legation, in de Martel to MAE, February 10, 1925; NCH, January–June 1925.

22. MAE, 16 E515.4 Wilden to MAE, July 9, 1923; 34 E515.4 Wilden to MAE, February 18, 1924; FMC. *Compte-Rendu 1924* (Police Report), 296; FMC, *Compte-Rendu 1925* (Police Report), 258.

23. NCH, December 6, 1924.

24. Willoughby 1925, 25–37.

25. The minutes of meetings and the text of the contract between Du Yuesheng and certain French officials and businessmen are provided in U.S. Dept. of State, 893.114 Narcotics/208 Jenkins to State, March 16, 1931. See also DLDYS 1965, 14–15; Xue Gengxin 1980, 163; U.S. Dept. of State, 893.114/528 Mayer to State, April 23, 1925; *Minguo Ribao*, July 25, 1925.

26. DLDYS 1965, 15; SMP Files (October 9, 1929) CS190.

27. U.S. Dept. of State, 893.114 Narcotics/208 Jenkins to State, March 16, 1931.

28. Ibid.

29. Ibid.

30. Ibid.; NCH, May 9, 1925.

31. U.S. Dept. of State, 893.114 Narcotics/208 Jenkins to State, March 16, 1931.

32. Ibid.

33. Ibid.

34. Ibid.; FO, F3570/184/87 Brenan to Legation, May 29, 1930; SMP Files (February 6, 1940) D9319; CWR, February 7, 1931; CWR, January 23, 1932.

35. NCH, November 22, 1924; SMP Daily Intelligence Report, July 21, 1925; Fan Shaozeng 1986, 208; MAE, 204 E515.4 Naggiar to MAE, September 10, 1927.

36. FMC, *Compte-Rendu 1926* (Meeting of the Council, July 5, 1926), 142.

37. MAE, 157 E515.4 Naggiar to Legation, August 15, 1926; MAE, 35 E515.4 Meyrier to MAE, September 21, 1925.

38. Dong Shu 1934b, 759; MAE, 157 E515.4 Naggiar to Legation, August 15, 1926; Clifford 1991, 156–157.

39. MAE, 33 E515.4 Naggiar to MAE, May 17, 1926.

40. The five Chinese members were Lu Baihong, Lu Songhou, Zhu Yan, Wu Zonglian and Wei Tingrong. NCH, January 15, 1927; Dong Shu 1934a, 1000–1001; *China Year Book 1928*, 928; MAE, 11 E515.4 Naggiar to MAE, January 17, 1927; FMC, *Compte-Rendu 1927* (Meeting of the Provisional Commission for Administration, January 24, 1927), 8; Clifford 1991, 207–209.

41. DLDYS 1965, 11–12; Huang Guodong 1986, 255–256; Chen Dingshan 1964, 98–100; Yang Hao and Ye Lan 1989, 159–160.

42. Yang Shi 1986, 88–89; Xue Gengxin 1980, 162–163; Fan Shaozeng 1986, 208.

43. NCH, May 9, 1925.

44. DLDYS 1965, 6; Xiang Bo 1986, 132.

45. NCH, October 25, 1924.

CHAPTER FOUR

1. Rankin 1971, 119, 209; Zhang Chengyu [1945–47] 1965, 270–297; Rodyenko 1914, 53, 94–95, 106–108, 121, 123; Chen Rongguang 1919, 1: 73–74; Mark Elvin 1984, 152–153.

2. Fan Songfu 1980, 156, who states that Chen belonged to the prestigious Da generational status group of the Green Gang; Huang Dezhao 1978, 106; Hu Shengwu 1987, 227–230. However, Chen Qimei's nephew, Chen Lifu, in his autobiography denies that Chen was a member of the Green Gang, but does note his "popularity" with the the Green Gang. Chen Lifu 1994, 63, 10.

3. "Xinhai Shanghai Guangfu qianhou: Zoutanhui jilu" 1981, 12–13; *Xinhai Geming zai Shanghai Shiliao Xuanji* 1981, 892–893; Geng Yuying 1934; SMP Files (September 19, 1916) IO585; Fan Songfu 1980, 155.

4. Loh 1971, 26.

5. The possibility of Chiang's membership in the Green Gang is mentioned in *China Year Book 1928*, 1361; Isaacs [1938] 1961, 81; Snow [1938] 1961, 19; Smedley 1972, 156; *Diyici Guonei Geming Zhanzheng Shiqi de Gongren Yundong* 1954, 528; Rong Mengyuan 1980, 8.

6. Rong Mengyuan 1980, 8–9.

7. Huang Zhenshi 1992, 335–337.

8. SMP Files (September 23, 1929) D529.

9. Chen Guoping 1946, 306. Chen's entry is for a "Jiang Dezheng" of Fenghua County, Jiang's native place in Zhejiang and the profession given is "politician" (*zhengjie*). It should be noted that *dezheng* is a close variant of Jiang's courtesy name *zhongzheng*. It could represent either a deliberate obfuscation or an error in transcription, with the latter being the more likely prospect. Another approach could be that *dezheng* (moral governance) represents the name that Jiang himself adopted when he entered the Green Gang.

10. SMP Files (February 6, 1940) D9319; Chen Lifu 1994, 64.

11. Zhang Jungu 1980, 1: 256; Ma Chaojun 1958, 2: 377; Rigby 1980, 31.

12. Ma Chaojun 1958, 2: 378–379; Zhang Jungu 1980, 1: 258; Rigby 1980, 36–37.

13. Shi Yi 1962, 95.

14. Chang Kuo-t'ao 1971, 1: 170; Inprecorr, June 23, 1927. For details of the baogong system, see Martin 1991, 194.

15. For a discussion of native place as an organizational basis for Shanghai workers, see Perry 1993, 11–64.

16. Chang Kuo-t'ao 1971, 1: 172–173; Inprecorr, June 23, 1927; Isaacs 1932; Deng Zhongxia [1946] 1978, 203; Ma Chaojun 1958, 1: 31–34.

17. Li Lisan. 1981, 143.

18. Chen Duxiu [1922] 1987, 597. See also Perry 1993, 73.

19. Li Lisan 1981, 142.

20. Chang Kuo-t'ao 1971, 1: 174; Chesneaux 1968, 171; Perry 1993, 74.

21. Chang Kuo-t'ao 1971, 1: 172–174; Perry 1993, 145–146; and *Douzheng de Wushinian* 1960, 19–27.

22. Chang Kuo-t'ao 1971, 1: 173, 174–175.

23. Li Lisan 1981, 144. Li Lisan described the three different approaches to the Green Gang that the CCP adopted in its first four years of trade union activity (1921–1925) as follows:

> When we first engaged in labour work we paid no attention to the Green Gang, with the result that the capitalists were able to use the Green Gang to defeat our struggle in the Japanese and Chinese cotton factories in Pudong. On the second occasion Li Qihan joined the Green Gang, but he was too trusting of the Green Gang, with the result that the Green Gang bosses betrayed him, [and this approach] also ended in failure. After I arrived, I studied the historical circumstances of the Shanghai labour movement and felt that it was inappropriate either to ignore or to join [the Green Gang]. I adopted another method which was to study who among the Green Gang "disciples" [*tudi*] was oppressed, in order to unite with the lower strata to oppose the bosses, and so to engage in class struggle within the Green Gang. The bosses were all in the pay of the imperialists, and their "disciples" were oppressed. (143–144)

24. Li Lisan 1981, 148; Zhu Xuefan 1986, 1.

25. Deng Zhongxia [1946] 1978, 137–138; Li Lisan 1981, 144.

26. Ma Chaojun 1958, 1: 261–262; Deng Zhongxia [1946] 1978, 120; Chang Kuo-t'ao 1971, 1: 420; Chesneaux 1968, 223; Li Lisan 1981, 144.

27. Li Lisan 1981, 144–145.

28. Deng Zhongxia [1946] 1978, 120.

29. Chang Kuo-t'ao 1971, 1: 420; Deng Zhongxia [1946] 1978, 120; Chesneaux 1968, 255.

30. Li Lisan 1981, 145–147; Chao Lin, 1925.

31. Li Lisan 1981, 145–146. For a discussion of Yu Xiaqing's policy during the strike, see Rigby 1980, 38–62 passim.

32. Ma Chaojun 1958, 2: 485–487; *Xiang Dao*, no. 131, September 25, 1925, 1199–1200.

33. SMP Daily Intelligence Report, August 3, 1925, August 28, 1925, September 19, 1925; NCH, August 8, 1925, August 15, 1925, December 12, 1925.

34. Inprecorr, June 23, 1927; *China Year Book 1928*, 968–970.

35. NCH, January 15, 1927.

36. Shi Yi 1962, 95.

37. Wan Molin 1973, 1: 21–22.

38. Liu Shaotang 1977, 2: 199.

39. *China Year Book 1928*, 1348; Zhang Jungu 1980, 1: 270; Chang Kuo-t'ao, 1: 586; C. Martin Wilbur and Julie Lien-ying How 1956, 525.

40. Zhang Jungu 1980, 1: 270.

41. Liu Shaotang 1977, 2: 199; Rankin 1971 *China Year Book 1935*, 398.

42. Inprecorr, January 13, 1927; Chesneaux 1968, 342; Xu Yufang and Bian Xingying 1987, 121–122.

43. Isaacs [1938] 1961, 131, 143; Mark Gayn 1944, 138; Inprecorr, January 13, 1927.

44. Isaacs [1938] 1961, 131, 143; Gayn 1944, 138.

45. Zhang Jungu 1980, 1: 276.

46. Ibid., 269–270.

47. Jiang Shaozhen 1978, 315; J. V. Davidson-Houston 1962, 135; Wan Molin 1973, 1: 21.

48. Minutes of the Special Committee of the Shanghai Area Committee for March 19, 1927, in Xu Yufang and Bian Xingying 1987, 210.

49. Wan Molin 1973, 1: 21–23; Zhang Jungu 1980, 1: 276–278.

50. Wan Molin 1973, 1: 21–23.

51. Zhang Jungu 1980, 1: 276–278; Wan Molin 1975, 192–194.

52. Guo Morou 1978, 3: 129.

53. Ibid., 127.

54. MAE, E515.4 Naggiar to MAE, November 13, 1926; SB, February 13, 1927; NCH, February 19, 1927.

55. Zhang Jungu 1980, 1: 277–278.

56. Hua Gang [1931] 1982, 214.

57. Chang Kuo-t'ao 1971, 1: 570.

58. Zhang Jungu 1980, 1: 271–272, 315; Wan Molin 1982b, 93; Chang Kuo-t'ao 1971, 1: 568–570; Huang Meizhen 1983, 63.

59. Minutes of the plenary meeting of the Shanghai District Committee for January 25, 1927, in Xu Yufang and Bian Xingying 1987, 186.

60. Chang Kuo-t'ao 1971, 1: 570; Shi Yi 1962, 95.

61. Only two incidents of attacks on factory foremen were reported in the *North-China Herald* for the period November 1926 to January 1927; NCH, November 27, 1926; NCH, January 15, 1927.

62. Chesneaux 1968, 341; Isaacs [1938] 1961, 131; Wilbur and How 1956, 525.

63. Zhang Jungu 1980, 1: 271.

64. Ibid., 274.

65. NCH, February 26, 1927.

66. NCH, March 5, 1927.

67. Chesneaux 1968, 355.

68. NCH, March 5, 1927; NCH, March 19, 1927; NCH, April 23, 1927.

69. Chesneaux 1968, 355, 531.

70. Boorman and Howard 1967–71, 1: 203; Guo Morou 1978, 3: 128–129, 132.

71. Chesneaux 1968, 352; Chang Kuo-t'ao, 1: 578; Isaacs [1938] 1961, 143; Liu Shaotang, 1978, 1: 354.

72. Liu Shaotang, 1978, 1: 354–355; Isaacs [1938] 1961, 127; Clark 1928, 147.

73. Chang Kuo-t'ao, 1: 578–579.

74. Chesneaux 1968, 352; Isaacs [1938] 1961, 143; NCH, April 2, 1927.

75. Chen's report is to be found in the Minutes of the plenary meeting of the Shanghai District Committee for April 1, 1927, in Xu Yufang and Bian Xingying 1987, 220; Guo Morou 1978, 3: 129, 134–135; Isaacs [1938] 1961, 143; NCH, April 2, 1927.

76. This account is based largely on Guo Morou 1978, 3: 123–127, 136–140 and Chen Lifu 1994, 53–54. Both Guo and Chen were present in Anqing during the coup.

77. Guo Morou 1978, 3: 139–140; Zhang Jungu 1980, 1: 309–310.

78. *China Year Book 1928*, 821–822; Isaacs [1938] 1961, 135; Zhang Jungu 1980, 1: 283–284; Liu Shaotang 1978, 1: 355.

79. Zhang Jungu 1980, 1: 280.

80. NCH, March 12, 1927; Zhang Jungu 1980, 1: 281–282.

81. Zhang Jungu 1980, 1: 284–285; NCH, March 19, 1927; Liu Shaotang 1978, 1: 355.

82. Isaacs [1938] 1961, 137.

83. Liu Shaotang 1978, 1: 358; NCH, April 2, 1927; NCH, April 9, 1927; Jordan 1976, 285.

84. Chesneaux 1968, 355–356.

85. Hua Gang [1931] 1982, 224; Chesneaux 1968, 357.

86. NCH, March 26, 1927; Hua Gang [1931] 1982, 216–226.

87. Zhang Jungu 1980, 1: 288.

88. Hua Gang [1931] 1982, 216–226
89. Zhang Jungu 1980, 1: 287–289; Hua Gang [1931] 1982, 219; *Diyici Guonei Geming Zhanzheng Shiqi de Gongren Yundong* 1954, 476.
90. Zhang Jungu 1980, 1: 290; Mark Gayn 1944, 145; Hua Gang [1931] 1982, 221–222.
91. Zhang Jungu 1980, 1: 292–294; Hua Gang [1931] 1982, 219–220; *Diyici Guonei Geming Zhanzheng Shiqi de Gongren Yundong* 1954, 476–477; Isaacs [1938] 1961, 139.
92. Hua Gang [1931] 1982, 220; *Diyici Guonei Geming Zhanzheng Shiqi de Gongren Yundong* 1954, 477.
93. Zhang Jungu 1980, 1: 297.
94. Isaacs [1938] 1961, 146, 360; Chesneaux 1968, 358, 362; Li Zongren 1980, 1: 459.
95. NCH, April 21, 1927.
96. Li Zongren 1980, 1: 458–459; Chitarov, "Report to the 16th Session of XV Congress of the CPSU, December 11, 1927," in Trotsky [1938] 1967, 270. For Xue Yue's entry into Zhabei on March 22, see Hua Gang [1931] 1982, 223–224; and *Diyici Guonei Geming Zhanzheng Shiqi de Gongren Yundong* 1954, 478.
97. Li Zongren 1980, 1: 457–460.
98. Chitarov, in Trotsky [1938] 1967, 270; Vishnyakova-Akimova 1971, 310.
99. Xue Gengxin 1986, 91.
100. *Diyici Guonei Geming Zhanzheng Shiqi de Gongren Yundong* 1954, 528.
101. Zhang Jungu 1980, 1: 301, 322, 327; Guo Morou 1978, 3: 127; Zhu Zijia 1964, 49.
102. Zhang Jungu 1980, 1: 301–313; Lu Chongpeng 1967, 71.
103. Lu Chongpeng 1967, 71, 73; Zhang Jungu 1980, 1: 312.
104. Zhang Jungu 1980, 1: 314; Chen Guoping 1946, 284, 294; Zhu Zijia 1964, 50; Liu Hong 1943, 90; Shi Yi 1962, 189; Jiang Shaozhen 1978, 314.
105. Lu Chongpeng 1967, 71.
106. NCH, March 12, 1927; Wang Qingbin et al. 1928, 472; Zhu Shaozhou 1952, 25(a).
107. Isaacs [1938] 1961, 152; Gayn 1944, 149; Wang Qingbin 1928, 2: 41–42; Ma Chaojun 1958, 2: 660.
108. Zhang Jungu 1980, 1: 320; *Diyici Guonei Geming Zhanzheng Shiqi de Gongren Yundong* 1954, 528; Liu Hong 1943, 89.
109. SB, April 8, 1927; DLDYS 1965, 23; Jiang Shaozhen 1978, 315.
110. Zhang Jungu 1980, 1: 312; Shi Yi 1962, 96; DLDYS 1965, 22.
111. Zhu Zijia 1964, 48; Shi Yi 1962, 97; Zhang Jungu 1980, 1: 320–321; *Diyici Guonei Geming Zhanzheng Shiqi de Gongren Yundong* 1954, 528–529; DLDYS 1965, 22.
The twelve leaders of the MPA were

1. Huang Jinrong   3. Zhang Xiaolin
2. Du Yuesheng   4. Jin Tingsun

5. Gu Jiatang	9. Ma Xiangsheng
6. Ye Chuoshan	10. Gu Zhuxuan
7. Rui Qingrong	11. Pu Jinrong
8. Gao Xinbao	12. Yang Shunchuan

DLDYS mentions five other Green Gang leaders whose assistance was sought in setting up the MPA: Fan Jincheng, Liu Chunpu, Xu Langxi, Jiang Baiqi and Yuan Hanyun. None of these leaders, however, played a prominent part in the MPA's activities.

112. Zhang Jungu 1980, 1: 331.

113. Zhu Zijia 1964, 48; Shi Yi 1962, 97.

114. These were Gu Jiatang, Ye Chuoshan, Rui Qingrong, Gao Xinbao and Yang Qitang. Shi Yi 1962, 97; Zhu Zijia 1964, 48.

115. Shi Yi 1962, 190; Zhang Jungu 1980, 1: 130.

116. Zhang Jungu 1980, 1: 321; Zhu Zijia 1964, 48.

117. Chen Guoping 1946, 296–297, 302. Both Gu and Ye belonged to the Tong generational status group of the Xing Wu Liu Branch of the Green Gang.

118. Zhang Jungu 1980, 1: 336.

119. Zhang Jungu 1980, 1: 315; Wan Molin 1973, 1: 22; Shi Yi 1962, 97.

120. Isaacs [1938] 1961, 360; Jiang Shaozhen 1978, 315.

121. Powell 1945, 159. See chapter 5 for a discussion of the involvement by the French authorities in the coup of April 1927.

122. On the political background to the April 12 Purge see Wu 1976a. See also Li Zongren 1980, 1: 460–463; Huang Xuchu 1968, 13–14; Huang Shaoxiong 1969, 175–177; Chang Kuo-t'ao 1971, 1: 587–588.

123. NCH, April 9, 1927; Liu Hong 1943, 89.

124. Chesneaux 1968, 364.

125. Liu Shaotang 1978, 1: 358; NCH, April 9, 1927; Chang Kuo-t'ao 1971, 1: 587.

126. *Diyici Guonei Geming Zhanzheng Shiqi de Gongren Yundong* 1954, 494.

127. NCH, April 16, 1927; Inprecorr, June 23, 1927; Zhu Zijia 1964, 51; Shi Yi 1962, 95; Zhang Jungu 1980, 2: 9; Chang Kuo-t'ao 1971, 1: 589; Isaacs [1938] 1961, 177; Huang Meizhen 1983, 64; Gayn 1944, 153; Powell 1945, 158–160.

128. Chang Kuo-t'ao 1971, 1: 569–570; Chesneaux 1968, 358; Zhu Zijia 1964, 50; Shi Yi 1962, 95–96; Zhang Jungu 1980, 2: 7.

129. Xu Yufang and Bian Xingying 1987, 316–318; Zhang Jungu 1980, 2: 1–5.

130. Zhang Jungu 1980, 2: 7–12; Zhu Zijia 1964, 51; Shi Yi 1962, 96; Liu Hong 1943, 89; DLDYS 1965, 25.

131. *Diyici Guonei Geming Zhanzheng Shiqi de Gongren Yundong* 1954, 531–532.

132. Powell 1945, 158–160; Zhang Jungu 1980, 1: 332–334. For biographical details on Fessenden see *The Directory and Chronicle for Corea, Japan and China for the Year 1916* 1916, 845, and Powell 1945, 326–327.

133. Powell 1945, 158–159; Zhang Jungu 1980, 1: 332–334.

134. Zhang Jungu 1980, 1: 331–332.

135. Ibid.; *Diyici Guonei Geming Zhanzheng Shiqi de Gongren Yundong* 1954, 494, 529; SMP Files (February 6, 1940) D9319; Chesneaux 1968, 362.

136. NCH, April 16, 1927; Zhu Shaozhou 1952, 25(a).

137. Gayn 1944, 153; NCH, April 16, 1927; *Diyici Guonei Geming Zhanzheng Shiqi de Gongren Yundong* 1954, 494–495; *China Year Book* 1928, 1362; the SMP monthly report for April in NCH, May 21, 1927.

138. *Diyici Guonei Geming Zhanzheng Shiqi de Gongren Yundong* 1954, 495–497; Isaacs [1938] 1961, 176; Vishnyakova-Akimova 1971, 308.

139. *Diyici Guonei Geming Zhanzheng Shiqi de Gongren Yundong* 1954, 495–500; NCH, April 16, 1927.

140. *Diyici Guonei Geming Zhanzheng Shiqi de Gongren Yundong* 1954, 495–500.

141. NCH, April 16, 1927.

142. *Diyici Guonei Geming Zhanzheng Shiqi de Gongren Yundong* 1954, 523; Wang Qingbin et al. 1928, 2: 42; Ma Chaojun 1958, 2: 659; Inprecorr, June 23, 1927; Vishnyakova-Akimova 1971, 311; NCH, April 16, 1927.

143. Isaacs [1938] 1961, 179; Liu Shaotang 1978, 1: 359; NCH, May 21, 1927, April 16, 1927; Zhu Shaozhou 1952, 25(b); Inprecorr, June 23, 1927; *Diyici Guonei Geming Zhanzheng Shiqi de Gongren Yundong* 1954, 529–530.

144. Zhu Zijia 1964, 49; Liu Shaotang 1978, 1: 362; Wan Molin 1973, 1: 10.

145. Jun Xing 1933, 175.

146. Zhang Jungu 1980, 2: 77–78; Wan Molin 1973, 8–12, 13; Zhu Zijia 1964, 49; *Diyici Guonei Geming Zhanzheng Shiqi de Gongren Yundong* 1954, 525–526.

147. Inprecorr, June 23, 1927.

148. Zhu Zijia 1964, 49–50

149. DLDYS 1965, 25; Zhang Jungu 1980, 2: 79–80.

150. *Yijiu'erqinian de Shanghai Shangye Lianhehui* 1983, 247; DLDYS 1965, 26.

151. NCH, April 30, 1927, May 14, 1927.

152. "Jiangsu zuijin gongzuo zongbaogao: guanyu zhigong yundong" (General report on [our] most recent work in Jiangsu: The labor movement), November 12, 1927. In *Zhonggong "Gongren Yundong" Yuanshi Ziliao Huibian* 1980, 1: 220.

153. NCH, June 18, 1927.

154. Ma Chaojun 1958, 2: 734; Jun Xing 1933, 175.

155. Lu Chongpeng 1967, 73; Isaacs [1938] 1961, 177.

156. Chapman 1928, 231–232; Coble 1980, 32–36. Owen Chapman described the extension of the "White Terror" to the Shanghai bourgeoisie in the following terms:

[What] created a [great] sensation in Shanghai was the extension and abuse of the anti-communist campaign.... When ... it became necessary to raise forced "loans" and contributions from the wealthy classes, it was convenient to use the machinery which had already been created. The charge of "communist" ... obviated all awkward questions or criticisms. Wealthy Chinese would be arrested in their homes or mysteriously disappear from the streets; and those who reappeared came back as poorer men, but could in no case be induced to open their mouths to inform on their oppressors. A sense of insecurity and foreboding was in men's minds, which they feared to speak of to their nearest friends. Millionaires were arrested as "communists"! ... Under no previous regime in modern times had Shanghai known such a reign of terror; and the pressure became heavier as the military situation became more desperate. (231–232)

157. *Yijiu'erqinian de Shanghai Shangye Lianhehui* 1983, 269. According to this source Huang Jinrong was the Head of the Self-Defense Militia and both Du Yuesheng and Zhang Xiaolin were his deputies.

158. Letter from Du Yuesheng and Zhang Xiaolin to Zhang Jingjiang, August 12, 1927, in MBY 1993, 95.

159. NCH, September 10, 1927; Powell 1945, 154; Snow [1938] 1961, 54.

160. NCH, May 21, 1927; Zhang Jungu 1980, 2: 81; Zhu Zijia 1964, 48; Shi Yi 1962, 97; Wan Molin 1973, 24; Liu Hong 1943, 90; DLDYS 1965, 27.

CHAPTER FIVE

1. MAE, 232 E515.4 MAE Minute to Colonial Ministry, February 26, 1927; MAE, E515.4 MAE to Colonial Ministry, January 10, 1927. For a detailed discussion of the foreign response to the Shanghai crisis of early 1927, see Clifford 1991, 177–256.

2. MAE, E515.4 Minute of the Council of Ministers, January 10, 1927.

3. MAE, E515.4 Minute of the Council of Ministers on the Defense of the Shanghai French Concession, January 10, 1927; MAE, 45 E515.4 Naggiar to MAE, February 11, 1927.

4. FO, F1380/7/87 Ingram to FO (enclosing memorandum of Woodhead's interview with Wilden, French Minister, October 21, 1932), December 26, 1932; MAE, 386 E515.4 MAE Minute to the War Ministry, March 2, 1927; MAE, 118 E515.4 de Martel to MAE, March 5, 1927; MAE, 57 E515.4 Naggiar to MAE, March 6, 1927; MAE, 444 E515.4 MAE Minute to the War Ministry, March 9, 1927.

5. *Diyici Guonei Geming Zhanzheng Shiqi de Gongren Yundong* 1954, 528.

6. Powell 1945, 158–159.

7. AMAE, Asie: Affaires Communes, vol. 56, Meyrier to Legation, August 30, 1928. I would like to thank Dr. Nicholas Clifford for having brought this dispatch to my attention together with that in n. 61, below.

8. MAE, 130 E515.4 Naggiar to MAE, May 29, 1927.

9. Personal communication from Professor Jean Chesneaux; FO, F1380/7/87 Ingram to FO, December 26, 1932; FO, F3570/184/87 Brenan to Legation, May 29, 1930.

10. Woodhead 1931, 58.

11. AMAE, Naggiar to MAE, January 7, 1928.

12. AMAE, de Martel to MAE, February 10, 1928; AMAE, Meyrier to Legation, August 30, 1928.

13. FO, F42990/127/87 Lampson to FO, May 29, 1928.

14. FO, F3621/244/87 Henderson [Paris] to FO, July 7, 1928.

15. U.S. Dept. of State, Narcotics/419 Graves to Adams, September 29, 1932.

16. DLDYS 1965, 34; SMP Files (February 6, 1940) D9319; Xue Gengxin 1980, 163; CWR, July 25, 1931; Zhang Jungu 1980, 2: 86–89; Shi Yi 1962, 68–69.

17. *Shanghai Shi Nianjian 1936*, V45–V46; SMP Files (October 8, 1938) D4683; *Gendai Chūka Minkoku Manshūkoku Jimmeikan 1932*, 171.

18. For details see Martin 1992, 289; *Shanghai Shi Nianjian 1936* 1935–37, V45–V46.

19. Dong Shu 1934a, 1022.

20. NCH, July 9, 1927, July 19, 1927, July 30, 1927; *Shanghai Shi Nianjian 1936*, V46; DLDYS 1965, 29; Dong Shu 1934a, 1022; AMAE, Meyrier to Legation, August 30, 1928.

21. SB, November 17, 1927, cited in Dong Shu 1934a, 1021.

22. NCH, January 21, 1928, February 4, 1928; Dong Shu 1934a, 1021–1023; U.S. Dept. of State, 893.114 PR Shanghai/1 Cunningham to State, February 11, 1928; MAE, 7 E515.4 Naggiar to MAE, January 9, 1928; FMC, *Compte-Rendu 1928* (Meeting of the Provisional Commission, January 16, 1928), 9.

23. FMC, *Compte-Rendu 1929*, (Meeting of the Provisional Commission, July 17, 1929), 138; MAE, 96 E515.4 Koechlin to MAE, August 9, 1929.

24. FO, F6548/69/87 Lampson to FO (enclosing SMP confidential report on Shanghai opium traffic), October 22, 1929; FO, F3570/184/87 Brenan to Legation, May 29, 1930; *Shanghai Shi Nianjian 1936*, V46; Fan Shaozeng 1986, 208.

25. CWR, July 5, 1930; Dong Shu 1934a, 1023–1024; *Shanghai Shi Nianjian 1936*, V46; Zhu Menghua 1983, 81.

26. FO, F3570/184/87 Brenan to Legation, May 29, 1930.

27. For a detailed analysis of Du's involvement with the French Tramways Union, see Martin 1985.

28. NCH, July 15, 1930, October 7, 1930. On the origin and development of the French Tramways Company, see Zhu Bangxing et al. [1939] 1984, 273–274; Zhou Jianfeng 1982, 348–350; Roux 1974, 4–5; Hammond 1978, 174–177.

29. For the Wu Tonggen Affair, see Martin 1985, 108–109; for the Xin Dingxiang Affair, see Ma Chaojun 1958, 3: 1019–1021.

30. In the case of the Wu Tonggen Affair, the indemnity paid to the family was Ch$3,500, of which the French authorities and the French Tramways Company each contributed Ch$1,000, with Du Yuesheng making up the balance of Ch$1,500. Du also undertook to pay Wu's widow a monthly maintenance allowance of Ch$30 for ten years. Du's total financial contribution, therefore, amounted to Ch$5,100. Zhang Jungu 1980, 2: 121–122.

31. On the 1928 strike, see Martin 1985, 112–118; Roux 1974, 3–35; Hammond 1978, 185–193; Zhu Bangxing et al. [1939] 1984, 301–313; Ma Chaojun 1958, 3: 843–847.

32. CWR, January 5, 1929; NCH, December 22, 1928; SB, December 19, 1928. Xu belonged to He Mengxiong's "real work" faction of the CCP's Jiangsu Provincial Committee; see Jiang Peinan 1984, 3: 189, 204–205. On the "real work" faction, see Harrison 1972, 151, 162, 171, 182, 186–188.

33. NCH, December 22, 1928; Ma Chaojun 1958, 3: 847; Zhang Jungu 1980, 2: 128.

34. Ma Chaojun 1958, 3: 847; Zhang Jungu 1980, 2: 130; Roux 1974, 21–22.

35. Zhu Bangxing et al. [1939] 1984, 305.

36. *Zhongguo Gongren* (Chinese Worker), vol. 5 (January 1929): 28–33, translated by Roux in appendix 1, Roux 1974, 32–35; Ma Chaojun 1958, 3: 847; CWR, January 5, 1929; Zhu Bangxing et al. [1939] 1984, 306–310; Jiang Peinan 1984, 201–202.

37. DLDYS 1965, 30; Zhu Bangxing et al. [1939] 1984, 362–363; Shi Yi 1962, 7.

38. Jiang Peinan 1984, 204; NCH, March 30, 1929; Zhu Bangxing et al. [1939] 1984, 312–313.

39. Zhu Bangxing et al. [1939] 1984, 316–318.

40. Ibid., 319–320; Jiang Peinan 1984, 209.

41. On the 1930 strike, see Martin 1985, 122–129; Hammond 1978, 193–204; Zhu Bangxing et al. [1939] 1984, 316–339; Ma Chaojun 1958, 3: 994–997.

42. Jiang Peinan 1984, 214–215; "The Shanghai Trade Union Federation's report to the Shanghai workers on the strikes in the French Tramways Company and Jardine, Matheson's" (Shanghai Gonghui Lianhehui wei Fadian, Lao Yihe bagong gao quan Shanghai gongyou), July 21, [1930], in *Shanghai Gonghui Lianhehui* 1989, 404.

43. NCH, July 22, 1930.

44. NCH, July 15, 1930, July 22, 1930.

45. Hammond 1978, 199–200.

46. NCH, July 22, 1930; CWR, July 26, 1930; Ma Chaojun 1958, 3: 995; Zhang Jungu 1980, 2: 156; *China Year Book 1931*, 579; Jiang Peinan 1984, 210.

47. NCH, July 29, 1930; Ma Chaojun 1958, 3: 995.

48. NCH, July 29, 1930; NCH, August 5, 1930; Ma Chaojun 1958, 3: 996; Zhang Jungu 1980, 2: 156.

49. Yang Guanbei 1952, 30(b); Zhang Jungu 1980, 2: 156; Gu Jiatang 1952, 28(a).

50. *China Year Book 1931*, 579; NCH, July 29, 1930.

51. Xue Gengxin 1979, 156.

52. CWR, August 9, 1930.

53. Yang Guanbei 1952, 30(b); Shi Yi 1962, 7; NCH, August 5, 1930; CWR, August 9, 1930.

54. Zhang Jungu 1980, 2: 157–158; Yang Guanbei 1952, 30(b); Gu Jiatang 1952, 28(b); Shi Yi 1962, 7; "Xinshishuo" 1954, 57(b)–58(a).

55. NCH, September 8, 1931.

56. Xue Gengxin 1979, 156.

57. Dong Shu 1934a, 1026.

58. FO, F6548/69/87 Lampson to FO, October 22, 1929.

59. FO, F3225/22/37 Lampson to FO, April 13, 1931.

60. CWR, July 18, 1931.

61. AMAE, Meyrier to MAE, May 16, 1932, AMAE, Asie: Affaires communes, vol. 111.

62. CWR, July 18, 1931.

63. FO, F1380/7/87 Ingram to FO, December 26, 1932; NCH, June 24, 1930.

64. FO, F3225/22/87 Lampson to FO, April 13, 1931; CWR, May 23, 1931, May 30, 1931, June 6, 1931, June 13, 1931.

65. U.S. Dept. of State, 893.00 PR Shanghai/36 Cunningham to State, June 5, 1931.

66. Martin 1985, 129–130, 133; NCH, July 7, 1931; CWR, July 18, 1931; U.S. Dept of State 893.00 PR Shanghai/38 Cunningham to State, August 5, 1931; FMC, *Compte-Rendu 1931* (Police Report), 300; Dong Shu 1934a, 49–52.

67. CWR, September 5, 1931, September 19, 1931, September 26, 1931.

68. *La Lumiere*, June 18, 1932, cited in CWR, September 10, 1932; SB, February 19, 1932, cited in DLDYS 1965, 32; *Peking and Tientsin Times*, June 28, 1932; CWR, March 19, 1932.

69. FO, F1380/7/87 Ingram to FO, December 26, 1932.

70. "Shanghai Fazujie dangju youguan yi'erba shibian wenjian xuankan" 1985, 26; FMC, *Compte-Rendu 1932* (Meeting of the Provisional Commission, February 29, 1932), 34; DLDYS 1965, 29.

71. FMC, *Compte-Rendu 1932* (Meeting of the Provisional Commission, March 14, 1932), 44; FMC, *Compte-Rendu 1932* (Meeting of the Provisional Commission, March 24, 1932), 53–54; NCH, March 15, 1932, March 22, 1932, March 29, 1932; CWR, March 26, 1932.

72. Tiltman 1937, 57.

73. AMAE, Meyrier to MAE, May 16, 1932, vol. 111.

74. FO, F1380/7/87 Ingram to FO, December 26, 1932; CF, April 16, 1932; DLDYS 1965, 36.

75. Martin 1985, 134–135; Zhu Bangxing et al. [1939] 1984, 360–361; Da Yun 1932, 123–125; NCH, July 13, 1932.

76. Da Yun 1932, 126.

77. FO, F1380/7/87 Ingram to FO, December 26, 1932.

78. FMC, *Compte-Rendu 1932* (Meeting of the Provisional Commission, March 14, 1932), 44.

79. FMC, *Compte-Rendu 1935* (Meeting of the Provisional Commission, January 7, 1935), 4; NCH, January 16, 1935.

80. FMC, *Compte-Rendu 1935* (Meeting of the Provisional Commission, January 7, 1935), 4–5; Huang Guodong 1986, 256.

81. *Central China Post*, September 26, 1932, September 27, 1932; NCH, September 28, 1932.

82. FMC, *Compte-Rendu 1932* (Police Report), 341.

83. FMC, *Compte-Rendu 1935* (Police Report), 197; FMC, *Compte-Rendu 1936* (Police Report), 215.

84. FMC, *Compte-Rendu 1935* (Police Report), 197–198; FMC, *Compte-Rendu 1936* (Police Report), 215.

85. AMAE, Meyrier to MAE, May 16, 1932, AMAE, Asie: Affaires communes, vol. 111.

86. FMC, *Compte-Rendu 1933* (Meeting of the Provisional Commission, January 9, 1933), 3; FMC, *Compte-Rendu 1934* (Meeting of the Provisional Commission, January 15, 1934), 3; FMC, *Compte-Rendu 1935* (Meeting of the Provisional Commission, January 7, 1935), 5; FMC, *Compte-Rendu 1936* (Meeting of the Provisional Commission, January 20, 1936), 3; FMC, *Compte-Rendu 1936* (Meeting of the Provisional Commission, June 22, 1936), 56.

87. *Shanghai Shi Nianjian 1936*, V47; *Heng She Sheyuan Lu 1934*, 369, 372, 373, 379.

88. *Shishi Xinbao*, January 10, 1935.

89. For the SMC reforms, see Wright 1991, 76–111.

90. *Chen Bao*, July 30, 1935, July 31, 1935, August 4, 1935; *Min Bao*, August 5, 1935; SMP Files (August 6, 1935) D5670; SMP Files (August 7, 1935) D5670; *Xinwen Bao*, August 8, 1935; SMP Files (August 9, 1935) D5670; *China Times*, August 10, 1935; Ma Chaojun 1958, 3: 1245–1246.

CHAPTER SIX

1. Liu Shaotang 1978, 1: 366; FO, F522/127/87 Lampson to FO, December 20, 1927; FO, F4749/4749/87 memorandum by Pratt, August 10, 1929; Tyau 1930, 305–309. On the politics of opium in the Guomindang period, see Marshall 1976.

2. FO, F522/127/87 Lampson to FO, December 20, 1927.

3. NCDN, November 23, 1927; FO, F522/127/87 Lampson to FO, December 20, 1927; U.S. Dept. of State, 893.114 602 Cunningham to State, December 12, 1927; FO, F4749/4749/87 memorandum by Pratt, August 10, 1929.

4. FO, F4749/4749/87 memorandum by Pratt, August 10, 1929; FO, F522/127/87 Lampson to FO, December 20, 1927; FO, F4920/127/87 Lampson to FO, May 29, 1928.

5. FO, F4749/4749/87 memorandum by Pratt, August 10, 1929; FO,

F441/69/87 Garstin to Legation, November 21, 1928; FO, F6548/69/87 Lampson to FO, October 20, 1929.

6. On the Jiang'an opium scandal, see NCH, December 1, 1928, December 8, 1928, December 15, 1928, December 22, 1928, December 29, 1928; U.S. Dept. of State, 893.114 Narcotics/16 [Jiang'an Opium Case]; Wakeman 1989, 190–194.

7. NCH, December 1, 1928; U.S. Dept. of State, 893.114 Narcotics/16.

8. Huang Meizhen and Hao Shengchao 1987, 168; NCH, December 29, 1928; U.S. Dept. of State, 893.114 Narcotics/16.

9. NCH, December 1, 1928.

10. *Shanghai Times*, December 7, 1928.

11. FO, F441/69/87 Garstin to Legation, November 21, 1928; FO, F109/69/87 Lampson to FO, November 27, 1928.

12. NCH, December 8, 1928.

13. NCH, December 8, 1928; FO, F5428/69/87 Garstin to Legation, August 9, 1929.

14. FO, F3570/184/87 Brenan to Legation, May 29, 1930.

15. NCH, December 8, 1928, December 29, 1928; U.S. Dept. of State, 893.114 N16.

16. NCH, December 8, 1928.

17. U.S. Dept. of State, 893.00 PR Shanghai/2 Cunningham to State, March 7, 1928.

18. FO, F370/184/87 Brenan to Legation, May 29, 1930; FO, F3634/184/87 Brenan to Legation, May 31, 1930; FO, F5008/792/87 Brenan to FO, July 30, 1930; FO, F5392/792/87 Brenan to FO, August 14, 1930.

19. U.S. Dept. of State, 893.114 Narcotics/208 Jenkins to State, March 16, 1931.

20. U.S. Dept. of State, 893.114 Narcotics/625 State to Legation, January 29, 1934. On Rajchman's missions to China, see Balinska 1992, 168–207.

21. CWR, August 1, 1931.

22. Ibid.

23. *Dagong Bao* (L'Impartial), April 30, 1931; CWR, August 15, 1931; Isaacs 1932, 18.

24. CWR, July 11, 1931; Sues 1944, 70–71.

25. U.S. Dept. of State, 893.00 PR Shanghai/38 Cunningham to State, August 4, 1931; CWR, July 18, 1931.

26. U.S. Dept. of State, 893.00 PR Shanghai/39 Cunningham to State, September 17, 1931; Isaacs 1932, 18.

27. Fan Shaozeng 1992; Fan Shaozeng 1986, 195, 196, 198; Yi Wen 1988, 32–34; FO, F4098/184/87 Fitzmaurice to FO, June 14, 1930; U.S. Dept. of State, 893.114 Narcotics/178 Lockhart to State, December 12, 1930; FO, F6293/184/87 Toller to Legation, August 14, 1930; U.S. Dept. of State, 893.114 Narcotics/208 Lockhart to State, March 4, 1931; U.S. Dept. of State, 893.114 Narcotics/419 Graves to Adams [Hankow], October 3, 1932; U.S. Dept. of State, 893.114, Narcotics/738 Clubb to Adams [Hankow], April 28, 1934.

28. See chapter 4 for a discussion of Du's involvement with the UUC.

29. Jun Xing 1933, 174–178; "Jiangsu zuijin gongzuo zongbaogao," November 12, 1927, 220; Ma Chaojun 1958, 2: 659; Zhang Jungu 1980, 2: 113.

30. Li Zongren 1980, 2: 531–533.

31. Jin Feng 1954, 51(a); Xinshishuo 1954, 56(b).

32. Isaacs 1932, 18.

33. Jiang Hao 1986a, 65.

34. SMP Files (September 15, 1938) D8185.

35. Yan Ran 1934, 87, 92.

36. Jiang Nan n.d., 44.

37. SMP Files (February 6, 1940) D9319.

38. Chen Zu'en and Wang Jinhai 1990, 135–163; Elvin 1974, 257. For similar developments in Hankou, see Rowe 1984, 317–321.

39. Yang Guanbei 1952, 31; DLDYS 1965, 54; Du Weifan 1954, 19.

40. *Who's Who in China* 1931, 106; DLDYS 1965, 54; Sues 1944, 100–103.

41. Yang Guanbei 1952, 31.

42. DLDYS 1965, 52, and chapter 2, above.

43. Chen Zu'en and Wang Jinhai 1990, 343.

44. *Who's Who in China* 1931, 106; Chen Zu'en and Wang Jinhai 1990, 343.

45. On Yang Du's career, see Peng Guoxing, ed., "Yang Du shengping nianbiao" (A chronology of the life of Yang Du), in Liu Qingbo 1986, 805–826; Liu Shaotang 1977, 3: 263–264; Boorman and Howard 1967–71, 4: 13–16. Yang's membership in the CCP is intriguing, to say the least, and would suggest that Yang probably spied for the CCP while he was a member of Du's household. Although it should be noted that, as yet, there is no hard evidence to support this hypothesis. See Liu Qingbo 1986, 799–803.

46. Yang Guanbei 1952, 30.

47. Yang Du, "Du shi jiasi luocheng song" (A eulogy on the completion of the family temple of the Du clan), in Liu Qingbo 1986, 783–784.

48. Yang Du, "Du shi jiasi ji" (Essay to commemorate the family temple of the Du clan), in Liu Qingbo 1986, 785.

49. Liu Qingbo 1986, 785.

50. Shi Yi 1962, 176–177.

51. Ibid., 180–183.

52. Fan Shaozeng 1986, 221–224; DLDYS 1965, 48–49; Zhang Jungu 1980, 2: 284–311; Shi Yi 1962, 149–158; *Du Shi Jiasi Loucheng Jiniance* 1932.

53. Liu Shaotang 1978, 1: 480, 481; U.S. Dept. of State, 893.00 Legation to State, March 5, 1932; U.S. Dept. of State, 893.00 Legation to State, March 8, 1932.

54. U.S. Dept. of State, 893.00/11899 Peck to State, March 12, 1932.

55. Eastman 1974, 1.

56. On the Shanghai Incident, see Henriot 1991, 83–124; Jordan 1991; Coble 1991, 39–55.

57. For a discussion of the Zhabei puppet government, see Wakeman 1989, 229–230, 235–239.

58. SMP Files (April 5, 1932) D3445, (April 8, 1932) D3445; NCH, May 3, 1932, May 24, 1932, August 17, 1932.

59. SMP Files (May 2, 1932) D3445, (May 5, 1932) D3445.

60. *Shanghai Shimin Difang Weichihui Baogao Shu* 1932, 1: 1–15.

61. Guo Xiaoxian 1933, 481–482.

62. *Shanghai Shimin Difang Weichihui Huiyuan Lu* [1932].

63. *Shanghai Shimin Difang Weichihui Baogaoshu* 1932, 8:11–13; Ma Chaojun 1958, 3: 1071–1073.

64. Shen Yunlong 1981, 331–349; Liu Jingyuan 1933, 111–120; NCH, April 12, 1932; CF, April 16, 1932.

65. Zhang Jungu 1980, 3: 2; Jordan 1991, 94.

66. Zhang Zhang 1933, 165–169.

67. Isaacs 1932, 18.

68. FMC, Police, Compte Rendu d'Enquête 113/8, November 2, 1932; SMP Files (September 1, 1932) D3904, (November 8, 1936) D7667.

69. Powell 1945, 157–158; Liu Lianke 1940, 143.

70. *Shanghai Shimin Difang Weichihui Baogao Shu* 1932.

71. Guo Xiaoxian 1933, 481.

72. CF, April 16, 1932; Isaacs, 1932, 18; Shen Yunlong 1981, 336–337; SMP Files (April 20, 1932) D3176/17.

73. Coble 1980, 115–119; U.S. Dept. of State, 893.00 PR Shanghai/49 Josselyn to State, September 9, 1932; U.S. Dept. of State, 893.00 PR Shanghai/53 Cunningham to State, January 19, 1933.

74. SMP Files (May 2, 1932) D3445, (May 5, 1932) D3445; CWR, June 4, 1932.

75. SMP Files (April 10, 1932) D3445, (April 18, 1932) D3344.

76. U.S. Dept. of State, 893.114 Narcotics/738 Clubb to Adams [Hankow], April 24, 1934; *Peking and Tientsin Times*, June 23, 1932.

77. *Peking and Tientsin Times*, November 11, 1932; FO, F1380/7/87 Ingram to FO, December 26, 1932; FO, F4503/87/87 Cadogan to FO, June 11, 1934; SMP Files (December 28, 1932) D3648, (February 6, 1940) D9319.

CHAPTER SEVEN

1. See chapter 8 for a discussion of Du's economic interests in the 1930s.

2. Schmitter 1979, 13.

3. Ibid., 31.

4. Mihail Manoilesco, cited in Schmitter 1979, 7.

5. Dirlik 1989, 128. On the Guomindang conception of the state, see Bedeski 1981.

6. Eastman 1974, 68.

7. Ibid., 54.

8. On Guomindang policy toward trade unions in the 1930s, see Perry 1993, 92–103, 106–108.

9. Ma Chaojun 1958, 3: 905–911, 980–981; Wales 1945, 67–68; Henriot 1991, 56–58, 225–226, 247–269.

10. Ma Chaojun 1958, 3: 755, 784.

11. Ibid., 1170–1171.

12. Fewsmith 1985, 159–166.

13. NCH, March 22, 1932; NCH, April 12, 1932; *Shen Bao Nianjian 1933*, U13.

14. *Shanghai Shimin Difang Weichihui Baogao Shu* 1932, 1: 81–82.

15. DLDYS 1965, 61; SMP Files (December 27, 1935) D4683.

16. *Shanghai Shi Nianjian 1935*, F51–F57; Henriot 1991, 76–81.

17. NCH, October 19, 1932.

18. Hatano 1943, 460–462; SMP Files (June 20, 1933) D4685; Tien 1972, 49–51; Eastman 1976, 196–200.

19. SMP Files (February 6, 1940) D9319.

20. *Shanghai Shi Nianjian 1937*, E2–E6.

21. Huang Jingzhai 1986, 134. Several leading members of the CC Clique's Shanghai organization found membership in the Green Gang useful in furthering their intelligence activities. For example, Li Shiqun, the head of the Action Club's intelligence section in the mid-1930s, joined the Green Gang in 1928 when he became a follower of the Shanghai Gang boss Ji Yunqing. Li's membership of the Green Gang proved very useful in his relations with Du Yuesheng. See Huang Meizhen and Shi Yuanhua 1987, 351–352; Huang Meizhen 1986, 429–430; Zhao Yulin 1988, 194.

22. Zhang Jungu 1980, 3: 121–123; CF, May 28, 1932; NCH, June 7, 1932; Ma Chaojun 1958, 3: 1098–1100.

23. Zhang Jungu 1980, 3: 117–121; Huang Jingzhai 1986, 133; *Shanghai Shi Nianjian 1935*, F20.

24. SMP Files (June 16, 1936) D7382.

25. For details of the Endurance Club, see below.

26. *Shanghai Shi Nianjian 1937*, E2–E5; Guo Lanxin 1986, 306.

27. Huang Jingzhai 1986, 131–139; SMP Files (June 20, 1933), (August 22, 1933) D4685.

28. Huang Jingzhai 1986, 142–155. On the Guomindang regime's policies toward Shanghai students, see Wasserstrom 1991, 156–161.

29. SMP Files (August 22, 1933), (July 18, 1935) D4685; Huang Yuanqi 1982, 1: 352–353; Chen Shaoxiao 1965, 2–3, 35–6.

30. *Shanhai Mainichi*, July 8, 1933, cited in SMP Files (July 8, 1933) D4685.

31. On the Blue Shirts, see Eastman 1974, 31–84 and Chang 1985.

32. Chen Shaoxiao 1965, 43–46; Huang Jingzhai 1986, 151–153.

33. Guo Xu 1986, 321–322.

34. Shen Zui 1985, 47–50.

35. Guo Lanxin 1986, 319; DLDYS 1965, 56; SMP Files (March 9, 1933) D9638.

36. Zhang Jungu 1980, 3: 126; Huang Jingzhai 1986, 136; SMP Files (February 19, 1936) D4685, (May 1, 1936) D4797; FMC, Police, Compte Rendu d'Enquête 1123/2, June 2, 1936.

37. Wakeman 1989, 239–250.

38. *Shanghai Haiyuan Gongren Yundong Shi* 1991, 37–38, 111; Ma Chaojun 1958, 3: 1165–1166. See also Wakeman 1989, 185.

39. SMP Files (December 28, 1932) D3648, (April 18, 1936) D3648, (October 24, 1939) [no number].

40. NCDN, July 24, 1937; SMP Files (July 26, 1937) D7584.

41. Zhu Xuefan 1986, 5; DLDYS 1965, 56.

42. Ma Chaojun 1958, 3: 921–922.

43. CF, January 20, 1932.

44. CF, January 20, 1932, January 27, 1932, April 23, 1932, May 21, 1932.

45. Hammond 1978, 162–167; CF, May 28, 1932, June 4, 1932, June 18, 1932; U.S. Dept. of State, 893.00 PR Shanghai/47 Cunningham to State, June 8, 1932.

46. CF, September 18, 1933.

47. DLDYS 1965, 50–51.

48. CF, October 22, 1933; *Shanghai Evening Post and Mercury*, November 25, 1936; *Shanghai Times*, April 24, 1937; Ma Chaojun 1958, 3: 1197–1201; SMP Files (July 16, 1936) D7020, (February 23, 1937) D7803, (April 8, 1937) D7836.

49. Zhu Xuefan 1986, 8–10, 18–19.

50. SMP Files (May 11, 1937) D7870.

51. On Shi's political activities, see Narramore 1989, 107–132.

52. Huang Yanpei 1982, 93–94.

53. SMP Files (February 6, 1940) D9319; Shen Zui 1985, 161; Coble, 1991, 216.

54. SMP Files (April 27, 1936) D7382, (May 22, 1936) D7382, (July 1, 1936) D7382; *Min Bao*, July 2, 1936.

55. NCH, April 10, 1935.

56. Sues 1944, 71–72.

57. DLDYS 1965, 64.

58. *Ci Hai* 1974, 107; Wen Juntian 1939; Hsiao Kung-chuan 1960, 43–83; Kuhn 1970, 24–28, 33.

59. Tien 1972, 111–112; *Jiaofei Zhanshi* 1967, 6: 1189–1197.

60. DLDYS 1965, 64.

61. Tsao 1947, 17–19.

62. In some respects the Guomindang process of defining who was a "citizen" was not dissimilar from the CCP practice after 1949 of deciding who did and who did not belong to "the people." Liu Shaotang, 1: 536; Tsao 1947, 19; SMP Files (August 19, 1936) D7493.

63. SMP Files (August 11, 1936) D7493, (August 12, 1936) D7493; *Xinwen Bao*, August 14, 1936.

64. SMP Files (August 17, 1936) D7493.

65. SMP Files (August 19, 1936) D7493.

66. *Shanghai Evening Post and Mercury*, May 25, 1937; Tsao 1947, 19.

67. SMP Files (July 17, 1937) D7493.

68. SMP Files (July 26, 1937) D7493.

69. Huang Meizhen and Hao Shengchao 1987, 261. On the December Ninth Movement, see Israel 1966, 111–156, and Wasserstrom, 158–161.

70. DLDYS 1965, 62; Israel 1966, 301.

71. DLDYS 1965, 63.

72. The best general account of the Xi'an Incident is Wu 1976b.

73. DLDYS 1965, 63–64; Zhu Wenyuan 1993, 1: 292.

74. U.S. Dept. of State, 893.00 PR Shanghai/56 Cunningham to State, April 1, 1933.

75. DLDYS 1965, 63–64.

76. *Shanghai Shi Difang Xiehui Jibao* (The Shanghai Civic Association Quarterly), 12 (1937), cited in DLDYS 1965, 62.

77. U.S. Dept. of State, 893.114 Narcotics/738 Clubb to Adams [Hankow], April 21, 1934; U.S. Dept. of State, 893.114 Narcotics/625 State to Legation, January 29, 1934; Xiao Juetian 1980, 157, 159–160; DLDYS 1965, 36–37.

78. SMP Files (November 25, 1933) [no number].

79. Guo Lanxin 1986, 308; SMP Files (December 19, 1935) D7143.

80. DLDYS 1965, 37; SMP Files (November 25, 1933) [no number].

81. SMP Files (November 25, 1933) [no number], (November 30, 1933) [no number], (February 6, 1940) D9319; U.S. Dept. of State, 893.114 Narcotics/738 Clubb to Adams [Hankow], April 24, 1934.

82. SMP Files (July 2, 1935) D7138; U.S. Dept. of State, 893.114 Narcotics/1308 Nicholson [Treasury Attaché] to Customs, July 5, 1935.

83. U.S. Dept. of State, 893.114 Narcotics/1574 Johnson to State, March 21, 1936.

84. Sues 1944, 73–74, 94.

85. U.S. Dept. of State, 893.00 PR Shanghai/94 Gauss to State, August 5, 1936; *Shanghai Times*, May 22, 1937; SMP Files (July 7, 1937) D7318.

86. Guo Lanxin 1986, 305; DLDYS 1965, 57–58; Zhang Jungu 1980, 3: 61.

87. Zhu Xuefan 1986, 6; DLDYS 1965, 57–58; Guo Lanxin 1986, 307–308.

88. DLDYS 1965, 57; *Heng She Yuekan*, nos. 16–17 (May 1937): 106.

89. *Heng She Sheyuan Lu 1934*, 369–382; *Heng She Yuekan*, nos. 16–17 (May 1937): 119–122.

90. *Heng She Sheyuan Lu 1934*, ibid.; *Heng She Yuekan*, ibid.

91. DLDYS 1965, 59; Zhang Kechang 1936, 18.

92. Zhang Kechang 1936, 10–11.

93. *Heng She Shezhang* n.d., 367–368; *Heng She Yuekan*, nos. 16–17 (May 1937): 107–111; Guo Lanxin 1986, 307-308; DLDYS 1965, 59.

94. Lu Jingshi 1936, 9.

95. Its very success inspired imitation both from among Du's followers and from his Green Gang colleagues and rivals. Guo Lanxin 1986, 301, 309; DLDYS 1965, 57; Wang Yangqing and Xu Yinghu 1982, 64.

96. Report of Guomindang Intelligence Agent "205," February 18, 1939, in MBY 1993, 104.

97. For information on the early career of Gu Zhuxuan, see chapter 1.

98. SMP Files (December 30, 1930) CA178, (October 8, 1938) D4683, (April 7, 1932) D3445, (October 26, 1935) D7057.

99. Xue Gengxin 1986, 96; SMP Files (October 26, 1935) D7057; *Li Bao*, December 18, 1936; *Dagong Bao*, March 5, 1937; *Shanghai Evening Post and Mercury*, June 25, 1937; Wang Yangqing and Xu Yinghu 1982, 64; Jiang Hao 1986a, 61.

100. Yu Yunjiu 1986, 348; SMP Files (February 8, 1934) D5532.

101. Zhu Jianliang and Wu Weizhi 1984, 163.

102. Huang Zhenshi 1986, 176–177.

103. Cheng Xiwen 1986, 163–164; Huang Zhenshi 1986, 177. In an article published in 1985 I suggested that this incident occurred in 1927. I am now persuaded by other evidence that this date is too early, and that the incident actually occurred in early 1936, possibly April 1936. My supposition rests on the facts that Lu Jingshi did not take up his post as head of the Martial Law Division of the Wusong-Shanghai Garrison Command until September 1935; and that Yang Hu was not appointed to the post of Wusong-Shanghai Garrison Commander until the end of March 1936, and did not in fact take up the post until mid-April. Martin 1985, 106; U.S. Dept. of State, 893.00 PR Shanghai/91 Gauss to State, May 7, 1936; SMP Files (April 18, 1936) D3648.

104. SMP Files (December 7, 1936) D7682, (December 15, 1936) D7862; Shi Jun 1986, 352.

105. Yu Yunjiu 1986, 349.

106. Xue Gengxin 1986, 91–92.

107. Sakai 1970, 327.

108. Jiang Hao 1986a, 59–60, 61, 62; Jiang Hao 1986b, 82–83; Xu Xiaogeng 1986, 126; Ling Lei 1992.

109. Sakai 1970, 328–330; Jiang Hao 1986b, 81; Liu Lianke 1940, 145–146; Fan Songfu 1980, 157–158.

110. Jiang Hao 1986b, 83–84; Sakai 1970, 332.

111. Zhang Jungu 1980, 3: 59; Jiang Hao 1986b, 82–83.

112. Zhang Jungu 1980, 3: 63; *Heng She Yuekan*, nos. 10–11 (November 1936): 18; *Heng She Sheyuan Lu 1934*, 376; Jiang Hao 1986b, 80–81, 83–84; Sakai 1970, 328–329, 332; Fan Songfu 1980, 158.

CHAPTER EIGHT

1. DLDYS 1965, 39–40; Jiang Shaozhen 1981, 248; Xu Zhucheng 1983, 50–52.

2. *China Year Book 1935*, 367–368; Boorman and Howard 1967–71, 1: 380; NCH, May 17, 1933.

3. Fan Shaozeng 1986, 219; Zhu Kuichu 1954, 40; DLDYS 1965, 40.

4. DLDYS 1965, 41.

5. *Shanghai Yanjiu Ziliao Xuji 1937*, 270.

6. DLDYS 1965, 40; Yu Yongfu 1986, 278; Gui Yongding 1982, 83.

7. DLDYS 1965, 40; Gui Yongding 1982, 87.

8. DLDYS 1965, 43–44; *Who's Who in China 1931*, 106; Gui Yongding 1982, 88; Zhang Jungu 1980, 2: 251–257.

9. SMP Files (January 27, 1931) D1949.
10. SB, January 30, 1931; *Xinwen Bao*, February 7, 1931.
11. SB, January 21, 1931.
12. Wang Renze and Xiong Shanghou 1984, 273–274; SMP Files (January 28, 1931) D1949.
13. *Shishi Xinbao*, April 1, 1931; SMP Files (May 29, 1931) D1949.
14. DLDYS 1965, 41; *Shanghai Jinrong Gailan* 1947, 119; *Shanghai Yanjiu Ziliao Xuji* 1937, 270.
15. *Shen Bao Nianjian 1935*, 499; *Zhongguo Jingji Nianjian* 1935, vol. 1, E88; Tamagna 1942, 161.
16. DLDYS 1965, 41; *Shanghai Jinrong Gailan* 1947, 119; Sues 1944, 88.
17. *Shanghai Jinrong Gailan* 1947, 198, 184.
18. Ibid., 135, 152.
19. Ibid., 231, 279.
20. Coble 1980, 140–147, 161–197; Wright 1989, 133–163.
21. Coble 1980, 178–180.
22. SMP Files (February 6, 1940) D9319.
23. Coble 1980, 178–180.
24. Ibid.
25. Wright 1989, 151, citing the "Autobiography of Chang Chia-ao" (unpublished manuscript, Columbia University).
26. SB, April 2, 1935.
27. Leith-Ross 1968, 208; Friedman 1940, 64–70.
28. Coble 1980, 178–180. The other two banks were the Ningbo Commercial and Savings Bank (*Siming Shangye Chuxu Yinhang*) and the National Industrial Bank of China (*Zhongguo Shiye Yinhang*).
29. Feuerwerker 1970, 225–241; Chen Zhen et al. 1961, 3: pt. 2, 985.
30. Bergère 1986, 240–241, 243; Wang Renze 1984, 156–157; *China Year Book 1928*, 1119.
31. Hu Baoqi 1986, 165–168.
32. Ibid., 168–171; *Shanghai Jinrong Gailan* 1947, 58–60; Chen Zhen et al. 1961, 3: pt. 2, 985–986.
33. DLDYS 1965, 41.
34. Leith-Ross 1968, 208.
35. For a discussion of Shanghai stevedores and Communist organizing among them, see Perry 1993, 233–235. See also Zhu Bangxing et al. [1939] 1984, 634–668.
36. Liu Nianzhi 1982, 54.
37. Huang Yongyan 1986, 284.
38. *Liu Hongsheng Qiye Shiliao* 1981, 1: 315; Liu Nianzhi 1982, 54.
39. CF, January 20, 1932; NCH, January 12, 1932; SB, January 9, 1932, January 11, 1932, January 12, 1932; SMP Files (January 12, 1932) D3531, (January 13, 1932) D3531.
40. Huang Yongyan 1986, 284; Zhang Jungu 1980, 2: 218–219; Wang Youcheng 1987, 249; Boorman and Howard 1967–71, 1: 36–37.
41. Huang Yongyan 1986, 285; Zhang Jungu 1980, 2: 219–220; Wang Youcheng 1987, 246–247.

42. Huang Yongyan 1986, 286; Zhang Jungu 1980, 2: 221; NCH, June 28, 1932.

43. Wang Youcheng 1987, 247; Huang Yongyan 1986, 286.

44. Zhang Jungu 1980, 2: 220; Huang Yongyan 1986, 284–285; Wang Youcheng 1987, 247.

45. Wang Youcheng 1987, 247; Huang Yongyan 1986, 287.

46. Huang Yongyan 1986, 287.

47. Ibid.; *Shanghai Shi Nianjian 1935*, O38.

48. Huang Yongyan 1986, 288; Wang Youcheng 1987, 248.

49. Huang Yongyan 1986, 288.

50. Jiang Hao 1986a, 59; Xie Tianmin 1935, sect. 2, p. 15; Zhang Jungu 1980, 2: 223–224.

51. Finnane 1993, 216–224; Honig 1992, 18–35.

52. Wu Choupeng 1935; NCH, February 23, 1929, April 13, 1929, April 27, 1929, December 2, 1930.

53. Zhang Jungu 1980, 2: 225–226.

54. Huang Yongyan 1986, 288–289; Zhang Jungu 1980, 1: 124; Zhu Wenwei 1984, 240; *Shanghai Shi Nianjian 1935*, O39.

55. *Shanghai Shi Tongji* 1933, sect. 11, p. 8.

56. Huang Yongyan 1986, 290–291.

57. Chen Changhe 1983, 124; CWR, February 22, 1930, July 26, 1930; NCDN, July 21, 1930, July 24, 1930.

58. SMP Files (July 19, 1930) D1462.

59. Chen Changhe 1983, 125; NCH, February 22, 1933, March 8, 1933.

60. Chen Changhe 1983, 125; *Liu Hongsheng Qiye Shiliao* 1981, 1: 308.

61. *Liu Hongsheng Qiye Shiliao* 1981, 1: 308–309.

62. Ibid., 309; Chen Changhe 1983, 125.

63. *Shanghai Times*, May 13, 1936; *Shanghai Evening Post and Mercury*, May 22, 1936.

64. Xue Gengxin 1988, 192.

65. Huang Zhenshi 1986, 186; Xue Gengxin 1988, 192.

66. DLDYS 1965, 44; *Shanghai Shi Nianjian 1936*, 28, 32.

67. *Shanghai Evening Post and Mercury*, May 22, 1936.

68. *Shanghai Times*, May 13, 1936.

69. DLDYS 1965, 44.

70. Huang Zhenshi 1986, 177.

71. *Heng She Sheyuan Lu 1934*, 369, 372, 373; *Heng She Yuekan*, no. 12 (December 1936): 50.

72. *Shanghai Evening Post and Mercury*, May 22, 1936.

73. DLDYS 1965, 44; *Shanghai Shi Nianjian 1937*, Q71. For the membership of the executive committee, see Martin 1991, 423–424.

74. *Shanghai Shi Nianjian 1937*, Q71; DLDYS 1965, 44; SMP Files (February 6, 1940) D9319.

75. *Heng She Yuekan*, nos. 10–11 (November 1936): 19.

76. *China Press*, May 12, 1936.

77. NCDN, May 19, 1936; *Shanghai Evening Post and Mercury*, May 22, 1936.

78. *Shanghai Times*, May 28, 1936; *China Press*, May 28, 1936.

79. *Shanghai Times*, June 3, 1936.

80. Xue Gengxin 1988, 192; DLDYS 1965, 44; *Shanghai Times*, June 8, 1936.

CONCLUSION

1. Blok 1974; Arlacchi 1979, 1988.

2. Arlacchi 1988, 5–6.

3. Hobsbawm 1965, 36. Hobsbawm later developed this theme further in Hobsbawm and Ranger 1983.

4. Snow 1934, 206; Gunther 1939, 267. For a comparison of the situation in Shanghai with that in Chicago, see Woodhead 1931, 57.

5. Sues 1944, 68.

6. Finch 1953, 295.

7. Fried 1980, 141–142.

8. Cashman 1981.

9. Nelli 1976, 162.

10. Fried 1980, 106.

11. Nelli 1976, 191.

12. For a general discussion of gangsters and labor racketeering in the United States, see Hutchison 1972, 65–138, 229–270.

13. Fried 1980, 160–166; Hutchison 1972, 74–92.

14. Short 1984, 232–235, 246–255; Hutchison 1972, 93–109, 229–270.

15. Cribb 1991.

16. Ibid., 21.

17. Ibid., 30–31.

18. Kaplan and Dubro 1986.

19. Ibid., 29.

Glossary

an 庵
Andong 安東
Anfu 安福
Anqing Daoyou 安清道友
Anqing Zhongxing 安清中興
antang 庵堂
Ba Gu Dang 八股黨
Bai Chongxi 白崇禧
baishitie 拜師帖
baixiangren 白相人
baixiangren saosao 白相人嫂嫂
Ban Gu 班固
ban shitou 搬石頭
bang 幫
Bao Da 寶大
Bao Haichou 鮑海籌
Bao Xing Li 寶興里
Bao Xinzhai 鮑心齊
baogong 包工
baogongtou 包工頭
baojia 保甲
ben 本
Bi Shucheng 畢庶澄
biaojun 彪軍
Bingzi She 丙子社

bukuaitou 捕快頭
Cai Futang 蔡福棠
Cai Hongtian 蔡洪田
Cai Jingjun 蔡勁軍
Cai Tingkai 蔡廷鍇
Cai Yuanpei 蔡元培
Cai Zengji 蔡增基
Cao Kun 曹錕
Chang Yuqing 常玉清
Chang Zhiying 常芝英
Chao Bang 潮幫
Chaozhou 潮州
Chen Bao 晨報
Chen Dazai 陳達哉
Chen Duxiu 陳獨秀
Chen Gongbo 陳公博
Chen Guofu 陳國夫
Chen Guoping 陳國屏
Chen Jieru 陳潔如
Chen Junyi 陳君毅
Chen Kunyuan 陳坤元
Chen Lifu 陳立夫
Chen Peide 陳培德
Chen Qimei 陳其美
Chen Qun 陳群

Chen Runqing 陳潤青
Chen Shichang 陳世昌
Chen Tiaoyuan 陳調元
Chen Yiting 陳翊庭
cheng 成
Cheng Huang Miao 城隍廟
Cheng Yanqiu 程硯秋
Cheng Zhusun 程祝蓀
Cheng Ziqing 程子卿
Chewubu Tongren Julebu 車務部同仁俱樂部
chuanbi 川幣
Chunbao Shantang 春寶山堂
Cui Fu 崔福
Cui Ruiting 崔瑞亭
Cui Shuxian 崔叔仙
Cui Xilin 崔錫麟
Cui Yangchun 崔陽春
Da 大
Da Ba Gu Dang 大八股黨
Da Da—Da Tong Lianhe Banshichu 大達大通聯合辦事處
Da Da Lunchuan Gongsi 大達輪船公司
Da Da Matou 大達碼頭
Da Gongsi 大公司
Da Sheng Shachang 大生紗廠
Da Shijie Riye Yinhang 大世界日夜銀行
Da Shijie Yule Zhongxin 大世界娛樂中心
Da Tong Renji Hangye Gongsi 大通仁記航業公司
Da Xing Maoyi Gongsi 大興貿易公司
Da You 大有
Dai Buxiang 戴步祥
Dai Fushi 戴浮石

Dai Jieping 戴介屏
Dai Li 戴笠
Dalian 大連
dao 道
daoyi qianqiu 道義千秋
daoyi zhengzong 道義正宗
dashanshi 大善士
Datong Wuxue 大通武學
de 德
Deji Qianzhuang 得記錢莊
Deng Zuyu 登祖禹
Ding Yongchang 丁永昌
Dinghai Dao 定海島
Donghai 東海
Du Aqing 杜阿慶
Du Fengju 杜風舉
Du Jiasi 杜家祠
Du Wenqing 杜文慶
Du Yuesheng 杜月笙
Duan Qirui 段祺瑞
dudu 都督
Dujiazhai 杜家宅
Dunhe Gongsuo 郭和公所
duoshou 舵手
E Shen 鄂森
fa 法
fabi 法幣
Fadian Gonghui 法電工會
Fan Huichun 范回春
Fan Jincheng 樊瑾成
Fan Shaozeng 范紹曾
Fazujie Nashui Huaren Hui 法租界納稅華人會
Feizhi Neizhan Da Tongmeng 廢止內戰大同盟
fen dawang 糞大王
fengjian wangguo 封建王國

Fengtian 奉天

Feng Yuxiang 馮玉祥

fo 佛

Fu Xiao'an 傅筱庵

Furu Jiuji Hui 婦孺救濟會

Fusheng 福生

Fuxing She 復興社

Gan She 幹社

ganniang 干娘

Gansi Dui 敢死隊

Ganyu 贛榆

Gao Shikui 高士奎

Gao Xinbao 高鑫寶

Gaoqiao 高橋

Gaoqiao Nongcun Gaijinhui 高橋農村改進會

Gelaohui 哥老會

Geng Jiaji 耿嘉基

gong 工

gong 功

Gong Wutai 共舞臺

Gongda Yuhang 公大漁行

Gongren Xingdong Da Dui 工人行動大隊

Gu Jiacai 顧嘉才

Gu Jiatang 顧嘉堂

Gu Shunzhang 顧順章

Gu Songmao 顧松茂

Gu Zhuxuan 顧竹軒

Guan Yu 關羽

Guangxu 光緒

Guangzhou 廣州

guanshang heban gongsi 官商合辦公司

guanxi 關係

Guo Haishan 郭海珊

Guo Morou 郭沫若

Guo Shun 郭順

Guomin Dahui 國民大會

Guomin Jinyan Ju 國民禁煙局

Guomindang 國民黨

Guomindang Zhonghua Hai-yuan Tebie Dangbu Guonan Huiyi 國民黨中華海員特別黨部

Guonan Huiyi 國難會議

Guoxin Yinhang 國信銀行

guoying 國營

Guoying Zhaoshangju 國營招商局

Guoyu Ji 郭煜記

Guyun Shan 峪雲山

Han Fuju 韓復矩

Han Hui 韓恢

Hang San 杭三

Hangzhou Jifang Xue 杭州機房學

haoxia 豪俠

He Fenglin 何豐林

He Mengxiong 何夢雄

He Yingqin 何應鈜

Heng She 恆社

hong 紅

hong 洪

Hong Bang 紅幫

Hong Men 洪門

Hong Xing Xiehui 洪興協會

hongjinzei 紅巾賊

Hongkou 虹口

Hongze 洪澤

Hou Dachun 后大椿

Hou Quangen 侯泉根

Houzu 後祖

Hu Hanmin 胡漢民

Hu Lifu 胡立夫

Hu Mei'an 胡梅庵

Huai Hai 淮海

Huang Bingchuan 黃炳泉

Huang Chujiu 黃楚九

Huang Huilan 黃惠蘭

Huang Jiafeng 黃家豐

Huang Jinrong 黃金榮

Huang Xianggu 黃香谷

Huang Zhenshi 黃振世

huangse gonghui 黃色工會

Hubei Teshui Qinglihui 湖北特
税清里會

hui 慧

huiguan 會館

hunhun'r 混混兒

Ji Yunqing 季雲青

jia 家

Jia Bai 嘉白

Jia Hai Wei 嘉海衛

jiali 家里

jiamiao 家廟

Jiang Ganting 江幹廷

Jiang Hao 姜豪

Jiang Huai Si 江淮四

Jiang-Huai Tongxianghui 江淮
同鄉會

Jiang Jieshi 蔣介石

Jiang Zhe Shangye Chuxu
Yinhang 江浙商業儲蓄銀行

Jiang'an 江安

Jiangbei 江北

jianghu 江湖

Jiangnan 江南

Jiangsu Dangwu Weiyuanhui
江蘇黨務委員會

Jiangsu Sheng Jinyan Ju 江蘇省
禁煙局

jianxia 劍俠

jiaomen 教門

Jiaotong Yinhang 交通銀行

Jin Bifeng 金碧峰

Jin Jiulin 金九林

Jin Tingsun 金廷蓀

jing 淨

jingkou 淨口

jinshi daxia 今世大俠

Jiuguo Ansha Tuan 救國暗殺團

Jiuguo Juan 救國捐

Jiuguo Kangri Anchatuan 救國
抗日暗察團

Jubao Chalou 聚寶茶樓

jue 覺

Jufeng Maoyi Gongsi 聚豐貿易
公司

Juntong 軍統

junzi 君子

Kangdi Weilao Jin Chuli Weiyuanhui 抗敵慰勞金處理委
員會

Kong Xiangxi 孔祥熙

kongzi 空字

lai 來

lao'an 老安

laoguan 老官

laoshi 老師

laotang 老堂

laotangchuan 老堂船

laotou 老頭

li 理

li 裡

Li Baozhang 李寶章

Li Guojie 李國杰

Li Lisan 李立三

Li Linshu 李麟書

Li Qihan 李啟漢

Li Shiqun 李士群
Li Xiutang 李休堂
Li Yaozhang 李耀章
Li Yingsheng 李應生
Li Zhengwu 李徵五
Li Zongren 李宗仁
Liang Huai 兩淮
Liang Qichao 梁啟超
Liangshanbo 梁山泊
Lin Ji Muhang 霖記木行
Lin Kanghou 林康侯
Liu Bei 劉備
Liu Dengjie 劉登階
Liu Fubiao 劉福彪
Liu Hongsheng 劉鴻生
Liu Luyin 劉蘆隱
Liu Nianzhi 劉念智
Liu Ruiheng 劉瑞恆
Liu Xiang 劉湘
Liu Zhi 劉峙
liumang 流氓
liumang gonghui 流氓工會
Liwei Ji 李偉記
Longhua 龍華
Lu Baihong 陸伯鴻
Lu Chongpeng 陸沖鵬
Lu Jingshi 陸京士
Lu Kui 陸逵
Lu Lanchun 露蘭春
Lu Liankui 陸連奎
Lu Songhou 陸崧侯
Lu Xiaojia 盧筱嘉
Lu Yongxiang 盧永祥
Lunchuan Zhaoshangju 輪船招商局
Lunchuan Zhaoshangju Matou Gongsi 輪船招商局碼頭公司

Luo Guanzhong 羅貫中
Luo Qing 羅清
Luo Yinong 羅亦農
Luo Zu Jiao 羅祖教
Ma Chaojun 馬超俊
Ma Lianliang 馬連良
Ma Xiangsheng 馬祥生
mafei da wang 嗎啡大王
Mahong Ji Fenhang 馬鴻記糞行
Manting Fang 滿庭芳
Mao Yun 毛雲
mapi Jinrong 麻皮金榮
Mei Guangpei 梅光培
Mei Lanfang 梅蘭芳
Meizhenhua Ji 美珍華記
mensheng 門生
mianzi 面子
Minfu Shangye Chuxu Yin-hang 民孚商業儲蓄銀行
ming 明
Ming De 明德
Ming She 銘社
Minguo Ribao 民國日報
Minli Bao 民立報
Nandao 南道
Nantong 南通
Nanmin Jiuji Hui 難民救濟會
neng 能
Ningbo 寧波
Niu Yongjian 鈕永建
Pan Gongzhan 潘公展
Pan Jia 潘家
Pan Men 潘門
Pan Qing 潘清
Pan Shengtai 潘盛泰
Paoge 袍哥
paotui 跑腿

Peng Baiwei 彭柏威

Pingmin Ribao 平民日報

pingyi hui 評議會

Pu Jinrong 浦金榮

Pu Xianyuan 浦賢元

Pudong 浦東

Pudong Linshi Bao'anju 浦東臨時保安局

Pudong Qu Geye Renmin Daibiao Dahui 浦東區各業人民代表大會

Pudong Shangye Chuxu Yinhang 浦東商業儲蓄銀行

Pudong Tongxianghui 浦東同鄉會

Qi Xieyuan 齊燮元

Qian Jian 錢堅

Qian Xinzhi 錢新之

Qianfeng 乾豐

qianhuaiziyi 謙懷自仰

Qianlong 乾隆

Qing 青

Qing 清

Qing Bang 青幫

Qingdao 青島

Qinghe 清河

Qinghong Bang 青紅幫

Qinghong Bang Shi Yanyi 青紅幫史演義

qingpi 青皮

Qiu Jin 秋瑾

ren 仁

renren 仁人

Ren Lu 忍廬

Ren She 仁社

Renlicheye Gonghui 人力車業公會

Rong Zongjing 榮宗敬

ru 儒

Rui Qingrong 芮慶榮

San Bei Lunchuan Gongsi 三北輪船公司

san daheng 三大亨

San Guo Zhi Yanyi 三國志演義

San Zu Jiao 三祖教

Sandianhui 三點會

Sanhehui 三合會

Sanmin Zhuyi 三民主義

Sanpai Lou 三牌樓

Sanshiliu Gudang 三十六股黨

Sanxin Gongsi 三鑫公司

Shang Mujiang 尚慕姜

Shanghai Beishi Renmin Difang Weichihui 上海北市人民地方維持會

Shanghai Dongbei Nanmin Jiuji Hui 上海東北難民救濟會

Shanghai Ge Zishan Tuanti Zhenji Dongbei Nanmin Lianhehui 上海各慈善團體振濟東北難民聯合會

Shanghai Gonghui Zizhi Tongyi Weiyuanhui 上海工會組織統一委員會

Shanghai Gongjie Lianhe Zonghui 上海工界聯合總會

Shanghai Gongren Yundong Zujinhui 上海工人運動促進會

Shanghai Gongtuan Lianhehui 上海工團聯合會

Shanghai Hangzhengju 上海航政局

Shanghai Huashang Shabu Jiaoyisuo 上海華商紗布交易所

Shanghai Nantong Dichan Gongsi 上海南通地產公司

Shanghai Qu Weiyuanhui 上海區委員會

Shanghai Shangye Chuxu Yinhang 上海商業儲蓄銀行

Shanghai Shangye Lianhehui 上海商業聯合會

Shanghai Shi Bao'andui 上海市保安隊

Shanghai Shi Bingxianye Tongye Gonghui 上海市冰鮮業同業公會

Shanghai Shi Difang Xiehui 上海市地方協會

Shanghai Shi Gong'an Ju 上海市公安局

Shanghai Shi Jinyan Ju 上海市禁煙局

Shanghai Shi Jinyan Weiyuanhui 上海市禁煙委員會

Shanghai Shi Kangri Jiuguo Weiyuanhui 上海市抗日救國委員會

Shanghai Shi Linshi Shi Canyihui 上海市臨時市參議會

Shanghai Shi Qingdang Weiyuanhui 上海市清黨委員會

Shanghai Shi Shanghui 上海市商會

Shanghai Shi Shanghui Choumu Yuanjiu Dongbei Juankuan Weiyuanhui 上海市商會籌募援救東北捐款委員會

Shanghai Shi Shehui Ju 上海市社會局

Shanghai Shi Shiye Gongren Jiujihui 上海市失業工人救濟會

Shanghai Shi Xin Shenghuo Yundong Zujinhui 上海市新生活運動促進會

Shanghai Shi Yuye Shichang 上海市漁業市場

Shanghai Shi Zonggonghui 上海市總工會

Shanghai Shimin Difang Weichihui 上海市民地方維持會

Shanghai Shimin Gonghui 上海市民公會

Shanghai Yinhangye Tongye Gonghui 上海銀行業同業公會

Shanghai Zhengzhifan Jiaohui Weiyuanhui 上海政治犯教誨委員會

Shanghai Zonggonghui 上海總工會

Shangtuan Wenti Yanjiu Weiyuanhui 商團問題研究委員會

shangxiang 上香

Shao Lizi 邵力子

Shao Ziying 邵子英

Shaohou 紹後

Shaoxing 紹興

Shen Bao 申報

Shen Xingshan 沉杏山

Shendong Pai 紳董派

Sheng Xuanhuai 盛宣懷

Shenghuo Huzhu She 生活互助社

Shengli Gongsi 勝利公司

Shi Chuanfu 石全福

shi da banggui 十大幫規

shi jiemei 十姐妹

Shi Liangcai 史量才

shifu 師父

Shiliupu 十六舖

shimu 師母

shoujie 受戒

shourong suo 收容所

Shuiguo Yuesheng 水果月笙
Shuihu Zhuan 水滸傳
shuishou banghui 水手幫會
sili 司禮
Sima Qian 司馬遷
Siming Shangye Chuxu Yin-hang 四明商業儲蓄銀行
Song Ailing 宋藹齡
Song-Hu Chajin Siyun Zhuijin Pinwu Chu 淞滬查禁私運追禁品物處
Song-Hu Jingbei Siling 淞滬警備司令
Song-Hu Jingbei Silingbu de Junfa Chuzhang 淞滬警備司令部的軍法處長
Song Jiang 宋江
Song Jiaoren 宋教仁
Song Meiling 宋美齡
Song Ziwen 宋子文
Su Jiashan 蘇嘉善
Subei 蘇北
Sun Baoqi 孫寶琦
Sun Chuanfang 孫傳芳
Sun Jiefu 孫介福
Sun Ke 孫科
Sun Meiyao 孫美瑤
Sun Wen Zhuyi Xuehui 孫文主義學會
Tang Chengzhong 唐承宗
Tang Jiapeng 唐嘉鵬
Tang Shaoyi 唐紹儀
Teshui Zongju 特稅總局
Tewu Bu 特務部
Tiandihui 天地會
Tianshan Wutai 天蟾舞臺
tong 通
tongcao 通草

Tonghui Xintuo Yinhang 通匯信託銀行
Tongmenghui 同盟會
tongxiang 同鄉
tongxianghui 同鄉會
tudi 徒弟
Wan Molin 萬墨林
Wang Boling 王伯齡
Wang Gang 王剛
Wang Jingwei 汪精衛
Wang Manyun 汪曼雲
Wang Shijie 汪世杰
Wang Shouhua 汪壽華
Wang Xiaolai 王曉籟
Wang Xinheng 王新衡
Wang Yansong 王延松
Wang Yiting 王一亭
Wang Yucheng 王禹丞
Wang Ziliang 王子良
Wei Tingrong 魏廷榮
wen 文
Wen Lanting 聞蘭亭
Weng Guanghui 翁光輝
Weng Yan 翁岩
Wu 悟
Wu Choupeng 吳壽彭
Wu Kaixian 吳開先
Wu Kunshan 吳崑山
Wu Laoyao 吳老么
Wu Liande 伍連德
Wu Peifu 吳佩孚
Wu Tiecheng 吳鐵城
Wu Tonggen 吳同根
Wu Xingya 吳醒亞
Wu Xintai 鄔信泰
Wu Yong 吳用
Wu Yugong 吳虞公

Wu Zonglian 吳宗濂
Wusong 吳淞
Wuxing Shan 五行山
Wuxing Shan 五聖山
Xi Han Yanyi 西漢演義
xia 俠
Xia Chao 夏超
Xia Ji Gongsi 洽記公司
Xianfeng 咸豐
xiansheng 先生
Xiang Songpo 向松坡
xiangtang 香堂
xiao 孝
Xiao Ba Gu Dang 小八股黨
xiao bisan 小癟三
xiao Changjiang xian 小長江線
Xiaodaohui 小刀會
xiayi qingshen 俠義精神
Xie Baosheng 謝葆生
xin 信
Xin Dingxiang 忻鼎香
Xin Shenghuo Laodong Fuwu Tuan 新生活勞動服務團
xin'an 新安
xing 興
Xing Wu Liu 興武六
Xing Wu Si 興武四
Xingdong Dadui 行動大隊
Xinliantang 信廉堂
Xinwen Bao 新聞報
Xiong Shihui 熊式輝
Xu Amei 徐阿梅
Xu Baoshan 徐寶山
Xu Guoliang 徐國梁
Xu Langxi 徐朗西
Xu Maotang 徐懋棠
Xu Shichang 徐世昌

Xu Shuzheng 徐樹錚
Xu Xilin 徐錫麟
Xu Yefu 許也夫
Xu Yihe 徐挹和
xue 學
Xue Yue 薛岳
Xuehun Chujian Tuan 血魂除奸團
xuesheng 學生
Yan Fuqing 顏福慶
Yan Xishan 閻錫山
Yan Zhong 嚴重
Yang Guanbei 楊管北
Yang Hu 楊虎
Yang Qingshan 楊慶山
Yang Qitang 楊啟堂
Yang Shande 楊善德
Yang Shunchuan 楊順銓
Yang Shuzhuang 楊樹莊
Yang Zaitian 楊在田
Yang Zhixiong 楊志雄
Yangshupu 楊樹浦
yanyi 演義
Yao Zhisheng 姚志生
yapian da wang 鴉片大王
Yazhou Yinhang 亞洲銀行
Ye Chucang 葉楚滄
Ye Chuoshan 葉綽山
Ye Qinghe 葉清和
yi 義
Yi She 毅社
Yibailingba Jiang 一百零八將
Ying Guixin 應桂馨
Yinhang Lianhe Junbei Wei-yuanhui 銀行聯合準備委員會
yinjian 引見
Yongcheng Yinhang 永成銀行

yongyin 用印

youxia 游俠

Yu Bingwen 余炳文

Yu Hongjun 俞鴻鈞

Yu Xianting 俞仙亭

Yu Xiaqing 虞洽卿

yuan 元

Yuan Ludeng 袁履登

Yuan Shikai 袁世凱

yuba 魚霸

Yuye Yinhang 漁業銀行

Zang Ruiqing 藏瑞卿

Zhabei 閘北

zhai sangye 摘桑葉

Zhang Binghui 張秉輝

Zhang Binglin 張炳麟

Zhang Boqi 張伯岐

Zhang Cha 張警

Zhang Dingfan 張定璠

Zhang Guotao 張置濤

Zhang Fei 張飛

Zhang Fubao 張福寶

Zhang Heng Da 張恆大

Zhang Jia'ao 張嘉敖

Zhang Jian 張謇

Zhang Jingjiang 張靜江

Zhang Jinkui 張金奎

Zhang Junyi 張君毅

Zhang Kechang 張克昌

Zhang Qun 張群

Zhang Renkui 張仁奎

Zhang Rongchu 章榮初

Zhang Shichuan 張石川

Zhang Xiaolin 張嘯林

Zhang Xiaoruo 張孝若

Zhang Xueliang 張學良

Zhang Yuanming 張元明

Zhang Zaiyang 張載陽

Zhang Zhijiang 張之江

Zhang Zilian 張子廉

Zhang Zongchang 張宗昌

Zhang Zuolin 張作霖

zhangbu 掌布

Zhao Shiyan 趙世炎

Zhao Tieqiao 趙鐵橋

Zhaoshangju Wumatou Lian-gonghui 招商局五碼頭聯工會

Zhejiang Wubei Xuetang 浙江武備學堂

Zheng Yuxiu 鄭毓秀

Zheng Ziliang 鄭子良

zhengjie 政界

Zhengli Hangxian Weiyuanhui 整理航線委員會

Zhengshi Zhongxue 正始中學

Zhengxia Ji 鄭洽記

zhi 智

Zhongguo Hongshizi Hui 中國紅十字會

Zhongguo Jinan Hui 中國濟難會

Zhongguo Shiye Yinhang 中國實業銀行

Zhongguo Tongshang Yinhang 中國通商銀行

Zhongguo Tongshang Yinhang Daxia 中國通商銀行大廈

Zhongguo Yinhang 中國銀行

Zhonghua Gemingdang 中華革命黨

Zhonghua Gongjiao Jinxing Hui 中華公教進行會

Zhonghua Gongjin Hui 中華共進會

Zhonghua Haiyuan Gonghui 中華海員工會

Zhonghua Matou Gongsi 中華碼頭公司

Zhonghua Minguo Gongjin Hui 中華民國共進會

Zhonghui Dalou 中匯大樓

Zhonghui Yinhang 中匯銀行

Zhongxin She 忠信社

Zhongyang Yinhang 中央銀行

zhongyi haoxia 忠義豪俠

Zhou Enlai 周恩來

Zhou Fengqi 周鳳歧

Zhou Mengyue 周夢月

Zhou Zhiyuan 周致遠

Zhoushan Tongxianghui 舟山同鄉會

Zhu Baosan 朱葆三

Zhu Kaiguan 朱開觀

Zhu Minyi 褚民誼

Zhu Rushan 朱如山

Zhu Xuefan 朱學範

Zhu Yan 朱炎

Zhu Yangsheng 朱揚聲

Zhu Zhiyao 朱志堯

Zhu Zhuowen 朱卓文

zhuandao 傳道

zhuye 主爺

zi 字

zibei 字輩

Zifeng Qianzhuang 滋豐錢莊

Ziwei Tuan 自衛團

zujie zhi'an de changcheng 租界治安的長城

Bibliography

BIBLIOGRAPHICAL REFERENCES

Chan, Ming K. 1981. *Historiography of the Chinese Labor Movement, 1895–1949: A Critical Survey and Bibliography of Selected Chinese Source Materials at the Hoover Institution.* Stanford: Hoover Institution Press.

Dongfang Zazhi Zongmu (A Complete Table of Contents of the *Dongfang Zazhi*). 1957. Beijing: Sanlian Shudian.

Guowen Zhoubao Zongmu (A Complete Table of Contents of the *Guowen Zhoubao*). 1957. Beijing: Sanlian Shudian.

Nathan, Andrew J. 1973. *Modern China, 1840–1972: An Introduction to Sources and Research Aids.* Ann Arbor: Center for Chinese Studies, University of Michigan.

Shen Bao Suoyin, 1919–1920 (An Index to Shen Bao, 1919–1920), edited by Shen Bao Suoyin Bianji Weiyuanhui (The Shen Bao Index Editorial Board). 1987. Shanghai: Shanghai Shudian.

Skinner, G. William, ed. 1973. *Modern Chinese Society: An Analytical Bibliography.* 3 vols. Stanford: Stanford University Press.

Teng Ssu-yu, ed. 1981. *Protest and Crime in China: A Bibliography of Secret Associations, Popular Uprisings, Peasant Rebellions.* New York: Garland Publishing.

Wei Jianyu, ed. 1985. *Zhongguo Huidang Shi Lunzhu Weiyao* (An Annotated Bibliography of Works on Chinese Secret Societies). Tianjin: Nankai Daxue Chubanshe.

"Wenshi Ziliao Xuanji" Pianmu Fenlei Suoyin, Diyi zhi yilingling Ji (A Table of Contents and Classified Index to "Selections of Literary and Historical Materials," nos. 1–100). 1986. [Beijing]: Zhongguo Wenshi Chubanshe.

NEWSPAPERS

Central China Post
Chen Bao ("Morning Post")
China Forum

China Press
China Times
China Weekly Review
Dagong Bao ("L'Impartial")
Guowen Zhoubao ("Kwowen Weekly")
International Press Correspondence (Inprecorr)
Li Bao
Min Bao
Minguo Ribao ("The Republican Daily News")
North-China Daily News
North-China Herald
Peking and Tientsin Times
Shanghai Evening Post and Mercury
Shanghai Times
Shen Bao
Shishi Xinbao
Xiang Dao ("The Guide Weekly")
Xinwen Bao

WORKS CITED

Adshead, S. A. M. 1970. *The Modernization of the Chinese Salt Administration, 1900–1920.* Cambridge: Harvard University Press.

Alley, Rewi. 1976. *Yo Banfa!.* Auckland, N.Z.: The New Zealand-China Society.

An Wensheng et al. 1983. "Anqing, Wuhu, Tongcheng Qing Bang jianwen" (What is known of the Green Gang in Anqing, Wuhu and Tongcheng). *Anhui Wenshi Ziliao* (Historical and Literary Materials on Anhui) 16: 93–105.

Arlacchi, Pino. 1979. "The Mafioso: From man of honour to entrepreneur." *New Left Review*, no. 118 (November–December): 53–72.

———. 1988. *Mafia Business: The Mafia Ethic and the Spirit of Capitalism.* Oxford: Oxford University Press.

Balinska, Marta Alexandra. 1992. "Ludwik W. Rajchman (1881–1965): Précurseur de la Santé Publique Moderne." Doctoral dissertation, Institut d'Etudes Politiques de Paris.

Bedeski, Robert E. 1981. *State-Building in Modern China: The Kuomintang in the Prewar Period*, Berkeley: Institute of East Asian Studies, University of California.

Bergère, Marie-Claire. 1986. *L'Âge d'Or de la Bourgeoisie Chinoise, 1911–1937.* Paris: Flammarion.

Bianco, Lucien. 1970. "Sociétés secrètes et autodéfense paysanne (1921–1933)." In *Mouvements Populaires et Sociétés Secrètes en Chine aux XIXe et XXe Siècles*, edited by Jean Chesneaux, Feiling Davis and Nguyen Nguet Ho. Paris: Francois Maspero., 407–420.

Blok, Anton. 1974. *The Mafia of a Sicilian Village, 1860–1960: A Study of Violent Peasant Entrepreneurs.* Oxford: Basil Blackwell.

Boorman, Howard L., and Richard C. Howard, eds. 1967–71. *Biographical Dictionary of Republican China*. 4 vols. New York: Columbia University Press.

Cai Shaoqing. 1984. "On the origins of the Gelaohui." *Modern China* 10, no. 4 (October): 481–508.

———. 1987. *Zhongguo Jindai Huidang Shi Yanjiu* (Studies on the History of Modern Chinese Secret Societies). Beijing: Zhonghua Shuju.

———. 1989. *Zhongguo Mimi Shehui* (Chinese Secret Societies). Hangzhou: Zhejiang Renmin Chubanshe.

———. 1993. *Minguo Shiqide Tufei* (Banditry in the Republican Period). Beijing: People's University Press.

Cashman, Sean Dennis. 1981. *Prohibition: The Lie of the Land*. New York: The Free Press.

Chan, Anthony B. 1982. *Arming the Chinese: The Western Armaments Trade in Warlord China, 1920–1928*, Vancouver, B.C.: University of British Columbia Press.

Chang, Maria Hsia. 1985. *The Chinese Blue Shirt Society: Fascism and Developmental Nationalism*. Berkeley: Institute of East Asian Studies, University of California.

Chang Kuo-t'ao. 1971. *The Autobiography of Chang Kuo-t'ao*. 2 vols. Lawrence: University Press of Kansas.

Chang Shengzhao. 1935. *Anqin Xitonglu* (A Genealogy of the Green Gang). N.p.

Chao Lin. 1925. "Diguozhuyide gongju zhiyi—gongzei" (Scabs—one of the tools of imperialism). *Xiang Dao*, no. 127 (August 31, 1925): 1165–66.

Chapman, H. Owen. 1928. *The Chinese Revolution, 1926–1927*. London: Constable.

Chen Bingzhi, Kuai Mingsun and Wang Bingjun. 1981. "Yangzhou Xu Baoshan pianduan" (A fragment on Xu Baoshan of Yangzhou). In *Jiangsu Wenshi Ziliao Xuanji* (Selections of Historical and Literary Materials on Jiangsu) 1: 40–44.

Chen Changhe, "1927–1949 nian Zhaoshangju zuzhi gaikuang" (Changes in the organization of the China Merchants' Steam Navigation Company in the years 1927–1949). 1983. In *Lishi Dang'an* (Historical Archives) 2: 124–128.

Chen Dingshan. 1964. *Qunshen Jiuwen* (Old Tales of Shanghai). Taibei: Chenguang Yuekan.

Chen Duxiu. [1922] 1987. *Duxiu Wencun* (The Collected Writings of Chen Duxiu). Anhui: Renmin Chubanshe.

Chen Guoping. 1946. *Qingmen Kaoyuan* (The Origins of the Green Gang). Shanghai: Lianyi Chubanshe.

Ch'en, Jerome. 1970a. "The origins of the Boxers." In *Studies in the Social History of China and South-East Asia: Essays in Memory of Victor Purcell*, edited by Jerome Ch'en and Nicholas Tarling. Cambridge: Cambridge University Press, 57–84.

——— 1970b. "Rebels between rebellions: Secret societies in the novel *P'eng Kung An*." *Journal of Asian Studies* 29, no. 4 (August): 807–822.

Chen Lifu. 1994. *The Storm Clouds Clear over China: The Memoir of Ch'en Li-fu, 1900–1993.* Edited by Sidney H. Chang and Ramon H. Myers. Stanford: Hoover Institution Press.

Chen Rongguang. 1919. *Lao Shanghai* (Old Shanghai). 3 vols. Shanghai: Taidong Tushu Ju.

Chen Shaoxiao 1965. *Heigang Lu* (The Record of the Black Net). Hong Kong: Xianggang Zhicheng.

Chen Siyi. 1986. "Lincheng jieche an" (The train hold-up at Lincheng). In *Minguo Si Da Qi'an* (Four Very Strange Cases from the Republic), edited by Shi Peng et al. Hong Kong: Zhongyuan Chubanshe, 1–89.

Chen Xizhang. 1982. *Xishuo Beiyang* (Detailed Discussion of the Northern Warlords). 2 vols. Taibei: Zhuanji Wenxue.

Chen Zhen et al., eds. 1961. *Zhongguo Jindai Gongye Shi Ziliao* (Materials on the History of China's Modern Industry). 4 vols. Beijing: Sanlian.

Chen Zu'en and Wang Jinhai, eds. 1990. *Haishang Shi Wenren* (Ten Notable Individuals of Shanghai). Shanghai: Renmin Chubanshe.

Cheng Xiwen. 1986. "Wo dang Huang Jinrong guanjia de jianwen" (What I saw and heard as Huang Jinrong's butler). In JSBH, 138–166.

Chesneaux, Jean, ed. 1965. *Les Sociétés Secrètes en Chine (XIXe et XXe Siècles).* Paris: Julliard.

———. 1968. *The Chinese Labor Movement, 1919–1927.* Stanford: Stanford University Press.

———. 1973. *Peasant Revolts in China, 1840–1949.* London: Thames and Hudson.

Chesneaux, Jean, Feiling Davis, and Nguyen Nguet Ho, eds. 1970. *Mouvements Populaires et Sociétés Secrètes en Chine aux XIXe et XXe Siècles.* Paris: Francois Maspero.

China. Maritime Customs. *Decennial Reports.* Shanghai: Kelly and Walsh, various years.

The China Year Book, 1914–35.

Ci Hai (Sea of Words). 1974. Hong Kong: Zhonghua Shuju.

Clark, Grover. 1928. "China in 1927." *The Chinese Social and Political Science Review* 12, no. 3 (July): 136–196.

Clifford, Nicholas R. 1991. *Spoilt Children of Empire: Westerners in Shanghai and the Chinese Revolution of the 1920s.* Hanover, N.H.: University Press of New England.

Coble, Parks M., Jr. 1980. *The Shanghai Capitalists and the Nationalist Government, 1927–1937.* Cambridge: Council on East Asian Studies, Harvard University.

———. 1991. *Facing Japan: Chinese Politics and Japanese Imperialism, 1931–1937.* Cambridge: Harvard University Press.

Cribb, Robert. 1991. *The Jakarta People's Militia and the Indonesian Revolution, 1945–1949.* Sydney: Allen and Unwin.

Cui Xilin. 1992. "Wo suo zhidao de Qing Hongbang" (What I know of the Green and Red Gangs). In *Jindai Zhongguo Banghui Neimu,* vol. 1, 111–156.

Da Liumang Du Yuesheng (Big Gangster Du Yuesheng). 1965. Edited by

Shanghai Shehui Kexue Yuan Zhengzhi Falu Yanjiusuo Shehui Wenti Zu (The Social Issues Section of the Political and Legal Institute of the Shanghai Academy of Social Sciences). Beijing: Chunchong Chubanshe.

Da Yun [pseud.]. 1932. "Fadian bagong yu women de lingdao" (The French Tramways strike and our leadership) (August 6). In *Zhonggong "Gongren Yundong" Yuanshi Ziliao Huibian*, vol. 4, 123–128.

Dai Xuanzhi. 1973. "Qing Bang de yuanliu" (The origins and evolution of the Green Gang). *Shihuo Yuekan* (Sustenance Monthly) 3, no. 4 (July): 172–179.

Dangdai Shisheng (Fragments of Contemporary History). 1933. Shanghai: Shanghai Zhoubao.

Daoyi Zhinan (A Guide to the Neglected Way). 1931. N.p.

Davidson-Houston, J. V. 1962. *Yellow Creek: The Story of Shanghai*. London: Putnam.

Davis, Fei-Ling. 1971. *Primitive Revolutionaries of China: A Study of Secret Societies in the Late Nineteenth Century*. London: Routledge and Kegan Paul.

Deng Zhongxia. [1946] 1978. *Zhongguo Zhigong Yundong Jianshi (1919–1926)* (A Brief History of the Chinese Labor Movement, 1919–1926). Hong Kong: Wenhua Ziliao Hongying She.

The Directory and Chronicle for Corea, Japan and China for the Year 1916. 1916. Hong Kong: Hong Kong Daily Press.

Dirlik, Arif. 1989. *The Origins of Chinese Communism*. New York: Oxford University Press.

Diyici Guonei Geming Zhanzheng Shiqi de Gongren Yundong (The Workers' Movement in the Period of the First Civil War). 1954. Beijing: Renmin Chubanshe. Documentary collection on the Chinese labor movement for the years 1921–27.

Dolby, William. 1976. *A History of Chinese Drama*. London: Paul Eleck.

Dong Shu. 1934a. "Shanghai fazujie de duoshi shiqi" (An eventful period in the Shanghai French Concession). *Shanghai Shi Tongzhiguan Qikan* (The Journal of the Shanghai Municipal Gazetteer Office) 1, no. 4 (March): 975–1024; vol. 2, no. 1 (June): 49–83.

———. 1934b. "Fazujie shizheng yange" (The evolution of the French Concession administration). *Shanghai Shi Tongzhiguan Qikan* 2, no. 3 (December): 721–761.

Douzheng de Wushinian (Fifty Years of Struggle). 1960. Edited by Zhonggong Shanghai Chuanyuan Yichang Weiyuanhui Xuanzhuanbu (The Propaganda Unit of the Communist Party Branch of the Shanghai First Rolled Tobacco Company). Shanghai: n.p.

Du Shi Jiasi Loucheng Jiniance (Commemorative Volume on the Foundation of the Du Family Temple). 1932. Shanghai: Zhongguo Fanggu Yinshuju.

Du Weifan. 1954. "Guoting lu" (For the record). In *Du Yuesheng Xiansheng Jinian Ji*, vol. 2, 18–20.

Du Yuesheng Xiansheng Jinian Ji (Collection in Commemoration of Mister Du Yuesheng). 1952–54. 2 vols. Taibei: Heng She.

Eastman, Lloyd E. 1974. *The Abortive Revolution: China under Nationalist Rule, 1927–1937.* Cambridge: Harvard University Press.

———. 1976. "The Kuomintang in the 1930s." In *The Limits of Change: Essays on Conservative Alternatives in Republican China*, edited by Charlotte Furth. Cambridge: Harvard University Press, 91–210.

Elvin, Mark. 1974. "The administration of Shanghai, 1905–1914." In *The Chinese City Between Two Worlds*, edited by Mark Elvin and G. William Skinner. Stanford: Stanford University Press, 239–262.

———. 1984. "The 1911 Revolution in Shanghai." *Papers on Far Eastern History* 29 (March): 119–161.

Esherick, Joseph W. 1987. *The Origins of the Boxer Rebellion.* Berkeley: University of California Press.

Fan Shaozeng. 1986. "Guanyu Du Yuesheng" (Concerning Du Yuesheng). In JSBH, 195–247.

———. 1992. "Wo yu Chuan Paoge ji Chuanjun hunzhan" (The Sichuan Paoge and conflicts among the Sichuan warlords and myself). In *Jindai Zhongguo Banghui Neimu*, vol. 2, 397–407.

Fan Songfu. 1980. "Shanghai banghui neimu (The inside story of the Shanghai secret societies)." *Wenshi Ziliao Xuanji* (Shanghai series) 3: 150–159.

Fass, Joseph. 1970. "L'insurrection du Xiaodaohui à Shanghai (1853–1855)." In *Mouvements Populaires et Sociétés Secrètes en Chine aux XIXe et XXe Siècles*, 178–195.

Feetham, Richard. 1931. *Report of the Hon. Richard Feetham, C.M.G., to The Shanghai Municipal Council.* Shanghai: North-China Daily News and Herald.

Feuerwerker, Albert. 1970. *China's Industrialization: Sheng Hsuan-huai (1844–1916) and Mandarin Enterprise.* New York: Atheneum.

Fewsmith, Joseph. 1985. *Party, State, and Local Elites in Republican China: Merchant Organizations and Politics in Shanghai, 1890–1930.* Honolulu: University of Hawaii Press.

Finch, Percy. 1953. *Shanghai and Beyond.* New York: Charles Scribner's Sons.

Finnane, Antonia. 1993. "The origins of prejudice: the malintegration of Subei in late imperial China." *Comparative Studies in Society and History* 35, no. 2 (April): 211–238.

Fitzgerald, John, ed. 1989. *The Nationalists and Chinese Society, 1923–1937: A Symposium.* Melbourne: History Department, University of Melbourne.

Fitzsimmons, John, and Paul Maguire, eds. 1939. *Restoring All Things: A Guide to Catholic Action.* London: Sheed and Ward.

FMC (Conseil d'Administration Municipale de la Concession Française à Changhai). *Compte-Rendu de la Gestion pour les Exercices 1917–1937.* (These annual reports also contain the official minutes of the fortnightly meetings of the French Municipal Council and, after 1927, the Provisional Commission).

France. Archives de la Ministère des Affaires Etrangères. Asie: Affaires Communes, Volume 56.

————. Ministre des Affaires Etrangères. *Direction des Affaires Politiques et Commerciales.* Asie: Océanie E515.4.

Fried, Albert. 1980. *The Rise and Fall of the Jewish Gangster in America.* New York: Holt, Rinehart and Winston.

Friedman, Irving S. 1940. *British Relations with China: 1931–1939.* New York: Institute of Pacific Relations.

Fu Runhua. 1948. *Zhongguo Dangdai Mingren Zhuan* (Biographies of Contemporary Chinese Personalities). Shanghai: Shijie Chubanshe.

Gao Hongxing. 1988. "Kangzhanqian Shanghai de yapianye gaishu" (A general account of the opium industry in Shanghai before the outbreak of the War of Resistance). In JSYDC, 46–55.

Gayn, Mark. 1944. *Journey from the East: An Autobiography.* New York: Alfred A. Knopf.

Gendai Chūka Minkoku Manshūkoku Jimmeikan (Biographical Dictionary of Contemporary China and Manzhouguo). 1932. Tokyo: Gaimusho Johobu.

Geng Yuying. 1934. *Anqing Shijian* (A History of the Anqing Bang). N.p.

Glick, Carl, and Sheng-Hwa Hong. 1947. *Swords of Silence: Chinese Secret Societies Past and Present.* New York: Whittlesey House.

Goodman, Bryna. 1992. "New culture, old habits: native-place organizations and the May Fourth Movement." In *Shanghai Sojourners,* edited by Frederic Wakeman and Wen-hsin Yeh, 76–107.

Great Britain. Foreign Office. *Further Correspondence Respecting Opium, 1920–1936.* Facsimile reprint by Scholarly Resources, *The Opium Trade, 1910–1941.* 1974. 6 vols. Wilmington, Del.: Scholarly Resources.

Gu Jiatang. 1952. "Zhongyi haomai de Du Yuesheng" (The loyal hero, Du Yuesheng). In *Du Yuesheng Xiansheng Jinian Ji,* vol. 1, 28(a)–29(a).

Gu Shuping. 1986. "Wo liyong Gu Zhuxuan de yanhu jinxiang geming huodong" (How I used Gu Zhuxuan to secretly conduct revolutionary activities). In JSBH, 360–366.

Gui Yonding. 1982. "Zhonghui Yinhang yu Du Yuesheng" (The Zhonghui Bank and Du Yuesheng). In *Shanghai Zhanggu,* 81–88.

Gunther, John. 1939. *Inside Asia,* New York: Harper and Brothers.

Guo Lanxin. 1986. "Du Yuesheng yu Heng She" (Du Yuesheng and the Endurance Club). In JSBH, 300–320.

Guo Morou. 1978. *Morou Zizhuan* (The Autobiography of Guo Morou). 4 vols. Hong Kong: Sanlian Shudian.

Guo Xiaoxian. 1933. "Shanghai de neiguo yinhang" (The Chinese commercial banks of Shanghai). *Shanghai Shi Tongzhiguan Qikan* 1, no. 2 (September): 441–498.

Guo Xu. 1986. "Du Yuesheng yu Dai Li ji Juntong de guanxi" (The relations between Du Yuesheng and Dai Li and the Juntong). In JSBH, 321–341.

Guo Xuyin, ed. 1991. *Jiu Shanghai Heishehui Mishi* (The Secret History of the Secret Societies of Old Shanghai). Henan: Renmin Chubanshe.

Hammond, Edward Roy III. 1978. *Organized Labor in Shanghai, 1927–1937.* Ph.D. dissertation, University of California, Berkeley.

Hao, Yen-p'ing. 1986. *The Commercial Revolution in Nineteenth Century*

China: The Rise of Sino-Western Mercantile Capitalism. Berkeley: University of California Press.

Harrison, James P. 1972. The Long March to Power: A History of the Chinese Communist Party, 1921–1972. New York: Praeger.

Hatano Ken'ichi. 1943. Chūgoku Kokumintō Tsushi (A History of the Chinese Guomindang). Tokyo: Shonan.

Hauser, Ernest O. 1940. Shanghai: City for Sale. New York: Harcourt, Brace.

Heng She Sheyuan Lu 1934 (The Membership List of the Endurance Club for 1934). In JSBH, 369–382.

Heng She Shezhang (The Regulations of the Endurance Club). N.d. In JSBH, 367–368.

Heng She Yuekan (The Endurance Club Monthly), 1936–37.

Henriot, Christian. 1991. Shanghai 1927–1937: Elites Locales et Modernisation dans la Chine Nationaliste. Paris: Editions de l'Ecole des Hautes Etudes en Sciences Sociales.

Hershatter, Gail. 1986. The Workers of Tianjin, 1900–1949. Stanford: Stanford University Press.

Hinton, Harold. 1970. The Grain Tribute System of China (1845–1911). Cambridge: Harvard University Press.

Ho, Ping-ti. 1962. The Ladder of Success in Imperial China: Aspects of Social Mobility, 1368–1911. New York: Columbia University Press.

Hobsbawm, Eric. 1965. Primitive Rebels: Studies in Archaic Forms of Social Movements in the 19th and 20th Centuries. New York: W. W. Norton.

Hobsbawm, Eric, and Terence Ranger, eds. 1983. The Invention of Tradition. Cambridge: Cambridge University Press.

Hong Weiqing. 1986. "Zhang Renkui yu Ren She" (Zhang Renkui and the Benevolence Society). In JSBH, 108–114.

Hong Zhensheng. 1992. "Cong sanguang mazi dai Qinbang toumu de Jin Tingsun" (Jin Tingsun, from "numbers Sanguang" to Green Gang boss). In Jindai Zhongguo Banghui Neimu, vol. 1, 437–447.

Honig, Emily. 1986. Sisters and Strangers: Women in the the Shanghai Cotton Mills, 1919–1949. Stanford: Stanford University Press.

———. 1992. Creating Ethnicity: Subei People in Shanghai, 1850–1980. New Haven: Yale University Press.

Hsia, C. T. 1968. The Classic Chinese Novel: A Critical Introduction. New York: Columbia University.

Hsiao Kung-chuan. 1960. Rural China: Imperial Control in the Nineteenth Century. Seattle: University of Washington Press.

Hu Baoqi. 1986. "Toudi funi Fu Xiao'an" (The traitor Fu Xiao'an). Wenshi Ziliao Xuanji (Selections of Historical and Literary Materials) 6: 156–177.

Hu Junsu and Li Shufen. 1983. "Tianjin Qing Bang yu diguozhuyi shili de goujie" (The collaboration of the Tianjin Green Gang with the forces of imperialism). Tianjin Wenshi Ziliao Xuanji (Selections of Historical and Literary Materials on Tianjin) 24: 220–231.

Hu Shengwu. 1987. "Minchu huidang wenti" (The question of secret societies in the early Republic). In *Huidang Shi Yanjiu*, 221–238.

Hu Xunmin and He Jian. 1991. *Shanghai Banghui Jianshi* (A Brief History of Shanghai Secret Societies). Shanghai: People's Publishing.

Hu Zhusheng. 1979. "Qing Bang shi chutan" (A preliminary enquiry into the history of the Green Gang). *Lishi Xue* (Historical Studies) 3: 102–120.

Hua Gang. [1931] 1982. *Zhongguo Da Geming Shi: Yijiu'ershiwu zhi Yijiu'ershiqi* (The History of China's Great Revolution, 1925–1927). Beijing: Wenshi Ziliao.

Huang Dezhao. 1978. "Chen Qimei." In *Minguo Renwu Zhuan*, vol. 1, 105–110.

Huang Guodong. 1986. "Du Men huajiu" (Reminiscences about Du's household). In JSBH, 248–267.

Huang Jingzhai. 1986. "Guomindang CCxi de Gan She" (The Guomindang CC Clique's Action Club). *Wenshi Ziliao Xuanji*, 6: 131–155.

Huang Jinrong. 1951. "Huang Jinrong zi baishu" (The deposition of Huang Jinrong). *Wen Hui Bao*, May 20.

Huang Meizhen. 1983. "Wang Shouhua zhuanlue (A biographical sketch of Wang Shouhua)." *Jindai Shi Yanjiu* (Studies in Modern History) 1, no. 15: 62–64.

———, ed. 1986. *Wangwei Shi Hanjian* (Ten Traitors of the Wang Puppet Regime). Shanghai: Renmin Chubanshe.

Huang Meizhen and Hao Shengchao, eds. 1987. *Zhonghua Minguo Shi Shijian Renwu Lu* (A Record of Major Events and Leading Personalities in the History of the Republic of China). Shanghai: Renmin Chubanshe.

Huang Meizhen and Shi Yuanhua. 1987. "Wangwei tegong zongbu shimo" (The full story of the intelligence headquarters of the Wang Puppet Regime). In *Wang Jingwei Hanjian Zhengquan de Xingwang: Wang Wei Zhengquan Shi Yanjiu Lunji* (The Rise and Fall of the Wang Jingwei Traitor Regime: A Collection of Studies on the Wang Puppet Regime), edited by Fudan Daxue Lishi Xi Zhongguo Xiandai Shi Yanjiu Shi (The Study Group on the Contemporary History of China, Department of History, Fudan University). Shanghai: Fudan Daxue, 350–392.

Huang Shaoxiong. 1969. *Wushi Huiyi* (Reminiscences of Fifty Years). Hong Kong: n.p.

Huang Xuchu. 1968. "Li Zongren kouzhong de Wu Zhihui yu Wang Jingwei" (Li Zongren speaks of Wu Zhihui and Wang Jingwei). *Chunqiu* ("The Observation Post"), no. 253 (January 16): 12–14.

Huang Yanpei. 1982. *Bashi Nianlai* (Eighty Years On). Beijing: Wenshi Ziliao.

Huang Yongyan. 1986. "Du Yuesheng dajin Dada Lunchuan Gongsi jingguo" (The takeover of the Dada Steamship Company by Du Yuesheng). In JSBH, 284–292.

Huang Yuanqi. 1982. *Zhongguo Xiandai Shi* (A History of Contemporary China). 2 vols. [Kaifeng]: n.p.

Huang Zhenshi. 1986. "Wo suo zhidao Huang Jinrong" (The Huang Jinrong I knew). In JSBH, 167–194.

———. 1992. "Jiang Jieshi baishi Huang Jinrong neimu" (The inside story of Jiang Jieshi's submission to Huang Jinrong). In *Jindai Zhongguo Banghui Neimu*, vol. 1, 335–339.

Huidang Shi Yanjiu (Studies in the History of Secret Societies). 1987. Edited by Zhongguo Huidang Shi Yanjiu Hui (The Association for the Study of Chinese Secret Societies). Shanghai: Xuelin Chubanshe.

Hutchison, John. 1972. *The Imperfect Union: A History of Corruption in American Trade Unions*. New York: E. P. Dutton.

Ikemoto Yoshio. 1973. *Chūgoku Kindai Himitsu Kessha Ko* (An Investigation of Secret Societies in Modern China). Nagoya: Saika Shorin.

International Anti-Opium Association. 1926. *Opium Cultivation and Traffic in China*. Peking: International Anti-Opium Association.

Iriye, Akira. 1969. *After Imperialism: The Search for a New Order in the Far East, 1921–1931*. New York: Atheneum.

Isaacs, Harold R. [1938] 1961. *The Tragedy of the Chinese Revolution*. Stanford: Stanford University Press.

———. 1932. *Five Years of Kuomintang Reaction*. [Shanghai]: China Forum.

Israel, John. 1966. *Student Nationalism in China, 1927–1937*, Stanford: Stanford University Press.

Jiang Hao. 1986a. "Qing Bang de yuanliu ji qi yanbian" (The origins and evolution of the Green Gang). In JSBH, 51–67.

———. 1986b. "Hongmen lishi chutan" (An introduction to the history of the Triads). In JSBH, 68–86.

Jiang Nan. N.d. "Jiang Jieshi hunyin shenghuo kao" (An investigation of the married life of Jiang Jieshi). In *Lun Jiang Jieshi Chengbai* (On the Success and Failure of Jiang Jieshi). Taibei: Zheng Nanrong, 39–49.

Jiang Peinan. 1984. "Xu Amei." In *Zhongguo Gongren Yundong de Xianqu* (The Pioneers of the Chinese Labor Movement). 3 vols. Beijing: Gongren Chubanshe, vol. 3, 189–223.

Jiang Shaozhen. 1978. "Du Yuesheng." In *Minguo Renwu Zhuan*, vol. 1, 314–319.

———. 1981. "Qian Xinzhi." In *Mingu Renwu Zhuan*, vol. 3, 246–252.

"Jiangsu zuijin gongzuo zongbaogao: Guanyu zhigong yundong" (General report on [our] most recent work in Jiangsu: The labor movement [November 12, 1927]. In *Zhonggong "Gongren Yundong" Yuanshi Ziliao Huibian*, vol. 1, 219–223.

Jiaofei Zhanshi (A Military History of "Bandit Suppression"). 1967. Edited by Guofang Bu Shizheng Ju (The Military History Bureau of the Ministry of National Defense). 6 vols. Taibei: Guofang Bu Shizheng Ju.

Jin Feng. 1954. "Du Yuesheng Xiansheng liushinian jianghu chongyi" (The sixty year adventurous life of Mister Du Yuesheng). In *Du Yuesheng Xiansheng Jinian Ji*, vol. 2, 48(b)–53(b).

Jin Laofo. 1990. *San Jiao Jiu Liu Jianghu Mimi Guizhou* (The Rules and Regulations of the Secret Societies that Follow the Three Doctrines and the Nine Schools). Shanghai: Datong Tushu Chubanshe. Reprinted in series Minjian Mimi Jieshe yu Zongjiao Congshu (Collection on Popular Associations and Religions) Hebei: Renmin Chubanshe.

Jindai Zhongguo Banghui Neimu (The Inside Story of Secret Societies in Modern China). 1992. Edited by Hebei Wenshi Ziliao Bianjibu (The Editorial Board of *Hebei Literary and Historical Materials*). 2 vols. Beijing: Masses Publishing.

Jiu Shanghai de Banghui (The Gangs of Old Shanghai). 1986. Edited by Zhongguo Renmin Zhengzhi Xieshang Huiyi Shanghai Shi Weiyuanhui Wenshi Ziliao Gongzuo Weiyuanhui (The Work Committee of Historical and Literary Materials of the Shanghai Municipal Committee of the Chinese People's Political Consultative Conference). Shanghai: Shanghai Renmin Chubanshe.

Jiu Shanghai de Yan Du Chang (Opium, Gambling and Prostitution in Old Shanghai). 1988. Edited by Shanghai Shi Wenshi Guan (The Shanghai Municipal Cultural Center). Shanghai: Baijia Chubanshe.

Johnson, David, Andrew J. Nathan, and Evelyn Rawski, eds. 1985. *Popular Culture in Late Imperial China*. Berkeley: University of California Press.

Johnstone, William Crane. 1937. *The Shanghai Problem*. Stanford: Stanford University Press.

Jones, Susan Mann, and Philip A. Kuhn. 1978. "Dynastic decline and the roots of rebellion." In *The Cambridge History of China, Volume 10: Late Ch'ing, 1800–1911, Part 1*, edited by John K. Fairbank. Cambridge: Cambridge University Press, 107–162.

Jordan, Donald A. 1976. *The Northern Expedition: China's National Revolution, 1926–1928*. Honolulu: University of Hawaii Press.

———. 1991. *Chinese Boycotts versus Japanese Bombs: The Failure of China's "Revolutionary Diplomacy," 1931–1932*. Ann Arbor: University of Michigan Press.

Jun Xing [pseud.]. 1933. "Gongtonghui jiuhua" (Old talk about the Unification Committee). In *Dangdai Shisheng*, 74–178.

Kaplan, David E., and Alec Dubro. 1986. *Yakuza: The Explosive Account of Japan's Criminal Underworld*. Reading, Mass.: Addison-Wesley Publishing.

Kelley, David E. 1982. "Temples and tribute fleets: The Luo Sect and boatmen's associations in the eighteenth century." *Modern China* 8, no. 3 (July): 361–391.

Kotenev, A. M. 1927. *Shanghai: Its Municipality and the Chinese*. Shanghai: North-China Daily News and Herald.

Kuhn, Philip A. 1970. *Rebellion and Its Enemies in Late Imperial China: Militarization and Social Structure, 1796–1864*. Cambridge: Harvard University Press.

Latourette, Kenneth Scott. 1929. *A History of Christian Missions in China*. New York: Macmillan.

League of Nations. Advisory Committee on Traffic in Opium and Other Dangerous Drugs. Minutes of the Seventh Session (Geneva, August 24–31, 1925), C.602.M.192/1925.

Leith-Ross, Sir Frederick. 1968. *Money Talks: Fifty Years of International Finance*. London: Hutchinson.

Li Chien-nung. 1956. *The Political History of China, 1840–1928.* Stanford: Stanford University Press.

Li Lisan. 1981. "Li Lisan tongzhi dui Eryue Bagong he Wusa Yundong de huiyi" (The memoirs of Comrade Li Lisan regarding the February Strike and the May Thirtieth Movement). In *Wusa Yundong Shiliao,* vol. 1, 142–148.

Li Shiyu. 1963. "Qing Bang, Tiandihui, Bailianjiao" (The Green Gang, the Triads and the White Lotus Sect). *Wenshizhe* (Literature, History and Philosophy), no. 88 (June): 67–73.

———. 1987. "Qing Bang zaoqi zuzhi kaolue" (An investigation of the Green Gang during its early period). In *Huidang Shi Yanjiu,* 286–303.

———. 1988. "Qing Bang zai Tianjin de liuchuan" (The spread of the Green Gang in Tianjin). *Tianjin Wenshi Ziliao Xuanji* 45: 212–230.

Li Xin and Sun Sipai, eds. 1978–93. *Minguo Renwu Zhuan* (Biographies of Leading Personalities of the Republic). 7 vols. Beijing: Zhonghua Shuju.

Li Xiuzhang. 1988. "Guangdong Bang fanmai yapian de yilinbanzhao" (Fragments of the Guangdong Clique's trafficking in opium). In JSYDC, 56–58.

Li Zongren. 1980. *Li Zongren Huiyi* (The Memoirs of Li Zongren). 2 vols. [Guilin]: Guangxi Renmin Chubanshe.

Lieberthal, Kenneth G. 1980. *Revolution and Tradition in Tientsin, 1949–1952.* Stanford: Stanford University Press.

Ling Lei. 1992. "'Chaozhou daheng' Zheng Ziliang" ('The Chaozhou Boss' Zheng Ziliang). In *Jindai Zhongguo Banghui Neimu,* vol. 1, 448–450.

Liu Bainian. 1931. *San An Quanji* (The Complete Collection of the Three Monasteries). Tianjin: n.p.

Liu Hong. 1943. "Du Yuesheng lun" (On Du Yuesheng). *Za Zhi* (The Magazine) 11, no. 6 (September 10): 89–90.

Liu Hongsheng Qiye Shiliao (Historical Materials on the Enterprises of Liu Hongsheng). 1981. Edited by Shanghai Kexue Yuan Jingji Yanjiu Suo (The Economic Research Institute of the Shanghai Academy of Social Sciences). 3 vols. Shanghai: Shanghai Renmin Chubanshe.

Liu Jingyuan. 1933. "Guonan Huiyi yiwen zhuiji" (An anecdotal record of the National Emergency Conference). In *Xiandai Shiliao,* vol. 1, 111–120.

Liu Lianke. 1940. *Banghui Sanbainian Geming Shi* (A History of the Secret Societies' Three Hundred Years of Revolution). Macao: [Liuyuan Chubanshe].

Liu Nianzhi. 1982. *Shiye Liu Hongsheng Zhuanlue: Huiyi Wode Fuqin* (A Biographical Sketch of the Industrialist Liu Hongsheng: Memories of My Father). Beijing: Wenshi Ziliao.

Liu Qingbo, ed. 1986. *Yang Du Ji* (The Collected Writings of Yang Du). Hunan: People's Publishing.

Liu Shaotang, ed. 1977–92. *Minguo Renwu Xiaozhuan* (Brief Biographies of Leading Personalities of the Republic). 14 vols. Taibei: Zhuanji Wenxue.

———, ed. 1978. *Minguo Dashi Rizhi* (A Chronology of Major Events in the Republic). 2 vols. Taibei: Zhuanji Wenxue.

Lo Kuan-chung. 1925. *Romance of the Three Kingdoms: San kuo Chih Yen-I"*. Translated by C. H. Brewitt-Taylor. 2 vols. Shanghai: Kelly and Walsh.

Loh, Pichon P. Y. 1971. *The Early Chiang Kai-shek: A Study of His Personality and Politics, 1887–1924*. New York: Columbia University Press.

Lu Chongpeng. 1967. "Yang Hu yishi liangci" (A couple of anecdotes about Yang Hu). *Zhuanji Wenxue* (Biographical Literature) 11, no. 4 (October): 70–73.

Lu Hsun. 1959. *A Brief History of Chinese Fiction*. Peking: Foreign Languages Press.

Lu Jingshi. 1936. "Heng She zhi huigu yu qianzhan" (Retrospect and prospect on the Endurance Club). *Heng She Yuekan*, nos. 10–11 (November 22): 7–9.

Luo Binsheng. [1919] 1989. *Heimu Daguan* (Inside Story Spectacular). Beijing: Chunqiu Publishing.

Luo Zhiru. 1932. *Tongji Biao Zhong Zhi Shanghai* (Shanghai in Statistics). Nanjing: Academia Sinica.

Ma Baoheng. 1981. "Qi-Lu zhi zhan jilue" (A brief record of the War between Qi Xieyuan and Lu Yongxiang). In *Beiyang Junfa Shiliao Xuanji* (Selected Historical materials on the Northern Warlords), edited by Du Chunhe et al. 2 vols. Beijing: Zhongguo Shehui Kexue Yuan, vol. 2, 136–148.

Ma Chaojun. 1958. *Zhongguo Laogong Yundong Shi* (A History of the Chinese Labor Movement). 5 vols. Taibei: Zhongguo Laogong Yundong Shi Biansuo Weiyuanhui.

Ma Xisha and Cheng Xiao. 1984. "Cong Luo Jiao dao Qing Bang" (From the Luo Sect to the Green Gang). *Nankai Shixue* (Nankai Historiography) 1: 1–28.

Ma Xisha and Han Bingfang. 1992. *Zhongguo Minjian Zongjiao Shi* (A History of Popular Religions in China). Shanghai: People's Publishing House.

Ma Yinchu. 1928. "Guanyu jinyan wenti zhi jige yaodian" (Several important points concerning the question of opium suppression). In *Ma Yinchu Yanjiang Ji* (Collection of the Lectures of Ma Yinchu). 4 vols. Shanghai: Shangwu Chubanshe, vol. 4, 279–281.

Mackerras, Colin. 1975. *The Chinese Theatre in Modern Times: From 1840 to the Present Day*. London: Thames and Hudson.

Marshall, Jonathan. 1976. "Opium and the politics of gangsterism in Nationalist China, 1927–1945." *Bulletin of Concerned Asian Scholars* 8 (July-September): 19–48.

Martin, Brian G. 1983. "The Green Gang and 'Party Purification' in Shanghai: Green Gang-Kuomintang Relations, 1926–1927." Paper presented to the Symposium on the Nanking Decade, 1928–1937: Man, Government and Society, August 15–17, University of Hong Kong.

———. 1985. "Tu Yueh-sheng and labour control in Shanghai: the case of the French Tramways Union, 1928–1932." *Papers on Far Eastern History* 32 (September): 99–137.

———. 1989. "Warlords and Gangsters: The Opium Traffic in Shanghai and the Creation of the Three Prosperities Company to 1926." In *The Nationalists and Chinese Society, 1923–1937: A Symposium*, edited by John Fitzgerald, 44–71.

———. 1990. "The Green Gang and the Guomindang polity in Shanghai 1927–1937." *Papers on Far Eastern History* 42 (September): 59–96.

———. 1991. *The Green Gang in Shanghai: The Rise of Du Yuesheng, 1920–1937*. Ph.D. dissertation, Australian National University.

———. 1992. "'The pact with the devil': The relationship between the Green Gang and the French Concession authorities, 1925–1935." In *Shanghai Sojourners*, edited by Frederic Wakeman, Jr. and Wen-hsin Yeh, 266–304.

Miners, Norman. 1987. *Hong Kong under Imperial Rule, 1912–1941*. Hong Kong: Oxford University Press.

Minguo Banghui Yaolu (Essential Documents on Secret Societies in the Republican Period). 1993. Edited by Zhongguo Di'er Lishi Dang'an'guan (The Chinese Second Historical Archives). Beijing: The Archives Press.

Morse, Hosea Ballou. 1909. *The Gilds of China: With an Account of the Gild Merchant or Co-Hong of Canton*. London: Longmans, Green and Co.

———. 1913. *The Trade and Administration of China*. London: Longmans, Green and Co.

Murphey, Rhoads. 1953. *Shanghai: Key to Modern China*. Cambridge: Harvard University Press.

Nan Huaijin. 1966. "Qing Bang xingqi de yuanyuan yu neimu" (The origins and inside story of the rise of the Green Gang). *Xin Tiandi* (New Universe) 5, no. 8 (October): 12–14.

Naquin, Susan. 1976. *Millenarian Rebellion in China: The Eight Trigrams Uprising of 1813*. New Haven: Yale University Press.

———. 1981. *Shantung Rebellion: The Wang Lun Uprising of 1774*. New Haven: Yale University Press.

Narramore, Terry. 1989. "The Nationalists and the Daily Press: The case of *Shen Bao*, 1927–1937." In *The Nationalists and Chinese Society, 1923–1937: A Symposium*, edited by John Fitzgerald, 107–132.

Nelli, Humbert S. 1976. *The Business of Crime: Italians and Syndicate Crime in the United States*. Chicago: University of Chicago Press.

Overmyer, Daniel L. 1976. *Folk Buddhist Religion: Dissenting Sects in Late Traditional China*. Cambridge: Harvard University Press.

———. 1985. "Values in Chinese sectarian literature: Ming and Ch'ing pao-chuan." In *Popular Culture in Late Imperial China*, edited by David Johnson, Andrew J. Nathan, and Evelyn Rawski, 219–254.

Pal, John. 1963. *Shanghai Saga*. London: Jarrolds.

Pan Gongzhan. 1954. "Lun xia dao" (On the way of the knight). In *Du Yuesheng Xiansheng Jinian Ji*, vol. 2, 4(b)–5(a).

Pan Ling. 1984. *Old Shanghai: Gangsters in Paradise*. Hong Kong: Heinemann Asia.

Perry, Elizabeth J. 1980. *Rebels and Revolutionaries in North China, 1845–1945*. Stanford: Stanford University Press.

———. 1985. "Tax revolt in late Qing China: The Small Swords of Shanghai and Liu Depei of Shandong." *Late Imperial China* 6, no. 1 (June): 83–112.

———. 1993. *Shanghai on Strike: The Politics of Chinese Labor.* Stanford: Stanford University Press.

Peters, E. W. 1937. *Shanghai Policeman.* London: Rich and Cowan.

Powell, John B. 1945. *My Twenty-Five Years in China.* New York: Macmillan.

Qian Shengke. 1919. *Qinghong Bang zhi Heimu* (The Inside Story of the Green and Red Gangs). Shanghai: Qian Shengke Heimu Faxing Suo.

Qian Yongming. 1952. "Du Xiansheng zhuan" (A Biography of Mister Du). In *Du Yuesheng Xiansheng Jinian Ji,* vol. 1, 2(a)–4(b).

Qin Baoqi. 1988. *Qing Qianqi Tiandihui Yanjiu* (Studies on the Heaven and Earth Society in the Early Qing). Beijing: Zhongguo Renmin Daxue Chubanshe.

Qing Bang Ji Qi Yi'an (The Green Gang and its Mystery). N.d., n.p.

Rankin, Mary Backus. 1971. *Early Chinese Revolutionaries: Radical Intellectuals in Shanghai and Chekiang, 1902–1911.* Cambridge: Harvard University Press.

Rigby, Richard W. 1980. *The May 30 Movement: Events and Themes.* Canberra: Australian National University.

"The Rise and Growth of the 'Ch'ing Pang.'" 1934. *The People's Tribune,* n.s., 7, no. 3, 115–117.

Rodyenko, Stephen Piero Rudinger de. 1914. *The Second Revolution in China, 1913: My Adventures of the Fighting Around Shanghai, the Arsenal, Woosung Forts.* Shanghai: Shanghai Mercury.

Rong Mengyuan. 1980. *Jiang Jia Wangchao* (The Jiang Family Dynasty). Beijing: Zhongguo Qingnian.

Roux, Alain. 1974. "Une grève en 1928 à Changhai: Un détournement d'héritage." *Le Mouvement Social* 89 (October–December): 3–35.

Rowe, William T. 1984. *Hankow: Commerce and Society in a Chinese City, 1796–1889.* Stanford: Stanford University Press.

Ruan Renze and Gao Zhennong, eds. 1992. *Shanghai Zongjiao Shi* (A History of Religions in Shanghai). Shanghai: Renmin Chubanshe.

Ruffé, D'Auxion de. 1928. *Is China Mad?* Shanghai: Kelly and Walsh.

Sakai, Tadao. 1970. "Le Hongbang (Bande rouge) aux XIXe et XXe siècles." In *Mouvements Populaires et Sociétés Secrètes en Chine aux XIXe et XXe Siècles,* 316–343.

Schlegel, Gustaaf. 1866. *Thian Ti Hwei: The Hung League, or Heaven-Earth-League, a Secret Society with the Chinese in China and India.* Batavia: Lange and Co.

Schmitter, Philippe C. 1979. "Still the century of corporatism?" In *Trends Towards Corporatist Intermediation,* edited by Philippe Schmitter and Gerhard Lehmbruch. Beverly Hills, Calif.: Sage Publications, 7–52.

Seagrave, Sterling. 1985. *The Soong Dynasty.* London: Sidgwick and Jackson.

Shanghai de Gushi (Tales of Shanghai). 1982. Shanghai: Shanghai Renmin Chubanshe.

Shanghai Difang Shi Ziliao (Materials on Shanghai Local History). 1982–86. Edited by Shanghai Shi Renmin Zhengfu Canyi Shishi Wenshi Ziliao Gongzuo Weiyuanhui (The Work Committee on Literary and Historical Materials of the Shanghai Municipal Peoples' Political Consultative Office). 5 vols. Shanghai: Shanghai Shehui Kexue Yuan Chubanshe.

"Shanghai Fazujie dangju you guan yi'erba shibian wenjian xuankan" (Selections from French Concession documents relating to the Shanghai Incident of January 28, 1932). 1985. *Dang'an yu Lishi* (Archives and History), vol. 2, 24–31.

Shanghai Gonghui Lianhehui (The Federation of Shanghai Trade Unions). 1989. Edited by Shanghai Shi Dang'an'guan (The Shanghai Municipal Archives). Shanghai: The Archives Press.

Shanghai Haiyuan Gongren Yundong Shi (The History of the Shanghai Seamen's Movement). 1991. Edited by Zhonggong Shanghai Haiyun Guanliju Weiyuanhui Dangshi Ziliao Zhengji Weiyuanhui (The Committee for the Collection of Materials on Party History of the Shanghai Maritime Administrative Office of the Communist Party [Shanghai Municipal] Committee) and Zhonghua Haiyuan Gonghui Shanghai Haiyun Guanliju Weiyuanhui (The Committee of the Shanghai Maritime Administrative Office of the Chinese Seamen's Union). Beijing: Zhonggongdang Shi Chubanshe.

Shanghai Jinrong Gailan (A General View of Shanghai's Financial Institutions). 1947. Edited by Lianhe Zhengxin Suo Tiaocha Zu (The Investigation Unit of the United Credit Exchange). Shanghai: Lianhe Zhengxin Suo.

Shanghai Municipal Police. Special Branch. Investigation Files, 1895–1945.

Shanghai Shi Nianjian (The Shanghai Municipal Yearbook). 1935–37. 6 vols. Shanghai: Zhonghua Shuju.

Shanghai Shi Tongji (Statistics of the City of Shanghai). 1933. Edited by Shanghai Shi Difang Xiehui (The Shanghai Civic Association). Shanghai: Shanghai Shi Difang Xiehui.

Shanghai Shi Tongzhiguan Qikan (Journal of the Shanghai Municipal Gazetteer Bureau), January 1933—March 1935.

Shanghai Shimin Difang Weichihui Baogao Shu (The Report of the Shanghai Citizens' Maintenance Association). 1932. [Shanghai]: n.p.

Shanghai Shimin Difang Weichihui Huiyuan Lu (Membership List of the Shanghai Citizens' Maintenance Association). [1932]. Manuscript.

Shanghai Yanjiu Ziliao (A Collection of Materials for the Study of Shanghai). 1936. Edited by Shanghai Tongshe (The Shanghai Gazetteer Association). Shanghai: Shanghai Tongshe.

Shanghai Yanjiu Ziliao Xuji (A Further Collection of Materials for the Study of Shanghai). 1937. Edited by Shanghai Tongshe. Shanghai: Shanghai Tongshe.

Shanghai Zhanggu (Anecdotes of Shanghai). 1982. Shanghai: Wenhua Chubanshe.

Shen Bao Nianjian 1933 (The Shen Bao Yearbook for 1933). 1933. Shanghai: Shen Bao.

Shen Bao Nianjian 1935 (The Shen Bao Yearbook for 1935). 1935. Shanghai: Shen Bao.

Shen Yunlong. 1981. *Minguo Shishi yu Renwu Luncong* (Essays on the Historical Events and Leading Figures of the Republic). Taibei: Zhunji Wenxue.

Shen Zui. 1985. *Juntong Neimu* (The Inside Story of the Military Statistics Bureau). Beijing: Wenshi Ziliao.

Shi Jun. 1986. "Shanghai sandaheng de goujie he douzheng (Co-operation and conflict among Shanghai's three big bosses)." In JSBH, 350–356.

Shi Yi. 1962. *Du Yuesheng Waizhuan* (An Unofficial Biography of Du Yuesheng). Hong Kong: Daye.

Short, Martin. 1984. *Crime Inc.: The Story of Organized Crime*. London: Thames Methuen.

Shuai Xuefu. [1970]. *Zhongguo Banghui Shi* (A History of Chinese Secret Societies). Hong Kong: Xiandai Chubanshe.

Slawinski, Roman. 1970. "Les Piques rouges et la révolution chinoise de 1925–1927." In *Mouvements Populaires et Sociétés Secrètes en Chine aux XIXe et XXe Siècles*, 393–406.

Smedley, Agnes. [1956] 1972. *The Great Road: The Life and Times of Chu Teh*. New York: Monthly Review Press.

Snow, Edgar. 1934. *The Far Eastern Front*. London: Jarrolds.

———. [1938] 1961. *Red Star over China*. New York: Grove Press.

Su Zhiliang and Chen Lifei. 1991. *Jindai Shanghai Heishehui Yanjiu* (A Study of Secret Societies in Modern Shanghai). Zhejiang: People's Publishing.

Sues, Ilona Ralf. 1944. *Shark's Fins and Millet*. Boston: Little, Brown and Co.

Sun Yuemin. 1946. *Jiali Baojian* (A Precious Guide to Those in the Family). Shenyang: Zhongguo Sanli Shushe.

Tamagna, Frank. 1942. *Banking and Finance in China*. New York: Institute of Pacific Relations.

Tao Chengzhang. [1916] 1957. "Zhe an jilue" (An account of the Zhejiang case). In *Xinhai Geming* (The 1911 Revolution), edited by Chui Degeng et al. 8 vols. Shanghai: Renmin Chubanshe, vol. 3, 3–111.

Teng, S. Y. 1971. *The Taiping Rebellion and the Western Powers: A Comprehensive Survey*. Oxford: Clarendon Press.

Tianjing Diaosou [pseud.]. 1932. *Qingpu Jiyao* (Essential Aspects of the Genealogy of the Green Gang). Chengdu: Chongyi Wuxueshe.

Tien, Hung-mao. 1972. *Government and Politics in Kuomintang China, 1927–1937*. Stanford: Stanford University Press.

Tiltman, H. Hessell. 1937. *The Uncensored Far East*. London: Jarrolds.

Trotsky, Leon. [1938] 1967. *Problems of the Chinese Revolution*. Ann Arbor: University of Michigan.

Tsao, W. Y. 1947. *The Constitutional Structure of Modern China*. Melbourne: Melbourne University Press.

Tyau, M. T. Z. 1930. *Two Years of Nationalist China*. Shanghai: Kelly and Walsh.

United States. Department of State. Decimal File, 1910–29: China. Internal Affairs.
———. Department of State. Decimal File, 1930–39: China. Internal Affairs.
Vinacke, Harold M. 1950. *A History of the Far East in Modern Times.* New York: Appleton-Century Crofts.
Vishnyakova-Akimova, Vera Vladimirovna. 1971. *Two Years in Revolutionary China, 1925–1927.* Cambridge: Harvard University Press.
Wakeman, Frederic, Jr. 1970. "Les sociétés secrètes du Guangdong (1800–1856)." In *Mouvements Populaires et Sociétés Secrètes en Chine aux XIXe et XXe Siècles,* 90–116.
———. 1988. "Policing modern Shanghai." *The China Quarterly* 115 (September): 408–440.
———. 1989. "The Shanghai Public Security Bureau, 1927–1932," unpublished manuscript.
Wakeman, Frederic, Jr., and Wen-hsin Yeh, eds. 1992. *Shanghai Sojourners.* Berkeley: Institute of East Asian Studies, University of California.
Wales, Nym. 1945. *The Chinese Labor Movement.* New York: John Day Company.
Wan Molin. 1973. *Hushang Wangshi* (Past Events in Shanghai). 4 vols. Taibei: Zhongwai Tushu Chubanshe.
———. 1975. "Zhang Zongchang zai Jiangnan" (Zhang Zongchang in the Jiangnan). In *Renhai Souqi Lu* (Searching for Those Who Stand Out from the Crowd), edited by Wan Molin. Taibei: Zhongwai Tushu Chubanshe, 189–222.
———. 1982a. "Shanghai wenren Huang Jinrong zhiba: cong tiaojie Lincheng jieche'an dao shemo bingshi" (Shanghai notable Huang Jinrong, part eight: From mediation of the Lincheng Incident to his death). *Shidai Wenzhe* (Current Digest) 4, no. 5 (May): 173–179.
———. 1982b. "Jianghu qiren Du Yuesheng (Secret Society notable Du Yuesheng)." *Shidai Wenzhe* 4, no. 6 (June): 6–20; vol. 5, no. 1 (July): 92–94; vol. 5, no. 2 (August): 78–94; vol. 5, no. 3 (September): 160–179; vol. 5, no. 4 (October): 110–130; vol. 5, no. 5 (November): 178–203.
Wang Delin. 1986. "Gu Zhuxuan zai Zhabei faji he kaishe Tianshan Wutai" (On Gu Zhuxuan's rise to power in Zhabei and the establishment of the Moon Theatre). In JSBH, 357–359.
Wang Qingbin et al., eds. 1928. *Diyici Zhongguo Laodong Nianjian* (The First Chinese Labor Yearbook). 2 vols. Beiping: Beiping Shehui Diaocha Bu.
Wang Renze. 1984. "Fu Xiao'an." In *Minguo Renwu Zhuan,* vol. 4, 154–159.
Wang Renze and Xiong Shanghou. 1984. "Huang Chujiu." In *Minguo Renwu Zhuan,* vol. 4, 268–274.
Wang, Y. C. 1967. "Tu Yueh-sheng (1881–1951): A tentative political biography." *Journal of Asian Studies* 26, no. 3 (May): 433–455.
Wang Yalu. 1988. "Qingbang 'Da' zibei Zhang Renkui he Zhao Chenglou" (Zhang Renkui and Zhao Chenglou, members of the "Da" generational status group of the Green Gang). In JSYDC, 238–241.

Wang Yangqing and Xu Yinghu. 1982. "Shanghai Qinghong Bang gaishu" (A general account of the Green and Red Gangs in Shanghai). *Shehui Kexue* (Social Sciences), no. 5: 63–65.

Wang Youcheng. 1987. "Du Yuesheng, Da Da matou yu 'xiao Changjiang'" (Du Yuesheng, the Da Da wharves and the 'Little Yangzi run'). In *Shanghai Yishi* (Anecdotes of Shanghai), edited by Tan Weikang et al. Shanghai: Wenhua Chubanshe, 245–256.

Wang Zichen. 1983. "Wo suo zhidao de Qinghong Bang zai Tianjin" (What I knew of the activities of the Green and Red Gangs in Tianjin). *Tianjin Wenshi Ziliao Xuanji*, no. 24: 206–219.

Ward, Barbara. 1985. "Regional operas and their audiences: Evidence from Hong Kong." In *Popular Culture in Late Imperial China*, 161–187.

Wasserstrom, Jeffrey N. 1991. *Student Protests in Twentieth Century China: The View from Shanghai*, Stanford: Stanford University Press.

Watanabe, Atsushi. 1984. "Secret societies in modern China: Ch'ing Pang, Hung Pang—late Ch'ing and early Republic of China [sic]." In *Zhonghua Minguo Chuqi Lishi Yantaohui Lunwen Ji: 1912–1927* (Collection of Papers from the Conference on the History of the Early Period of the Republic of China: 1912–1927), edited by Zhongyang Yanjiu Yuan Jindai Shi Yanjiu Suo (The Research Institute of Modern History of the Academia Sinica). 2 vols. Taibei: Academia Sinica, vol. 2, 797–815.

Wei, Grand Master. 1946. *Bang: Zhongguo Banghui; Qing, Hong, Hanliu* (Gangs: Chinese Secret Societies; the Green and Red Gangs, and the Han Remnants). Chongqing: Shuowen She.

Wen Juntian. 1939. *Zhongguo Baojia Zhidu* (The Baojia System of China). [Shanghai]: Shangwu Yinshu.

Who's Who in China 1931. 1931. Shanghai: China Weekly Review.

Wilbur, C. Martin, and Julie Lien-ying How, eds., *Documents on Communism, Nationalism and Soviet Advisers in China, 1918–1927*. 1956. New York: Columbia University Press.

Willoughby, W. W. 1925. *Opium as an International Problem: The Geneva Conferences*. Baltimore, Md.: Johns Hopkins University Press.

Woodhead, H. G. W. 1931. *The Truth about Opium in China*. Shanghai: Shanghai Evening Post and Mercury.

Wou, Odoric W. K. 1978. *Militarism in Modern China: The Career of Wu P'ei-fu, 1916–1939*. Canberra: Australian National University Press.

Wright, Mary C. 1969. *The Last Stand of Chinese Conservatism: The T'ung-chih Restoration, 1862–1874*. New York: Atheneum.

Wright, Tim. 1989. "Coping with the world depression: The Nationalist Government's relations with Chinese industry and commerce, 1932–1936." In *The Nationalists and Chinese Society, 1923–1937: A Symposium*, edited by John Fitzgerald, 133–166.

———. 1991. "Shanghai imperialists versus rickshaw racketeers: The defeat of the 1934 rickshaw reforms." *Modern China* 17, no. 1 (January): 76–111.

Wu Choupeng. 1935. "Douliu yu nongcun jingji shidai de Xuhai geshu" (The tarrying of the Xu-Hai region in the period of the village economy). In *Zhongguo Nongcun Jingji Ziliao* (Materials on the Rural Economy of

China), edited by Feng Hefa. Shanghai: Liming Chubanshe, 330–361.

Wu Rui. 1971. "Tan Qing Bang" (Discussing the Green Gang). *Changliu* (Free Flow) 43, no. 11 (July): 35–40.

Wu, Tien-wei. 1976a. "Chiang Kai-shek's April 12th Coup of 1927." In *China in the 1920's: Nationalism and Revolution*, edited by F. Gilbert Chan and Thomas H. Etzold. New York: New Viewpoints, 147–159.

———. 1976b. *The Sian Incident: A Pivotal Point in Modern Chinese History*. Ann Arbor: Center for Chinese Studies, University of Michigan.

Wu Yugong. [1922] 1991. *Qinghong Bang Shi Yanyi* (The Romance of the Green and Red Gangs). Shanghai: Guji Publishing.

Wusa Yundong Shiliao (Historical Materials on the May Thirtieth Movement). 1981–86. Edited by Shanghai Shehui Kexue Yuan Lishi Yanjiu Suo (The Institute for Historical Research of the Shanghai Academy of Social Sciences). 2 vols. Shanghai: Renmin Chubanshe.

Wusi Yundong zai Shanghai Shiliao Xuanji (Selected Historical Materials on the May Fourth Movement). 1980. Edited by Shanghai Shehui Kexue Yuan Lishi Yanjiu Suo (The Institute for Historical Research of the Shanghai Academy of Social Sciences). Shanghai: Renmin Chubanshe.

Xiandai Shiliao (Materials on Contemporary History). 1933–34. 4 vols. [Shanghai]: Haitian Chubanshe.

Xiang Bo. 1986. "Huang Jinrong shilue" (A biographical sketch of Huang Jinrong). In JSBH, 131–137.

Xiang Xiongxiao. 1981. "Xinhai Geming zai Zhejiang" (The 1911 Revolution in Zhejiang). In *Zhejiang Xinhai Geming Huiyi Lu* (Reminiscences of the 1911 Revolution in Zhejiang), edited by Zhongguo Renmin Zhengzhi Xieshang Huiyi Zhejiang Sheng Weiyuan Hui Wenshi Ziliao Yanjiu Weiyuan Hui (The Committee for the Study of Historical and Literary Materials of the Zhejiang Provincial Committee of the Chinese People's Political Consultative Conference). Hangzhou: Zhejiang Renmin Chubanshe, 168–179.

Xiao Juetian. 1980. "Jiang Jieshi jinyan de neimu" (The inside story of Jiang Jieshi's opium suppression). *Wenshi Ziliao Xuanji*, no. 34: 157–174.

Xiao Yishan. [1935] 1986. *Jindai Mimi Shehui Shiliao* (Historical Materials on Modern Secret Societies). Hunan: Yuelu Shushe.

Xie Tianmin. 1935. *Linji San An Shi* (A History of the Three Monasteries of the Linji Sect). N.P.: Zhongzheng Tang.

Xinhai Geming zai Shanghai Shiliao Xuanji (Selected Historical Materials on the 1911 Revolution in Shanghai). 1981. Edited by Shanghai Shehui Kexue Yuan Lishi Yanjiu Suo (The Institute for Historical Research of the Shanghai Academy of Social Sciences). Shanghai: Renmin Chubanshe.

"Xinhai Shanghai Guangfu qianhou: Zoutanhui jilu" (About the Liberation of Shanghai in 1911: Records of an informal discussion). 1981. In *Xinhai Geming Huiyi Lu* (Collection of Memoirs of the 1911 Revolution), edited by Zhongguo Renmin Zhengzhi Xieshang Huiyi Chuanguo Weiyuan Hui Wenshi Ziliao Yanjiu Weiyuan Hui (The Committee for Research into Historical and Literary Materials of the National Committee of the Chinese People's Political Consultative Conference). 8 vols. Beijing: Wenshi Ziliao Chubanshe, vol. 4, 1–19.

Xinshishuo [pseud.]. 1954. "Shuo Du Yuesheng Xiansheng (Speaking of Mister Du Yuesheng). In *Du Yuesheng Xiansheng Jinian Ji*, vol. 2, 55(a)–60(a).

Xu Xiaogeng. 1986. "Xianfu Xu Langxi shengping shilue" (An account of the life of my late father Xu Langxi). In JSBH, 126–130.

Xu Yufang and Bian Xingying, eds. 1987. *Shanghai Gongren Sanci Wuzhuang Qiyi Yanjiu* (Studies of the Three Armed Uprisings of the Shanghai Workers). Shanghai: Zhizhi Chubanshe. In addition to newspaper accounts and memoirs, this collection includes the minutes of the meetings of the Chinese Communist Party's Shanghai District Committee from August 1926 to April 1927.

Xu Zhucheng. 1983. *Du Yuesheng Zhengzhuan* (A True Biography of Du Yuesheng). Hangzhou: Zhejiang Renmin Chubanshe.

Xue Gengxin. 1979. "Wo yu jiu Shanghai Fazujie" (The Shanghai French Concession and myself). *Wenshi Ziliao Xuanji* (Shanghai series), no. 6: 149–169.

———. 1980. "Jindai Shanghai de liumang" (The gangsters of modern Shanghai). *Wenshi Ziliao Xuanji* (Shanghai series), no. 3: 160–178.

———. 1986. "Wo jiechu guode Shanghai banghui renwu" (My past contacts with leading Shanghai gangsters). In JSBH, 87–107.

———. 1988. "Jindai Shanghai heishehui jianwen" (What I saw and heard of the secret societies in modern Shanghai). In JSYDC, 179–195.

Yan Ran [pseud.]. 1934. "Shanghai de sichuan dahui" (The Fourth [GMD] Congress in Shanghai). In *Xiandai Shiliao* (Materials on Contemporary History). 1933–34. 4 vols. Shanghai: Haitian Chubanshe, vol. 2, 80–94.

Yan Zhongping. 1955. *Zhongguo Jindai Jingji Shi Tongji Ziliao Xuanji* (Selected Statistical Materials on the Modern Economic History of China). Beijing: Kexue Chubanshe.

Yang Guanbei. 1952. "Du Yuesheng Xiansheng yanxing jilue" (A brief record of the words and deeds of Mister Du Yuesheng). In *Du Yuesheng Xiansheng Jinian Ji*, vol. 1, 29(b)–32(b).

Yang Hao and Ye Lan. 1989. *Jiu Shanghai Fengyun Renwu* (Leading Personalities of Old Shanghai). Shanghai: Shanghai Renmin Chubanshe.

Yang Shi. 1986. "Shanghai tan liumang da heng yishi sance" (Three anecdotes about the Shanghai gangster bosses). *Dang'an yu Lishi*, no. 2: 88–91.

Yi Wen. 1988. "Yapian dafanzi Ye Qinghe" (The major opium trafficker, Ye Qinghe). In JSYDC, 28–45.

Yijiu'erqinian de Shanghai Shangye Lianhehui (The Shanghai Federation of Commerce and Industry in 1927). 1983. Edited by Shanghai Shi Dang'an Guan (The Shanghai Municipal Archives). Shanghai: Renmin Chubanshe.

Yu Yongfu. 1986. "Wo suo zhidao Du Yuesheng" (The Du Yuesheng I knew). In JSBH, 268–283.

Yu Yunjiu. 1986. "Wo suo zhidao de Zhang Xiaolin" (The Zhang Xiaolin I knew). In JSBH, 347–349.

Yu Zhi. 1925a. "Yapian wenti" (The opium question). *Dongfang Zazhi* 22, no. 4 (February 25): 2–3.

———. 1925b. "Yapian wenti yu Shanghai shizheng" (The opium question and the administration of Shanghai). *Dongfang Zazhi* 22, no. 12 (June 25): 1–2.

Zhang Chengyu. [1945–47] 1965. "Geming Jun Gansiduizhang Zhang Chengyu zhi zishu" (The memoirs of Zhang Chengyu, Dare-to-Die Commander in the Revolutionary Army). In *Geming Yishi* (Fragments of Revolutionary History), edited by Feng Ziyu. 5 vols. Taibei: Taiwan Shangwu Yinshu Guan, vol. 5, 270–297.

Zhang Jungu. 1980. *Du Yuesheng Zhuan* (The Biography of Du Yuesheng). 4 vols. Taibei: Zhuanji Wenxue.

Zhang Kechang. 1936. "Benshe di'erzhu lishihui yinianlai gongzuo gaikuang" (An outline of the work of our Club's Second Executive Committee over the past year). *Heng She Yuekan*, nos. 10–11 (November 22): 9–20.

Zhang Shusheng. N.d. *Tongcao Jiyao* (The Essentials of the Anqing Bang along the Grand Canal). N.p.

Zhang Zhang. 1933. "Guonan qizhongde Shanghai jiuji tuanti" (Shanghai relief agencies in the period of national emergency). In *Dangdai Shisheng*, 164–169.

Zhang Zhenyuan. 1940. *Daoyi Zhengsong* (The Orthodox Sect of the Truth and Proper Relationships). Beiping: n.p.

Zhao Yulin. 1988. "Zhongtong wo jian wo wen" (What I saw and heard in the Central Statistical Bureau). In Zhang Wen et al. *Tegong Zongbu: Zhongtong* (Intelligence Headquarters: The Central Statistical Bureau). Hong Kong: Zhongyuan, 189–221.

Zhonggong "Gongren Yundong" Yuanshi Ziliao Huibian (Collection of Original Documents on the Chinese Communist "Labor Movement"). 1980. Edited by Sifa Xingzheng Bu Tiaocha Ju (The Investigation Bureau of the Department of Judicial Administration). 4 vols. Taibei: Sifang Xingzheng Tiaocha Ju. This Guomindang collection of CCP documents covers the years 1921–35, with most coverage given to the period 1928–35.

Zhongguo Jingji Nianjian (The China Economic Yearbook). 1935. Edited by Shiye Bu (The Ministry of Industry). 3 vols. Shanghai: Shangwu Yinshu Guan.

Zhou Enyu and Liu Yanchen. 1988. "Tianjin Qing Bang wenjian zaji" (Notes on what is known of the Tianjin Green Gang). *Tianjin Wenshi Ziliao Xuanji*, 45: 231–244.

Zhou Jianfeng. 1982. "Fashang dianche" (The French Tramways Company). In *Shanghai de Gushi*, 348–360.

Zhou Yumin and Shao Yong. 1993. *Zhongguo Banghui Shi* (A History of Chinese Secret Societies). Shanghai: People's Publishing House.

Zhu Bangxing, Hu Linge and Xu Sheng. [1939] 1984. *Shanghai Chanye yu Shanghai Zhigong* (Enterprises and Workers in Shanghai). Shanghai: Shanghai Renmin Chubanshe.

Zhu Fugui and Xu Fengyi. 1985. *Yangzhou Shihua* (An Historical Account of Yangzhou). Yangzhou: Jiangsu Gujie Chubanshe.

Zhu Jianliang and Wu Weizhi. 1984. "Zhang Xiaolin." In *Minguo Renwu Zhuan*, vol. 4, 160–165.

Zhu Kuichu. 1954. "Du Yuesheng Xiansheng zhi zhongyi" (The loyalty of Mister Du Yuesheng). In *Du Yuesheng Xiansheng Jinian Ji*, vol. 2, 40(a)–40(b).

Zhu Menghua. 1983. "Shanghaifazujie de gongdongju ji xunbufang (The Municipal Council and Police Headquarters of the Shanghai French Concession). In *Shanghai Shi Difang Shi Ziliao*, vol. 2, 77–83.

———. 1984. "Jiu Shanghai de sige feipin dawang" (The four refuse potentates of Old Shanghai). In *Shanghai Difang Shi Ziliao*, vol. 3, 157–163.

Zhu Shaozhou. 1952. "Ji Du Yuesheng Xiansheng" (Remembrance of Mister Du Yuesheng). In *Du Yuesheng Xiansheng Jinian Ji*, vol. 1, 25(a)–26(a).

Zhu Wenwei. 1984. "Zhu Zhiyao." In *Minguo Renwu Zhuan*, vol. 4, 236–242.

Zhu Wenyuan. 1993. *Xi'an Shibian Shiliao* (Historical Materials on the Xi'an Incident). 2 vols. Taibei: Goushiguan.

Zhu Xuefan. 1986. "Shanghai gongren yundong yu banghui ersanshi" (One or two things about the Shanghai labor movement and the secret societies). In JSBH, 1–20.

Zhu Zijia [pseud. of Jin Xiongbai]. 1964. *Huangpu Jiang de Zhuolang* (The Turbid Waters of the Huangpu River). Hong Kong: Wuxing Jishu Bao She.

Index

Designer:	Barbara Jellow
Compositor:	Asco Trade Typesetting Ltd.
Text:	Sabon
Display:	Sabon
Printer:	Thomson-Shore, Inc.
Binder:	Thomson-Shore, Inc.